KYOTO-CSEAS SERIES ON ASIAN STUDIES
Center for Southeast Asian Studies, Kyoto University

MORAL POLITICS IN THE PHILIPPINES

KYOTO-CSEAS SERIES ON ASIAN STUDIES
Center for Southeast Asian Studies, Kyoto University

MORAL POLITICS IN THE PHILIPPINES

Inequality, Democracy and the Urban Poor

Wataru Kusaka

NUS PRESS
Singapore
in association with
KYOTO UNIVERSITY PRESS
Japan

The publication of this book is funded by the Japan Society for the Promotion of Science (JSPS) as Grant-in-Aid for Publication of Scientific Research Results.

© 2017 Wataru Kusaka

All rights reserved. No part of this publication may be reproduced or transmitted in any form or by any means, electronic or mechanical, including photocopy, recording, or any information storage or retrieval system, without permission in writing from the publisher.

NUS Press
National University of Singapore
AS3-01-02, 3 Arts Link
Singapore 117569
http://nuspress.nus.edu.sg

ISBN 978-981-4722-38-4 (Casebound)

Kyoto University Press
Yoshida-South Campus, Kyoto University
69 Yoshida-Konoe-Cho, Sakyo-ku
Kyoto 606-8315
Japan
www.kyoto-up.or.jp

ISBN 978-4-8140-0066-1 (Paperback)

National Library Board Singapore Cataloguing-in-Publication Data

Names: Kusaka, Wataru.
Title: Moral politics in the Philippines: inequality, democracy and the urban poor / Wataru Kusaka.
Other title(s): Inequality, democracy and the urban poor
Description: Singapore: NUS Press in association with Kyoto University Press, [2017].
Identifier(s): OCN 960841058 | ISBN 978-981-4722-38-4 (casebound)
Subject(s): LCSH: Political participation--Philippines | Urban poor--Political activity--Philippines | Democratization--Philippines | Political culture--Philippines.
Classification: DDC 320.9599--dc23

Cover image courtesy of Zenta Nishio. Photo taken in Tondo, Manila on November 27, 2011.

Typeset by: International Typesetters Pte Ltd
Printed by: Markono Print Media Pte Ltd

CONTENTS

List of Illustrations	vi
Preface	x
Introduction: Philippine Democracy and Moral Politics	1
1. Analytical Framework	21
2. Formation of the Dual Public Sphere	50
3. People Power and Moral Antagonism	81
4. Moral Antagonism in Elections	121
5. Moral Antagonism in Urban Governance	156
6. The Revival of Moral Nationalism	195
7. Beyond Moral Politics	235
Addendum: Duterte as a Drastic Medicine	260
Afterword	265
Notes	270
Bibliography	309
Index	332

LIST OF ILLUSTRATIONS

Map of Metro Manila   xiv

Photographs

(Photographs in this book are the author's personal collection unless otherwise stated.)

1.	Children playing with the street vendor's baskets	1
2.	Children playing in an informal settlement	21
3.	Men drinking liquor by a roadside during the day	37
4.	Driver trying to attract customers to a jeepney, a form of public transportation for ordinary people	50
5.	Children at a public elementary school	56
6.	At the root of urban poverty is rural poverty	71
7.	Alley in Pechayan	77
8.	People gather at the EDSA Shrine During People Power 2	81
9.	Cover of a book published in 1986 to commemorate People Power 1	86
10.	Demonstrators call for Estrada's resignation in front of the EDSA Shrine	100
11.	Pro-Estrada demonstrators confront police in front of Malacañang Palace	104
12.	Blood oozes onto the ground from the back of a demonstrator pinned down by police	117
13.	A voter education poster reading "Accept money, [but] vote your conscience"	121
14.	A street sweeper hired by an Arroyo project	125

List of Illustrations vii

15.	Resident asking for money from a mayoral candidate campaigning in a slum	128
16.	People crowding an outdoor polling place in Pechayan	148
17.	A voter education program by PPCRV entitled "Understanding My Vote. Do You Already Understand?"	150
18.	A resident of a squat watching his home being razed by the state	156
19.	A street vendor mother and her child	160
20.	A family whose house was razed by the MMDA	166
21.	A T-shirt made by a Philcoa street vendor reads, "I'm Proud to Be a Street Vendor"	178
22.	MMVA demonstration with a placard reading "Bayani, you're not a real bayani [hero]"	184
23.	Street vendors posing for a photo with a friendly MMDA employee	185
24.	Aquino supporters making the "L" sign (for laban, meaning "fight"), the symbol of People Power 1, at Benigno Aquino III's final speech of the 2010 election campaign	195
25.	A left-wing demonstration calling for the ouster of Arroyo, along with slogans such as "Awaken the nation's conscience!" and "Replace the rotten system!"	202
26.	Banners supporting Noynoy Aquino	210
27.	A pro-Estrada banner hangs over the entrance to Pechayan	225
28.	View of sunset from the Philcoa overpass	235
29.	Yoyoy talks about Duterte while holding a marijuana joint	260
30.	Teenagers play a coin gambling game all night long. Images of Duterte, marijuana and Christ are drawn on the game board	262

Figures

1.	Dual Public Spheres	5
2.	Employment in the Philippines by Occupation	25

3.	Net Satisfaction Ratings of Presidents of the Philippines	200
4.	Pre-election Approval Ratings of the Presidential Candidates	216
5.	Pre-election Approval Ratings of the Presidential Candidates among the Wealthy and Middle Classes (classes A, B, and C)	219
6.	Pre-election Approval Ratings of the Presidential Candidates among the Poor (class D)	219
7.	Pre-election Approval Ratings of the Presidential Candidates among the Very Poor (class E)	220

Tables

1.	Income Disparities and Poverty Rates in the Philippines	26
2.	Socioeconomic Status Indicators Used by SWS	27
3.	Education Level by Socioeconomic Status	27
4.	Income Disparities in Asian Countries	28
5.	Per cent of Labor Population in the Agricultural and Non-agricultural Sectors	29
6.	Per cent of GDP from the Agricultural, Industrial and Service Sectors	29
7.	Urban and Rural Percentages of National Population	29
8.	Overseas Contract Worker Population and Remittances	30
9.	Number of NPOs Registered with the Securities and Exchange Commission, and Estimated Number of NGOs	31
10.	Number of NGOs per One Million People in Asian Countries	31
11.	Types of Hegemonic Practice that Create Antagonistic Relations	46
12.	Media Owned by Family-owned Business Groups	61
13.	Circulation of Print Media	62
14.	Newspapers Published in Metro Manila	64

15.	Readership of Daily Newspapers in Metro Manila and Nearby Cities	64
16.	Household Ownership of Media Appliances	65
17.	Household Media Access Rates	65
18.	Comparing Distributional Strategies of Electoral Mobilization	127
19.	2010 Presidential Election Results (Top Four Candidates Only)	208

PREFACE

Before dawn on May 1, 2001, a riot broke out in the capital district of Manila when a group of poor demonstrators besieged the presidential palace. The police and armed forces attempted to suppress the revolt with tear gas and gunfire, and the demonstrators responded by throwing rocks. After seven hours, the riot was finally suppressed, but at least 4 demonstrators had died and 113 had been injured. I was extremely shocked and saddened by this incident. When I received the opportunity to study at the University of the Philippines starting the following year, I took up residence in a slum community and attempted to acquire an understanding of the political consciousness of the poor from the inside. The views expressed in this book are based on my experiences during this period.

The reason I took such an interest in the riot is as follows. At the time, I was a university undergraduate student in the process of writing my thesis. I had already become enamored with the Philippines through my participation in volunteer work-camp activities, and was becoming increasingly enthralled by the charm and wisdom of the country and its peoples. I became utterly absorbed in reading works such as Renato Constantino's *The Philippines: A Past Revisited* (1975) and *The Philippines: The Continuing Past* (1978), and Reynaldo Ileto's *Pasyon and Revolution: Popular Movements in the Philippines, 1840–1910* (1979). It was moving to learn how the community known as "Filipinos" was created through the actions of people who resisted harsh oppression and poverty to build a freer and more equal society. I was particularly impressed by the way in which Filipinos would rise up and act on their own initiative to reform politics when the state failed to protect their welfare and livelihood, in contrast to Japanese people, who tend to rely heavily on the state.

In January 2001, just as I was reaching a critical point in the work of writing my thesis, several hundred thousand citizens angered by the corruption surrounding President Estrada forced him out of office through a series of protests known as "People Power 2." Once again, I was filled with deep admiration for the Philippines. I decided to postpone my job search and enter graduate school to study more about the country. However, immediately after I started my graduate studies, another incident occurred. In May 2001, poor people engaged in protests and subsequent riots with the goal of seeking Estrada's reinstatement as president; this would come to be known as "People Power 3." Why would the poor go to such lengths for such a corrupt president? Just who were these Filipino "people" I admired so much? What did these riots signify? What were members of the poor really thinking? With questions like these swirling in my mind, I decided to live with the poor in the Manila slums and conduct live-in field research there.

In choosing a slum in which to reside, I intentionally avoided seeking introductions from leftists and non-governmental organizations (NGOs). For one thing, none of my acquaintances could provide such assistance. Moreover, I thought I would be unable to understand the "real" political relationships and consciousness of the poor by studying poor people who are affiliated with such organized groups. Instead, I became friendly with a number of street vendors, and through these connections I was able to rent a small, dark room (about four square meters) on the outskirts of the slum in which they lived. When lying down, I could hear cockroaches skittering around under the plywood floor. I would buy a bucket of water for one peso in the neighborhood and take care of my toilet and bathing needs at the same time. When I came home at night and switched on the light, the rats that had been chewing on my food would scamper noisily back to the open sewer outside my building. The landlord's son, who lived in the room next door, was a methamphetamine addict who would wander about every evening, yelling all night long, even when he was in his room. One night, a complete stranger tried to force his way into my room.

Fearing that I might be robbed or worse, and thinking it would help me to learn Tagalog if I lived with Filipinos, I decided to move in with the street vendor, who had so kindly found my room, and his family of five. We agreed that I would pay the rent for a new house and half of the electricity bill. I had no privacy, but I no longer felt anxious or lonely, and slum life became comfortable and pleasant.

Nearly every day, I drank with the men hanging out on the street corner or did my laundry with the women of the neighborhood. Gradually, I made a lot of friends. In the evening, I almost always helped the street vendors at their stalls. Sometimes we would all flee from crackdowns by the police and government agencies. When a heavy rainstorm came or a typhoon hit, I would help carry furniture and children to safer ground through stagnant, chest-deep floodwaters. Occasionally, I would go swimming with my friends in the equally stagnant Manila Bay. Although I rarely turned down an offer to have a drink, I did avoid drinking around a certain crowd who always got in fights when they were drunk. In fact, while I was living in the slum, three people died in such fights. At first, my friends in the slum couldn't understand why I lived there, and I wasn't able to explain myself well. Perhaps for that reason, I often heard the rumor that I had come from Japan to chase a Filipina woman but was jilted and ran out of money, and therefore I got stuck there.

At the same time, I was also attending graduate school at the University of the Philippines, and this proved to be a far more difficult adjustment than life in the slums. While attending university, I had to change not only my language, but also my appearance and behavior, so that educated Filipinos would accept me. In the slums, people were happy if I spoke broken Tagalog, but at university, everyone was expected to speak fluent English. However, I couldn't understand my English classes very well, and I could only respond to questions with a foolish laugh. I was also unable to follow discussions between Filipino teachers and my fellow students. I completely lost what little pride I had.

In effect, I lived a double life, shuttling back and forth every day between the "civic sphere," where the middle class engaged in sophisticated discussions in English in air-conditioned classrooms, and the "mass sphere," where the poor spoke in Tagalog about their desperate problems and difficult livelihoods in their crowded slums and streets. In the course of living this way, I came to see that between these two worlds, the way in which people talked about politics, as well as the morality they referenced in their political discussions, differed greatly. In addition to debating vastly different issues, they also judged the same points of contention using different notions of "correctness."

In the civic sphere, highly educated members of the middle class would lament that Filipino politics was forever doomed because the poor, in their ignorance, were easily duped by corrupt politicians and celebrity candidates. NGO activists would talk about how they needed to assist "the weak and ignorant poor" in order to improve Filipino politics. However, my experience living in the mass sphere instilled within me a discomfort with, and a resistance to, this civic-sphere attitude toward the poor. This was because the poor people I lived with had an unequivocally critical view of Filipino society and politics; moreover, they refused to follow the lead of not only the elite but also the NGOs and leftists. Above all, they felt a sense of tremendous pride.

Conventional theories of Filipino politics, which emphasize the continuity of rule by the elite and the potential for political engagement by NGO workers and moderate leftists, began to seem inadequate and even inapplicable in light of my daily participatory observations. In this book, I have used this experience and the awareness it has instilled as a basis for my analysis of contemporary Filipino politics, focusing on the conflict between the civic and mass spheres, with "morality" as a key concept. Through this case analysis of the Philippines, it has also been my intention to address general issues confronting democracy today.

In my view, democracy faces a serious predicament as neoliberalism exacerbates existing divisions in society with a growing "moralization of politics." By the "moralization of politics," I am referring to the transformation of interest politics, centered around resource distribution, into moral politics predicated on definitions of right and wrong. Whereas interest politics can be mediated through the distribution of resources, moral politics is based on right and wrong and therefore readily lends itself to zero-sum confrontations that make compromise difficult. By morally justifying the exclusion of others, it threatens the practice of democracy, which is predicated on plurality.

Today, as inequality spreads throughout the world in developed and developing countries alike, a politics of resentment, which incites fear of the "enemy" and uses brave words to call for the elimination of that "enemy," runs rampant and earns soaring praise. In most cases, this type of politics advances its cause by identifying itself with "moral citizens" and constructing an inferior "other" to be judged and condemned. In taking up this issue, it is my hope that the argument of this book, which stands in opposition to politics that lay claim to an "upright citizenry," can also provide some insight into surviving these troubled times.

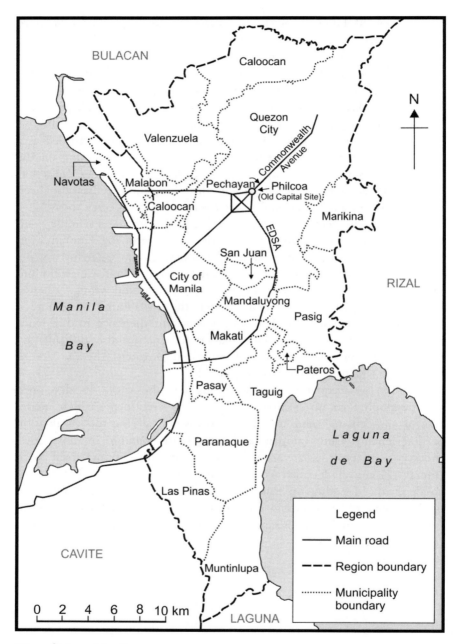

Map of Metro Manila

INTRODUCTION

Philippine Democracy and Moral Politics

Photo 1 Children playing with the street vendor's baskets (Pechayan, December 2007).

The subject of this book is contemporary Philippine democracy from the perspective of struggles in civil society associated with moral politics. By "moral politics," I mean politics that creates groups that are seen as either "good" or "evil" and draw a demarcation line between the two—in other words, politics concerned with definitions of good and evil. Moral politics is clearly distinguishable from "interest politics," which is concerned with the distribution of resources. In analyzing moral politics, it is absolutely imperative to scrutinize the hegemonic struggle in civil society and to identify which forces legitimize their own intellectual and moral leadership by defining themselves ("we") as representing "good."

In 1986, a movement known as the "People Power" revolution led to the collapse of the authoritarian Marcos regime and the subsequent democratization of the Philippines. However, it has been argued that the democratization process did little more than restore the "elite democracy" that had preceded Marcos.[1] Elite democracy refers to politics in which a very limited number of elite families rule over the rest of society by monopolizing electoral posts, with members of the same family serving such posts as town or city mayors, legislators, and provincial governors. Marcos amassed power by declaring martial law, dissolving Congress, and making local government-leadership positions appointive. With democratization, however, the elites who had lost opportunities to hold public office under Marcos reinstated themselves at the center of the political process. Even after democratization, elite-democracy discourse became the predominant framework for analyzing Philippine politics.[2]

Meanwhile, in the wake of democratization, middle-class activists formed a number of non-governmental organizations (NGOs) that participated actively in politics in diverse fields. NGOs monitored elections, hoping to enhance the legitimacy of this core aspect of democracy by preventing election rigging. NGOs supported the poor and other marginalized elements of society with the aim of furthering socioeconomic equality by making the interests of these social groups a part of public policy. Such practices when evaluated have been regarded as examples of middle-class independence of elite rule through participation in politics as citizens with a high moral consciousness, and thereby as contributors to the consolidation and deepening of democracy. The poor also now participate more freely in the political process, due to factors such as increased urbanization and economic migration, and have supported populist counter-elites who challenge traditional elites. These developments signify that the elite's hegemony does not penetrate civil society and that Philippine politics today can no longer be understood in terms of elite democracy alone.

However, despite the rise of various movements of counter-hegemony in civil society, political power in the Philippines remains dominated by the country's elite. Moreover, the Philippines has seen cases of what could be interpreted as the obstruction of democracy by the actions and discourse of a middle class that prides itself on moral citizenry. For example, in 2001, the urban middle class forced President Estrada out of office with a series of street demonstrations referred to as "People Power 2." Participants boasted that this was "a victory for democracy by civil society," but it cannot be denied that this extra-constitutional change of government posed a threat to the electoral process—in other words, to the consolidation of democracy. Furthermore, some members of the middle class, particularly those who viewed the poor as criminals dependent on illegal squatting and street vending for their subsistence, expressed negative attitudes toward movements designed to advance the interests of the poor by addressing socioeconomic inequality and "deepening democracy."

Based on these observations, I would like to consider the following three questions:

First, why did the middle class, self-identified as "citizens," play this ambiguous role vis-à-vis the consolidation and deepening of democracy? Many previous studies cannot precisely answer the question because they regard the middle class as essentially a democratic social force. In order to address this issue, it is helpful to adopt a constructivist approach that treats the political character of a particular social group not as established *a priori* but rather as inevitably determined by its contingent relationships with other social groups. The effects of a civil society on democracy must be analyzed from the dynamics of antagonistic relationships within that civil society, not merely the identification of its democratic social groupings. In fact, some studies have already focused on hegemonic struggles within Philippine civil society, but these were limited by their assumption of an unchallenged elite's hegemony, by their treatment of the antagonistic relationship between "citizens" and the "masses" as a fixed phenomenon, and by their exclusive focus on rivalries and expedient alliances among organizations.

My approach differs in that I focus on the fluid and contingent nature of antagonistic "we/they" relations, including the role of ordinary people unaffiliated with particular groups. I argue that the dynamics of contingent changes in morally antagonistic "we/they" relations constructed through the hegemonic struggles taking place in civil society are a powerful determinant in the advancement or obstruction of democracy. For example, the mobilization of "People Power" to oust the president, the support of specific politicians at election time, and the holding of street demonstrations over public issues, are all based on a collective identity as "we" in opposition to "them." Conversely, it would be exceedingly difficult to organize demonstrations or significantly influence electoral results through collective voting without the construction of such an identity.

Second, if this were the case, then what type of moral "we/they" relation would promote or advance democracy? My answer is that when moral antagonism of the "we/they" relation is so escalated as to justify elimination and destruction of "enemy," it threatens democracy. The danger increases particularly when a discourse on civic morality is superimposed upon class disparities, which transforms class conflict from a clash of interests to one framed as good versus evil. The moralization of class politics poses a pitfall for the counter-hegemony of the middle class against elite rule. When members of the middle class define themselves as upstanding "citizens" who morally challenge the elite's hegemony, it cannot help but construct bad "non-citizens" as a constitutive outside. Typically it is the poor who do not share the same morality with the middle class, which constructs them as bad "non-citizens"—that is, the "masses." As a result, not all people can be included in the "citizenry," and the discourse of good "citizens" paradoxically deprives the poor and other marginalized groups of legitimacy and negates the pluralistic nature of democracy.

Third, this perspective on moral politics offers new insight into why democracy in a stratified society is easily destabilized. Previous studies have addressed this question strictly from the standpoint of interest politics. For example, it is postulated that in a highly stratified society, class conflict over the distribution of resources will intensify, and inflammatory politicians who exploit the discontent of the poor will threaten democracy, not to mention an elite that harshly suppresses this discontent. From this, it may be surmised that if the middle class achieves power through economic development, thereby restraining the elite's power and ameliorating social stratification, then the democratic system will also be improved and stabilized. In this book, however, I argue that even if the middle class comes to power, should this be accompanied by the moralization of politics, it will promote discourses and political participation predicated on the belief that groups different from it are evil and must be excluded, which will damage democracy. To understand the issues that confront democracy in a stratified society, an examination of moral politics is imperative, because analysis from the perspective of interest politics has been shown to be insufficient.

In sum, the book criticizes the thesis that if the middle class grows larger and more people participate in the political process as highly

Introduction: Philippine Democracy and Moral Politics 5

moral "citizens," then the power of oligarchic elites will weaken, class tensions will dissipate and democracy will further consolidate and deepen. Many studies of Philippine politics criticize the interest politics of the country's elite and support the moral politics of its other citizens. On the contrary, I stress the paradoxical danger of moral politics to democracy by examining the moral antagonism inherent in the "we/they" relation constructed by hegemonic struggle within the civil society.

To demonstrate this thesis, I account for the societal constraints under which hegemonic struggles evolve. In the Philippines, class divisions have a particularly profound impact. In applying this fundamental fact to the analysis in this book, I wish to introduce the concept of "dual public spheres." These consist of a "civic sphere" and a "mass sphere" (see Figure 1), which represent the living environments and discourse spaces of the middle and impoverished classes, respectively—a division engendered by the language, education, media, and livelihood gaps that exist between the two classes. I use the term "contact zone" to refer to the space where these two spheres partially intersect—where disparate people and discourses encounter one another. There are two demarcation lines that engender an antagonistic "we/they" relationship between these

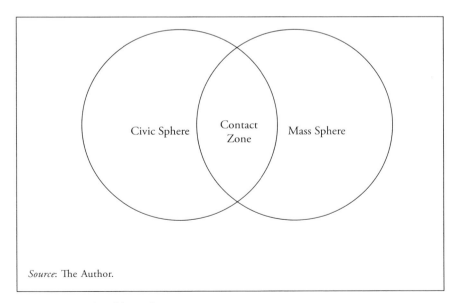

Source: The Author.

Figure 1 Dual Public Spheres

dual public spheres, one drawn between classes and the other between moralities. The class demarcation line, which derives from the unequal distribution of economic, occupational, educational, cultural and other resources, is fairly fixed due to divisions among people.[3] On the other hand, the moral demarcation line derives from differing concepts of good and evil, and is thereby more fluid.

The two antagonistic relationships created by these demarcation lines have played important roles in Philippine politics in recent years. The first antagonistic relationship is the "moral division of the nation," which is constructed when the legitimacy of "the other" is rejected in each of the dual public spheres. In this case, the moral line is superimposed over the class line, and this overlap transforms class antagonism over the distribution of resources into moral antagonism between "citizens" and the "masses" in the civic sphere, and between the "rich" and the "poor" in the mass sphere. This moral division of the nation, particularly between 1998 and 2004, obstructed democracy in the following three ways: People Power, electoral politics and urban governance. The second antagonistic relationship is the "moral solidarity of the nation," which is constructed when a moral demarcation line is drawn between bad politicians and the good "people" united in opposition.[4] In this case, solidarity in the name of "the people" has the effect of temporarily obscuring the demarcation line between classes. During the democratization process of 1986 and the presidential election of 2010, the moral solidarity of the nation had the paradoxical effect of preserving elite rule, even as this solidarity provided the underpinnings for political participation by those seeking a new politics that bade farewell to corruption.

Meanwhile, in the contact zone, a variety of social movements provided the medium for discourse between members of the civic and mass spheres. This interaction blurred the moral demarcation line and facilitated attempts to mediate the moral division of the nation. Rather than unduly foregrounding the moral antagonism between the middle and impoverished classes, these social movements sought to make the interests of the poor a part of public policy. Yet, while this effort has in practice achieved certain results, it has thus far lacked the leverage to effect major changes in Philippine politics.

This book aims to clarify how the dynamics of morally antagonistic "we/they" relations between dual public spheres have come to play a decisive role in both the advancement and obstruction of Philippine democracy, against a backdrop in which the hegemony of the elite is highly contested by various counter-hegemonies in civil society. The argument is also made that moral politics based on a perceived confrontation between good and evil undermines democracy by marginalizing interest politics over the distribution of resources. A democratic system that faces severe financial constraints and extreme inequality has above all a need for a deliberation-based distribution of resources. Instead, the moral division of a nation replaces interest-based conflict, which is amenable to amelioration through the distribution of resources, with morality-based conflict, which does not readily allow compromise, thereby further radicalizing antagonism. Meanwhile, moral nationalism temporarily conceals deep-seated inequalities under the rubric of "people's solidarity," although it cannot improve equality. The result is an accumulation of resentment toward an evil "enemy," which acts as a powerful destabilizing force in a democracy.

The growth of moral politics in the Philippines was greatly influenced by neoliberalism, and parallels what is happening in many other democracies, in developed and developing countries alike. In extolling and insisting upon unfettered market competition, neoliberalism confronts democracy with the thorny challenges of growing inequality and social fragmentation. The Philippines has experienced this problem under the conditions of deep class divisions, fragile democratic institutions, and limited financial resources. As a consequence, the problems posed by moral politics are fully exposed in the Philippines, as are numerous practices that seek to resolve this impasse. By studying the example of the Philippines, we hope to both identify and seek solutions to the problems of contemporary democracy associated with the moralization of politics under neoliberalism.

Social Conditions for Democracy

Studies on the Middle Class and Civil Society

In this book, the concept of "democracy" as I employ the term has two meanings. First, I use it in the sense of democracy as a system characterized by open competition for political power and the use of freely contested elections to select leaders. According to this definition, "consolidation of democracy" means a situation in which there is a consensus between the elite and the rest of the citizenry that democracy is the "only game in town" behaviorally, attitudinally and legally (Linz and Stepan 1996: 5). Second, I use "democracy" in the sense of an ideal that includes socioeconomic equality, according to which, "deepening democracy" involves exposing and remedying diverse forms of inequality and oppression that fail to be addressed as issues. When the word "democracy" is used, it refers to a concept embracing both meanings.

Most studies to date have postulated that democracy will advance with the growth of a highly educated and reasonably wealthy middle class and concomitant political participation by a growing number of people who possess an elevated "civic" consciousness. However, the influence of a specific social group on democracy is inevitably determined by antagonistic "we/they" relations that shift over time. It is from this standpoint that previous studies on middle class and civil society will be critiqued.

First, it has often been claimed that the growth of the middle class stabilizes and promotes democracy in such fields as modernization theory, which focuses on economic development and the modernization of society (Lipset 1959); historical sociology, which explains the establishment of democratic systems in terms of the transformation of social structure (Moore 1966; Rueschemeyer et al. 1992); "third wave" democratization theory (Huntington 1991); and game theory, which views democratization and stable democratic systems as being linked to interclass competition regarding redistribution (Persson and Tabellini 2000; Rosendorff 2001).[5] Similar views have been espoused in recent studies of Asian politics (Hsiao and Koo 1997). On the other hand, considerable research in Asian area studies rebuts this view by demonstrating that the nature of the middle class is ambiguous and not necessarily democratic, calling attention to the need to examine the individual context of each country rather than simply referencing the experience of Western Europe (Robison and Goodman 1996: 3).[6]

Studies of the Philippine middle class also remark upon its imprecise nature. Rivera (2000, 2007) asserts that, while the middle class has played a leading role in diverse movements across the spectrum from right to left, it has come to ally itself with other classes due to its small size. Shiraishi (2008) also argues that the middle class has a low degree of dependence on the state and provides the core of numerous social movements, but because it has been unable to gain control of the legislature and the government, it has split into establishment and anti-establishment factions. Tadem (2008) asserts that the middle class contains a sector that plays a significant role in the democratization of society as a supporter of voluntary associations, as well as a sector that supports the pursuit of profit under a free-market economy. Pinches (2010: 301–8) classifies the middle class as a sector that withdraws into a private world of consumption, reinforcing an exclusivist attitude toward the poor, as a left-wing NGO sector that continues to engage in patriarchal interventions with the poor, and as a sector that supports assistance to the poor through church-related NGOs. Kawanaka (2010) argues that the urban middle class became a factor in political instability through such actions as ousting a president with which it was dissatisfied, because he favored the rural poor in the interests of electoral politics.

Unquestionably, then, the Philippine middle class has a diverse political character. This diversity is partially defined by relations with other social groups; however, it cannot be explained strictly in terms of interest politics. This is demonstrated by the fact that even though the middle class and the poor might understandably have a common cause in opposing the interest politics under the control of the elite, conditions frequently arise in which the two classes become moral antagonists. However, the political consciousness of the middle class does reveal certain common denominators, including criticism of elite corruption and nepotism in traditional politics, and ambitions for modern political reform (Pinches 1996, 2010; Schaffer 2008: 132–6).

A paradox of this desire for modern political reform is that it tends to entail an exclusivist attitude toward the poor whenever the middle class believes that the poor pose an obstacle to such reform. For example, a deep-rooted belief can be seen within the middle class that the impoverished class, being easily deceived and bought off by incompetent and corrupt politicians, hinders the development of the Philippines. Although those who hold this belief identify themselves as educated and moral "citizens," they label the poor as "non-citizens," that is, the "masses," thus asserting their own intellectual and moral superiority. Although most studies on civil society have sought to identify the normative elements of "citizens" that contribute to democracy, none have adequately elucidated the politics associated with the labeling of "citizens" and "non-citizens."

Here, I define "studies on civil society" in a broader sense. The classic study by Almond and Verba (1963) asserts that the stable functioning of democracy requires not only the introduction of a system but also a suitable "civic culture." In recent years, Putnam (1993, 2000) has developed a theory of civic community that places emphasis on "social capital" in the form of trust, norms, and horizontal networks. The argument that democracy can be strengthened through active engagement with public issues by NGOs and other voluntary associations of citizens is also common. For example, Diamond (1999: 221) states: "Democracy— in particular, a healthy liberal democracy—also requires a public that is organized for democracy, socialized to its norms and values, and committed not just to its myriad narrow interests but to larger, common, 'civic' ends. Such a civic public is only possible with a vibrant 'civil society'." I refer to such arguments as "Tocquevillian civil society theory."

In addition, more than a few studies of civil society in Southeast Asia draw a connection between political participation by voluntary associations and the growth of the middle class, thereby viewing it as a factor that contributes to the advancement of democracy. In the wake of democratization, Tocquevillian civil-society theory also gained popularity in the Philippines. Bolstering this was the fact that activists from the middle class who had participated in the democratization movement formed numerous NGOs and began actively proposing policies aimed at "moral recovery" from the corruption of the state. According to studies of this phenomenon, political participation by NGOs has not only contributed to the checking of state power but also created a new, reformist "civic culture," altered the policy agenda with their proposals, and helped to actualize public policies reflecting the interests of social groups that had not been previously represented.[7] This theory of Philippine civil society is important for having brought into focus the conflict between elite democracy and citizens' political participation.

However, this "citizenry" standing in opposition to elite democracy is hardly harmonious or monolithic. What bears critiquing here is that this NGO activity and theory of Philippine civil society has been at least partially predicated on notions of a leadership role by self-styled "citizens" of the middle class and the dependency of the impoverished class. As Pinches (2010: 287) puts it, Philippine civil society "has been constructed as an alternate hegemonic space, seen to embrace the whole national citizenry, but molded on and in the interests of the growing middle class, in alliance with that section of the business elites which has publicly sought to distance itself from patrimonial politics, advocating instead modernist principles of free market capitalism, meritocracy, and legal-bureaucratic order." Also, as Kiba (2010: 28) has critically remarked, NGO members who pride themselves on being the representatives of Philippine civil society share a self-image of "people with a high degree of 'civil spirit' achieving social reform by organizing, assisting, or acting for poor people," and have prioritized the expansion of their own influence in the name of "aiding" the poor.[8] Moreover, as Garrido (2008: 456) argues, the notion of activists from the middle class instilling discipline in and leading an intellectually and morally inferior impoverished class (the "masses") has served the function of concealing a symbolic demarcation line that excludes the "masses" from civil society.[9]

In other words, most studies on civil society have sought only to identify the conditions under which "citizens" contribute to democracy from a specific normative viewpoint. Consequently, they have been incapable of critically analyzing the claim of the middle class to a position of moral superiority in civil society while labeling themselves as good "citizens" and the poor as "non-citizens" (that is, the "masses"). In order to analyze the politics of this moralistic "we/they" labeling, it is useful to adopt a constructivist approach that views the political process from the perspective of an ongoing hegemonic struggle.

Constructivism and Hegemonic Struggle

According to Laclau and Mouffe (1985), the identity and interests of a particular social group are neither *a priori* nor intrinsic but rather are constructed through diverse hegemonic practices that structure meaning. The structure of meaning is not fixed, but is instead contingent and provisional, and may be changed through the agency of people negotiating with it; the actual political process develops under the constraints of this shifting meaning structure, reflecting its characteristics.[10] Constructivism is characterized by an emphasis on the construction of an inter-subjective identity using interpretations of symbols and meaning; as a theoretical perspective, it is gaining increased acceptance in the field of comparative political science.[11]

This book applies the Gramscian theory of civil society, a constructivist theory that focuses on hegemonic struggles in which different forces compete for support by presenting different collective identities as "we." Gramsci himself viewed civil society as a realm in which hegemony by the state or a dominant group subjugated people to secure their voluntary submission through associations such as schools, churches, political parties and corporations. More recently, however, neo-Marxist scholars such as Laclau and Mouffe have developed Gramscian theory in order to clarify the possibility of counter-hegemonies that subordinate sectors seeking to expand by representing themselves as agents of change. To further develop their focus on counter-hegemony, I will elaborate on the struggle among competing counter-hegemonies and its varying outcomes.

I treat civil society as an arena of perpetual struggle in which mutually antagonistic "we/they" identities compete for both intellectual and moral leadership and also political power. This understanding opens the door to a critical analysis of the power characteristics of the moral concept of "citizens" that extends beyond the limitations of Tocquevillian civil-society theory, which habitually views civil society as an ideal democratic realm based on a specific moral foundation.[12]

To be certain, not all of the Philippine civil-society studies that take the Tocquevillian viewpoint turn a blind eye to the tension and antagonism existent in "we/they" relations. For example, Ferrer (1997b) raises concerns about the tense relationship between middle-class NGOs, which seek social reform for others' benefit, and "people's organizations" of the poor, which seek their own solutions to problems. It is widely assumed that harmonious cooperative relations between poor people's organizations and NGOs are indispensable to the achievement of political reforms that further the interests of the poor.[13]

However, the friction and discord between these two groups is considerable and difficult to reconcile. Boudreau argues that the friction between leftist NGOs espousing universal logic and grassroots people's organizations focusing on local issues is not something that can be resolved by the awakening of the latter's consciousness, and that this friction has a significant influence on the mobilization and dissolution of movements (Boudreau 2001). Moreover, the poor are not merely mobilized by NGOs, but rather use the NGOs to their own advantage. Magno (2003) and Karaos (2006) make note of a squatters' organization that operated independently of an NGO and that switched its allied organization from a church-related NGO to a pro-Estrada organization in the interest of furthering the land acquisition movement. In my own personal observations of a street vendors' organization, I noted that it worked with a moderate NGO adept at lobbying activities when the government appeared cooperative, but switched counterparts to a leftist group that held street demonstrations when the government shifted to a policy of harsh crackdowns (Kusaka 2010). According to Kiba (2010), squatters' organizations are able to achieve their objectives by skillfully controlling outside professionals and NGOs and allowing them to handle the procedures required for land acquisition. On the other hand, people's organizations that failed to achieve their goals have expressed disgust with NGOs and asserted their independence (Kiba 2012).

Case studies such as these are significant in demonstrating that attempts by NGOs to include the poor in the "we" of "we citizens" are easily frustrated, and in highlighting the need to recognize class antagonism in civil society as something that cannot be fundamentally resolved. However, while these studies have analyzed the effect of class antagonism between NGOs and people's organizations on the success or failure of individual social movements in civil society, they have not analyzed this effect on the more "macro" scale of promotion or obstruction of democracy. Furthermore, they have tended to view class antagonism solely in terms of interests and overlook its moralized character.

For a more "macro" political analysis, it is useful to examine the hegemonic struggles that produce antagonistic "we/they" relations. To the best of my knowledge, four previous studies have discussed hegemonic struggles in Philippine civil society from a Gramscian perspective. Hedman (2005) asserts that the dominant bloc (consisting of the church, big business and the US government) exercises a powerful hegemony in Philippine civil society. When confronted with a crisis in which presidential abuse of power and challenges from the "masses" threatens its vested interests, the dominant bloc subjugates people, primarily of the middle class, as moral "citizens," thereby mobilizing them to participate in anti-populist demonstrations and election-monitoring movements to ensure "free and fair" elections. This, Hedman says, stymies the challenge from the left and from populists with their support base among the "masses," resulting in the perpetuation of elite democracy.[14] In emphasizing the hegemony of the dominant bloc, however, she does not address the possibilities of change in elite democracy.

In another study, Garrido (2008) argues that in Philippine civil society the "masses" experience daily cultural and symbolic exclusion in the course of being treated as invisible by a "citizenry" that refuses to recognize them. He claims that the "mass" uprising known as "People Power 3" in May 2001 was actually a protest against this exclusion. This explanation is significant for the argument that hegemony by ruling forces does not always exercise an overwhelming dominance in civil society, and that it can be challenged by counter-hegemony. However, because this argument presupposes a fixed antagonistic relationship between "citizens" and "masses," it fails to explain the circumstances of change in the form of cooperation by the two forces.

Unlike the above studies, Quimpo (2008) treats hegemonic struggle between the two forces as fluid. He analyzes hegemonic struggle in civil society by introducing the convincing analytical framework of "contested democracy," which focuses on competition between elite democracy and "democracy from below" by the citizenry. However, by treating the moderate leftist group Akbayan as representative of "democracy from below," and legitimizing and privileging its role as such, Quimpo dismisses other forces opposing elite democracy as adulterating true "democracy from below." Although this framework is useful, the assumption is problematic in that it lacks a critical perspective for analyzing the exclusivist power of the "citizens" who lead Akbayan.[15]

From a more neutral stance, Igarashi (2011) studied the activities of numerous civic organizations and asserted that while activities by civic organizations led by members of the wealthy and middle classes may sometimes promote democracy, they may also exclude the poor and obstruct democracy at times. He explains the ambiguity of the effect of civil society on democracy as a product of the competition and expedient alliances among various organizations espousing different ideologies. However, in limiting his analysis to the expedient alliances and competition among various organizations, he overlooks the influence of unorganized ordinary people on the political process. In fact, ordinary people who do not normally engage in organized political activities have also played a crucial role in the political process through such actions as participating in People Power, voting for candidates and generating discourse on specific issues.[16] If we are to elucidate this role, we must examine how ordinary people have perceived, interpreted and engaged in Philippine politics.

In summary, while you cannot deny the persistence of the elite's hegemony in Philippine civil society, the new task for studies of this society is to explain how various forces have tried to expand their counter-hegemonies in civil society and what outcomes have been produced by the struggle among them. Construction and contestation of fluid and contingent "we/they" relations, both antagonistic and cooperative, among the elite, the "citizens" and the "masses," including ordinary people, provide the key for this analysis.

Subjects and Methodology of Research

To prepare for my analysis of hegemonic struggles within Philippine civil society, I first investigated previous studies and newspaper articles extensively. Next, at the field research stage, I conducted live-in participant observations and interview surveys with members of both the civic and mass spheres in the Metro Manila area (hereafter Manila). Some may object to the notion of discussing Philippine civil society based solely on research conducted in Manila; however, for analyzing the effect of hegemonic struggles in civil society on the political process, Manila is the most critical region in the Philippines.

First, Manila is significant to the analysis of antagonism and cooperation between the civic and mass spheres because, while it has the nation's largest concentration of middle-class residents, it also has a large number of poor residents who have emigrated from rural villages, and these populations coexist in proximity, their division into civic and mass spheres notwithstanding. Second, due to Manila's high concentration of mass media and media consumers, it is a region where both moral discourse about "how politics should be" enjoys widespread circulation and also politics that draws a demarcation line between "we" and "they" has seen vigorous growth. Third, because Manila is the capital, civil society and the state lie in relatively close proximity; this makes it the easiest place both for the state to put on ostentatious displays of its power vis-à-vis society and also for people to make their influence felt at comparatively little cost by mounting demonstrations and voicing policy proposals.

From April 2002 until April 2003, I lived in a squatters' settlement in Quezon City, part of Metro Manila. It was there that I conducted my first long-term survey of the mass sphere.[17] During this period, I spent as much time as possible with people from the impoverished class, endeavoring to gain an intrinsic understanding of their political consciousness and behavior. Because the Filipino family I lived with worked as street vendors, we spent nearly every evening together for a year selling fruits and sausages on the street. Since then, I have continued to engage in participant observation by living in this district for at least one month every year. My findings on life and discourse in the mass sphere are primarily based on this participant observation.

To supplement the information I had acquired through participant observation, in 2008, 2009 and 2010 I conducted interviews in the squatters' settlement with people with whom I had cultivated a certain degree of trust.[18] I asked questions on issues in three general categories, to which I have devoted Chapters 3, 4 and 5 in this book, namely, People Power, elections and urban governance, respectively. I encouraged people to speak freely in the interest of maintaining the flow of conversation. The language spoken was primarily Tagalog. Although I placed no limit on interview times, most of the interviews lasted between 30 minutes to an hour. The number of interviewees was 22 in 2008 and 37 in 2009, for a total of 59. In February 2010, I conducted interviews about the presidential election in the same squatters' settlement; this time, the number of interviewees was 20, some of whom I had interviewed previously.

As part of my research in 2008 and 2009, I also interviewed members of the civic-sphere middle class. Until then, I had relied mainly on English-language newspapers to reference discourse in the civic sphere, but I realized that I also needed to listen directly to people from the middle class. To this end, I conducted interviews in three middle-class residential subdivisions. Through introductions by acquaintances, I was also able to conduct separate interviews with lawyers, teachers and other professionals, company employees, and proprietors of small- and medium-sized businesses. These interviews were conducted mostly in English, but also in Tagalog when necessary. My middle-class interviewees numbered 17 in 2008 and 12 in 2009, for a total of 29.

The interviews were recorded and later transcribed by my Filipino college student assistants.[19] I analyzed the data derived from these interviews and identified the views and narratives that were articulated most frequently in the civic and mass spheres, respectively, as dominant discourses. I also focused on narratives that I believed to be significant in revealing the breadth of discourse in each sphere, for example, by taking a negative view of a dominant discourse. The names I use in this book for my informants are generally nicknames. Throughout this book, I have used several controversial terms such as "squatters," although I recognize that such terms may be seen as offensive to some and may contribute to further criminalization of these people. However, if I were to choose to use instead a "neutral" term, I fear that I might paradoxically strengthen the idea that "squatting" is morally evil. In reality, the poor themselves use the word and morally justify it as a means of survival. My intention is to question the hegemony of "civic" norms and highlight the moral contestation of concepts.

Organization of the Book

This book is organized as follows. Chapter 1 introduces the analytical framework. Previous Philippine studies generally argue that the elite have maintained elite democracy by doling out various benefits, as well as violence and coercion, to procure the votes of the poor. However, in recent years, increasing urbanization accompanied by overseas emigration for work have served to loosen the vertical ties between the elite and the poor, which now enables the poor to participate in politics more freely than ever. Hence, hegemony of the elite is seriously contested and phenomena that are unable to be explained by elite democracy discourse are on the rise. Civil society theory that focuses on political participation by voluntary associations has failed to adequately analyze the exclusivist power of the "citizenry." To resolve these shortcomings, I offer a new analytical framework, "hegemonic struggle in the dual public spheres," which focuses on the dynamics of morally antagonistic "we/they" relations inclusive of ordinary people who normally do not engage in organized political activities, and describes the role of these relations in the political process.

Chapter 2 surveys the historical process of formation of the dual public spheres—the civic sphere and mass sphere. First, linguistic and educational policies carried out under the colonial system created a division between a small intellectual elite with command of the colonizers' language (Spanish or English) and the vast majority of the poor without such command. Even after independence, this linguistic split was reflected in the division between the English media consumed by highly educated people and the indigenous-language media accessible to the poor. Moreover, the urban space of Manila developed with people's living environments separated by class. This division along class lines of living environments and the discourse arenas of the middle and impoverished classes resulted in the formation of dual public spheres.

In Chapters 3 through 5, I take up the cases of People Power, electoral politics, and urban governance, respectively, and argue that the moral division of the nation has had a deleterious effect on democracy.

Chapter 3 looks at the three People Power movements that sought the ouster of the president, and analyzes each event's antagonistic relations and effect on democracy. The first, in 1986, saw the formation of a "people" who opposed Marcos as the enemy of the nation, as well as the achievement of democratization through "People Power 1," a movement sustained by the moral solidarity of the nation. However, in 1998, when Estrada became president with the support of the poor, the dissolution of this "people" became apparent. In response to Estrada's populism, the mass sphere saw the formation of a moral antagonism defined as something between the virtuous "masses," who had suffered from poverty and the deprivation of their dignity, and the evil "rich" who despised and oppressed them. Meanwhile, in the civic sphere, moral antagonism arose between the "citizens" who criticized Estrada's corruption and the evil "masses" who continued to support him. In 2001, these "citizens" used "People Power 2" to oust Estrada from the presidency. However, in the same year, "People Power 3," rising from the mass sphere as "masses" increasingly frustrated with that very result, stormed the presidential palace demanding the ouster of President Arroyo and the reinstatement of Estrada. The hostile back-and-forth exchange between members of the People Power movements, which aimed to eliminate opposing presidents in 2001, posed a grave threat to the consolidation of democracy.

In Chapter 4, I argue that the moral division of the nation reduced trust in the electoral process. Even though the majority of eligible voters belonged to the impoverished class, their votes had long been dispersed and exploited in factional struggles among the elite, and had not served to advance class interests underpinned by horizontal solidarity. However, in 1998 and thereafter, in response to Estrada's appeals to "the poor" and "the masses," the impoverished class formed a loose voting bloc that gave it more influence in elections. Still, this did not lead to improved living conditions among the poor. Meanwhile, in the civic sphere, a sense of victimhood grew in tandem with the belief that we "citizens" were under the thumbs of politicians who had won the votes of the "masses" through bribery and the manipulation of images. This generated widespread mistrust of an electoral process over which the votes of the poor now wielded such influence, and of democracy itself. This is the paradoxical outcome that the emergence of counter-hegemonic voting blocs against the traditional elite in both spheres yielded. To remedy this problem, church-related NGOs held voter education campaigns in which they exhorted the poor to vote "correctly." However, this attempt by the civic sphere to enlighten the mass sphere cannot be said to have changed the voting behavior of the poor, even if it did succeed in opening a conduit in the contact zone for communication between disparate moralities.

In Chapter 5, I shift the focus to urban governance and argue that in the process of enforcing laws, the moral division of the nation worked against the interests of the poor. Many of the poor living in Manila survive by the illegal means of squatting and street vending. In 2002 the Metropolitan Manila Development Authority (MMDA) condemned these activities as infestations of disorder, announced a policy of strict enforcement of law and order, and embarked upon the large-scale forced demolition of squatter settlements and street stalls. This hardline, punitive approach to governance won approval in the civic sphere as a discourse treating the poor as criminals rather than as people deserving of help, and it gained widespread currency. In response, members of the impoverished class who felt their livelihoods threatened made an appeal from the mass sphere to both the civic sphere and state for recognition of their right to dignified livelihoods. In the civic sphere, however, support for the rule of law and order predominated, and these voices of desperation were not recognized as legitimate. Meanwhile, the state continued with its forced demolitions. Again, the desire for political reform divided the people. Even so, certain movements were emerging in the contact zone that sought to mediate this confrontation between the morality of the mass sphere, which placed emphasis on the survival of the poor, and the morality of the civic sphere, which prioritized the rule of law. These included efforts to establish a land-purchasing system for squatters and to legalize some street vending. Although these movements succeeded in setting up new systems, their implementation proved problematic.

Chapter 6 describes how elite rule was preserved, even as the moral division of the nation grew less clear-cut during the Arroyo administration and the moral solidarity of the nation reemerged during the 2010 presidential election. With the military and the House of Representatives as its power base, the Arroyo administration (2001–10) engaged in repeated acts of graft and corruption in nearly complete disregard of criticism from the public. As a result, Arroyo lost her moral legitimacy, even in the civic sphere, and moral nationalism that transcended the dual public-sphere schism led to the formation of a "people" that opposed her as an "enemy of the people." In the 2010 presidential election, this national backlash against Arroyo provided the backdrop for the sweeping victory by Benigno Aquino III, who ran as the morally clean, anti-corruption, "national" solidarity candidate, over two populist opponents. The anti-corruption moral politics of the

Aquino administration effectively neutralized the political rivals of the opposing elite. This case illustrates the paradox that counter-hegemony of the reformative "people" transformed Aquino, scion of a family of the traditional elite, into a moral agent of change who, by calling for morality and reform, served to obscure class contradictions and perpetuate rule by that elite.

In the final chapter, I summarize the knowledge gained about moral politics in the Philippines. First, the moral solidarity of the nation advanced democratization and acted as a force against political corruption. However, at the same time, it concealed deep-seated inequalities and preserved elite democracy by turning a member of a traditional elite into a moral leader of change and helping to form a weird coalition of elites and reformative "people." Second, the moral division of the nation replaced inter-class antagonism over resource distribution-related interests with moral antagonism in terms of good and evil, thereby exacerbating the mutual antipathy between classes and contributing to the instability of democracy. However, in the contact zone, one could see evidence of social movements by voluntary associations attempting to mediate this moral division of the nation. Nonetheless, efforts to incorporate the poor into the "citizenry" through moral education have not succeeded. If anything, greater possibilities for mediating the moral division of the nation can be found in efforts to improve the socioeconomic status of the poor through cooperation between the middle and impoverished classes at the level of interests, even while their moral antagonism persists. Based on these findings, I place Philippine moral politics among the structural conditions under which the Philippines has experienced a particularly severe version of the challenges posed to democracy by neoliberalism. Finally, I conclude with the argument that if we are to overcome this challenge, which is faced not only by the Philippines, but also by many other nations, it is necessary to curb the moralization of politics and engage more people in the interest politics of improving distribution of resources while building a new sense of community through expansion of the contact zone where people of different spheres can meet "others."

CHAPTER 1

Analytical Framework

Photo 2 Children playing in an informal settlement (Pechayan, December 2007).

Determining factors in the consolidation of a democracy include the international environment, the economy, the political system and the social structure. This book focuses on social structure—in other words, the social conditions for democracy. The Philippine social structure is characterized by profound class disparities and a high poverty rate, and these have had a particularly powerful impact on the practice of democracy.

According to elite democracy arguments, the stratified social structure of the Philippines fostered rule by oligarchic elites. However, scholars such as Kerkvliet (1995, 2005), Quimpo (2005, 2008) and Takagi (2016) put forth the critique that elite democracy discourses have reduced Philippine politics to mere factional competition and the pursuit of private profit by the elite while ignoring a broader diversity of values and struggles.[1] It is true that the emergence of non-traditional politicians in presidential and senatorial elections, as well as a surge in political participation by voluntary associations that oppose elite rule, has been seen in recent years. Consequently, one cannot understand Philippine politics strictly in terms of elite democracy. On the other hand, Tocquevillian civil society arguments, which focus on voluntary associations, are incapable of analyzing the hegemony of a middle class that calls itself the "citizenry," yet subordinates or excludes the poor. Previous Gramscian civil-society arguments about Philippine politics misjudged the elite's hegemony as penetrating civil society, viewed antagonism as fixed and failed to explain changes therein, or limited analysis to rivalries and expedient alliances among organized forces.

The study of Philippine politics requires a framework for analyzing how an increasingly fluid civil society—where various counter-hegemonies comprising both organized activities and a broader range of people challenge the elite's rule through voting, demonstrations and the creation of discourses—wields influence on the political process.

In this chapter, I will begin by reviewing the historical process that led to the inequalities and elite dominance of Philippine society. I will then describe how that structure has changed in recent years, from an era when the elite dominated the society in a top-down fashion to one in which politics is determined by the growing fluidity of society. In this context, I will also introduce the analytical framework of "hegemonic struggle in the dual public spheres" to explain Philippine politics in today's fluid society.

Changes in Philippine Society and Politics

The Formation of Inequality and Elite Rule

The origins of inequality in the Philippines lie in the system of large landholdings that developed under colonial rule and the growth of capitalism.² When Spain colonized the Philippines in the 16th century, it prohibited ships from other countries from entering Manila harbor. However, the spread of capitalism and world trade prompted Spain to open the port in 1834. The result was that the Philippine economy was incorporated into the world economy, and its exports of sugar, coconut palms and other cash crops proved extremely lucrative. Seeing this as an opportunity to accumulate wealth, Spanish religious orders and *mestizos* (people of mixed indigenous and Spanish or Chinese parentage) seized land from indigenous peoples and built huge plantations. With the advent of the American colonial period in 1898, Chinese mestizos, who had become wealthy running plantations on vast tracts of land purchased from the Spanish religious orders being expelled from the Philippines formed a traditional elite class.³

The American colonial government introduced democratic institutions to this stratified society; however, instead of weakening the power base of the elite, this action paradoxically reinforced it.⁴ The Americans employed members of the local elites as administrators and expanded the scope of elected offices from local governments to the Philippine Assembly (the equivalent of the subsequent House of Representatives), thereby paving the way for the acquisition of political power by the elite under the colonial system.⁵ However, the Americans concentrated the power to distribute economic resources and approve businesses in the central government. This produced a structure under which members of the elite elected to public office from localities all vied with one another for a share of the resources and the power of the central government (Fujiwara 1990: 44). The result was the creation of "strong societies and weak states" (Migdal 1988) in the Philippines, with local elites wielding tremendous influence in their home regions, leaving the state unable to exercise sufficient social control (Abinales and Amoroso 2005).⁶

Even after independence, the elite continued to utilize "rent" in the form of the state's authority over businesses in order to amass capital for their families, thereby maintaining a firm grip on power that continues to the present day (Hutchcroft 1998). In addition, unlike in Malaysia or Indonesia, overseas Chinese were effectively integrated into Philippine society, such that ethnic Chinese elites came to exercise powerful leadership as politicians and businessmen (Sidel 2008). Although elites divided by language engaged in fierce competition with one another for wealth and power, they still managed to construct a system of rule that protected their common class interests. Consequently, social cleavage along class became a more important factor than ethnic or language lines in the politics of the Philippines.[7]

Here I would like to take a moment to describe the Philippine class structure. I have adopted the approach of defining class in terms of occupation and characteristics of residences for the practical merit of being able to use the statistical data and to facilitate the identification of a social class of informants. The proportion of social class based on these two indicators are almost the same.

The wealthy class includes a traditional elite that has broadened its economic activities from plantation management to the manufacturing and service industries, as well as a new breed of ethnic Chinese entrepreneurs who have made noticeable strides in recent years. Middle-class occupations include professionals, technologists, business managers and executives, office workers, and the university students who fill these occupations. In the impoverished class, occupations include workers in the sales, service, farming, logging, fishing, production and transportation industries. Among these are factory workers, security guards, short-term contract laborers and others at the bottom of the formal sector, as well as street vendors, maids and others in the informal sector.

Public education introduced by the Americans formed the middle class professionals, technologists, business managers and executives, and office workers, especially in Metro Manila. The private sector played a bigger role than the public sector in providing job opportunities to the middle class. After the 1950s, however, the growth of the middle class stagnated, and after the 1980s, against the background of economic decline and labor policies, many members of the middle class migrated overseas. From the 1970s to the early 2000s, the middle class comprised about 10 per cent of the population nationwide and about 25 per cent of that in Metro Manila (see Figure 2). Nonetheless, Pinches (1996: 106) notes the advent of a "new rich" comprising new business entrepreneurs, overseas contract workers, and educated professionals, technologists and managers in the 1990s. Moreover, after the turn of the century, the gross domestic product (GDP) of the Philippines began to grow at a rate of 6 to 7 per cent. However, unlike other Southeast Asian countries, a radical increase in the proportion of the middle class in the Philippines has yet to be seen. The fact that reproduction of the middle class has been limited to within one-fourth that of better-off urban dwellers helped form an elitist self-identity as a social class superior to the rural and urban poor (Shiraishi 2008: 7–9).

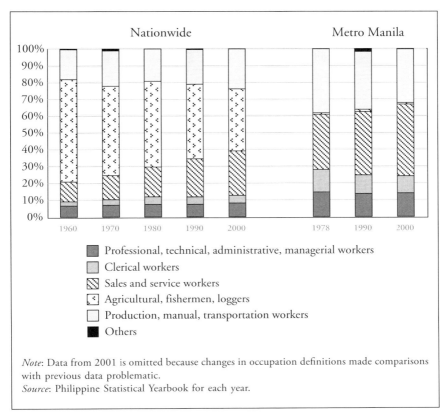

Figure 2 Employment in the Philippines by Occupation

Next, let us examine the characteristics of poverty in terms of indicators other than occupation (see Table 1). First, note that although the population below the poverty line as defined by the government-established benchmark of "basic consumption needs" has been declining, except for the sudden rise in Manila in the mid-2000s, the percentage of households subjectively regarding themselves as "poor" is much greater. According to a survey by Social Weather Stations (SWS), a private social research institution, 50 to 60 per cent of households nationwide, and about 35 to 50 per cent in Manila, perceive themselves as living in poverty.[8] Since the SWS survey uses the household as a unit, and poor households generally have more children than wealthier ones,

Table 1 Income Disparities and Poverty Rates in the Philippines

	Per cent of population below poverty line		Per cent of households self-rated as poor		Gini coefficients	
	Nationwide	Manila	Nationwide	Manila	Nationwide	Manila
1985	49.3	27.2	74.0	50.0	0.415	0.447
1988	45.5	25.2	66.0	38.5	0.426	0.445
1991	45.3	16.7	66.5	38.3	0.428	0.468
1994	40.6	10.5	68.3	48.5	0.397	0.451
1997	36.8	8.5	59.3	35.8	0.487	0.462
2000	33.0	7.8	56.5	34.6	0.482	0.445
2003	30.0	6.9	59.5	37.3	0.461	0.402
2006	32.9	10.4	54.3	52.5	0.458	0.399
2009	26.5	4.0	49.4	42.0	0.448	0.395

Sources: Gini coefficients and per cent of population below poverty line, National Statistical Coordination Board; per cent of households self-rated as poor (*mahirap*), Social Weather Stations, *Survey Sourcebook*; for the latter, mean values were calculated for each year in which national surveys were conducted.

the percentage of the population that considers itself poor may be even higher.

SWS also takes the approach of categorizing social classes by characteristics of residences (see Table 2).[9] If quality of residence is used as an indicator, trends identical to those when referencing occupation are found. At the beginning of the 2000s, the wealthy and middle classes constituted less than one tenth of the total population, while the impoverished class made up about 90 per cent. In Manila, the wealthy comprised about 10 per cent, the middle class 20 to 30 per cent and the impoverished class 60 to 70 per cent. Looking at education, we find that in Manila, those with a university or higher education made up 30 to 40 per cent, while those with a high school or lower education made up about 60 to 70 per cent; the higher the class, the higher the education level tended to be (see Table 3). In short, the Philippine social structure has a pyramidal shape with a very small wealthy class (the politico-economic elite) at the top, followed

Table 2 Socioeconomic Status Indicators Used by SWS (%)

	AB	C	D	E
Nationwide	2	7	67	24
Manila	12	24	44	20

Source: Social Weather Stations, *Survey Sourcebook*, 2002; mean values were calculated for results from four surveys per year. SWS employs a market survey approach, defining class by quality of residence with AB representing the wealthy class, C the middle class, and DE the impoverished class.

Table 3 Education Level by Socioeconomic Status (%)

	Elementary school unfinished	Elementary school graduate	High school dropout	High school graduate	University dropout	University graduate or higher
ABC	2	7	3	12	15	62
D	10	17	14	24	15	21
E	22	33	15	20	6	3
Nationwide	18	19	13	23	11	16
Manila	4	9	9	23	21	34

Source: Social Weather Stations, *Survey Sourcebook*, 2002, First Quarter. The term "university" includes vocational schools.

by a small middle class and an extremely large impoverished class at the bottom.

Moreover, the degree of inequality between these classes is extreme. Comparing Gini coefficients for various Asian countries roughly around the years 2000 and 2010, we see that the Philippines is a particularly stratified society (see Table 4). According to Yurika Suzuki, in 2003, households in the lowest 10 per cent of income earned barely 1.8 per cent of the total income in the Philippines, while households in the top 10 per cent of income earned 36.3 per cent of the total; the correlation between income and education level is evident. In Manila, 56 per cent of members of households earning the top 60 per cent of income, compared to only 27 per cent of those earning the bottom 40 per cent, were high school or higher graduates (Suzuki 2007: 21–3).

Table 4 Income Disparities in Asian Countries

	Gini coefficient (survey year)	
Philippines	0.461 (2003)	0.430 (2012)
Cambodia	0.450 (1999)	0.308 (2012)
China	0.447 (2001)	0.370 (2011)
Malaysia	0.443 (1999)	0.463 (2009)
Singapore	0.425 (1998)	0.464 (2014)
Thailand	0.420 (2002)	0.393 (2012)
Vietnam	0.370 (2002)	0.389 (2012)
Laos	0.347 (2002)	0.379 (2012)
Taiwan	0.345 (2002)	0.336 (2014)
Indonesia	0.343 (2002)	0.356 (2010)
India	0.325 (1999)	0.336 (2012)
Bangladesh	0.318 (2000)	0.320 (2010)
South Korea	0.306 (2003)	0.313 (2007)

Source: Asian Development Bank, *Key Indicators 2006*, for the data around year 2000 (left column). World Bank GINI Index and CIA World Factbook for the data around year 2010 (right column), accessed July 10, 2016.

Political Participation in a More Fluid Society

Although Philippine society retains deep-rooted inequalities, it has undergone a number of changes in recent years. These changes include increased urbanization, a decline in the percentage of the population engaged in agriculture, and a growing number of overseas contract workers. Since the 1980s, the agrarian population has fallen to less than half the total population (see Table 5). The shrinking of the agricultural sector has been accompanied by growth in the service sector, but not in the industrial sector (see Table 6). Meanwhile, by 2000, the majority of the nation's population was living in cities (see Table 7). Since the 1980s, the number of overseas contract workers has also surged, as has the amount of money being remitted from abroad (see Table 8).

These changes have been accompanied by an ongoing transformation in the social structure under which the elite dominate the poor. In rural society, with its stagnant economy and lack of social fluidity, the

Table 5 Per cent of Labor Population in the Agricultural and Non-agricultural Sectors

Year	Agricultural	Non-Agricultural
1956	59.0	41.0
1970	53.8	46.2
1980	47.6	52.4
1990	45.2	54.8
2000	37.4	62.6
2010	29.1	70.9

Source: National Economic and Development Authority, National Statistical Coordination Board, and *Philippine Statistical Yearbook* for each year.

Table 6 Per cent of GDP from the Agricultural, Industrial and Service Sectors

Year	Agricultural	Industrial	Service
1970	28.9	29.5	41.6
1980	25.6	36.1	38.3
1990	22.3	35.5	42.2
2000	19.9	34.7	45.4
2010	11.6	32.6	55.8

Source: National Economic and Development Authority, National Statistical Coordination Board, and *Philippine Statistical Yearbook* for each year.

Table 7 Urban and Rural Percentages of National Population

Year	Urban	Rural
1970	31.8	68.2
1980	37.3	62.7
1990	48.6	51.4
2000	48.0	52.0
2010	48.9	51.9

Source: National Economic and Development Authority, National Statistical Coordination Board, *Philippine Statistical Yearbook* for each year, and Asian Development Bank, *Key Indicators 2011*.

Table 8 Overseas Contract Worker Population and Remittances (× USD 1,000)

Year	Population	Remittance
1975	12,501	–
1980	156,018	–
1985	372,784	693,704
1990	446,095	1,203,009
1995	654,022	3,868,578
2000	841,628	6,050,450
2005	988,615	10,689,005
2010	1,470,826	18,762,989

Source: National Statistical Coordination Board, *Philippine Statistical Yearbook* for each year.

poor must often depend on the local elite when seeking employment or when borrowing money to cover family illnesses, funerals and other emergencies. However, when work overseas or new employment opportunities at home enable them to acquire their own resources, they no longer need to depend on the elite. In this way, increased urbanization and migration have engendered a more pluralistic and competitive political environment.

Amid these changes, voluntary associations set up by the urban middle class have emerged as important actors. NGOs engaged in various activities such as rural reconstruction and election monitoring after independence, and numerous "cause-oriented groups" participated in the democratization movement. That being said, Kimura (2002: 184) points out that prior to the imposition of martial law, most of the middle class was generally immersed in clientelist networks. With democratization, however, members of the middle class that had spearheaded the democratization movement acquired new confidence as social reformers and formed NGOs that engaged in social action on such issues as fair elections, poverty, indigenous people, women and so on. Although it is difficult to ascertain the specific number of NGOs, the number of nonprofit organizations (NPOs) registered with the Securities and Exchange Commission increased nearly threefold between 1984 and 1995 (see Table 9).[10] In addition, the number of NGOs per one million people in the Philippines far surpasses comparable figures in other Asian countries

Table 9 Number of NPOs Registered with the Securities and Exchange Commission, and Estimated Number of NGOs

	Number of NPOs	Estimated number of NGOs*
January 1984	31,719	23,800
January 1987	38,353	28,700
August 1990	54,925	41,100
April 1993	76,369	57,200
December 1995	93,597	70,200

Note: *The Securities and Exchange Commission estimates that 75 per cent of NPOs are NGOs.
Source: Abridged from Table 4-1 in Clarke (1998: 70).

Table 10 Number of NGOs per One Million People in Asian Countries

Country	NGOs	Population (× one million)	NGOs per one million
Philippines	6,000	64.8	92.59
Sri Lanka	500	17.9	27.93
India	12,000	898.2	13.36
Bangladesh	1,200	115.2	10.42
Nepal	140	20.8	6.73
Indonesia	1,000	187.2	5.34
Thailand	200	58.1	3.33

Source: Abridged from Table 6-1 in Fisher (1998: 164).

(see Table 10). Furthermore, the Local Government Code enacted in 1991 not only promoted decentralization, but also systematized the participation of voluntary associations in local politics.

Social change also loosened the grip of clientelism, enabling the poor to participate more freely and autonomously in politics. According to SWS surveys from 1998 to 2007, those who voted according to the dictates of the elite amounted to only about 2 in 10 eligible voters (15 per cent in the cities and 22 per cent in rural areas), with about 80 per cent voting for candidates of their own choosing.[11] How, then, did the clientelism that had restricted voters' freedom come to lose its grip?

Beginning in the latter days of the colonial era, as agriculture became commercialized and landowners started to engage in the accumulation of capital, rural areas of Southeast Asia saw landowners abandon their traditional obligations toward tenant farmers. This caused the collapse of patron-client relations and led to peasant revolts (Scott 1969b, 1972b, 1977, 1985). In the Philippines, peasant revolts began to break out around 1920, primarily in central Luzon. However, the government suppressed the revolts with military assistance from the United States. After independence, clientelism defined local politics in most parts of the Philippines (Lande 1965; Agpalo 1972). From the 1960s on, a growing population and the worsening of the rural economy prompted vast numbers of farmers to seek employment in the cities. The result was the emergence in urban areas of "machine politics," in which the elite and the poor traded resources for votes at election time (Scott 1969b, 1972a; Nowak and Snyder 1970; Machado 1971, 1974). Even after democratization, machine politics remains visible, particularly in regional cities, where elites continue to dominate the poor using coercion and violence (Sidel 1999) or top-down organization and effective resource distribution (Kawanaka 2002).[12] Local politics in the Metro Manila area has also seen the development of machine politics through which the elite have made slum-dwellers their constituency (F. Magno 1993; Gloria 1995).

However, Manila in recent years has also been the site of a continuing trend of the poor extricating themselves from domination by the elite. Although politicians endeavor to establish clientelist relations with slum-dwellers, they find it difficult to cultivate stable relationships due to the constant shifting of the slum population. Also, because the population is so large, most slum-dwellers miss out on the distribution of benefits from the elite. Furthermore, unlike rural areas, where a few elite families control politics and the economy, in the cities, not only a large number of elites, but also leftist and other NGOs, compete for the votes of the poor. Consequently, the poor in Manila now enjoy a wider range of options in their quest for the resources necessary for survival, and may readily "transfer" their allegiance to other elites or NGOs in opportunistic fashion. Although the elite can punish such fickle supporters by halting the distribution of resources, this is not a very effective tactic when people have other alternatives from which to choose. Thus, in Manila, maintenance of the dominant status of the elite through the vertical distribution of benefits has become fluid and unstable.

Another factor since the 1990s among the impoverished class has been the spread of television, through which images and moods conveyed by the media have come to exert a significant influence on voters (Magno 1994). However, the poor are not necessarily manipulated or controlled by media imagery. Whereas the poor formerly voted in accordance with the directives of local elites, they may now discuss information gleaned from the media with family or friends, and choose which candidates to vote for on that basis (David 2004; February 8). With the poor now participating in politics in a more autonomous manner, candidates feel the pressure to actively appeal to them not only through dole-outs, but also through the media.[13]

The changes in the political party system that accompanied democratization also facilitated freer political participation by the poor. Until Marcos abolished Congress under martial law in 1972, the poor were embedded in the clientelist politics of the Nationalist and Liberal Parties, which hampered their ability to vote freely. However, with democratization came the collapse of the two-party system and the rise of a multiparty system, as many ambitious candidates set up their own parties. After elections, legislators pursuing their respective interests would switch party affiliations and join in a ruling coalition with the president, thereby making the multiparty system fluid.[14] As observed by Sidel, in a situation where they were no longer fettered by a two-party system, vote gatherers called "*lider*" or "leaders" for a given candidate, seeing that their candidate's prospects for victory were poor, could begin pocketing campaign funds without fear of post-election punishment (Sidel 1998). This in turn caused a slackening of the reins on the vote-getting process, allowing voters more leeway in deciding for whom to cast their vote. Therefore, democratization was followed by greater freedom of political participation in Philippine civil society.

However, without a stable party system to ameliorate the antagonistic relationships in civil society through representation, these antagonisms now directly manifest themselves to polarize political processes and foment political instability. Because clientelist relationships extending from the elite to the poor served as the foundation for political parties in the Philippines, parties representing different social classes did not evolve.[15] Although the two main parties adopted opposing policy or ideological positions immediately after World War II over such issues as cooperation with Japan, trade with the United States and finance, the advent of the Cold War rendered these differences ambiguous, as both parties adopted the same anti-Communist, pro-American stance (Takagi 2008, 2016). After this, most of conflicts between the two main parties consisted of factional struggles among the elite. Then, with democratization came the dismantling of the stable party system itself. Most voters ignore political parties and simply focus on the personalities of the candidates.[16] Furthermore, without cohesive parties, conflicts among the president, the Senate, and the House of Representatives are more difficult to reconcile and readily devolve into political deadlock and disorder.[17] As a consequence, political parties cannot mediate social antagonisms within the democratic system.

How, then, are we to analyze the effect of increasingly fluid political participation in a dysfunctional system on the political process? Here I would like to propose the analytical framework of this book: a hegemonic struggle in the dual public spheres.

Hegemonic Struggles in the Dual Public Spheres

Plurality of Public Spheres

The "hegemonic struggle in the dual public spheres" is a framework for analyzing the contingent antagonistic relations constructed through contestation of counter-hegemonic discourses that represent different visions of change in a civil society divided along class lines, which play a decisive role in the political process. To define this framework, I would first like to conceptualize the public sphere as an arena in which collective "we/they" identities are constructed.[18]

Habermas (1990) treats the civic public sphere as a democratic realm that checks abuse of state power through rational deliberation. However, this argument has been criticized for idealizing the public sphere as one of wealthy, educated bourgeois citizens, and ignoring the power that excludes women or the poor from that sphere.[19] In a public sphere in which words are the medium of communication, people blessed with educational opportunities, the ability to gather, analyze and disseminate information, and free time tend to enjoy the hegemonic position.

Nonetheless, as Fraser points out, people denied free and equal access to the civic public sphere have developed alternative "subaltern counterpublics." Subaltern counterpublics are "parallel discursive arenas in which members of subordinated social groups invent and circulate counter-discourses, which in turn permit them to formulate oppositional interpretations of their identities, interests, and needs" (Fraser 1992: 123).

"On the one hand, they function as spaces of withdrawal and regroupment; on the other, they also function as bases and training grounds for agitational activities directed toward wider publics" (Ibid.: 124). In stratified societies, she argues that contestation among a plurality of competing publics would offset privileges of dominant social groups to some extent and approximate the ideal of equal participation (Ibid.).

Fraser thus anticipates that counter-hegemonies cultivated in these counter-publics will improve existing unequal power relations and contribute to democracy.[20] However, contestation among multiple public spheres does not necessarily facilitate democracy. Division into multiple public spheres hampers communication, which fosters distorted representations of those belonging to other spheres, as well as discourses that treat those others as enemies who must be eliminated. In doing so, such divisions can threaten the pluralism and equality of a democracy. If anything, it is essential to clarify the conditions under which hegemonic struggles arising among multiple public spheres would *not* threaten to destroy democracy.

The assumption that people can—and indeed, ought to—participate as free and equal citizens in a single public sphere is inappropriate when applied to a Philippine society with salient divisions in terms of language (fluent English vs. the vernaculars), education (private vs. public schools), media (English broadsheets vs. vernacular tabloids; English vs. Tagalog programming) and living space (guarded subdivisions vs. squatters' settlements). Rather, it is both more appropriate, and more effective from an analytic standpoint, to treat the public sphere of Philippine civil society as "dual public spheres" composed of a middle-class "civic sphere" and an impoverished class "mass sphere." Here I treat the public sphere as comprising not only an abstract discursive arena, but also a concrete lifeworld. In addition, I use the term "contact zone" to describe the area of overlap between the civic and mass spheres where different people and discourses encounter one another, giving rise to diverse power relationships.

Overview of the Dual Public Spheres

As I will be discussing the historical process of formation of dual public spheres in the next chapter, here I will describe the characteristics they display today. First, the present-day civic sphere is a discursive space consisting of media, forums for discussion and the like that use English, and a living space that includes guarded subdivisions (gated communities) and high-rise condominiums, business districts lined with multinational corporations, and shopping malls sporting high-class brand names.

As Bautista points out, middle-class residents of subdivisions and condominiums may interact with their neighbors, but their most significant relationships are those that extend beyond geographic limits, such as those with colleagues, friends, relatives, and members of groups in which they participate. However, subdivision residents do participate together in organized efforts vis-à-vis the environment, crime and other issues they share in common, or in religious activities with such groups as the Catholic lay organization Couples for Christ (Bautista 1998: 32–3).

To attract listeners in the civic sphere, one must be in possession of "cultural capital" (Bourdieu 1979), that is, fluent in English, versed in modern concepts and capable of using language perceived as logical and intelligent. English ability is seen in the civic sphere as a reflection of learning and intellect; one's views are likely to be ignored if they are not expressed in fluent English. English and power are intimately linked, and people of high social status often use language to display their superiority and authority over their subordinates. Of course, members of the middle class use Tagalog or "Taglish," a mix of Tagalog and English, when conversing with intimates. However, it is common to switch to English when engaged in "public" discourse. One reason for this is that most members of the middle class were educated in English from childhood, and therefore find it difficult to express complex, abstract thoughts in Tagalog.[21] Moreover, the civic sphere prizes not only English, but also the possession of refined tastes, proper etiquette, tact and discretion (*delicadeza*); speech and behavior lacking these qualities is criticized as unsophisticated, lowbrow and boorish.[22]

English-language newspaper columns penned by intellectuals play a particularly important role in forming discourses in the civic sphere. According to Maslog (2007: 160), in 2007, there were a total of 250 columnists in nine English-language newspapers in the Philippines, an exceedingly high number by global standards. Among these, columnists for the *Philippine Daily Inquirer* and the *Philippine Star* are particularly prominent as opinion leaders.

Now let us look at the mass sphere. This is the lifeworld of the poor and a discursive space in which vernacular languages predominate. In poor rural areas and the squatters' settlements of Manila, residents interact with one another throughout their daily lives, leaving their doors open except when they are sleeping. Benches are everywhere people hang out —in front of the general stores known as *sari-sari* stores, at bus stops, and so on. Slum alleyways are not merely spaces for transit; women can be seen washing by the roadside or gambling and trading gossip. When men come into a bit of money, they start drinking, sometimes even from the morning. Young men spend all day playing and betting small change on basketball and stroll around until late at night with guitars in hand. Through these daily contacts, they exchange information—rumors of all sorts as well as tips on reliable employers or moneylenders. They also discuss politics. Their sources of information include accounts of someone's first-hand experiences, rumors spread by word of mouth, Tagalog tabloids, and radio and television.

The mass sphere is sustained by the close relationships established among intimate relationships, including family, relatives, friends and colleagues. People are more prone to empathize with emotional stories rooted in personal experience than with objective, logical arguments. When seeking the sympathy of others, women will often touch one another's hands, and men will put their arms around each other's shoulders or share a glass of liquor; therefore, physical contact also plays an important role as an expression of intimacy. Through this sharing of problems, the individual's troubles often become "our" problems shared by the group.[23] As Berner (1997) notes, this collective "we" consciousness that arises from the local lifeworld of the poor sometimes serves as the foundation for organized resistance.

Photo 3 Men drinking liquor by a roadside during the day (Pechayan, April 2008).

Because people from regions with diverse mother tongues gather in the mass sphere of Manila, Tagalog is used as the *lingua franca*. However, due to the large number of people who come from non-Tagalog speaking regions, "deep Tagalog" (*malalim na Tagalog*), the more complex and abstract form of the language, is not used. Abstract Western-originating concepts are generally expressed in English- or Spanish-derived words.[24] On the other hand, the use of English in everyday conversation is viewed as a sign of snobbery and rejected. For example, someone, even a politician, who carelessly speaks in English might be put down as "stuck-up" (*Ang yabang niya*) or a "show-off" (*suplada* or *suplado*). In addition, people in the mass sphere also tell innumerable jokes about their own poor English ability. One example is a joke about someone who, when asked to speak English, puts their hand to their nose and says, "I've got a nosebleed" (*Dumudugo ang ilong ko*).[25] The idea is that they cannot respond in English because their nose is bleeding.

In both the civic and mass spheres, groups that to some degree share the same vocabulary and cultural codes circulate discourses within their respective sphere. Nevertheless, both spheres contain diverse competing discourses, and neither can be said to be a homogeneous discursive space. Furthermore, as I will explain below, not everyone belongs exclusively to one sphere or the other. Diverse social relationships are constructed, not only cooperation but also relations tinged with enmity and antagonism in contact zones.

Morality in the Civic and Mass Spheres

Any discourse that proclaims a specific "we" identity for which it seeks political support is able to establish hegemony if and only if it resonates with a morality championed by the civic or mass sphere. How, then, is "politics as it should be" conceived within these respective spheres, and what are its associated values?

First, let us look at the civic sphere, where notions of "correct" politics are articulated by concepts such as "policy-based debate," "accountability," "transparency," "good government" and "rule of law." As a whole, this is often described as "new politics" (Schaffer 2008: 132–6). According to the well-known Filipino sociologist Randy David (February 2, 2008), "new politics evolutionarily aims to reform institutions and revise existing routines and procedures to strengthen the foundations on which to build the new, not to revolutionarily invent something completely new. Its immediate objective is to end mass poverty and political illiteracy as a condition for the progressive democratization and modernization of society." The middle class also has a tendency to accept "benevolent authoritarianism" if it is associated with the economic growth of the country (Bautista 1999: 27–9; Karaos 1999). Needless to say, political consciousness in the middle class varies broadly from person to person, as do opinions on any specific issue. However, one can see a common thread of rejecting traditional Philippine politics and desiring modern political reform.[26]

Conversely, what the civic sphere tends to oppose is politics characterized by corruption, cronyism, personality, and elite domination of the poor through clientelism. Politicians who favor this type of politics are known as *trapo*, an abbreviation of the English "traditional politician" that also means "old rag" in Tagalog. According to David (1997, November 2), a *trapo* "refers to a politician who uses wealth to buy power, exploits the poverty of his constituents through selective patronage and treats public funds and facilities as if they were his own personal resources." A *trapo* employs any means to ensure their election or re-election, makes promises they have no intention of keeping. Based on these perceptions, the view within the civic sphere is that the abuse of democracy and freedom by a corrupt elite and their manipulation of the poor has caused disorder and stagnation in the Philippines, a condition criticized as a case of "too much democracy."

The dissemination of this moral discourse in the civic sphere began after democratization. Prior to martial law, the middle class was for the most part embedded in the clientelist system, and therefore did not strongly criticize the political status quo (Kimura 2002: 184). However, once they acquired self-esteem as primary actors in the democratization movement, members of the middle class began to see themselves as morally superior to the state, the elite and the poor, and increasingly, as the true leaders of a movement for moral, social, and political reform (Pinches 2010: 289–91). Behind the deep-seated antipathy of the middle class to current political realities lies a strong perception of themselves as taxpayers. As workers in the formal sector, they pay a high income tax of around 30 per cent on their earnings. However, under the corrupt political system, they see their taxes go into the pockets of the elite or doled out to the poor as a means of securing votes; this situation frustrates them immensely.[27]

Most members of the middle class support the morality of capitalism as a means of reforming a corrupt, inefficient, elite-dominated state. With the promotion of neoliberal economic reforms in the wake of democratization, terms like privatization, liberalization and equal opportunity have become common parlance in the civic sphere. Pinches notes that business magazines extol virtues such as initiative, vision, industriousness, resourcefulness, perseverance, and creativity, and run special features with success stories about the new breed of ethnic-Chinese entrepreneurs touted as the driving force of the nation's future growth.[28] Under the influence of this neoliberal idealization of market competition, the civic sphere has seen the spread of a morality that defines those who create wealth in the market through self-discipline, ingenuity and hard work as "good", and the elites who cling to their vested interests through cronyism and corruption, as well as the poor who depend on dole-outs without creating wealth themselves, as "bad".

Granted, not everyone in the civic sphere subscribes to the morality of capitalism, nor does everyone dismiss values supporting the right of the poor to dignity and subsistence. For example, motivated by a fear that extreme inequalities in land ownership could provide a breeding ground for communism, support can be seen in the civic sphere for land reform. Many are also of the view that, for humanitarian reasons, evicted squatters should be provided with alternative living quarters. In short, the civic sphere contains a specific axis of morality that extends between two antagonistic positions: one a neoliberalist morality that advocates the unabashed exclusion of the poor, and the other a morality that asserts inclusion of the poor by redistribution.

Meanwhile, in the mass sphere, the notion of "correct" politics that enjoys the most widespread support is politics based on fairness without regard for wealth or the poor, and on concern for and generosity toward those in need. Conversely, members of the mass sphere decry politics that displays a callous and disinterested attitude toward the needs of those who try to make an honest living and treats the weak unjustly (Schaffer 2008: 136–8). According to my own surveys, "democracy" (*demokrasya*) in the mass sphere is generally linked to the values of "freedom" (*kalayaan*) and "equality" (*pantay-pantay*), while "inequality in democracy," according to which the wealthy receive all the benefits, is perceived as a problem. This political viewpoint reflects the morality of the mass sphere, which supports protecting the livelihood and dignity of the poor.

According to Scott (1977), the traditional community norms of rural society in Southeast Asia were defined by a "moral economy" that ensured risk avoidance and the survival of all members of the community.[29] A morality of mutual assistance that places priority on the "survival/lives" (*buhay*) and "livelihood" (*hanapbuhay*) of community members is still conspicuous in the mass sphere of the Philippines today. Moreover, Kerkvliet (1990: 242–73) reports that in the 1980s in central Luzon, poor farmers, no longer content with mere subsistence, and perceiving that they were being deprived of wealth, asserted their "need" (*kailangan*) for and "right" (*dapat, karapat-dapat, karapatan*) to "fair and equal" (*pantay-pantay*) access to a broader range of resources.[30] However, he also notes that the traditional norm that "people with more should help those with less" was being eroded by capitalist values that defined the pursuit of personal wealth as "good." It is true that even within the mass sphere, discord occurs because the more successful people are, the more they tend to espouse capitalist morality of entrepreneurship expressed by such words as "self-reliance in business" (*sariling sikap sa negosyo*), whereas the poorer they are, the more they appeal to the morality of mutual assistance (*tulong*).[31]

Another value of great importance to the poor is "dignity" (*dangal, dignidad, pagkatao*). Poorer individuals are more likely than the wealthy to be viewed with contempt and denied the dignity of making an honest living.[32] According to Pinches, poor residents of the Manila slums are compelled to feel "shame" (*hiya*) under the prevailing social order and value system, and inevitably experience feelings of inferiority regarding their education, work, language, speech, etiquette, skin color, hair, teeth and clothing.[33] This crisis of dignity can be avoided to some degree by staying within the slums. But in workplaces, hospitals, government offices, churches, shopping malls and the like, the poor are not treated in the same manner as "the rich," and therefore must endure being ignored, ridiculed and scorned.[34] In the workplace, they must often put up with the contemptuous attitudes of bosses or superiors for the sake of their livelihood. Yet, at the same time, these feelings of shame and humiliation arouse intense anger, thereby serving as an impetus for resistance to the ruling order and its values.[35] As Shimizu (1995) has pointed out, it is precisely in circumstances in which the strong wound the dignity of the weak and force them into disadvantageous compromises that the longing for justice as "power to help the weak" grows acute.

According to Soon (2008), the morality of the mass sphere, which champions the livelihood and dignity of the poor, derives from the perspective of popular Catholicism. Soon describes this as the belief that if the poor walk the path (*lakaran*) of Christ, endure their long-term sufferings, purify their hearts inside (*loob*), strive to be patient, industrious and self-reliant (*sariling sikap*), obey the word of God, love one another without prejudice and help their neighbors (*kapwa*), it will bring about a society filled with light (*liwanag*), liberate them from their wretched livelihoods, and enable them to achieve happiness. Based on this religious view, he says, the impoverished class seeks honest, pure-hearted politicians who care about the lives and dignity of their compatriots.

Thus, even while the capitalist morality of "the pursuit of personal wealth is good" has made some inroads into the mass sphere, the morality of "above all, support your neighbor's life and dignity" has endured. In addition, politicians and people of high social status who deny the right of the poor to livelihood and dignity have become targets of indignation and outrage. In this regard, the morality of the mass sphere differs markedly from that of the civic sphere.

However, the moralities of the two spheres do have several things in common. First, they share feelings of dissatisfaction and antipathy toward the elite. For example, the word *trapo* is used in both spheres as a pejorative for corrupt politicians. In the civic sphere, the elite are criticized as a regressive force that impedes the modernization and economic development of the Philippines; in the mass sphere, they are denounced as a malevolent presence that oppresses the poor. Second, for the Catholics who make up over 80 per cent of the population of the Philippines, religion is also a moral reference point that transcends the boundary between the dual public spheres. Philippine Catholicism is characterized by a deep-seated empathy for the suffering of Christ, which translates into identification with and sympathy for Filipinos who suffer at the hands of excessive power.[36] As Shimizu (1991) has noted, this sympathetic sensibility provides the basis for a sense of community that opposes ruling authorities who deprive "we Filipinos" of their rightful livelihoods and dignity, and that demands justice.

Rule, Resistance and Cooperation in the Contact Zone

In traditional rural societies, landowners and tenants may not have shared precisely the same living space and discursive space, but both had a common arena in which they could negotiate or struggle over relative degrees of obligation and loyalty, based on their respective interpretations of the morality of clientelism.[37] Compared with those conditions, divisions are greater between the discursive and living spaces of the middle and impoverished classes in Manila today, and the two classes have only limited opportunities for substantial interaction. However, "contact zones" in which members of both classes can cross this dividing line and encounter people and discourses from the other side do exist. These contact zones serve an important function, as the complex interplay of power relations within them generates various contestations over dominant and subordinate relationships.[38] At the same time, deliberation or cooperation between people of different backgrounds also has the potential to mediate antagonisms between the civic and mass spheres.

Let us first examine the exercise and penetration of hegemony from the civic into the mass sphere. In the course of their lives, the poor interact with many modern institutions, including media, schools, churches and various associations. In Gramscian terms, these institutions are a means by which the civic sphere exercises day-to-day hegemony over the mass sphere, forcing the poor into an inferior position in the class hierarchy. Images of success in capitalist society as purveyed by the media imbue the poor with a sense of relative deprivation. Associations belonging to the civic sphere exercise hegemony in the form of moral or cultural "enlightenment." The Catholic Church views drinking and gambling as morally degenerate and seeks to correct these lifestyle habits among the poor. NGOs attempt to educate the poor and transform them into "proper citizens." Bosses and superiors warn poor employees against laziness and try to instill in them the morality of the work. In this way, by making the poor painfully aware of their lack of etiquette or skills in manners, speech, behavior, literacy, and familiarity with bureaucratic procedures interactions with schools, churches, businesses and government offices, their dignity is wounded.

Yet, poor Catholics do not attend church every week, and NGOs have not succeeded in mobilizing the majority of the poor. Furthermore, most members of the impoverished class manage to avoid critical affronts to their dignity by dropping out of school, ignoring bureaucratic procedures and shunning jobs in the formal sector. The hegemony exercised by the civic sphere does not necessarily extend throughout the mass sphere via the contact zone. To the contrary, it is challenged by the morality of the mass sphere and disputed on a daily basis.

Next let us look at the counter-hegemony of the mass sphere vis-à-vis the civic sphere. The stance of the poor toward the morality of the civic sphere is not always passive, and frequently aggressively active. For example, poor people express their opposition to traditional elite rule and socioeconomic inequality by voting for populists who espouse a politics of benevolence. The poor also assert their rights to a livelihood and dignity through demonstrations and policy proposals that address their problems and attack injustices, often enlisting the help of leftists or NGOs. These practices represent an effort to penetrate the civic sphere with a mass sphere counter-hegemony that asserts the rights of the poor and challenges the stratified social structure. However, insofar as these discourses or practices are often subject to backlash in the civic sphere, this counter-hegemony is not ensured of success.

Finally, there are also circumstances in which cooperation arises between the civic and mass spheres, as when middle-class activists and the poor team up to pursue social reform through social movements.[39] Conventional Tocquevillian civil society theory evaluates such movements as challenges to elite democracy by a moral citizenry. In this book, I instead choose to evaluate these movements as opportunities that provide a point of contact between the civic and mass spheres, thereby creating deliberative spaces in which people from different spheres can exchange sometimes antagonistic views. Although deliberations in social movements are not necessarily held on an equal footing, such interaction has the potential to problematize and deconstruct the dichotomous relationship between "citizens" and "masses."

In fact, I have encountered many activists from the middle class who fancy themselves as part of "the masses," despite having graduated from top universities and speaking fluent English. As they explain, this identification with the masses would be a reflection of their self-regard as oppressed members of a stratified society who have taken on a leadership role in social reform. Some of them actually find their origins in the lower or lower-middle class, but thanks to higher educational opportunities provided by scholarships or remittances from family members working abroad, have succeeded in elevating their social status. They therefore play an important role in shuttling between the civic and mass spheres and serving as intermediaries between the two. Whenever middle-class leaders speak as self-styled representatives of "the masses," however, it always entails the risk of depriving the poor of their own voices.[40]

Antagonism and "Agonism"

For politicians or social forces who wish to secure popular support, it is generally an effective strategy to propagandize about an enemy that threatens to hurt "us." They denounce the evil enemy as the cause of people's sufferings, insecurities, and fears, and present themselves as the best leaders in a moral battle against that enemy.[41] Such appeals enable politicians to procure the support of society even without engaging in resource distribution. The strategy to establish a "we/they" antagonism, defined in terms of good vs. evil, is especially effective in fluid societies. Granted, an appeal to a larger "we" may also seek to include "them," insofar as certain people are either subordinated inside or expelled outside the "we," antagonistic relations cannot be reconciled. This antagonism becomes most salient on particular occasions when the collective sense of crisis vis-à-vis the enemy intensifies; then, when the perception of a threat recedes, it grows more ambiguous in the course of day-to-day life.

According to Mouffe, antagonism is the essence of politics, and is impossible to remove through conciliation or consensus. Rather, what is crucial is to transform antagonism into "agonism" by conceiving "they" not as enemies to be destroyed, but as legitimate "adversaries" who share support for liberal democracy. "Agonism is a we/they relation where the conflicting parties, although acknowledging that there is no rational solution to their conflict, nevertheless recognize the legitimacy of their opponents." Moreover, she argues, if channels for legitimate protest are lost because agonistic relations cannot be achieved, violent manifestations of discontent will subsequently threaten democracy (Mouffe 2005: 19–21).

Viewing "they" as an enemy that must be destroyed is precisely what I conceptualize as blatant moral antagonism that denies "their" legitimacy and threatens the plurality of democracy. In contrast, the agonism presented by Mouffe can be viewed as a relationship of contestation with a legitimate "they" under which both sides share a democratic space while maintaining a moral antagonism that does not readily admit of compromise, yet is not excessively aggravated. Because an agonistic relationship acknowledges both struggle and coexistence with an adversarial "they," it is compatible with the plurality of democracy. However, Mouffe does not fully explore the conditions that generate the moral antagonisms that deny the legitimacy of "they," and conversely, those that produce agonism in which each side acknowledges the legitimacy of the other.

One circumstance that permits the emergence of agonism is the failure of a hegemonic practice by powerful actors to generate moral antagonism. When politicians or social forces attempt to construct antagonistic "we/they" identities, they may be confused, ignored, or opposed, and thus efforts to establish hegemony do not always succeed.[42] When a moral antagonism-constructing hegemony fails, it opens up the possibility of establishing agonistic relations between hostile forces. Another possible scenario is that interaction with the other may result in a partial internalization of the views and values of the other, effecting a transformation in one's identity.[43] In terms of a deliberative democracy theory, even if a full consensus cannot be achieved in a plural society, the realignment of mutual identity or preferences brought about by deliberation with the other can still yield a meta-consensus that structures continued dispute (Dryzek 2010).[44] Such occasions make it feasible to establish agonistic relations in the contact zone wherein both sides may not resolve their right/wrong, "we"/"they" moral antagonism, yet still recognize one another's legitimacy even as they continue to struggle.

Types of Antagonistic Relations and the Political Process

In the dual public spheres, both ruling elites and various social forces struggle for hegemony and antagonistic "we/they" relations are constantly being constructed, deconstructed and reconfigured, exerting a profound impact on the political process. The hegemonic discursive practices that played a particularly significant role in the post-democratization politics of the Philippines can be classified into the following four types (see Table 11).[45] The discursive power that constructs these antagonistic relations is decentralized, and discourse of ruling elites and counter-discourse of various social forces are often intertwined. Therefore, the success of hegemonic discursive practice depends upon whether it creates resonance of moral discourse among different actors, and no one can ultimately dictate the outcome of the hegemonic struggle.

First, there is *moral nationalism*, which constructs a national solidarity of "the people" transcending divisions between the civic and mass spheres in opposition to presidential corruption and abuses of power.[46] Leadership

Table 11 Types of Hegemonic Practice that Create Antagonistic Relations

	Moral Nationalism	*Civic Inclusivism*	*Civic Exclusivism*	*Populism*
Main arena	Dual public spheres	Contact zone	Civic sphere	Mass sphere
"We"	"People" in solidarity against corruption	Educated, skilled, moral "citizens"	Educated, skilled, moral "citizens"	Oppressed, righteous "poor people"
"They"	Corrupt politicians	Corrupt politicians	Corrupt politicians and uneducated, immoral "masses"	"Rich" who oppress the poor

Source: The Author.

in moral nationalist discourses and movements derives from the business community, the church, the moderate left and some traditional elite. Although the first three entities are typically critical of the traditional elite and not always in harmony with each other, they tend to cooperate with them when opposing the "common enemy" of corrupt politicians. Presence of "common enemy" facilitates resonance of counter-discourses among the different actors including the middle class and the poor to construct the "the people." However, this national solidarity does not lead to substantial redistribution or deliberation, and therefore cannot be sustained once the common enemy is vanquished.

Next, there is *civic inclusivism*, with which middle-class activists engaged in social movements seek to include the poor in the "citizenry" by providing them with education, resources and civic morality, and aim to achieve social reform through policy proposals to the state. These activists are members of different organizations with varying ideologies from Communism, left-of-center and Catholicism but they share the objective of extending their respective hegemony to the civic and mass spheres by spreading their social movement via the contact zone. While civic inclusivism resembles moral nationalism in its opposition to corrupt state officials, it differs in that it seeks to cooperate with state officials while maintaining a critical stance. Also, unlike moral nationalism, which conceals inequalities through temporary solidarity, civic inclusivism continually strives for concrete remedies to various forms of inequality.

Third, there is also *civic exclusivism,* which builds up moral antagonism between good "citizens" in the civic sphere and bad "masses." Government leaders and members of the middle class, the business community, and the church work together in the construction of the antagonistic relation despite of their different political stands when they feel threatened by "irrational" political participation and illegal livelihoods of the poor. This resembles civic inclusivism in its construction of a good "citizenry," but differs in its aggressive attempts to exclude the "masses," who are their target of harsh criticism. The discourse of civic exclusionism has an affinity with the neoliberal morality that sees poverty not as a structural problem, but as one of personal responsibility. While civic exclusivism once realized as an expulsion movements against a populist, it more frequently exercises an influence on the political process through their generation of various discourses, such as defining squatters and street vendors as "criminals."

Finally, there is *populism*, with which counter-elites make an issue of poverty and inequality in the mass sphere and appeal to the poor to oppose the vested-interest classes.⁴⁷ Populism constructs an antagonistic relationship between the good "masses" (*masa*) or "poor" (*mahihirap*) and the evil "rich" (*mayayaman*).⁴⁸ Populists of the counter-elite have sought to wrest power from the traditional elite by gaining the support of the poor through a melding of populist discourses with the mass sphere morality of protecting people's livelihoods and dignity. Only when the poor believe integrity of a populist leader after their critical moral scrutinization, his or her populism can take root in the mass sphere. Populism resembles Communism in its exploitation of interclass antagonisms; however, whereas Communism aspires to fundamentally transform the social structure through revolution by fanning these hostilities, populism seeks to restrict hostilities to a certain level so that they do not reach the stage of revolution.⁴⁹

These hegemonic discursive practices vie with one another in the dual public spheres and give birth to the following types of antagonistic relations, which play varying roles in the political process.⁵⁰

First, there is the case in which moral nationalism establishes hegemony, leading to the creation of *moral solidarity of the nation*. Here, the "people" constructed in solidarity transcend the divisions of the dual public spheres and can launch a democratization movement against an authoritarian regime or demand the resignation of a corrupt president. On the other hand, the discourse and practice of solidarity of the "people" conceals profoundly unequal power relations between classes. Moreover, once the leaders who are seen as the "common enemy" are ousted by People Power or elections, the base of this solidarity readily crumbles. Thus, it has paradoxical impacts on democracy.

A second case is the emergence of the *moral division of the nation*, which is the result of civic exclusivism and populism gaining hegemony in the civic and mass spheres, respectively. In this instance, a moral antagonism that denies the legitimacy of "they" takes hold in both the civic and mass spheres, generating increased discontent with a politics in which "they" wield influence. Fear and antipathy against the rise of populism in the civic sphere makes not small number of the middle class to choose traditional elite as "lesser evil." Also, because "good vs. evil"–based moral antagonisms do not easily lend themselves to mediation through compromise, there is a danger that participation by these polarized civic and mass spheres will destabilize the political process.

In a third case, social movement in the contact zone extends its *hegemony of civic inclusivism* into the civic and mass spheres, including not only the middle class, but also the poor in the "citizenry." Here, the organization and mobilization of the poor by NGOs and leftists promote politics based on "citizen" participation. Yet, even in this type of social movement, not everyone is included in a "citizenry" united in support of the same morality and interests. The resulting interclass discord and friction over initiative of social movement tends to marginalize the interests and morality of the poor, and the movement itself may stagnate or deadlock.

In a fourth instance, the failure of civic inclusivism in a contact zone-based social movement may lead to the *emergence of agonism*, according to which middle-class activists and the poor remain morally antagonistic toward one another over good vs. evil, yet avoid excessive aggravation and acknowledge each other's legitimacy, even as they engage in disputes. In this case, because the civic sphere does not marginalize mass sphere interests and morality, agonistic relations have the potential to contribute to democracy.

CHAPTER 2

Formation of the Dual Public Sphere

Photo 4 Driver trying to attract customers to a jeepney, a form of public transportation for ordinary people (Philcoa, Quezon City, 2002).

The coexistence of multiple public spheres exerts a significant influence on both the development of hegemonic struggles in civil society and the democratic political process. In this chapter, I would like to examine language, education, the mass media and living space in order to clarify the historical process by which the public sphere of Philippine civil society has come to be divided along class lines to form a dual public sphere, before embarking on a detailed analysis of the political process itself.

The Linguistic Divide

Language and Democracy

Colonialism transmitted the language of the ruling empire to non-Western societies in the name of benevolence and liberation that would bring civilization to an uncultured local populace. Local elites blessed with educational opportunities responded by actively studying the imperial language in an effort to join the broader intellectual world it represented. Non-elites also sought to improve their socioeconomic status by learning the imperial language. The language of empire as the very embodiment of power spread within colonies through a mix of coercion and voluntary initiative.

The Philippines boasts a tremendous diversity of indigenous languages —over 100 in all, including minority languages, and as many as ten major languages. With the aim of overcoming barriers between these indigenous languages and enabling communication on a national level, the United States introduced English as a common language. However, the introduction of English-language education on a nationwide level created a divide between elites fluent in English and masses who could only speak "inferior" indigenous languages. Considering that Filipinos would have found it much easier to learn a different indigenous language than to learn English, this was an ironic outcome.

The linguistic divide produced by English-language education cast a dark shadow on democracy and the public sphere in the Philippines. A public sphere arises from countless communication links achieved through language; hence, a division along linguistic lines inevitably means a division in the public sphere. Moreover, as Kymlicka (2002: 312) points out, the sharing of a common language is one of the fundamental preconditions for deliberative democracy. Also, as maintained by Schaffer (1998), imperial and indigenous languages differ in their respective interpretations of the concept of "democracy," and this can lead to contested political participations. A linguistic divide not only impairs communication between politicians and their constituents, thereby diluting the meaning of the representative system, it can also obstruct deliberation among fellow nations and exacerbate antagonisms.

Origins of the Divide

In the period before Spanish rule, the Philippines had no unified dynasty and diverse vernaculars were spoken in each region. With the arrival of the Magellan expedition in the Philippine islands in 1521 and Spain's subsequent establishment of colonial rule, the colonial government set up an educational system for Spanish citizens that employed Spanish through the higher-education level. In contrast, indigenous peoples were provided with an elementary education in the churches, where indigenous languages were used with the objective of spreading Christianity. In 1863, toward the end of Spanish rule, the influence of the European movement for free elementary education led to the institutionalization of elementary education for indigenous youth from age 7 to 12.[1]

Around the 1860s and 1870s, an intellectual elite fluent in Spanish emerged among indigenous Filipinos. Children of the Chinese *mestizos* who had accumulated wealth as plantation owners went to university in Manila or in Europe. They were known as *ilustrado*, a term meaning "enlightened ones." However, because religious orders opposed the spread of Spanish-language education to the masses, it is estimated that only about 5 per cent of the Philippine population was literate in Spanish at the time.[2] This is how a linguistic divide arose between the intellectual elite and the general masses.

When the armed struggle for Philippine independence began, Tagalog came into active use as a language of the movement. In 1897, the independence-movement leader Emilio Aguinaldo promulgated the Constitution of Biak-na-Bato, which declared Tagalog as the official language. However, this linguistic nationalism declined with the advent of English-language education under American rule.

Pros and Cons of English-Language Education

The change in colonizers switched the language of the intellectual elite. In 1898, the United States won the Spanish-American War and acquired the Philippines from Spain for USD 20 million. The United States suppressed the independence movement and set up a system of rule under a policy of "benevolent assimilation."[3] The American colonial government installed a public education system with English as its medium of instruction, and with the ostensible aims of cultivating a population of skilled modern professionals, unifying the nation and fostering democracy.[4] Elementary schools were built throughout the country, and numerous teachers and educational materials were brought from the United States. English was mandated as the official, and only, language of the curriculum and the use of vernaculars was banned in the classroom. Study in America was also promoted among the elite in order to nurture a class of colonial managers.[5]

The Americans justified these colonial policies with the rationale that the Filipinos themselves wished to be educated in English. Sustaining the policies, however, was the notion that English-language education could help to undermine support for the ongoing anticolonial struggle by converting the indigenous population into subservient, America-loving, "good" colonials.[6]

In response, the elite, swallowing their bitterness over defeat in the Philippine-American War, sought to master English in the hopes of gaining independence from the United States, and to demonstrate that Filipinos were capable of governing themselves. Meanwhile, those who fought for independence and rejected the adoption of English were suppressed and executed as "bandits" by America. In this way, English-language education played a part in reinforcing American rule by delegitimizing the anticolonial struggle and compelling the elite to submit, however reluctantly, to the United States.

The American colonial government promoted the use of English with its introduction of a democratic system. Official documents were now written in English, which required a degree of English ability from those hired to fill administrative positions. English ability was also a prerequisite for the right to vote in the local elections that were initiated in 1899. Thus, well into the 1940s, English replaced Spanish as the language of higher education and the executive, legislative and judicial branches of government. The number of English speakers continued to grow, reaching 38.5 per cent of the population according to a survey conducted after independence in 1946.[7]

The introduction of English-language education posed an opportunity for everyone in the Philippines—regardless of income or location—to learn a new language at the same time. In this respect, English symbolized "equality" and "democracy." People born into poverty did in fact manage to improve their social status to a certain level by learning English in public schools and going on to obtain employment as teachers, office workers or civil servants. It had become clear by the 1930s, however, that English-language education had also generated inequalities. Children of poor families could not spare sufficient time to receive an education and were dropping out of school. In contrast, children of the rich who attended private schools and studied in the United States gained greater proficiency in English, which smoothed the path to high-ranking positions in the public or private sector. Even as English-language education produced measurable improvements in literacy and school-enrollment rates, Filipinos who could make themselves understood in English on a sophisticated level remained in the minority.

Bilingual Education and the Search for a National Language

In 1934, the US Congress passed the Tydings-McDuffie Act, which stipulated that the Philippines would be granted independence on July 4, 1946. This also led to the establishment of a commonwealth government the following year, in 1935, under which the Philippine people were to receive training in self-rule under US supervision until independence arrived.

At a constitutional convention convened for this purpose in 1934, the thorniest issue proved to be the choice of a national language.[8] At the time, English speakers constituted less than 30 per cent of the population, making English an unrealistic option as a common language. Thus, it was deemed necessary to establish a national language that was rooted in Philippine life and culture. Delegates to the Constitutional Convention, who hailed from different regions of the country and spoke different indigenous languages as their mother tongues, communicated in English and Spanish. They engaged in heated debate over whether the national language should be Tagalog, which was the language of the capital and had played a significant role in the revolutionary movement, or a "fusion" language that would be created by incorporating indigenous languages including Tagalog. In the end, the proposal to make the national language Tagalog was rejected by delegates whose mother tongue was not Tagalog, and the alternative proposal to create a "fusion" language was adopted. Based on the decisions made at this convention, the Commonwealth government promulgated the 1935 Constitution, which stipulated that a national language should be developed as a fusion based on the native languages of various regions of the Philippines. To this end, the Institute of National Language was founded in 1937 with Manuel Quezon, the president of the Commonwealth, as its chairman. The institute approved Tagalog as the basis for the fusion language and set about compiling a grammar, a dictionary and a curriculum. However, the effort to develop a national language was interrupted by the Japanese occupation of the country from 1941 to 1945.[9]

Once the war was over and the country achieved its independence from the United States in 1946, the Philippine government defined the national language as "a language based on Tagalog," and declared English and Spanish as the official languages. In 1959, it gave the "language based on Tagalog" a name, "Pilipino." The non-Tagalog elite opposed this, pointing out that 75 per cent of the nation had a mother tongue other than Tagalog. The opposition of the non-Tagalog elite remained fierce at the 1971 Constitutional Convention, and a proposal to make Pilipino the national language was voted down. However, after seizing power by declaring martial law in 1972, President Marcos promulgated a new Constitution in 1973 that changed the name of the language from Pilipino to Filipino and recognized it as the national language and, along with English, an official language. Marcos wished to legitimize martial law by espousing a nationalist discourse that encouraged the use of Filipino; however, attempts to create a new Filipino language based on all of the country's major languages did not progress further, and Filipino remained substantially the same as Tagalog.

In 1974, Marcos issued detailed regulations in implementing a system of "bilingual education," under which, science courses would be taught in English and humanities courses in Filipino. To justify bilingual education, English was framed as a linguistic tool for gaining access to economic opportunities and Filipino as a linguistic symbol of national unity (Bernardo 2007: 8). Bilingual education won the support of elites of the various language groups that had engaged in bitter confrontation over the definition of a national language. Bilingual education enabled the Tagalog elite to promote Filipino as the national language while maintaining the privileged position of English. The non-Tagalog elites were also happy to preserve the privileges accruing to English even if they had to give up the dream of making their own indigenous language a national or official language (Tupas 2007: 73–5).

Thus, English-language education was retained even after independence. However, significant population growth caused a surge in the number of students, and this coincided with a decline in the quality of English teachers following the withdrawal of the Americans, resulting in a deterioration of English-language education in public schools (Sibayan and Gonzalez 1996: 142). This opened a substantial gap in the degree of English mastery between the private schools attended by children of the wealthy and middle classes, and the vast majority of public schools attended by the children of the poor. Meanwhile, the use of Tagalog was spreading in the realm of colloquial speech, even as English remained the written language of business, the judiciary, government bureaucracy, academia and other professions. In this way, English-language education continued to function as a means of reproducing class disparities.

Persistence of the Linguistic Divide

The bilingual education policy continued after democratization under the same rationale, according to which English-language education was needed as a practical tool, and Filipino-language education was needed for symbolic reasons. The advance of globalization has been accompanied by assertions that education in English is indispensable as a means of producing Filipinos capable of competing in the international arena, and that education in Filipino is more important than ever as a symbol of national identity (Bernardo 2007: 13).

There have also been proposals to reassess the bilingual education policy. In 1993, the Congressional Commission on Education determined that bilingual education was hampering the learning process, and thus proposed the use of native languages in the lower elementary grades.[10] Conversely, President Arroyo declared in 2003 that the decline in English skills had to be prevented if Philippine workers were to compete in the global market, and advocated the reinforcement of English-language education. Pro-English and pro-Filipino intellectuals argued over the pros and cons of this view.[11]

Photo 5 Children at a public elementary school (Tungko, Bulacan Province, February 1998).

Such issues aside, the most significant problems with bilingual education are its failure to create a nation capable of using either English or Filipino at will as circumstances necessitate, and its failure to eliminate the country's linguistic divide. Granted, since the 1990s, the permeation of Filipino-language education, the spread of Tagalog media, and increased population drift have seen Tagalog come to play the role of a *lingua franca*, thereby ameliorating the divisions among native languages.[12] However, an English skills gap rooted in socioeconomic inequalities remains conspicuous.[13] At the primary and secondary level, a substantial disparity persists in quality of education, between the private schools attended by children of the wealthy and middle classes and the public schools attended by children of the poor. Moreover, students entering public school in the 2000s were found to be dropping out at high rates— 30 per cent of those in elementary school and over half of those in secondary school.[14]

The English gap also reproduces inequality. Because English is the primary language of higher education[15] and is employed in all manner of powerful public systems, English ability is a determining factor in improving one's social status. Nearly all government and business documents are written in English, and state certification examinations of various types are conducted in the language. Employment and promotion opportunities are affected by one's ability in English, not Filipino. As a consequence, people with poor English skills are restricted in their opportunities for social advancement.[16]

To summarize, the class divide in language emerged under colonial rule in the Philippines, but post-independence language education has not only failed to unify the nation, but also actually exacerbated this divide, thereby impeding mutual communication among the Philippine people.[17]

The Media Divide

Hegemonic Struggle and a Divided Media

When the linguistic divide along class lines came to be reflected in the mass media, it divided not only the discursive space through which people perceive society, but also in their identity as "we." Anderson (1983) argues that print capitalism and print language played a significant part in the formation of national identities, that is, of national "imagined communities" consisting of "we" who share the same time and space. Today, broadcast media also serve an important role in the formation of a national sense of community. In the Philippines, however, the media divide increases the tendency for class divisions to be reflected in this "imagined community." Furthermore, this divided "we" embraces different perceptions of the same social or political circumstances. Lippmann (1922) feared that divergence between the real environment and the "pseudo-environment" created by the media would provoke irrational behavior in human beings, since they exercise influence on real environment with wrongly regarding the pseudo-environment as real. The problem is more complicated in the Philippines, where the pseudo-environment differs within the dual public sphere.[18]

How then does the media that divides "we" identity and the pseudo-environment influence the hegemonic struggle among various forces in the dual public sphere? Teodoro (1998) categorizes the Philippine mass media into a "dominant press" and an "alternative press."[19] He maintains that the dominant press has supported the ruling establishment in the name of American-style "objectivity" and fostered a stratified socioeconomic structure. On the other hand, the alternative press has criticized the government from a nationalistic standpoint and made active policy proposals on such issues as national independence, freedom and social reform.

Based on these categories, we can classify the media and their roles in the dual public sphere into four types. Dominant media contribute to the formation of a civic sphere in which colonizer languages (Spanish or English) circulate; at the same time, they convey the hegemony of dominant forces both domestic and foreign, such as the elite, big business, the church, the Vatican, and Spain or America. Additionally, there are dominant media, albeit few in number, that use native languages to convey the hegemony of dominant forces to the masses. In addition, there are alternative media that have used Spanish or English to foment counter-hegemonies in the civic sphere, employing modern political concepts like "liberalism," "independence" and "democracy." However, because the vast majority of people who could not understand the colonizer languages were excluded from the civic sphere, the influence of these media has been limited. Moreover, because even these alternative media used the language of the colonizers, they embodied a contradiction that exacerbated the division into civic and mass spheres. In contrast, alternative media that use indigenous languages have not only conveyed the antiestablishment discourses of the civic sphere to the mass sphere by translating them into indigenous languages, but also contributed to the creation of counter-discourses in the mass sphere.

Media and the Independence Movement

From the early to mid-19th century, newspapers in the Philippines, published in Spanish by the colonial government for Spanish nationals seeking news from home, were the dominant media.[20] The publication of alternative media by Filipinos began in the latter half of the 19th century with the propaganda movement launched by Jose Rizal and others. These were the *ilustrado*, neo-bourgeois intellectuals who had received higher education and studied in Europe. Through the publication of newspapers and novels, they carried out a propaganda movement that criticized oppression by Spain and asserted the rights of Filipinos. The opportunity to learn the language of the colonizer paradoxically created the intellectual elite that opposed colonialism. However, because their objective was to make the case for Filipino rights to the Spanish, most of their publications were in Spanish, and this posed a barrier to the creation of a counter-discourse in the mass sphere.

A more significant source of inspiration for mass rebellion against Spanish rule can be found in the Tagalog publication activities of Andres Bonifacio and other revolutionary leaders of lower-class origin.[21] They created an anti-Spain discourse by blending modern concepts that they had learned such as freedom, independence and revolution with the worldview of the *Pasyon*, a Christian epic narrative written in Tagalog. Originally, the *Pasyon* was published by a Filipino poet in 1704 to familiarize Christianity among the masses. Considering that Spanish friars proselytized Christianity to indigenous Filipinos in order to obtain vows of allegiance to the Church and Spain, it was paradoxical that the masses found elements in the *Pasyon* that seemed to oppose colonial rule. As Ileto has shown, in its narration of a series of events from Christ's passion, death and resurrection to Judgment Day, the *Pasyon* depicted the wealthy and noble as evil oppressors and Christ and his disciples as poor, oppressed illiterates. The masses interpreted this worldview as showing that good Christians struggling against the mayhem of this world could bring about a transformation of the world from darkness to light. This interpretation inspired many to devote themselves to the revolutionary movement (Ileto 1979).

American Rule and the Commercialization of Media

Whereas the media in the final years of Spanish rule played an important role as vehicles of political propaganda, under American rule, they acquired the pronounced character of commercial businesses.[22] However, these commercialized media were by no means apolitical. Print media funded by American capital functioned as a cultural means of supporting American interests. In 1920, nationalist alternative media such as the *Philippine Herald*, the first English-language newspaper published by Filipinos, also began to appear. However, the publication of newspapers more nationalist than the *Herald* was suspended under US orders.

After independence was achieved in 1946, Philippine print media thrived, earning praise as "Asia's freest media." However, as before, most of these media were actually funded by American capital and reflected its intentions.[23] For example, the *Manila Daily Bulletin* and *Manila Times* supported the unequal Bell Trade Act and the Military Bases Agreement that the Philippines signed with the United States.[24] The American-capitalized English-language newspapers also endorsed Manuel Roxas, who was backed by Douglas MacArthur, in the 1946 Philippine presidential election and, in line with their close relationship with the CIA, strongly supported Ramon Magsaysay in the 1953 presidential election. They also conducted negative campaigns, employing such pejoratives as "degenerate," "corrupt" and "Communist sympathizer," against nationalists and advocates of autonomy from America like Claro Recto and Carlos Garcia.

In contrast, the Philippine-capitalized *Philippine Herald* maintained a stance of prioritizing Philippine national interests, while the Tagalog newspaper *Bagong Buhay* was particularly outspoken in its opposition to the Bell Trade Act.[25] A media-nationalization bill, which would eliminate the influence of foreign-owned media, was submitted amid periods of rising nationalist sentiment in 1961 and 1965, and the same demand was voiced again at the Constitutional Convention of 1971; however, these proposals were not enacted.[26]

Nonetheless, direct ownership of media by Americans gradually decreased. Beginning in the 1960s, powerful Philippine family-owned business groups began to assemble huge multimedia conglomerates that included newspapers, magazines, and radio and TV stations. Thus, media ownership came to be concentrated in the hands of a few big business groups (see Table 12). These entities, which maintained diverse business portfolios, sought to use the media to wield influence over trade policy with the United States, over competition with other groups, and so on. In this manner, the dominant media became a device through which capitalists pursued profit.[27]

Another significant problem was the limitation imposed on readership by the use of English. The English print media contributed to the formation of a civic sphere that shared, through English, a variety of issues and

Table 12 Media Owned by Family-owned Business Groups

	Newspapers	*Radio*	*TV*
Lopez family	*Manila Chronicle*	ABS-CBN: Alto Broadcasting System-Chronicle Broadcasting Network	ABS-CBN
Roces family	*Manila Times*	ABC: Associated Broadcasting	ABC
Soriano family	*Philippine Herald*	RMN: Radio Mindanao Network	IBC: Inter-Island Broadcasting
Elizalde family	*Evening News*	MBC: Metropolitan Broadcasting	MBC

Source: Prepared by author.

concerns; however, at the same time, it excluded the great majority of Filipinos from that sphere. English-language newspapers and magazines targeted only the limited number of English speakers living in the Metro Manila area. The high price of such media also impeded their dissemination in the mass sphere.[28] Furthermore, geared as they were toward the minority of urban dwellers who enjoyed a Western lifestyle, articles appearing in the English print media had no relevance to the experiences of the mass majority.[29] As a result, the greater part of the population that lacked fluency in English turned to vernacular-language magazines, which were laced with entertaining photographs, for their news and information (see Table 13).[30]

Turning to the broadcasting media, we find that the first commercial radio broadcasts in the Philippines were launched with American capital in 1922. Initially, American capitalists owned and operated nearly all of the country's radio stations, with broadcasts handled by American announcers and musicians. However, as radio use spread, vernacular-language broadcasts also proliferated. With the entry of family-owned business groups into the market after the war, the number of radio stations soared from seven prewar stations to 213 by 1968, and radio dramas and news programs in Tagalog and other vernaculars became increasingly popular.[31] Radio rapidly gained in mass appeal during this period. Meanwhile, the first TV broadcasts took place in 1953, and, once again, with the entry of family-owned business groups, the number of TV stations rose from 5 in 1962 to 18 in 1966. However, because imported sets were so expensive,

Table 13 Circulation of Print Media

	English-language newspapers	Indigenous-language newspapers	English-language magazines	Indigenous-language magazines
1966	443,000	24,000	829,000	636,000
1968	519,000	77,000	911,000	931,000

Source: Compiled from Ofreneo (1984: 130).

TV remained a luxury limited to the rich and did not enjoy mass proliferation. What was more, programs imported from the United States were cheaper than programs produced domestically; hence, the latter made up only one-tenth of all programming in the 1960s.[32]

Media under Martial Law

When Marcos declared martial law in 1972, he shut down all communications media and arrested media owners and journalists who criticized his regime. After this, the only media permitted to operate (pending screening by the regime) were those state-owned and dominant media owned by Marcos's cronies. In response to these restraints, Filipinos developed an interpretive framework through which people spread numerous rumors (*tsismis*) about Marcos and his wife Imelda, and subjected official information transmitted by the media to critical scrutiny. The most adamant opponent of the Marcos regime, the Communist Party of the Philippines (CPP), actively employed Tagalog in its publishing activities, as in the party organ *Ang Bayan*. The use of Tagalog by the Communist movement derived from its ideology of anti-Americanism, as well as the desire of its leaders, who came from the civic sphere, to spread Communist discourse to the mass sphere and mobilize peasants and workers.

It was under these circumstances that the 1983 assassination of former Senator Benigno Aquino Jr. sparked impassioned calls, primarily from the civic sphere, for "accurate information." After this incident, anti-regime forces launched a boycott of government media. When Marcos, under both domestic and foreign pressure, loosened his grip on the media, the publication of English-language alternative media, known by the English term "alternative press," burgeoned. Newspapers and magazines such as *We Forum, Malaya, Mr. & Ms.* and the *Philippine Daily Inquirer* gained avid readership, and their articles were copied and passed from person to person. The Catholic Church, too, disseminated information critical of the regime through its own radio station *Veritas* and publications with funding from the business community. These English-language alternative media outlets served as conduits through which business circles, the church and the urban middle class disseminated information, built networks and initiated a new political debate within the democratization movement (D. Smith 2000: 146). In this manner, the democratization process saw the achievement of hegemony by forces in the civic sphere that used English-language media. On the other hand, the CPP, which had instigated the anti-Marcos movement while gathering support in the mass sphere through the use of Tagalog media, was marginalized from the political process after the Aquino assassination, and was unable to make its influence felt on the democratization process.

Mass Popularization of the Media

Once democratization had freed the media from constraints, publication activities grew rapidly. Between 1986 and 1990, 27 newspapers were launched in Manila alone (D. Smith 2000: 113). Among the most popular of these were *Malaya* and the *Philippine Daily Inquirer,* both of which had opposed Marcos.

Nevertheless, the English-language newspapers did not lose their dominant-media characteristics in the wake of democratization. Due to the restriction of media ownership to domestic capital stipulated by Article 16, Section 11 of the new constitution enacted in 1987, American capital no longer exercised direct control. Still, the major newspapers continued to use English and substantially exclude the impoverished class. Control by the family-owned business groups also remained entrenched. After democratization, a new breed of Filipino Chinese entrepreneurs in became owners of such major papers as the *Manila Bulletin*, the *Philippine Star* and the *Manila Times*.[33] As Coronel (1999: 10–13) maintains, to one degree or another, these business groups intervened in the content of their newspapers to maximize profits of their business portfolios.[34]

In the 1990s, the quantity and circulation of inexpensive Tagalog tabloids also began to soar.[35] Tabloids enjoyed remarkable growth, especially in Manila, where their circulation outnumbered that of English papers (see Table 14). Among dailies, Tagalog papers also boasted greater circulation than their English-language counterparts (see Table 15). These figures demonstrate the penetration of tabloids into the mass sphere and the general popularization of newspaper media.

Table 14 Newspapers Published in Metro Manila

		Broadsheet		Tabloid	
		English-language	Chinese-language	English-language	Tagalog-language
1993	No. of papers	10	5	4	8
	Total circulation	1,519,338	180,650	860,841	1,372,914
1998	No. of papers	19	5	8	18
	Total circulation	2,011,272	293,000	1,486,481	3,449,303
2005	No. of papers	9	3	2	17
	Total circulation	2,337,911	191,000	835,275	4,069,084

Note: Chinese-language newspapers target an ethnic-Chinese readership and are mostly published in Binondo, Manila's Chinatown.
Source: Philippine Information Agency, *Philippine Media Factbook 1993, 1998,* and *2005.*

Table 15 Readership of Daily Newspapers in Metro Manila and Nearby Cities (%)

	Per cent of readership
English-language dailies	20
English-language Sunday editions	28
Tagalog-language dailies	31
Tagalog-language Sunday editions	27

Note: Survey subjects were people aged 15 and above, excluding those with a monthly income of 8,000 pesos and below (the poorest of the poor), in the greater Manila area (Metro Manila; Meycauayan, Bulacan Province; Bacoor, Cavite Province; San Pedro, Laguna Province; Cainta and Antipolo, Rizal Province).
Source: Synovate, Media Atlas Survey, 2006.

The Tagalog tabloids were not only inexpensive, but they also had content of interest to the poor such as crime reports, gossip columns, love stories, horoscopes, help-wanted ads and personal mobile phone numbers for "wanted textmates." They also carried logos with catchphrases that emphasized that they catered to the masses, such as "*Ang Diaryo ng Masa*" (Newspaper for the Masses) for *Remate* (Another Chance of Fight) and "*Mata ng Masa, Boses ng Masa*" (Eyes of the Masses, Voice of the Masses) for *Bulgar* (Scandalize). By far the most successful tabloid was *Abante*. According to Alibutud (1999: 41–2), the secret to its success was its targeting of the poor with erotic content and nude photos on the front page. Once it had upped its circulation, *Abante* sought to broaden its appeal to advertisers by reducing its most dubious content and becoming a more sophisticated paper. This strategy was also adopted by later tabloids.

Following democratization, television, which had been primarily a mode of entertainment for the civic sphere, also grew increasingly popular in the mass sphere. As of 2005, TV ownership and access rates had exceeded those of radio (see Tables 16 and 17).[36] The mass popularization of TV was most visible in the two major networks, ABS-CBN and GMA. When the Lopez family purchased back ABS-CBN from Marcos in 1986, its viewership was the lowest among the big five stations, but it quickly leapt to the top. The key to its success was that while the other stations were broadcasting American programs in English, ABS-CBN targeted the poor by broadcasting self-produced programming in Tagalog (Rimban 1999: 47–51). For example, its flagship news program, *TV Patrol*, upped its entertainment quotient by devoting considerable screen time to news about celebrity scandals and crime that viewers were likely to face in daily life.[37] Members of the impoverished class could be seen talking about their experiences and voicing opinions as parties to various incidents. From 2005 to 2010, a program called *Wowowee* was a huge hit with the impoverished class; it featured poor people displaying their talents in song and dance

Table 16 Household Ownership of Media Appliances (%)

	Radio	*TV*	*Personal computer*
Metro Manila	90	96	17
Rural villages	82	85	7
Nationwide	86	90	12

Source: Philippine Information Agency, *Philippine Media Factbook 2005*.

Table 17 Household Media Access Rates (%)

	Newspapers	*Magazines/Books*	*Comics*	*Radio*	*TV*	*Movies*
Metro Manila	70.5	35.7	6.8	61.7	79.4	16.6
Rural villages	48.5	37.6	58.3	58.3	63.0	10.5
Nationwide	46.5	35.7	56.7	56.7	61.8	9.3

Source: Philippine Information Agency, *Philippine Media Factbook 2005*.

and participating in quizzes and games that offered big cash prizes to the winners.[38] In short, the mass popularization of TV was characterized by media participation by the poor through talking, singing, dancing and viewing.[39]

The mass popularization of TV on the heels of newspapers and radio carries with it the potential to accelerate the use of Tagalog in the media and erode divisions in the dual public sphere. However, the wealthy and middle classes decry the sensationalism and popular orientation of Tagalog programming and have gravitated toward viewing domestic and foreign English-language programs on cable TV. Since democratization, cable TV has become a fixture in the Philippines, and Manila today is one of the top regions in Asia for cable TV access (Robles and Tuazon 2007: 255). Thus, the mass popularization of the media has also generated a backlash within the civic sphere.

Cell phones and the Internet have also proliferated since the late 1990s. Through these new forms of media, people do not merely consume information; they transmit their thoughts to a greater number of people. Interest in the potential of new media was kindled by their role in "People Power 2," which ousted President Estrada in 2001; members of the middle class used text messaging on their cell phones to spread information critical of the Estrada administration and to communicate with each other and organize demonstrations. However, the new media themselves do not have the power to neutralize the authority of the state or the elite, and the mobilization of demonstrations via cell phones does no more than reflect the status quo of power relationships within civil society (Pertierra et al. 2002: 101–24). To be sure, email communications engender a feeling of constant connection to others and may create a sense of community that transcends the divisions of the dual public sphere. But while the poor tend to seek "textmates" among strangers, the wealthy and middle classes utilize text messaging mainly for work purposes or to reinforce existing relationships (Pertierra 2006: 6). Hence, it appears that texting reproduces a sense of community in line with existing class divisions.

In sum, the divide in the media has had the effect of splitting the discursive space where people obtain and disseminate information, and experience a sense of community as "we." Although the mass popularization of media has the potential to create a common discursive space through the use of Tagalog, it also reinforces the inclination of the wealthy and middle classes toward English-language newspapers and cable TV. Therefore, English-language media impede communications among the class-divided nation, as well as between political leaders and constituents, and thereby inhibit democracy (Ofreneo 1984: 197).

The Fragmentation of Living Space

Fragmentation in the Urban Space

The United Nations World Urbanization Project (2014) reported that between 1950 and 2014, the global urban population surged from 746 million to 3.9 billion. Currently, about 56 per cent of the global population lives in cities. Up to 90 per cent of the increase in the urban population has occurred in Asia, and as of 2015, 25 of the 34 global "megacities" (metropolitan areas populated by more than 10 million people) are in developing or emerging countries.

According to Harvey (2012), the urbanization of the global population is intimately connected to the capitalist process of increasing production. He argues that the construction of urban space as a target of investment to absorb surplus capital has become indispensable to capitalism. Furthermore, as many scholars have discussed, the rise of information communication technologies that link cities around the world has created a deepening technological divide and led to polarization between an elite class that works in high-level information- and finance-related professions and performs executive functions within the economy and an increasingly large number of poor people and immigrants whose job opportunities are primarily limited to basic manual labor (Friedmann 1986; Sassen 2001; Castells 2002). This polarization among the urban population is also reflected in urban spaces. For example, Davis (1990) depicts Los Angeles as a space fragmented into suburbs inhabited by a fearful middle class who live in fortress-like gated communities and an inner city inhabited by immigrants and workers who live amid frequent crime and violence.

This urban divide serves to exacerbate resentment and violence. As Smith (1996) maintains, the advance of a gentrification process in which decaying inner cities are redeveloped for middle-class habitation inevitably drives out the poor. Moreover, the sluggish economy and neoliberal policies of recent years have resulted in the emergence of "revanchist cities," where members of the middle class, feeling fear and frustration over job insecurity and cutbacks in welfare, call for the removal of immigrants, laborers and the unemployed in the name of civic morality, family values, and law and order. Meanwhile, the poor experience socioeconomic exclusion, even while simultaneously subsumed to an excessive degree in the success-extolling culture of capitalism. This results in a profound and unrelenting sense of deprivation that increasingly tempts the poor to resort to crime. In response, a growing perception is shared among the relatively well off that criminals should be punished severely, with "zero tolerance" (Young 1999, 2007).

Similar to the megacities in developed countries that were the main focus of previous studies, megacities in the global South are also undergoing social fragmentation under global capitalism. However, whereas the urban poor in developed countries have been in the context of the post-welfare state, the poor in the cities of the global South remain as they always have been—socioeconomically excluded by the state. Furthermore, even as financial and real estate businesses thrive, and modern high-rises buildings and shopping malls proliferate in the cities, the urban problems of poverty, squatting, flooding, poor sanitation and traffic congestion remain. One reason for this is that the governments of developing and emerging nations, when faced with the dilemma of choosing between capitalist demands to lower taxes, which encourages investment and increases global competitiveness, and democratic demands to raise taxes, which provides funds for improving social welfare and urban infrastructure, have chosen to prioritize the former. The developed countries used to resolve this dilemma by fostering both economic growth and a welfare state; however, the global South, driven by fierce competition for investment, now lacks the temporal and financial wherewithal to pursue such a solution.

Furthermore, as Davis (2006) argues, the International Monetary Fund (IMF) and the World Bank have pressed governments in the global South to implement agricultural deregulation, financial reform and structural adjustment programs. Consequently, growing numbers of impoverished farm workers flow into the cities, where insufficient industrial or economic growth is unable to absorb them; this leads to the reduction of formal employment in the cities, declining wages and a collapse in revenues. The upshot is that in the cities, the wealthy and middle classes enjoy a high level of city services and a regressive taxation system, while the poor in the slums are criminalized by capitalists and the state, becoming targets for forced removal. Under these conditions, as AlSayyad and Roy (2004) point out, the urban poor expanded squatter settlements into the suburbs, where they work unstable, irregular jobs in the informal sector; this results in a marked expansion of urban informality.

However, as Shatkin (2006, 2008) points out, urban development is multifarious and determined by conditions specific to each locality. For example, conversely to the example of Europe and North America, where the middle class appears to be vanishing, the middle class in Asia is growing, and no clear division is seen between the suburbs and the inner city. In the next section, I will examine and identify the characteristics of the fragmentation of the urban space in Metro Manila.

Urban Planning by the State

The urban development of Manila began under the rule of Spain. In 1571, Miguel López de Legazpi, who had been appointed by Spain as the first Governor-General of the Philippines, founded the city of Manila (*Insigne y siempre leal Ciudad de Manila*) after using military force to eliminate the resistance of indigenous rulers.[40] The city of Manila was originally composed of what would later be developed into the citadel-like walled city of Intramuros, where only the Spanish were permitted to live. Intramuros was constructed as a space that visually represented the authority of Spain, housing the Governor's Palace, the Archbishop's Palace, City Hall, churches, convents, educational institutions, a hospital and a plaza. However, damage from repeated earthquakes hastened the decline of its function as an economic center. Meanwhile, the suburb of Binondo flourished as a residential area for wealthy merchants, mainly Chinese *mestizos*. When the Port of Manila was opened to world trade in the late 18th century, the city enjoyed rapid economic growth. This led to the designation of seven suburban *pueblos* (towns) as regional administrative districts called *arrabales* (suburbs) and their representation in the Manila City Council.[41]

The American colonial government designated an administrative district equivalent to the current city of Manila as the capital of the Philippines. It attempted to improve the poor public hygiene and infrastructure of the city by introducing hospitals, waterworks, electricity, railroads, telephone lines, radio and other elements of a modern urban infrastructure. In 1905, Chicago city planner Daniel H. Burnham developed a master plan for Manila.[42] According to Shatkin, this plan was for the most part unrealized, but the construction of numerous government offices and the Legislative Building near Luneta Park, with its easy public access, was meant to visualize American democratic values (Shatkin 2005: 581–5).

In 1936, Commonwealth President Quezon founded Quezon City to serve as the nation's capital in the suburbs of Manila, where he had planned to build a new complex of government offices; however, these plans were interrupted by the invasion of Japanese forces. In 1948, to restore the nation's devastated capital functions, President Roxas designated Quezon City as the capital, and subsequently set up the Capital City Planning Commission to preside over postwar urban planning.[43] However, as Caoili

(1988: 126) notes, the commission lacked adequate personnel and funding, and proposals to unify administrative functions that had been dispersed among local governments were not realized. As a result, the development of Manila, based on short-term decisions without any comprehensive long-term plan, proceeded in haphazard fashion.[44]

The declaration of martial law by Marcos in 1972 marked a turning point. In 1975, Marcos established the Metro Manila Commission (MMC) as a regional administrative structure that would integrate local governments, and appointed his wife Imelda as its governor.[45] In 1976, the capital was changed from Quezon City to Metro Manila, an entity consisting of 16 neighboring municipal governments. Using funds from the World Bank as seed money, Marcos implemented a series of ostentatiously modern large-scale projects. The Culture Center of the Philippines is of particular note for its modern design and grandiosity. The Marcoses, hoping to impress people both inside and outside the Philippines with the modernity and future potential of the Philippines, used the Culture Center to host events such as an international film festival and the Miss Universe Pageant. However, the exorbitant costs run up by cronies of the regime who received contracts for these urban development projects adversely affected public finances. What is more, the plan to concentrate all capital functions at the National Government Center in Quezon City remained incomplete; only some government offices were actually relocated.

After the democratization of 1986, President Aquino abolished the MMC and created a new regional administrative structure, the Metro Manila Authority (MMA), whose chair would be elected from among the mayors of the local governments making up Metro Manila. However, the local mayors serving concurrently as MMA chairs came to be viewed as a problem; therefore, in 1995, President Ramos established a new entity, the Metro Manila Development Authority (MMDA), whose chair would be appointed by the president. Due to budgetary constraints, the MMDA, unlike the MMC under Marcos, which had engaged in large-scale urban development projects, was primarily mandated to improve traffic congestion, waste disposal and flood control.

Encroachment on State Planning by the Urban Poor

The state's efforts to create a modern living space in Manila were stymied by the influx of poor people from the countryside. Alternatively, it could be said that the poor arriving from the countryside created their own urban mass sphere, which encroached upon the state's urban projects. An example

Photo 6 At the root of urban poverty is rural poverty (Mat-e village, Merida, Leyte, March 2006).

of this phenomenon is the National Government Center in Quezon City, where Marcos attempted to concentrate the functions of the capital; today it is a massive squatters' settlement that is home to some 300,000 poor people.

Spurred by population growth and the impoverishment of the rural economy, the Philippines started undergoing a full-scale population shift from rural to urban areas in the 1960s.[46] However, due to the lack of industrial development in Manila, this resulted in an oversupply of labor ("urbanization without industrialization") and a population exceeding the limits of the city's capacity ("over-urbanization"). Unable to formally buy or rent land at Manila's high prices, people flooding into the city from the countryside instead squatted illegally on public and private lands, forming slums. Based on data from the National Housing Authority, squatter households in Metro Manila increased from 432,450 in 1995 to 726,908 in 2002.

Because employment in the formal sector is difficult to come by, informal sector jobs such as street vendor, domestic worker, pedicab and jeepney driver, and security guard have become crucial sources of income for the urban poor.[47] According to a 1995 survey by the International Labour Organization and the National Statistics Office, informal sector workers made up 17.3 per cent (539,000 people) of total employment (3,113,000) in Metro Manila.[48] An increase has recently been seen in the number of people who make their living at the unstable bottom of the formal sector work as janitors, guards, drivers, shop clerks and so on; underlying this trend is the growth in short-term contract labor that has accompanied moves toward greater hiring flexibility.[49] As providers of cheap labor, these workers make an important contribution to the urban economy by supporting the lives and businesses of the wealthy and middle classes; however, their jobs are low paying and unstable.

In developed countries, apartment complexes have been constructed to provide urban workers with housing, but similar social policies in the Philippines have not made any headway. Consequently, in building a base for their livelihood, the urban poor have tended to circumvent state regulations. This typically begins with the occupation of relatively inconspicuous public or private lots, usually by several families at a time, on which they build simple dwellings. Once they ascertain that they are not in danger of immediate eviction, more people converge on the area, and the slum expands. Residents give the squatters' settlement a name and register it with the local government as a *barangay* (the smallest administrative unit in the Philippines) or a *sitio*, an enclave within a *barangay*, thereby obtaining voting rights as well as basic services such as water and electricity.[50] Sometimes people make unofficial payments to a criminal "syndicate" to "buy" or "rent" part of a squat in order to secure the safety of their homes. Street vendors also pay "protection money" (*lagayan*) to the police or street-level bureaucrats for use of the streets or sidewalks where they make their living. In this way, the urban poor have constructed a living space based on an informal order that exists outside the legal framework of the state, and in so doing, have ended up encroaching on the urban space the state has attempted to create.

Urban Development by the Private Sector

In the Philippines, the private sector has been more successful than the state in creating modern urban spaces. In the postwar era, developers belonging to family-owned business groups have taken the initiative in building American-style gated communities for the wealthy and middle classes. Since the mid-1990s, urban development in Manila has increasingly been left in the hands of private developers. Behind this trend is the implementation of liberalization, deregulation, privatization and other economic reforms at the urging of the World Bank and IMF in the wake of democratization. To alleviate its financial distress, the government has aggressively sold off public lands to private developers. For their part, the family-owned business groups and ethnic-Chinese entrepreneurs have pursued redevelopment projects in Manila intended for the wealthy and middle classes, as well as overseas contract workers. Here I would like to refer to Shatkin (2008) for an overview of redevelopment in Manila by the private sector.

Developers purchase public land with financing obtained from foreign corporations or overseas Chinese networks and construct massive projects such as high-rise condominiums and office complexes, gated communities, shopping malls, and export-oriented industrial parks that are subject to their own special traffic and architectural regulations, so as to maintain an attractive modern appearance and high security. Since the 1950s, the Ayala Group, a leading private conglomerate, has developed the infrastructure in the city of Makati, transforming it into the most prominent modern business center in the Philippines. Recently, the Ayala Group has been involved in major development projects in Bonifacio Global City and the Manila suburb of Alabang. The group also develops transportation infrastructure and seeks to promote even greater prosperity by constructing traffic links between the areas it has developed around the capital area.[51]

Shatkin asserts that the extreme extent to which urban planning is privatized in Manila has generated a division between the "private city" developed by private corporations and the increasingly impoverished "public city" left in the wake of its development. In his analysis of this type of urban development, he introduces the concept of "bypass-implant urbanism," in the sense that private capital "bypasses" the impoverished public city as it promotes greater mobility of people and capital, and "implants" new centers of production and consumption at various sites in the urban space. In this way, he says, private corporations overwrite the existing urban space as they plan and develop an entire urban system.

Saddled with chronic financial woes, the Philippine national government has formed joint ventures with private corporations in order to curb development costs and optimize efficiency in developing and maintaining railways, waterworks, toll roads and other key components of the urban infrastructure. The principal system employed for this purpose is build-operate-transfer (BOT), in which a developer contracted to build urban infrastructure operates a facility for a certain period of time until the initial investment is recovered, whereupon it is transferred to the state. In such joint ventures, public–private partnership (PPP) is installed to entice private sectors, through which the state guarantees rent and compensation for loss regardless of earnings so that the developer can reduce the risk of their investment. Such contracts tend to guarantee profits for private entities and place the burden of risk on the government.

Shatkin asserts that private sector-led urban development of this sort adversely impacts transparency and accountability in government and exacerbates social stratification and fragmentation. Even as it subsidizes infrastructure development and maintenance by private developers, the state cuts back on outlays needed for living space and transportation infrastructure for lower-income people. As a result, the public city, abandoned by the private sector, suffers from problems such as extreme traffic congestion and an impoverished living environment (Shatkin 2008: 394–5).

Friction between Two Urban Spaces

Manila today therefore consists of a modern urban space created by private capital (the civic sphere) and an impoverished but lively space created by the poor on their own initiative (the mass sphere); these two spaces coexist adjacent to one another in a fragmented, mosaic-like layout. The former space is filled with office buildings and shopping malls, where people come and go dressed in sophisticated fashions. These people live in high-rise condominiums or gated subdivisions with security personnel and commute in private cars between their homes and offices or commercial centers; they never set foot in squatters' settlements. The living space of the poor consists of informal settlements lined with shanties made of corrugated metal and scrap lumber, where half-naked men loiter, women gossip while they do laundry, and barefoot children in ragged clothing scamper about. Aside from live-in maids and chauffeurs, residents of the squats rarely set foot in the wealthy and middle-class neighborhoods.

Though these two living spaces are a study in contrasts, they are intimately linked due to the fact that the poor who live in the informal settlements supply the cheap labor that is indispensable to the urban lifestyles of the wealthy and middle classes. As pointed out by Pinches (1994), these two living spaces are the outcome of the different methods of pursuing advancement and modernity employed by people of different classes, and profound antagonisms exist between the two. For the state, the capitalists and the middle class, the squatters are an impediment to the modernization of Manila and the maximization of profits. Conversely, for the squatters, the state and the capitalists who subject them to forced evictions continue to be an impediment to advancement and the ability to live a better life.

The Philippine government came to view squatters as an obstacle to urban modernization.[52] In particular, the Marcos regime, in its desire to attract foreign capital, develop the economy, and create a beautiful, modern Manila, attacked the problem head-on. In 1978, Marcos appointed his wife Imelda as the Minister of Human Settlements, which subsequently implemented Bagong Lipunan Improvement of Sites and Services (BLISS), a low-income housing construction program. However, due to a combination of corruption and Imelda's aesthetic concerns, the housing that was built proved to be too expensive for the poor to purchase. Starting in 1977, the NHA, acting on the recommendation of the World Bank, began efforts to improve the slums "on-site," but the project stalled when the NHA, unable to recover the cost of its land purchases, fell into financial disarray. Furthermore, back in 1975, Marcos declared squatting a crime with Presidential Decree No. 772, paving the way for a series of massive forced evictions.[53] These strong-arm tactics motivated the urban poor to organize and launch resistance movements. The Zone One Tondo Organization (ZOTO) initiated an active movement in the Tondo district, home to a large squatters' settlement, and succeeded in frequently forcing the government to modify its development projects.[54] However, as Karaos (1993, 1995) has noted, this movement was limited to a particular district and was perennially put on the defensive, eventually fragmenting and weakening with the intervention of leftist activists.

After democratization, numerous NGOs and peoples' organizations engaged in a lobbying effort that culminated in the passing of the 1992 Urban Development Housing Act (UDHA), which made the issue of squatters' settlements part of housing policy.[55] This law stipulated that the resettlement of squatters living along riverbanks and in other high-risk areas required developers to build social housing, and it established a Community Mortgage Program (CMP) under which resident organizations could obtain low-interest financing for land purchases. It also imposed strict conditions on evictions, including consultations with residents and the provision of alternative sites. Introduced in tandem with decentralization policies, these housing policies called on local governments to engage in adequate consultation with NGOs and people's organizations. However, the local governments stood to profit from the property taxes they could levy by redeveloping the squats and constructing commercial establishments and subdivisions. Consequently, they ignored the requests of NGOs and people's organizations and continued to carry out forced evictions (Shatkin 1999, 2004: 2473–5). As a result, through the early 2000s, the number of households that had acquired land through the Community Mortgage Program came merely to less than 5 per cent of the total number of squatter households in Manila.[56] Thus, the friction over urban space between the state, the capitalists and the middle class on the one hand, and the poor on the other, remained unresolved, even after democratization.[57]

As urban development by the state stagnated and vast slums proliferated in Manila, private entrepreneurs took over the reins of post-democratization urban development for the wealthy and middle classes. The result was a split, and subsequent friction, between a civic sphere and a mass sphere inhabited by the poor.

Overview of Survey Sites

Survey Site in the Mass Sphere

In order to better understand and collect data from the mass sphere, I began conducting live-in field research in 2002 in Barangay Old Capitol Site, Quezon City, which is part of the district where President Quezon intended to move the capital. On its periphery are government agencies that were built by Marcos in the 1970s, such as the Philippine Coconut Authority and the Department of Agrarian Reform. Because the district is adjoined to the University of the Philippines, it is home to a large number of university students and employees. It also contains the "UP Village" subdivision, home to many NGO offices. There is also a small commercial district, Philcoa, where people associated with the university congregate.[58]

Several families took up residence in Old Capitol Site in the 1960s and began growing crops for a living. In the mid-1980s, large numbers of people began to migrate from rural areas and squat on the land. By 2010, some 10,000 people lived within the site's 20-hectare administrative zone, most of them concentrated in a four-hectare squatters' settlement adjacent to the University of the Philippines Arboretum.[59] Residents commonly refer to the district by the name "Pechayan." *Pechay* is a type of Chinese cabbage; thus the name is a vestige of the days when this was a flourishing vegetable-growing area. Today, however, the land is covered with numerous shacks, and vegetables are grown only on the periphery. In the early 2000s, many of the residents of Pechayan were first-generation arrivals from the countryside who engaged in various kinds of mutual aid with relatives and

Photo 7 Alley in Pechayan (November 2012).

people from the same locale; they tended to distrust residents outside this circle. However, second-generation residents who view Pechayan as their hometown tend to form more solid networks of mutual trust with one another.[60] Third-generation residents are also on the increase in the 2010s.

The principal means of livelihood for Pechayan residents are found in the informal sector or at the bottom of the formal sector doing short-term contract and other such labor. Street vending in the busy Philcoa district is especially common. Young people often find short-term contract service jobs in shopping malls or restaurants, or earn irregular income from construction work. Tagalog, not English, is spoken on an everyday basis in Pechayan, but people from the same locale also speak to one another in their own native languages. In terms of educational background, very few first-generation residents have attended university. There are more university attendees among the second generation, but the universities they attend are generally low-caliber institutions where they do not acquire sufficient English fluency to function freely in the professions or in positions of responsibility in business or government.

Close to 90 per cent of all Pechayan households owned television sets by the 2010s. Residents are particularly fond of the Tagalog programming on ABS-CBN and GMA. While they may watch English-language sports programs, cartoons and films, they do not watch English-language news. Tagalog magazines and tabloids circulate widely, but hardly anyone buys English-language newspapers on a daily basis. In 2002, cell phones were expensive and ownership was limited, but by the end of the decade, it was common for a single household to own more than one phone. Personal computer use has also gradually spread since around 2010. The Internet cafes of Philcoa, once patronized mainly by students from the University of the Philippines, were by the late 2000s also being frequented by Pechayan residents.

Pechayan sits on public land owned by the National University of the Philippines, but no indications of impending eviction have been seen, at least into the 2010s. Because NGOs and leftists give priority to organizing residents in areas where forced evictions seem imminent, the organization of residents by outside forces has not progressed in Pechayan. Similarly, the Community Mortgage Program, which facilitates organization for people who wish to purchase land, was not conducted in the district. Therefore, compared to squatters' settlements, where leftists and NGOs have actively intervened and residents have launched aggressive land acquisition movements, one may surmise that the political views of Pechayan residents are relatively moderate.[61]

Nonetheless, despite the lack of eviction activity, Pechayan residents feel that they are in danger of being forcibly evicted. The Ayala Group is proceeding with redevelopment along Commonwealth Avenue, the main thoroughfare passing through Philcoa. In 2005, Ayala leased land adjacent to Pechayan from the University of the Philippines and built UP-Ayala Land Techno Hub. They then invited IBM and other multinational corporations to set up call centers, restaurants, hotels and other businesses. There is an undeniable possibility that this is only the first phase in Ayala Group's redevelopment plans in this area, and that it aims to redevelop a larger area that includes Pechayan in the near future.

Survey of the Civic Sphere

For my survey of the civic sphere, I collected research materials in the form of columns and letters to the editor appearing in the three English-language dailies with the largest circulations, the *Philippine Daily Inquirer*, the *Philippine Star* and the *Manila Bulletin*.[62] To supplement this documentary research, I conducted interviews in 2008 and 2009 in the following three subdivisions: Caras de Andalucia and Metro Heights in Quezon City, and Dela Costa Homes in Marikina City. Introduced through networks of professionals and business colleagues, I also interviewed lawyers, university employees, bank employees, workers at international agencies and members of the Philippine Chamber of Commerce and Industry who owned small and medium-sized businesses.

Most of the middle-class individuals I interviewed lived in gated communities. The origins of subdivisions in the Philippines can be dated to the American colonial period, during which the elite made efforts to give concrete form to the imagined American home described in magazines (Yamaguchi 2006). After the war, the Ayala Group developed subdivisions for the rich. Since the 1990s, subdivisions for the middle class have also proliferated. In 2001, there were over 1,000 subdivisions, and more continue to be built, particularly in the suburbs (Tanate and Omura 2004). The three communities where I conducted my interviews were all middle-class subdivisions developed with private capital in the 1980s or 1990s. The highest land prices are in Metro Heights, followed by Caras de Andalucia and Dela Costa Homes.

Metro Heights and Caras de Andalucia are gated communities enclosed by walls. When non-residents want to enter the community, they must present their identification to a gun-carrying guard. The subdivisions contain facilities for common use such as churches, chapels and basketball courts. Individual homes have their own walls and iron gates, but are not uniform in appearance; diverse materials and designs reflect the income of the inhabitants. Most of the homes in Metro Heights and Caras de Andalucia have carports in which the residents keep their own cars. Although most car owners drive themselves, some families hire full-time chauffeurs. In Dela Costa homes, however, a fair number of households did not own cars.

All of the people who consented to be interviewed had at least an undergraduate university degree. Their children were all sent to private schools, and if the household budget permitted, domestic workers were typically hired to look after them and do housework. Every family subscribed to cable TV and enjoyed watching CNN and other American news channels, as well as Hollywood movies. Newspaper delivery services were not available, but most residents frequently purchased English-language newspapers at or on their way to work. They owned at least one cell phone per person, and every home had an Internet connection.

Subdivision residents jointly managed common facilities and implemented crime-prevention measures through their homeowners association. Most residents were members of a number of organizations both inside and outside their subdivision, such as hobby clubs, charities, church groups and NGOs. However, there was nothing resembling a political movement that involved all of a subdivision's residents.

CHAPTER 3

People Power and Moral Antagonism

Photo 8 People gather at the EDSA Shrine During People Power 2 (Ortigas, Quezon City, January 2001; Leo A. Esclanda/BAGWIS).

The most explicit manifestation of the dynamics of "we/they" antagonism in the dual public sphere, and one that had a profound influence on the political process, was the extra-constitutional mobilization of people pressing for a change in presidents in a show of force that bypassed the constitutional system.

To date, the Philippines has seen three instances of the massive protests known as "People Power" in which hundreds of thousands of people took to the streets demanding the resignation of a president. The term "People Power" originated with the protests that culminated in the ouster of

President Marcos in February 1986 and the restoration of democracy. It articulates the idea that it was, literally, the power of "the people" that overthrew the dictatorial Marcos regime. When President Estrada was ousted in January 2001 by the massive protests referred to as "People Power 2," the movement that had deposed Marcos became known as "People Power 1." Then, in May 2001, demonstrations took place that called for the resignation of President Arroyo. Although these protests were subsequently suppressed, they were labeled "People Power 3." All of these protests took place primarily on Epifanio de los Santos Avenue (EDSA) in Manila; therefore, they are also referred to as "EDSA 1," "EDSA 2," and "EDSA 3."

The majority of previous studies on People Power have analyzed the political process in terms of the actions of various forces and key individuals.[1] However, the great majority of participants in People Power were ordinary people who had not typically engaged in organized political activities; hence, it is inappropriate to view these events simply as organized mobilizations. These protest actions, in which hundreds of thousands of people took to the streets, arose from the formation of a powerful, albeit temporary, perception of a righteous "we" opposing an evil "they." What sort of moral discourse produced these antagonistic "we/they" relations that gave birth to People Power?

There is considerable research that explains People Power in terms of moral politics in the civic sphere. Fujiwara (1988: 69–78) writes that a moral politics arose in the wake of the 1983 assassination of former Senator Benigno Aquino Jr., spread via church masses in various locales that formed a "Yellow Community" supporting Aquino's widow Corazon, and culminated in People Power 1. Ileto (1998: 165–86) and Shimizu (1991) assert that Manila's middle class participated in People Power 1 out of a deep empathy for Benigno and Corazon Aquino that was inspired by the Catholic story of the *Pasyon* (Passion). Thompson (2007) argues that in People Power 1 and 2, Aquino and Arroyo played revolutionary roles as women who, wearing a mantle of "moral capital," ousted dictatorial or corrupt male presidents.

As Claudio argues, to the church, the middle class, the intelligentsia, the business world and politicians, the "People Power narrative" provided the basis for a nationalism that awakened the solidarity and aspirations of the nation, and thus became a moral reference point that continued to define political legitimacy, even after democratization. However, the farmers forced to live in abject poverty on the Hacienda Luicita owned by the Aquino-Cojuangco families have rejected this hegemony. This has been cited as proof that the People Power narrative serves to obscure class politics and perpetuate elite rule (Claudio 2013). However, the People Power narrative has not always succeeded in concealing class politics. Furthermore, the mass sphere has on occasion temporarily threatened elite rule with more aggressive actions against the civic sphere.

What, then, is the moral politics that provided the impetus for People Power in the mass sphere? Pinches (1991) vividly describes the alienation of the poor from Marcos and their support for Corazon Aquino and People Power 1 in terms of the restoration of denied self-esteem and the "politics of shame." Rafael (2003) compares People Power 2 and 3, describing the nonviolence of the former as being rooted in a sense of community among members of the middle class who aspired to a "'justice of promise' which is always yet to come," and the violence of the latter as arising from demands for immediate approval from members of the impoverished class and a "justice of revenge." In a discussion of People Power 3, del Rosario (2004) asserts that the poor participated in those protests because they associated Estrada's trials and suffering with the Passion of Christ, thereby intensifying their perception of injustice.

While these studies describe the roles played by various moral discourses that gained hegemony in the civic and/or mass spheres, they do not give sufficient consideration to the mutual relations between the two spheres. In this chapter, to explain how the "people" of People Power 1 were formed but then came apart, culminating in clashes between the "citizens" and "masses" in People Power 2 and 3, I examine the moral politics contested in the dual public sphere. I then describe how the emergence in electoral politics of a populism based in the mass sphere elicited a moral backlash by "citizens" and how People Power arising out of the moral division of the nation severely destabilized democracy.

Democratization through National Solidarity

The Marcos Regime's Collapse and Democratization

In February 1986, global attention was drawn to the Philippines. President Ferdinand Marcos had ruled the country for over 20 years since his election in 1965.[2] In the protests known as People Power, hundreds of thousands of people opposing Marcos filled Manila's streets day after day and eventually succeeded in achieving democratization through nonviolent means.[3] But just who were the "people" who led this democratization revolution?

In September 1972, Marcos declared martial law and then proceeded to imprison his opponents and shut down Congress. His primary objective was to remain in power by suspending the 1935 Constitution that prohibited presidents from serving a third term.[4] Replacing this with his own 1973 Constitution, Marcos granted himself both executive and legislative powers. At the same time, to maintain the appearance of democracy, he instituted a system of national referendums at the *barangay* (village) level, calling this new system "constitutional authoritarianism." He justified martial law as a means of building a more affluent "New Society" by crushing elite rule through a state-led "revolution from the center."

Business circles and the middle class, who had long been frustrated with the inefficiency and corruption of legislative politics, and who also feared the rise of the left, anticipated that martial law would restore public order and improve economic growth.[5] It is true that this authoritarian system was epochal insofar as it replaced political rule by local elites with a system of state-initiated social control and economic development.[6] Eventually, however, the corruption and inefficiency of the Marcos regime became conspicuous. With the rampant inflation that followed the second oil crisis of 1979, people's livelihoods grew increasingly untenable.[7] Amid an intensifying mood of despair over politics and the economy, anti-Marcos forces expanded to include not only the Communist Party of the Philippines (CPP), which espoused armed revolution, as well as social movements that sought to restore elections, but also the business community and the elite.[8] Still, none of these forces could topple the Marcos regime single-handedly, and their ideological differences hampered the formation of an alliance.

However, when former Senator Aquino was assassinated in September 1983, national discontent with Marcos exploded. As Marcos's chief political enemy, Aquino had been incarcerated immediately after the imposition of martial law; however, he developed heart disease during his eight years of confinement and was permitted to undergo treatment in the United States, where he sought asylum. In 1983, ignoring the regime's "warnings" that his safety could not be guaranteed if he returned home, he flew to Manila International Airport and was shot in the head from behind while still on the airplane gangway, just before setting foot once more on his native soil. Despite rigid censorship, the image of Aquino, collapsed with arms spread in broad daylight at the airport, was broadcast via the foreign media, shocking the nation. For Aquino's mass at Santo Domingo Church, throngs of people lined up from morning to night in hopes of getting a glimpse of his body. Even though it took 11 hours to make it from the church to the cemetery, crowds lined the route of the funeral procession. The masses of people who endured stifling heat and heavy rain to mourn Aquino were the harbinger of the "we" identity that eventually came to oppose Marcos.

After these events came repeated protest demonstrations, primarily in the business district of Makati.[9] Finally, in February 1986, Marcos, facing increasing criticism and pressure from the United States, announced a snap election. At this point, anti-Marcos forces, which mainly consisted of business factions, found it difficult to unite behind a single candidate. However, they soon turned their attention to Aquino's widow, Corazon, and urged her to run. Despite initial hesitation, she eventually agreed on the condition that one million people sign a petition supporting her candidacy; this quickly came to fruition and consequently made her determined to run. During the campaign, Marcos derided her as an "inexperienced housewife," to which Aquino sarcastically retorted, "I concede I cannot match Mr. Marcos when it comes to experience. I admit that I have no experience in cheating, stealing, lying, or assassinating political opponents." She also frequently reiterated her commitment to "honesty, sincerity, simplicity and religious faith" (Thompson 1995: 144–6). The Aquino "family color" was yellow, so her supporters wore yellow shirts, making it easy to recognize each other as kindred spirits without having to shout slogans.[10] Fearing violence and misconduct by the Marcos regime during the election, some 500,000 people nationwide volunteered to serve as monitors in the National Citizens' Movement for Free Elections (NAMFREL).[11]

After Marcos was declared the winner by the National Assembly (*Batasang Pambansa*), over one million Aquino supporters gathered at Luneta Park in protest. Aquino denounced Marcos for rigging the election and called for nonviolent civil disobedience in the form of labor strikes and a boycott of businesses linked to the regime. Amid these rising tensions, on February 22, the government learned of a *coup d'état* plot by officers disgruntled with Marcos and ordered army troops to surround the plotters in a military base next to EDSA. In desperation, the insurgents appealed to Cardinal Jaime Sin, the Catholic Archbishop of Manila, for help. Cardinal Sin then used the church radio station Veritas to urge citizens to protect the insurgents from Marcos.[12] Believing that the rebel troops were Aquino supporters, hundreds of thousands of people poured onto EDSA and stood in the path of

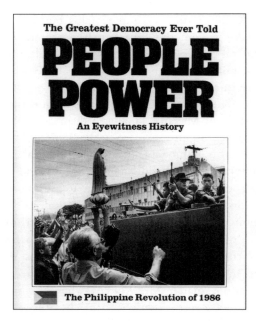

Photo 9 Cover of a book published in 1986 to commemorate People Power 1. People raise their arms and statues of the Virgin Mary as they attempt to halt the advance of an armored vehicle on EDSA.

tanks and machine guns, holding rosaries and holy statues in their hands. Women and children walked around passing out flowers to the soldiers. This response effectively neutralized the firepower of the army, and troops began to defect in growing numbers. Having lost even the support of US President Reagan, Marcos was forced to flee to Hawaii, and Corazon Aquino was sworn in as president. This was the famous triumph of democratization by "People Power."

The Catholic Narrative in the Civic Sphere

The main protagonist in this democratization movement was the middle class of the civic sphere, which had initially welcomed martial law under Marcos and had long acquiesced to his regime. Why did these people suddenly grow critical of the regime after the Aquino assassination, to the point of risking their lives in street protests?

Shimizu (1991) argues that this shift occurred because people felt a deep empathy, rooted in the Catholic worldview, for Benigno and Corazon Aquino. Aquino, cut down by an assassin's bullet upon his return from the United States, had spoken beforehand of the risk to his life. His death was therefore associated with that of Christ, who had prophesied his own death, but accepted it for the sake of saving humanity, and of Jose Rizal, who gave his life for his homeland when it had suffered under Spanish rule. In this worldview, martyrdom for country was equated with martyrdom for religion. Moreover, in losing her husband, Mrs. Aquino was likened to Mary, the bereaved mother of Christ. Filipinos were also profoundly moved by words that Aquino uttered before his assassination, "The Filipino is worth dying for," which rekindled awareness of the value of "Filipinos" as a community. Under the moral leadership of the Catholic Church, even members of the middle class who had been immersed in their private lives acquired a new sense of solidarity as "we Filipinos," which motivated them to participate in the movement.

The middle class of the civic sphere came to demonize Marcos and to view the Aquinos as morally "good." When Marcos denied his involvement in the Aquino assassination, people called him "Pontius Pilate" after the man who sent Christ to his death while denying his own responsibility (Thompson 2007: 6). Marcos himself complained that he had been turned into a "combination of Darth Vader, Machiavelli, Nero, Stalin, Pol Pot, and maybe even Satan himself" (Burton 1989: 312). The English-language newspapers and magazines circulating in the civic sphere were purveyors of this good-evil dichotomy. Responding to the demands of people seeking the truth about the Aquino assassination, English-language publications—including the *Philippine Daily Inquirer*, *Malaya* and *Mr & Ms Special Edition*—featured the late Aquino's words and deeds, thereby actively disseminating the discourse of Aquino as a martyr for his country.

It should be noted that while People Power 1 was a movement of the civic sphere led by the urban middle class, its participants shared a perception of "we" that transcended class boundaries. Together in the streets, they repeatedly sang *Bayan Ko* ("My Country"), a song that calls for the liberation of an oppressed homeland. They also wore yellow shirts and showed their support for Aquino by making the "L" (for *laban*, meaning "fight") sign with their fingers or honking their car horns. In so doing, they solidified their self-perception as one of the "people" seeking the liberation of their country. This memory was resonating powerfully in the civic sphere even while I was conducting research in the

2000s. In my interviews, members of the middle class reminisced about sharing the joy of solidarity with everyone, regardless of class.

> I was very proud of that time because of the thing we created as *a nation* and shared with the entire world. Imagine only *the people* in the streets—the priests, the nuns, the poor and the rich. Everyone was mixed, including the poor, the rich, and the middle class. I was a high school student, and me and my friends always went there. As I said, it was mixed with priests, nuns, politicians and businesspeople; the mix was very, very good. (Joey, 37, male, employed by a foreign corporation, February 15, 2009)

> I was a volunteer. "Doctors For Cory." At that time, the clamor for change was insurmountable, so all of us professionals formed a crusade against the government. I was very much involved with DFC. I think the unity was very prominent. Everyone there was united and helping each other, not just physically. And at that time, I couldn't see any gap between rich and poor. (Elmer, 50, male, medical doctor, March 7, 2009)

Behind this rare sense of solidarity lay both the uncertain hope that it might be possible to oust Marcos, and the fear that everyone might be killed *en masse* by Marcos's troops. Precisely because all participants shared a determination to accept the same fate, even if it meant sacrificing their lives for the Philippines, a sense of community transcending class differences was born. The following accounts testify to this:

> Just hearing Cardinal Sin calling the people, I was nervous, but there was a vast majority of people on EDSA. And once you entered the circle, there was no *takot* [fear]. It was just a miracle that before you reach the vast people, you were so scared, but once you're there, *wala nang takot* [the fear disappeared]. Whatever happens there I will accept, even if I shed my blood, I will accept it—that was the feeling. (Alberto, 70, male, electrician, February 21, 2009)

> All Filipinos really united on EDSA to get rid of Marcos. When I was there, I felt both fear and joy at the same time. We didn't know if the tanks right in front of us would stop or not. Everybody's ideals were there. We were fighting not for ourselves, but for all Filipinos, to make a better Philippines. We were in solidarity—no matter how hard it got, we laughed together. We had barbecues and laughed as we shared the food. We were in such high spirits, everyone was happy. We had everything there. (Esther, 63, female, private school administrator and teacher, February 21, 2009)

Even if someone had tossed a bomb, I wouldn't have been scared. Priests, nuns—all kinds of people were there. Rich people offered us food. It didn't matter who was rich and who was poor. (Louie, 51, female, university clerk, February 21, 2009)

In this way, members of the middle class in the civic sphere experienced a sense of solidarity in the streets as "people" opposed to Marcos and encouraged one another to commit themselves to the democratization movement. It might be said that the various hierarchies and power relations that order and structure society were dismantled at the site of People Power, and that a horizontal community of equals—in other words, *communitas* (Turner 1974)—arose there. The "people" of People Power represented nothing less than the entire Philippine nation in solidarity, beyond class.

The Politics of Shame in the Mass Sphere

Although the poor in the mass sphere also participated in the People Power, they did so in a political context different from that of the middle class. A rare example of a study analyzing this political watershed from the perspective of the poor is that by Pinches (1991). Based on a survey of the Tatalon squatters' settlement in Quezon City, Pinches says that the participation of the poor in People Power can be understood as a consequence of a "politics of shame" over not being treated equally as human beings by society, rather than as an expression of opposition to Marcos. Let us examine, with reference to Pinches, the logic that spurred the poor to take part in People Power.

According to Pinches, the Marcoses spoke patronizingly during the election campaign about how much they had improved the lot of the poor, showering them with land and gifts. In reality, however, forced evictions had continued unabated in the squatter settlements, and the poor felt that far from improving their lives, the Marcoses had insulted them. Despite this, the Marcoses claimed that the poor should repay them with loyalty for the "blessings" they had bestowed, thus inviting a backlash. As political tensions heated up, the number of people attending Aquino rallies steadily grew, even in Tatalon. However, this participation was not motivated by solid support for Aquino, but rather simply by "curiosity" or the notion that "everyone was there."[13] The streets were full of a fiesta-like mood of camaraderie, energy and good feelings, with everyone laughing, dancing and greeting one another. In other words, through the *communitas* of People Power, the impoverished class gained the approval and self-esteem that they had been denied under the existing hierarchy.

This analysis by Pinches shows that the streets where these demonstrations took place had become a contact zone. The experience of *communitas* on the streets signified the dissolution of the dichotomy of "rich" (*mayaman*) vs. "poor" (*mahirap*) that the poor normally experienced on an everyday basis.[14] A friend who lived in the squatters' settlement of Pasay City had this to say about the experience of People Power: "I was so happy. Everybody, rich and poor alike, was sharing food and water. I was outdoors all day, and no matter how far I walked, I never got tired." (Nilo, 37, male, unemployed May 2002). Precisely because they experienced this dissolution of hierarchical divisions, the poor were able to feel that they were part of the "people."

This class-transcending sense of community prompted the poor to anticipate the coming of a new world. Motivated by the hope that if democratization succeeded, the new government would give land to squatters, several hundred thousand people moved to Manila from the countryside (Shatkin 2004: 2478). However, it soon became acutely clear that the cooperation between the civic and mass spheres was based on different expectations. The joy and unity of *communitas* was short-lived. After this "revolution," one young man told the following to Pinches (1991: 186): "On EDSA, rich and poor came together, but now it is as it was before—they can't be bothered with us". As if to underscore these words, the following year, the police massacred farmers demonstrating for land reform on Mendiola Street near the presidential palace.

In the interviews I conducted, poor people who recall that period reminisce less about the feelings inspired by People Power than about the virtues of the Marcos era in terms of low prices and services to the people:

> I think things were better in the Marcos days. Today's democracy is only good for the rich. We felt more benefits and good will under Marcos. Sure, society wasn't entirely equal, but food got delivered for free to the *barangay*, and Marcos really did give us many things. I was only around 17 then, and I didn't realize how important People Power was. But in my opinion, we might have been better off if People Power hadn't happened. During Marcos's time, prices were kept under control, and they didn't keep going up like they do now. (Gil, 42, male, tailor, March 12, 2009)

These accounts by the poor of their nostalgia for the Marcos era stand in marked contrast to the stories of the middle class about the joy and solidarity of People Power. Perhaps this class disparity in memory is due to a disparity in experience during the intervening decades since democratization—between those still capable of sentimentality about the good feelings of People Power, and those who have lived a life too harsh to allow such reminiscing. It is a common enough tendency to deny the present by idealizing the past.

"Solidarity of the People" According to the Powerful

In truth, democratization did not ameliorate the dire poverty and inequality of the Philippines. The CPP, an exponent of equality, boycotted the presidential elections due to its commitment to revolution by armed struggle, and hence failed to retain influence over the democratization process or the Aquino administration. For her part, President Aquino, in order to stabilize her power base, was obliged to compromise with the existing elite, including her own relatives who owned vast plantations. The elite who had lamented their plight under the Marcos regime made a comeback with the reinstatement of Congress, where they watered down land reform legislation. Elements from moderate social movements who initially participated in the Aquino administration also found themselves gradually edged out. The fact that the "people" in solidarity transcending class differences became the protagonist of the "revolution" under the hegemony of moral nationalism marginalized the issue of remedying deep-seated inequalities.[15]

It is true that elements from non-CPP moderate social movements attempted to institutionalize the political participation of NGOs and reduce inequality amid the new political conditions that followed democratization. Both the Aquino and Ramos administrations displayed a cooperative stance toward citizen participation-based politics. The Aquino years saw the promulgation of the Local Government Code (1991), which institutionalized the participation of NGOs and people's organizations. The Fidel Ramos administration that followed also implemented a "Social Reform Agenda" that attempted to address the poverty problem through cooperation between government agencies and groups representing farmers, workers, indigenous people and the urban poor. Although these practices sought to implement continuous social reform through civic inclusivism, they did not bring about immediate, fundamental social reform.

In this context, state leaders began to actively exploit the moral nationalist discourse of "solidarity of the nation." Used in this manner, such discourse took on the characteristic of actively concealing, in the name of solidarity, the inequalities and disparities that existed between classes. This was the paradoxical outcome in which desire for democratization and emancipation from oppression in civil society transformed the elites into moral agents of change. Both Aquino and her successor Ramos took every opportunity to bring up the memory of People Power, attempting to maintain their legitimacy by securing the support of the entire "nation". For example, in her inaugural address, Aquino cited the death of her husband in calling for the nation to unite:

> Ninoy believed that only the united strength of a people can overturn a tyranny so evil and well organized. It took the brutal murder of Ninoy to bring about the unity, the strength, and the phenomenon of People Power. . . . And now, I would like to appeal to everyone to work for national reconciliation, which is what Ninoy came home for. . . . So I call on all those countrymen of ours who are not yet with us to join us at the earliest possible time so that together, we can rebuild our beautiful country. (Quoted in Malaya and Malaya 2004: 254)

In the 1992 presidential election, Ramos used the slogan "EDSA 1992" to identify himself to voters as a leader of the rebel forces and People Power. He even chose "Lakas," short for *Lakas ng Tao* (People Power Party), as the name of the new political party he launched prior to the election. In short, Ramos was declaring that the "power of the people" would have to be rallied once more if the hope for a better society embodied in People Power was to be fulfilled.

Yet, however many exhortations might be made for unity of the "people," the obvious inequalities could not be concealed indefinitely. In other words, the hegemony of moral nationalism could not be sustained because although it includes the poor among "the people" morally, it excludes them socioeconomically. This limitation was made indubitably clear by the populism of Joseph Estrada during the presidential election of 1998.

A Clash between Civic and Mass Protests

Philippine Populism

Because Joseph Estrada was a movie actor, studies of Philippine populism have inevitably focused on the influence of Tagalog cinema on the poor. According to Flores (1998), these studies share a thesis that Estrada won the support of the poor by reenacting in the political world the theme of longing for social reform and justice that appeared in Tagalog films. It is also asserted that Estrada used his movies to construct active subjects of "the masses," turning them into both his base of support and his victims. According to Hedman (2001), this populism, which had its origins in the "social imagery" offered to the poor in Tagalog films and the fetishizing of movie stars by the poor, came to "haunt reformists and radicals alike." Tolentino (2010) also argues that the aspirations of the "masses" for liberation were assigned meaning and collectively subjectified by Estrada, thereby depriving the masses of a voice, marginalizing them and alienating them from one another.[16]

However, there are several problems with these earlier studies. First, while their cinematic analysis is excellent, they do nothing more than attempt to corroborate the common belief that the poor are manipulated by populists because they are unable to distinguish between movies and political reality. These studies do not pay adequate heed to the voices of the poor themselves to learn how they interpreted and imparted meaning to Estrada. Consequently, there is a need for a renewed focus on discourses in the mass sphere.

Second, the argument that populists exploit the poor and render them powerless is problematic. The votes of the poor had been divided by clientelism and competition among the elite. In the 1998 presidential election, however, for the first time in the history of Philippine elections, the poor responded to Estrada's appeals and engaged in class voting behavior. Through this exercise of their own power, they made the critical problem of inequality a political issue. Precisely because their collective vote wielded significant influence, the voting behavior of the poor became a focus of interest in every subsequent election. It must be recognized that populism did not divide the "masses" so much as it enabled their collective participation in politics.

A third problem is the too-facile argument that populism impedes political reform. There is no dearth of Philippine political studies—not only those in relation to cinema—that treat populism as an obstacle to political reform. For example, Doronila (1998, May 18; 2003,

December 15) criticizes populism based on "personality" and "image" as obstructing policy-based political reform. Aquino (1998) also criticizes situations in which "star-ization" takes priority over policy issues. Meanwhile, Magno (1998) expresses concern that pork-barrel politicking to buy the support of the poor may impede economic reform and give pause to foreign investors.

Yet, populism is indispensable to democracy insofar that it seeks to legitimize the participation of ordinary people, and to reject it is ultimately to reject democracy itself (Canovan 1999, 2002). Moreover, populism that calls for equality can acquire a revolutionary character by providing a foundation for opposition to elite rule (Laclau 1977, 2005). In this light, populism cannot be readily dismissed as a pathology that undermines democracy or political reform.

As mentioned in Chapter 1, I treat populism as a counter-discourse that constructs an antagonistic relationship between the good, oppressed "masses" (*masa*) or "poor" (*mahihirap*) and the "rich" (*mayayaman*) by appealing to the former and making poverty and inequality an issue in the mass sphere. The "masses" constructed by populism must be acknowledged as a subject that is not merely manipulated by populists, but that often exceeds the latter's intentions or control in the desire for transformation of the stratified socioeconomic structure. Furthermore, the effect of populism on the political process must be analyzed, not by focusing on populism alone, but rather in terms of conflict with the existing power structure.

The Rise of Populism

Joseph Estrada, known by the nickname "Erap," is an action film star turned politician.[17] He was born into an upper-middle-class family in the downtown Manila district of Tondo and grew up in the town of San Juan.[18] He entered the elite private Ateneo de Manila High School but was subsequently expelled. He then attended the Mapúa Institute of Technology and the Polytechnic Colleges of the Philippines, but eventually dropped out of both.[19] He made his film debut in 1954, and scored his first hit in 1962 with *Asiong Salonga*, in which he played the protagonist, Nicasio Asiong Salonga, a notorious gangster in postwar Tondo. His performance made Estrada one of the top movie stars in the Philippines. In the 1960s, his *Batang* series, in which he played a young man of the streets whose hopes are crushed by society's oppression, earned him a dedicated fan base among the poor.[20]

Among his most highly rated films is *Geron Busabos: Batang Quiapo*, which was released in 1964. As Hedman (2001) points out, "busabos" can mean "enslaved," but also connotes "dirty" in the sense of the "dirty masses." Geron, the dockworker hero played by Estrada, is adored by poor people—including street vendors, beggars and prostitutes—who he protects from crooked cops and syndicate gangsters.[21] Hedman analyzes this film in terms of suppression, eruption and failure of desire. Geron's feelings of entrapment in poverty and his powerlessness to change the cruel realities of slum life drive him to reject the friends, women and orphans who depend on him. Eventually, however, he is unable to suppress his desire to help and opens his heart. But now he is beset by a host of woes—betrayal by a friend, breakup with a woman and the death of an orphan he cared for. Finally, he is framed for a murder he did not commit and beaten to death by thugs and cops. He draws his final breath in the arms of the woman he loves.

In the many action films in which he appeared, Estrada played roles such as farmer, jeepney or taxi driver, street vendor, day laborer and street punk (*kanto boy*), earning him recognition as "the Estrada hero, the rebel with a cause, fighting for the underdog and for what he believes in, fighting against the pressures from a harsh, cruel world."[22] The heroes of these action movies, played by Estrada and others, recall the legends of "social bandits" (*taong labas, tirong, tulisan*) who were active during the colonial era or the chaotic postwar years (Gealogo 2000; Tolentino 2010: 80). These social bandits, who established their own justice and morality outside of the ruling order, live on in the collective memories of the oppressed poor.[23] Also, as noted by Lumbera (2000: 12), action films of this period were heavily influenced by the American popular-culture motif of the young man who defies social norms, characters similar to that played by James Dean in *Rebel Without a Cause*. Estrada himself personified the theme of rebellion against his own middle-class roots and elite education, and as noted by del Rosario (2004: 57), he even adopted the style of James Dean in his haircut and cool demeanor.

This image was extremely useful to Estrada in launching his political career. In 1967, at age 31, he was elected mayor of the municipality of San Juan and served as a faithful supporter of the Marcos regime.[24] When Aquino appointed new mayors in the wake of democratization, Estrada organized his supporters to protest and refuse to step down. In the 1987 election, he ran for the Senate as a candidate of the Grand

Alliance for Democracy (GAD), a pro-Marcos opposition party, and won a seat despite the overwhelming popularity of the Aquino side. In the 1992 election, he ran as a candidate of his own small party, *Partido ng Masang Pilipino* (PMP, "Party of the Filipino Masses"), and won election to the vice-presidency.

On the national political stage, Estrada cultivated an image of being "tough on crime". While serving in the Senate, he hosted a TV program entitled *Hotline sa Trese* ("Hotline to Channel 13"), which urged viewers to call in with information on unsolved crimes. While vice-president, he served as chair of the Ramos administration's "Presidential Anti-Crime Commission," and would show off his tough-guy image by arresting bank robbers, drug dealers and kidnappers, and marching them in front of the TV cameras. Additionally, Estrada transformed his overall image from loyal Marcos ally to anti-American nationalist politician. While still a senator, he starred in the 1989 film *Sa Kuko ng Agila* ("In the Claws of the Eagle"), playing a jeepney driver who denounces human-rights abuses by US troops stationed in the Philippines, and leads the masses in a nationalist movement. In 1991, Estrada won praise as one of the "Magnificent 12" senators who opposed extending the contracts of US bases in the Philippines and successfully terminated the base agreement.

When Estrada ran for president in 1998, he criticized elite rule and pledged to implement a new politics for the poor.[25] Speaking in Tagalog, he wooed the poor with such slogans as *Erap para sa mahirap* ("Erap for the poor"), *ama ng masa* ("father to the masses"), and "champion of the poor." When exhorting the people of the nation, he used the word *kababayan*, meaning "countryman," to signify his solidarity and fraternity with the "masses" (*masa*). His political coalition, *Laban ng Makabayang Masang Pilipino* (LAMMP, "Struggle of the Patriotic Filipino Masses") took the jeepney, the indispensable mode of transportation for working people, as its symbol, and "Justice, Economy, Environment and Peace" (JEEP) as its slogan. When coalition candidates delivered their applications to the Commission on Elections, they rode in a jeep driven by Estrada. LAMMP also tried to organize the poor at the grassroots level by screening Estrada's films in urban slums, followed by a video touting his record in eradicating crime and aiding the poor.[26] The radio program "Erap's JEEP" was set up so that poor people could talk about their problems directly with Estrada, who would promptly solve them.

Estrada also likened himself to Andres Bonifacio, the hero from a plebeian background who launched the armed struggle against the Spanish. Building on this theme, he asserted that his mission as "centennial president" (1998 being the centennial of independence from Spain) was to complete the unfinished revolution and achieve a Philippines free of poverty and inequality, as Bonifacio had envisioned.[27]

Estrada's populism was extremely effective in the Philippines, a country where 60 to 70 per cent of the population was poor. Although the presidential vote was split among seven candidates, Estrada nearly claimed a majority of the votes of the poor.[28] As a result, he won easily with 39.86 per cent of the total vote, nearly double that of the ruling party candidate, who was better funded and more organized. Estrada became the first president in Philippine history to give his inaugural address in Tagalog and declared the advent of the time of Filipino masses (*panahon ng Masang Pilipino*):

> The common people have waited long enough for their turn, for their day to come. That day is here. . . . It is time. Time to speed up the improvement of the living conditions of the common people. Time for them to have a fairer share of the national wealth they create and a bigger stake in their own country. . . . This time, why not to the common people as well, for a change? Must we always measure progress only by the golf courses of the rich? . . . [S]urely, it is time for the masses to enjoy first priority in the programs of the government. As far as resources permit, to the best of our ability and the limit of our energy, we will put a roof over their heads, food on their tables and clothes on their backs. We will educate their children and foster their health. We will bring peace and security, jobs and dignity to their lives. . . . This I promise the people.[29]

With this pledge to the masses of a government that would be generous to the poor, Estrada made the presidency his own.

Moral "Citizens" in People Power 2

Estrada's appeal was not directed exclusively at the mass sphere. To placate fears among business circles that pork-barrel largesse aimed at the poor would adversely impact the economy, he hired economists from the University of the Philippines to serve as the "brains" of his administration and subsequently pledged to continue economic reforms.[30] Meanwhile, by appointing the veteran leftist and NGO activist Horacio Morales as

Secretary of Agrarian Reform, and another famous NGO activist, Karina Constantino-David, as presidential advisor on housing, Estrada sought to show the NGOs and the left that he was serious about tackling poverty issues.

However, Estrada's actual approach to carrying out policy measures could only be termed inappropriate.[31] He would not look over materials in advance to prepare for cabinet meetings, and he delegated legislative strategy entirely to his chief cabinet secretary. He spent nearly every evening lavishly wining and dining politicians and businesspeople in his circle, and he often made policy decisions while mahjong gambling. Moreover, by appointing these same intimates as presidential advisors and the like, he created redundancies in jurisdiction with his official cabinet, creating confusion in the executive branch. The English-language press accused this "midnight cabinet" of ignoring official decisions. English-language newspapers critical of the Estrada administration unearthed one scandal after another, including suspicions of insider trading and reports of a mansion (complete with a pool) inhabited by his mistress. Estrada responded by threatening to sue the *Manila Times* for libel and having his corporate friends withdraw their advertising from the *Inquirer*. However, the pressure on the media only intensified the criticism of his administration.

In October 2000, Luis Singson, governor of Province of Ilocos Sur, claimed that Estrada had pocketed "protection money" payoffs from *jueteng*, an illegal numbers game popular among the poor, as money paid to the government.[32] The alleged amount was some 400 million pesos over the course of two years. Singson further accused Estrada of pilfering 130 million pesos in tobacco taxes. These allegations sent Estrada's popularity plummeting, especially among the wealthy and middle classes. According to an opinion survey by SWS, wealthy and middle-class support for Estrada fell from 17 to 7 per cent between October and December 1999 alone.[33]

Those upset with Estrada expressed their wrath through street protests. As early as August 1999, Cardinal Sin and former president Aquino, the living symbols of People Power 1, had been leading large protests against Estrada in the Makati business district. When the *jueteng* scandal broke, they led a prayer rally demanding Estrada's resignation. Other elements—ranging from Bayan Muna, the alleged legal arm of the CPP, and CPP splinter groups Sanlakas and Akbayan on the left, to the Makati Business Club and other business leaders—also began calling for

Estrada to step down.³⁴ Though this broad range of forces held vastly disparate views on ideology and the composition of a post-Estrada government, the single issue of Estrada's resignation led to the formation of an unlikely alliance.

Challenges to Estrada also gathered momentum in Congress. In the House of Representatives, a large number of congressmen seceded from the ruling party and submitted a motion to impeach Estrada, and in early December 2000, an impeachment trial began in the Senate with the aim of ousting Estrada from the presidency.³⁵ Every session of the trial received live television coverage and attracted a huge viewership as the proceedings unfolded.³⁶ On January 16, 2001, a vote was held on whether to open an envelope that was purported to contain evidence of Estrada's secret bank account. As a result of maneuvers by Estrada to secure a majority, votes against opening the envelope edged out those in favor, 11 to 10. In protest, the Senate president and the other members of Congress who served as prosecutors resigned from their posts, and the impeachment trial collapsed in a stalemate.³⁷

Many members of the urban middle class used cell phones to communicate and to urge each other to take to the streets and join in a protest demonstration centered around the EDSA Shrine, which had been built to commemorate People Power 1. On the night of January 16, Cardinal Sin and former president Aquino stood on the stage and called for a reenactment of People Power; this marked the beginning of "People Power 2." Participants demonstrated daily and nightly, holding up signs saying "Erap is Guilty" (*Guilty si Erap*), "Erap Resign," and "Oust Erap," and demanding Estrada's resignation. The number of demonstrators swelled to over 200,000 at the peak of the protests.³⁸ An organization, *Kongreso ng Mamamayang Pilipino* (*Kompil*) *II* (Congress of Filipino Citizens II), was formed to coordinate the numerous citizens' groups that were participating in the movement.³⁹ According to Arugay (2004: 85–6), the "frame" (that is, the system of meaning and belief undergirding their activities) of the protesters' collective action was "to launch a moral crusade against corruption with civil society as the claimant for the citizen's rights to transparent and accountable governance."⁴⁰ Ads pronouncing Estrada guilty appeared almost daily in the English-language papers, and Ateneo de Manila and other Catholic universities cancelled classes, tacitly facilitating student participation in the demonstrations. The demonstrators wore black shirts symbolizing protest and the "death of Philippine democracy."⁴¹

Photo 10 Demonstrators call for Estrada's resignation in front of the EDSA Shrine (January 2001; Leo A. Esclanda/BAGWIS).

In answer to this growing criticism, the Estrada administration defended its legitimacy, maintaining that their supporters outnumbered the protesters in the streets.[42] To demonstrate their unwavering loyalty, *Iglesia ni Cristo* and *El Shaddai*, two religious groups that served as a major support base for the administration, held large prayer rallies at Luneta Park.[43] The administration's press secretary asserted that People Power 2, led as it was by a small, wealthy segment of the citizenry, did not represent the Philippine people, and that the ten million citizens who had voted for Estrada did not want him to step down. Estrada made the rounds in poor urban areas, where he likened the elite's personal attacks against him to the cruel and unjust treatment experienced by the poor on a daily basis at the hands of the rich. Before a crowd of poor people on Tondo, he declared, "I am being beaten up, and I let them beat me up. I remember when I was still an actor with FPJ

[Fernando Poe Jr., a famous film star and close friend of Estrada], I let my enemies beat me up. But in the end, all of my enemies would be knocked out." These brave words earned him an ovation.[44] Finally, he made a desperate appeal to the poor that they should fight to the end, to the last man, until there was "nothing left" (*walang iwanan*), in an expression of solidarity (*barkadahan*) of comradeship beyond right and wrong.[45]

However, as People Power 2 gathered momentum with each passing day, members of Estrada's cabinet began to resign one after the other. On January 20, the fourth day of protests, the heads of the army and the police stood before the crowd at the EDSA Shrine and announced they were withdrawing their support from the administration.[46] Hoping to resign with dignity, Estrada requested a four-day reprieve; however, the Supreme Court promptly approved the installation of Vice President Gloria Macapagal-Arroyo as president. Arroyo took the oath of office, and a beleaguered Estrada left Malacañang Palace under his own power.[47]

In her inaugural address, citing the support of the "people" to legitimize the extra-constitutional change of administrations, Arroyo stated that "People Power and the oneness of will and vision have made the new beginning possible." She also vowed to promote a "national healing" of the wounds caused by enmity between classes, and asserted that she was not the enemy of the poor.[48] Yet ultimately, People Power 2 was led by the middle class of the civic sphere and did not result in the formation of a "people" transcending class. Though it is true that some members of the impoverished class participated in People Power 2 when mobilized by Catholic lay groups or the left, the vast majority continued to support Estrada.[49] The poor felt no affinity for Arroyo, a member of the elite who was the daughter of former president Macapagal, had studied in the US, and held a doctorate in economics.

Revolt by the "Masses" in People Power 3

Among Estrada's supporters, some not only watched People Power 2 unfold on TV, but also took to the streets and engaged in counter-demonstrations. Several thousand Estrada supporters held rallies on the Mendiola Bridge near Malacañang Palace and got involved in skirmishes with anti-Estrada groups. Pro-Estrada groups even made forays into the Makati business district where they clashed with middle-class workers. A witness to one such incident, an American living in the Philippines, posted this account on his website:

> A group of 300 or so pro-Erap rallyists, mostly head-banded teenagers in raggedy shorts, tank tops, and the flip-flops ubiquitous among the Filipino working class, had assembled on Ayala Avenue to have a little demonstration. Many looked pretty drunk, and more than a few were carrying pointed sticks. Initially, they minded their own business. . . . However, when the white collars (mostly from the Philippine Stock Exchange) started coming out for lunch, things escalated quickly. Most of the white collars were dressed in black, and several carried "Erap Resign" streamers. The only thing separating the two groups was the median island of Ayala Avenue and a small squad of cops. Perhaps predictably, the white collars couldn't resist taunting the tank tops. Equally predictably, the tank tops reacted with angry, obscene gestures. The white collars responded with more taunting and chants of "Erap Resign!" Back and forth it went. Chaos ensued, including screaming curses, obscene gestures, and flying rocks, which caused the white collars the scurry. . . . Once safely back inside, a fair number of the white collars ascended to the roofs of their buildings and began showering the tank tops with plastic water bottles, rocks, and miscellaneous building materials.[50]

Amid this inter-class strife, the Arroyo administration was confronted with a severe dilemma over how to deal with Estrada. The forces behind People Power 2 demanded that the administration thoroughly investigate and prosecute Estrada; however, a hardline stance posed the risk of inspiring a sympathy vote by the poor for the pro-Estrada opposition coalition *Puwersa ng Masang* (Force of the Masses) in the midterm elections slated for May 14. In the end, Arroyo went with a hardline policy, and in early April, Estrada was indicted on charges of plundering for illegally amassing 4.1 billion pesos during his tenure in office. Under Philippine law, persons indicted for plundering are to be held without bail, and if found guilty, may be sentenced to life in prison or death.[51] On April 25, around 3,000 Estrada supporters erected barricades in front of Estrada's residence to prevent his arrest. They were greeted by some 2,000 police, who fired tear gas and water cannons, broke through the barricades, and arrested Estrada. Images of weeping and moaning elderly women and bloodied men who had been beaten by the police appeared on TV. When Estrada was brought to police headquarters, located on EDSA, his supporters gathered at the adjacent EDSA Shrine and began to shout *Ibalik si Erap* ("Return Erap [to the presidency]"). This marked the beginning of what came to be called "People Power 3."⁵²

Providing transport, food, and money so as to encourage participation in the demonstrations, politicians of the opposition coalition *Pwersa ng Masang* attempted to exploit People Power 3 for the purpose of elections or of seizing power.⁵³ They incited the masses by repeatedly declaring, "Estrada is persecuted by the elite because he is the defender of the masses," and "We will take back Malacañang Palace!" To attract more demonstrators, they provided entertainment on the stage, including dancing by sexy female performers. Seeking a better vantage point from which to view the stage, throngs of people climbed onto the roof of the EDSA Shrine, causing part of the roof to collapse under the weight. Graffiti was painted on the statue of Mary, Queen of Peace, Our Lady of EDSA. The shopping mall next to the EDSA Shrine had cordially offered the use of its toilets and trash cans to participants in People Power 2, but locked its doors to those in People Power 3. As a result, the area around the shrine was transformed into a massive public toilet and garbage heap, causing a terrible stench.⁵⁴

The Catholic Church loudly denounced People Power 3 and forbade participation in the demonstrations, but most of the poor turned a deaf ear.⁵⁵ Many of the demonstrators were members of the grassroots, pro-Estrada Peoples' Movement Against Poverty (PMAP) or of the religious groups *Iglesia ni Cristo* or *El Shaddai*. Although the major TV stations did not televise People Power 3, it was covered 24 hours a day by TV and radio stations owned by *Iglesia ni Cristo*.⁵⁶ The demonstrations continued day and night on a scale eclipsing People Power 2, with as many as 300,000 people.⁵⁷ In an effort to cool the situation, the Arroyo administration negotiated with leaders of the two religious groups and persuaded them to stop mobilizing demonstrators in exchange for promises to improve the treatment of Estrada, among other conditions.

Meanwhile, with the goal of overthrowing the Arroyo administration and setting up a provisional government, opposition politicians made plans with elements within the army to launch a *coup d'état*. When it failed to occur on the predicted day of April 29, the administration claimed victory over a "foiled *coup d'état*." But before dawn on May 1, some 40,000–50,000 demonstrators overturned barricades set up by the police and stormed Malacañang Palace with shouts of "We're here, our victory is close at hand! (*Nandito na kami, malapit na tagumpay!*)" and "Get rid of Gloria, return Erap! We are coming! Get ready! (*Patalsikin*

Photo 11 Pro-Estrada demonstrators confront police in front of Malacañang Palace (May 2001; Leo A. Esclanda/BAGWIS).

si Gloria, ibalik si Erap! Nandyan na kami! Maghanda na kayo!)" Opposition legislators and Estrada's son incited the crowd, but then disappeared from view. Sometime after 5 a.m., a fierce clash between demonstrators, police, and army troops involving exchanges of rocks, gunfire and tear gas ensued in front of Malacañang. Seven hours later, the demonstrators had been suppressed, but at least 4 had been killed and 113 injured.

Having narrowly averted disaster, the Arroyo administration declared a "state of rebellion" and began rounding up and arresting opposition legislators, hoping to quell the crisis once and for all.

This sequence of events dramatically demonstrated how the "people" who had once ousted Marcos became divided into two clashing entities: the "citizens" who acted in People Power 2, and the "masses" who acted in People Power 3.[58] How did members of the civic and mass spheres experience and interpret these political upheavals?

Victory by a Moral Citizenry and Fear of the Mob

The Triumph of Moral "Citizens"

To the middle class of the civic sphere, People Power 2 was nothing less than an action undertaken by "citizens" to guide the Philippines along the path of progress by returning a democracy warped by a corrupt leader to its proper state. They felt that Estrada had "hurt" the Philippines, as suggested by a 30-year-old female teacher: "We thought it was the most natural thing to do—we were hurt and angry, so we trooped to EDSA." (quoted in San Juan 2001: 5–7).

However, in a departure from People Power 1, the subject "we" here clearly refers to the middle class. In the interviews I conducted, participants in People Power 2 recalled the demonstrations as being something like a party for the middle class:

> You could see that all have cars. And so it started with the middle class and continued with a flow of communication. There were masses also but mostly just curious onlookers. The middle class people were the ones feeling the crunch at that time whenever the government was not doing good, particularly at the time of Erap. Everyone was smiling, they were socializing, it's like you've known them for quite some time. Friendly atmosphere. (Joey, 37, male, employed at a foreign corporation, February 15, 2009)

> It was like a party, the energy and the atmosphere. It was an exciting way to fight for something. If you have food, you can share it with everybody. The participants were the middle class who were at their tipping point. Everyone brings food, and organizations like Couples for Christ had tents. Companies and schools excused absences on that day. (Jason, 32, male, lawyer, April 23, 2008)

To justify this extra-constitutional change of administrations, those in the civic sphere asserted that Estrada had abused his power, betrayed the democratic system's trust, and enriched himself through graft and corruption. Yet unlike Marcos, who had held power as president for 21 years, Estrada had been in office for only a year and a half. Moreover, a tendency toward heavy-handedness notwithstanding, Estrada neither imprisoned nor assassinated his opponents. Furthermore, no severe economic crises occurred during his administration. Above all, he did not declare martial law, and therefore his presidency could be challenged in the next election. So why was Estrada so demonized—one might say excessively—in the civic sphere? The answer is that his very presence posed a threat to the moral order championed by the civic sphere. Estrada was known for his "bad habits" (*bisyo*) of drinking, gambling, and womanizing. These "habits" were associated with those of poor male Filipinos, and were effective in inspiring a sense of kinship with Estrada within the mass sphere. But in the civic sphere, he was criticized for lacking *delicadeza* (refined manners and taste).

From the time Estrada declared himself a candidate for president in 1998, the Catholic Church, the business community, and the English-language newspapers expressed intense moral animosity toward him. For example, the *Philippine Daily Inquirer* ran a front-page headline on Election Day quoting the words of Cardinal Sin, "Anybody but Erap." The article quoted a pastoral letter by the Catholic Bishops' Conference of the Philippines trumpeting the Church's message that "voting for a womanizer would be dealing a 'death blow' to democracy."[59] The Makati Business Club said of Estrada's election to the presidency, "Heaven forbid!"[60] In short, the Church, business leaders and columnists for the English-language newspapers all voiced their objections to Estrada's candidacy, asserting that a presidential candidate must "have a high IQ, a college degree, scholarly capabilities, courage, honesty, humility, and the ability to lead moral lives and love their spouses."[61]

More than anyone else, Cardinal Sin continued to castigate Estrada's personal lifestyle—which was characterized by his gambling and drinking and numerous mistresses and illegitimate children—as failing to serve as a "role model" for the Catholic faithful.[62] When suspicions of Estrada's involvement in illegal gambling came to light, Cardinal Sin called for his resignation, declaring that Estrada had lost the "moral ascendancy to govern." When People Power 2 began, he repeatedly uttered, "Stay here until evil is conquered by good. Stay here until corruption is overcome by integrity. Stay here and pray."[63] Active political engagement of this sort on the part of Cardinal Sin and the Catholic Church reflected the fact that since People Power 1, the bishops had assumed a role in guiding the government and the people, and had come to believe they had a "moral right" to demand the resignation of a "failed president."[64] The civic sphere welcomed Cardinal Sin's active political intervention. One 64-year-old housewife said, "When we saw Cardinal Sin come out to deliver Mass, without prior notice, security, or a sound system, we knew a miracle was due." (quoted in San Juan 2001: 5–7).

Estrada was attacked and scorned in the civic sphere not only for his moral decadence, but also for his "lack of intelligence," particularly what was perceived as his poor English. Numerous "Erap jokes" ridiculing

Estrada circulated in the civic sphere via texting, adding a humorous side to the protest movement.[65] Examples of some of these texts are as follows.

> Stewardess: sir r u DONE?
> ERAP: no im ERAP
> S: no I mean r u FINISHED?
> E: no im PILIPINO
> S: I mean r u THRU?
> E: wat do u think me FALSE?!

> HOT NEWS!!! Ascnation attempt on Erap failed. D Pres was shot in d hed w/ a 45 clber but survivd *dahil walang utak na natamaan* (because he had no brain).

> Q: Why can't Erap resign?
> A: Because that would be the intelligent thing to do.

Erap jokes of this sort had two distinctive aspects: they were satirical in nature ridiculing someone in power, and they were a display of superiority over a social and intellectual inferior. As one lawyer said, "Erap's words and deeds felt like an insult to my intelligence, as if I were being taken for a fool." (Shelia, 35, female, lawyer, April 14, 2008). Such comments suggest that members of the civic sphere were angered that someone such as Estrada, supposedly their intellectual and moral inferior, should leap to the apex of Philippine politics and behave as if he were their superior. Through Erap jokes, the middle class expressed its resentment and sought to restore the proper intellectual and moral order.

People Power 2 was extolled in the civic sphere as a victory for democracy in which moral citizens once again brought down a corrupt politician. For example, the *Inquirer* ran an editorial entitled, "Triumph of the People", which read, "The people acted to save a democracy that was subverted by an unworthy and corrupt leadership in an upheaval ignited by a spontaneous explosion of rage.... EDSA 2 was a triumph of civil society."[66] Academics also positively evaluated People Power 2 as "a massive exercise in direct democracy after the institution of impeachment had failed" (Abueva 2001: 83) and "a demonstration of democracy in action" (Hernandez 2001: 65).[67]

Fear and Loathing of the "Masses"

In the civic sphere, the solemn passing of judgment on Estrada's crimes was viewed as the perfect opportunity both to show that no one was above the law and to demonstrate the systemic maturity of Philippine democracy.[68] However, the result was that Estrada's prosecution triggered People Power 3, vividly revealing the "masses" as a threat to the middle class of the civic sphere. One columnist described the shock of this realization as follows: "Isn't it amazing that in this day and age there still exist undiscovered islands in our archipelago? . . . In early May, we discovered one such island: a colony of smelly, boisterous, and angry people. They are the poor among us" (Coronel 2001, May 19). Another columnist, Doronila (2001, April 30), expressed a sense of extreme crisis: "We are a nation sitting on the edge of civil war." Fears subsequently spread that Philippine politics was sinking into a bottomless pit of mayhem.

As the target of moral outrage in the civic sphere expanded from Estrada to the poor, civic exclusivist sentiment intensified. The poor, with their blind devotion to Estrada and their determination to return him to the presidency, were seen as no longer true "citizens." The English-language newspapers reported that EDSA had become a lawless outpost of rowdy, undisciplined mobs and vandalism by thugs and hooligans. Jokes portraying the demonstrators as a "shirtless, toothless,[69] bathless (*hindi naliligo*), mindless mob" who were *dugyot* (filthy), *mabaho* (smelly), *tarantado* (stupid), *mangmang* (ignorant) *kriminal* (criminals) circulated via texting. One such message read, "The world is looking at the Philippines again. The rally at EDSA will go into the Guinness Book of World Records as the largest ever gathering of fools, idiots, and imbeciles."[70] Another parodying text written by demonstrators said, "Calling all the filthy and the ignorant, the toothless and the unclothed, let's prove we have no brain—go to EDSA, please pass."[71] Another message implied that the poor were latent criminals, stating, "As a result of the current rally at the EDSA Shrine, Metro Manila has experienced a zero crime rate."[72]

Meanwhile, a senior police official in the Arroyo administration claimed that the demonstrators were being given weapons, alcohol and methamphetamines (*shabu*), and that most of those who had been arrested tested positive for methamphetamine use: "They were mobilized with money, given drugs, and were really high. This may sound like a joke, but they kept dancing even after they'd been shot."[73]

The "disorderly," "vulgar," and "violent" behavior of People Power 3 was in direct contrast to the orderly, disciplined, and peaceful behavior of the moral citizens of People Power 2. One columnist asserted that whereas People Power 1 and 2 "involved moral issues in ousting corrupt and immoral leaders," People Power 3 did not (Olivares-Cunanan 2001, May 1). Another columnist argued that unlike the poor, the middle class had "justifiable cause" to depose a president when necessary (Romano III 2001, May 2). The *Philippine Daily Inquirer* published a letter from a reader who wrote that a "noble reason" was a prerequisite for "People Power" and, referring to the pro-Estrada demonstrations, "Please don't call 'it' People Power 3."[74] A businessman I interviewed personally also cited a notable absence of morality in People Power 3:

> The crowd was rude. EDSA III was just like there were groups of gangs. [It was] not violent, but like mealtime in EDSA II and everyone was sharing food. [But] in EDSA III *agawan sa pagkain* [they were grabbing for food], like they were fighting (Joey, 37, male, employed at a foreign corporation; February 15, 2009)

Those in the civic sphere perceived the estimated 300,000 participants in People Power 3 as nothing more than an ignorant, easily manipulated mob that had been mobilized with handouts of money and food from opposition politicians. They referred to the demonstrators as *hakot crowd* (load-in crowd), *bayaran* (paid for), and "rent-a-crowd." Among the jokes that made the rounds via texting were the following:

> They are paying different rates to people who go to EDSA: P300 for those who go there daily, P500 for those who come from the provinces, P700 for those who bring lead pipes and P300 for the toothless and ugly.[75]

> EDSA 1: free the nation from a dictator. EDSA 2: free the nation from a thief. EDSA 3: free lunch, dinner, breakfast and snacks too . . . let's go![76]

In fact, the objective of the opposition politicians who supported People Power 3 was neither to return Estrada to the presidency nor to solve the poverty problem, but rather to seize power for themselves, whether through elections or a *coup d'état*. Hence Doronila's lament: "The *masa* (masses) were again exploited by the counter-elite, including former President Estrada, for causes which didn't help the poor at all, but instead that promoted the political objectives of the counter-elites themselves." (Doronila 2001, May 2). Similar views were expressed by my interviewees:

> The *masa* was easily swayed. Most of the *masa* were very poor, and to brainwash them into supporting a lost cause was very easy. You tell them what to do and they do it without knowing that they are being manipulated. (Alberto, 70, male, electrician, February 21, 2009)

> I felt it was stupid. I didn't see why they had to do it, why they supported Erap to begin with. To me it was barbaric. A typical *masa* movement. The method they used was violent, so it would never get support. I think they were blindly supporting Erap and there were reports that they were getting paid. *Kasi mahihirap tong mga to kaya tingin ko totoo yun* [They're poor, so I suppose it's true]. (Ellen, 42, female, employee of Asian Development Bank, March 11, 2009)

The Catholic Church also bestowed legitimacy upon this civic sphere discourse. Cardinal Sin complained that "impolite and discourteous guests on Catholic property" had "profaned" the EDSA Shrine, and recited the following prayer at mass: "Father, forgive them, for they know not what they do."[77]

Although few in number, some people in the civic sphere questioned this contemptuous attitude toward the poor. For example, the columnist Conrado de Quiros (2001, April 30) wrote: "[T]o dismiss the throng as nothing more than riffraff that should be disposed of like garbage, that is not to be anti-Erap, to be anti-people. . . . [T]he people who converge at EDSA today are *not* the enemy; they are the people, the same people we fought EDSA for, the same people we want to jail Erap for, the same people we want to build a future for."[78] Some of those among my middle-class interviewees also reflected on their prejudices toward the poor:

> When People Power 3 began, I was overwhelmed by a desire to see them all killed. They embodied the worst of the Philippines. They were misguided by politicians. But I also felt a sense of guilt, and I couldn't reconcile these two emotions. I might despise them, but they were also my fellow Filipinos. I was able to get an education, but they could not. I cannot just sit back and criticize. Maybe Erap gave them food and houses. I should try to understand the masses, I thought. (Shelia, 35, female, lawyer, April 14, 2008)

> The elite led the revolt of People Power 2. Were we insensitive to the *masa*? Does Erap's corruption and mismanagement even matter to the *masa*? We ignored the *masa*. We mistakenly thought that if we just get rid of Erap, everything will be fine, and that's it. Everybody participating in People Power 2 smelled nice. No one from the *masa* was there.

The elites said to the *masa*, "You don't know anything, listen to us. We will lead the revolution." Then the *masa* replied, "Look at what you've done." (Luie, 43, male, lawyer, April 16, 2008)

Therefore, in contrast to People Power 2, which was hailed as a triumph of moral "citizens" who peacefully compelled a corrupt politician to resign, those in the civic sphere—with the exception of a few people expressing second thoughts—condemned People Power 3 as a riot by "masses" who lacked moral legitimacy. The poor appeared to them not as a legitimate adversary with different interests and values competing in the same democratic space, but as an ominous, incomprehensible threat that needed to be eliminated. Members of the civic sphere feared the poor and criticized them as "dumb" *masa*, but, in fact, the latter had their own clearly defined logic and values. Let us now turn our attention to the mass sphere.

Self-Righteousness of the Rich and Defeat of the Poor

Estrada and the Wounded Dignity of the Poor

When Estrada visited impoverished neighborhoods, he cultivated an image of kindness toward the poor, showing his respect by touching the foreheads of the elderly with the back of his hand, eating with his fingers along with local residents, passing out gifts of food and other goods—and in this manner, he won their support. Yet Estrada's anti-poverty policy consisted of nothing more than dispersing largesse to a limited number of households; it cannot be said that he accomplished any systematic, substantive redistribution of wealth.[79] Evidence indicating a dramatic improvement in the lives of the poor during his administration is lacking. Moreover, even in the mass sphere, a gradual increase was seen in the number of individuals who suspected that Estrada was corrupt. Despite all of this, why was there such deep-seated support for Estrada in the mass sphere?

One explanation, as seen in the populist theory discussed earlier, was that the poor confused cinema with political reality and persisted in the illusion that Estrada was truly "a friend to the poor" like the characters he had played in the movies. However, this argument does not lend itself to analysis of how the poor's support for Estrada came to challenge the dominant value system and social order. Another explanation, which is cited in studies of squatter movements, holds that the poor did not blindly support Estrada, but rather supported People Power 3 because they had been promised a transfer of public land by the Estrada administration (Magno C. 2003; Karaos 2006; Kiba 2010, 2012). However, while this analysis applies to the peoples' organizations that negotiated land acquisitions, it fails to explain why so many of the poor continued to support Estrada despite receiving no concrete benefits.[80]

Here I would like to analyze the mass-sphere discourse with a focus on the opportunity to regain dignity experienced by the poor. According to David (2001, July 29), the election of Estrada as president in a country long ruled by the elite was of symbolic significance to the poor in that it represented the restoration of their wounded self-esteem. Then, when Estrada was ousted, the poor perceived the many humiliations visited upon him by the elite as being identical to the treatment to which they had been subjected. They also viewed the ouster of Estrada, someone from a non-elite background, as indicative of the limits imposed on their own social advancement and symbolic of their social exclusion.

According to del Rosario (2004), the poor's understanding of the series of events encompassing Estrada's ouster, his arrest, and People Power 3 was based on the *Pasyon* narrative of Christ's sufferings recited during Holy Week, and the "hidden transcript" (Scott 1990) of Christ's persecution, execution, and retribution as reenacted in Philippine films and TV dramas. In this "hidden transcript," a hero (*bida*) bearing the Christ-like virtues of "patience, goodness of heart, a love for the unfortunate, tenderness, [and] the ability to sacrifice especially for one's family" long endures cruel trials and suffering at the hands of a "rich, unscrupulous, scheming, and exploitative" villain (*kontrabida*) but, in the end, achieves "glorious redemption."

As del Rosario argues, the poor viewed the ridicule, derision, insults, indignities, persecution and punishment heaped upon Estrada by the "rich" as equivalent to the trials of Christ and, above all, to their own personal experience. Governor Singson's accusations were equated with Judas's betrayal of Christ to the Pharisees. The arrest and parading of Estrada by several thousand police resembled the arrest of Christ as depicted in the *Pasyon*. And, just as Christ was unjustly treated after his arrest, Estrada was subjected to extreme indignities—his mug shot was taken, he was fingerprinted, and then incarcerated in a small cell while TV newscasters spoke of the possibility of execution. Shots of Estrada behind bars were broadcast nationwide, rousing intense feelings of injustice among the poor supported by a sense of shared humiliation.[81] This, Rosario says, is what triggered the explosion of long pent-up discontent that produced People Power 3.

Del Rosario's analysis is persuasive in its application to contemporary politics of Ileto's framework, which references the worldview of the *Pasyon* to explain the anticolonial struggle by the lower classes (Ileto 1979). However, we must retain reservations about this dualistic portrayal of the civic sphere as the domain of a secularized modern discourse and the mass sphere as the domain of a religious discourse. In reality, religious and secular discourses have come to coexist in both the civic and mass spheres. In the civic sphere, too, religious discourse guided political behavior in People Power 1.[82] Also, as we shall see below, the poor people that I interviewed spoke of the events surrounding Estrada not in religious but in secular terms.

Empathy with an Estrada Persecuted by the "Rich"

Let us next examine the politics of self-esteem and approval in the mass sphere as articulated by the poor. There is no question that the poor regarded People Power 2 as an attack on both Estrada and themselves. As one street vendor told me, the poor felt an acute alienation from People Power 2 as "different from us."

> We saw them on TV. When Erap was kicked out, there were only rich people on the streets. Do you think there'd be any poor people? It was just the rich. They all came by car and had nice shiny skin. (Beng, 42, female, food vendor, February 7, 2009)

To the poor, the arrest and incarceration of Estrada by several thousand police when he had already lost the presidency was insulting, gratuitous and uncalled for. Consequently, they voiced outrage: "I'm an Erap supporter. What they did stinks. He's the only president they've ever thrown in jail, right? They beat Erap really bad. All the things he helped with seem to be gone too. It pisses me off!" (Boboy, 37, male, unemployed, 1 April 2008). Meanwhile, Cardinal Sin and other prominent church leaders continued to hurl vitriol regarding Estrada's character, prompting fierce reactions such as: "Those priests have no heart. Poor Erap, to be insulted like that on top of getting thrown in jail" (Lidenia, 36, female, street vendor, January 21, 2003). Such remarks demonstrate that even a self-styled moral leader like Cardinal Sin could not gain hegemony in the mass sphere.

As the poor watched their champion Estrada forced to endure scorn, ouster from the presidency, and imprisonment, they experienced feelings of pain (*sakit*), empathy (*damay*), pity (*awa*) and helplessness (*walang magawa*). "Poor Erap. I felt so sorry for him when he was kicked out of Malacañang. My heart ached. They betrayed him." (Baby, 49, female, housemaid, February 7, 2009) "Only the rich supported Gloria. Estrada's supporters were poor, so they had no choice but to give up and withdraw." (Lito, 48, male, janitor, January 20, 2003). These shared feelings of humiliation and powerlessness fostered an even stronger sense of community and empathy with Estrada among the poor.

Moreover, Estrada's quiet departure with his family by boat from the rear of Malacañang Palace was viewed as his effort to protect the poor by avoiding a violent confrontation:

> The other side resorted to force. Erap shouldn't have had to leave, but he quit on his own because he didn't want there to be any trouble. He wanted to keep people from getting hurt. Those people who did People Power 2 have no values. They don't even know what 'freedom' is. (Henry, 22, male, unemployed, 2 April 2008)

> He left of his own accord. We felt terrible, our hearts ached, because we didn't want Erap to go. But he decided to so people wouldn't get hurt. We couldn't do anything, we were just in pain. There was nothing we could do but accept the situation and try to understand it. We felt sorry for the president. (Cion, 58, female, street vendor, February 16, 2009)

However, the poor did not simply appeal to emotion in their criticisms of People Power 2, they also spoke of institutions and the importance of reason. They pointed out the impropriety of ignoring constitutional institutions in ousting a duly elected leader. "It's wrong to steal someone's job. Arroyo was not really elected by the people." (Gloria, 42, female, street vendor, January 20, 2003). "First, they should have finished the impeachment trial and proven whether Erap was guilty. They shouldn't have suddenly forced him out by demonstrating" (Marilyn, 35, female, street vendor, January 23, 2003). The poor also criticized supporters of People Power 2 for being swayed by the general mood and the words of leaders without due deliberation or any strong convictions. "They made a mistake. They acted on their feelings without giving it careful thought." (Lina, 40, female, general store proprietor, April 2, 2008). "The elite just used them to get rid of the president. If a leader says something, they just blindly follow, whether it's good or bad." (Ate, 55, female, general-store proprietor, April 4, 2008).

Even in the mass sphere, suspicions about Estrada's corruption were not rejected across the board; however, they gradually gained credence. Nonetheless, many people continued to support him even while acknowledging his guilt, citing such reasons as the fact that life had been easier under Estrada than under Arroyo, and that he had helped the poor:

> Erap's only crime was *jueteng*, right?[83] Life was good under Erap, so People Power 2 upset us. I guess he stole a lot of money, but I heard he has funds [to help the poor]. I support Erap. I don't understand why they kicked him out or why they put him on trial. Maybe he really is guilty. But why did Gloria become president? I still support Erap. (May Anne, 35, female, housewife, March 12, 2009)

> His trial was just about gambling, wasn't it? He didn't steal anyone's money. There was no need to impeach him. It didn't cause any problems while he was president. Gambling was just like a sideline. Life was easier under Erap. (Lina, 40, female, general-store proprietor, April 2, 2008)

The question of Estrada's guilt per se was therefore not really an issue in the mass sphere. Rather, the question raised was why Estrada's corruption was so relentlessly attacked while the major misdeeds of the rich were overlooked, and while no one, from the president down to the lowest-echelon politician or bureaucrat, was completely free of corruption. A plausible explanation, that Estrada had been deposed because his policies favored the poor without regard for the interests of the rich, enjoyed widespread acceptance: "They kicked Erap out of the presidency because he supported the masses" (May Anne, 35, female, housewife, March 12, 2009).

Subsequently, a consensus arose in the mass sphere that life had become more difficult under the Arroyo administration; this generated and reinforced memories of "the good old days" under Estrada. Complaints such as the following could be heard daily: "Gloria says our lives are better, but it doesn't feel that way at all. We were better off under Erap. Look at the price of rice nowadays—it's gone way up" (Emma, 49, female, housewife, March 12, 2009). "Under Erap we could buy a kilo of *galunggong* [a species of scad] at the market for 10 pesos, but now, even a half kilo costs 40 or 50 pesos." (Rosalinda, 48, female, manicurist, March 10, 2009).

A Defeated Uprising and Feelings of Powerlessness

Let us now turn to the discourse in the mass sphere about People Power 3, first taking a look at the narratives of those who participated. Immediately after the upheaval, a pro-Estrada NGO held political meetings in various poor neighborhoods throughout Metro Manila and its surroundings in which the personal experiences of participants were recorded (Global Call to Action Against Poverty Philippines 2001). All of the witnesses were members of peoples' organizations in squatter settlements to whom Estrada had promised land transfers, and who had lost that opportunity with Estrada's resignation. The following quote is rather long, but bears noting:

> I participated in EDSA 3 for a personal reason—because I supported former president Erap. I went with [my friend] Pilar to Polk Street in front of Erap's house [in the town of San Juan], set up a cardboard house, and moved in. We brought food, a gas stove, water and other necessities. We didn't expect anyone to bring us food. I'd heard on Channel 2 [ABS-CBN] that demonstrators were fighting over food because they were hungry and tired.
>
> That was the place where I first experienced getting tear-gassed and sprayed by water cannon trucks. I was afraid the other people occupying the area would evacuate. But the media lied when it said that Erap supporters were gone from the streets. The media was in cahoots with Arroyo. When Erap was arrested, they attacked us with tear gas and water cannons again. The water from the cannon trucks hit with so much force that an old woman next to us who said she'd come from Antipolo was knocked into a drainage ditch. She had come only because she felt sorry for Erap. The army, police, and government were shameless like that. That poor old woman died. A lot of people died just on Polk Street. But that wasn't reported by the news. They made everyone keep quiet.
>
> When they arrested Erap, we headed for the EDSA Shrine, set up a hut under the MRT [overhead tracks], and moved into that. More and more people arrived. But people coming from out of town were blocked by the government. I just wanted to change the system. That's why I was there, because they were not enforcing the law fairly. They called us terrible names, like 'maggot' (*uod*) and 'stinking' (*mababaho*). Only Channels 5 and 25 [owned by *Iglesia ni Cristo*] reported the truth, but then they were shut down. You can't imagine how hungry and tired people were after Polk Street, EDSA, and Mendiola Bridge. . . .

Politicians dropped by EDSA 3 because elections were coming up. But we poor people knew exactly why we were there. It was to change the system under which they taxed us and made us suffer at the hands of the police and the army. Our dream of having our own homes had disappeared. When we poor folks felt so angry we couldn't stand it, we banded together and stormed Malacañang Palace. Lots of people were killed by sniper fire from the roof of Malacañang Palace or in the streets. (Ibid.: 5; Juanie, North Triangle, Quezon City [English Translation])

People like this committed themselves to People Power 3 of their own free will with the goal of changing an unjust society and the dream of owning their own land and housing. In contrast with the narratives of happiness and a festival-like atmosphere reported by participants in People Power 1 and 2, most of the narratives from People Power 3 involve hunger, fatigue, callous violence by the government, biased coverage by the media and contemptuous looks from the "rich." From the civic sphere came criticism that People Power 3 had no causes or beliefs. However, considering that this was the only People Power in which participants suffered significant casualties, it is fair to say that People Power 3 was the uprising that manifested the most heroic resolve.

Photo 12 Blood oozes onto the ground from the back of a demonstrator pinned down by police (in front of Malacañang Palace, May 2001; Leo A. Esclanda/BAGWIS).

Accusations of drunkenness and drug use by participants in People Power 3 also circulated in the civic sphere. There is a response to this claim that is of great interest, so I quote it here:

> Most of those who headed for Malacañang were drunks or speed users, that's for sure. But what kind of system is it where Filipinos would take speed and drink booze to go there? I admit, I was one of those drunk and high people. We were looking for the justice and rights that had been denied us as Filipinos. I was using speed at the time. Because I wanted something those bastards had denied us for years. That's why the struggle continued until we could achieve that. I used speed. Because I wanted to reclaim the dignity the bastards had stolen from us poor Filipinos. I was drunk. Because they wouldn't give us equality. They have to treat the Filipinos living in this country as equals. I got drunk for the sake of the rights and justice that were stolen and trampled by the elite of this country and its brutal government.
>
> Now is the time to rethink what is most important for Filipinos. To live for ourselves, or for our country? Or for the future of our children? That's the ideal we are trying to achieve. That's what we were trying to get by getting drunk or using speed. Now is the time for us to stick together and keep fighting for our hopes and rights. For our right to have land and a house. For the right to send our kids to school and give them a good education. That's what we have to keep fighting for. (Ibid.: 21–2; Nolly, Balara, Quezon City [English Translation])

It is easy to dismiss People Power 3 as nothing more than a riot by drunks and drug users. Consider, however, that it would have been no easy thing to storm Malacañang Palace, guarded by soldiers and police, with nothing but rubber sandals, sticks, and stones, in a normal state of mind. Just as soldiers in many countries used amphetamines during World War II, one can well understand why people used alcohol and amphetamines to help muster the courage to do battle with a powerful enemy for a cause they believed in. To these people there was no contradiction whatsoever between drinking alcohol or taking speed and trying to get land and housing or a good education for their children.

Next, let us hear the narratives of members of the impoverished class who did not participate in People Power 3. In Pechayan, Estrada had never promised to give residents land, nor were there any pro-Estrada peoples' organizations; consequently there was no organized participation in People Power 3.[84] Nonetheless, the dominant discourse was one of support for People Power 3.

> If Erap could actually come back, that would be better. The ones who kicked him out never proved for certain that he committed any crimes. Erap was only in office for a short time, during which he was viciously criticized. I wish they would give him a chance. He did good things for us, so I wish he could come back. (Jonathan, 28, male, construction worker; April 4, 2008)

Yet, even while most people endorsed the idea of ousting Arroyo and returning Estrada, then under house arrest, to the presidency, the tragic outcome of People Power 3 made them painfully aware of how difficult it was for the poor to challenge the powerful and the state. "Nothing will change. Even if the poor put up a fight against the rich, they can't win" (Maria, 28, female, street vendor. January 21, 2003). This feeling of powerlessness originates in the perception that it is impossible to prevail against the violence of an army controlled by money.

> It wouldn't be easy to get rid of Arroyo because she has the army's backing. From what I can see, people are so full of anger, she has to pay off the military and keep them well fed so they don't desert her. (Susan, 47, female, street vendor; March 31, 2008)

> No matter how much we demonstrate, it's useless. Arroyo controls the army. She just buys people off. Forget it. The little people can demonstrate all they want, but unless the army's top brass switch sides, nothing's going to happen. (Taba, 40, female, general-store proprietor, April 9, 2008)

People also described how the government had engaged in flagrant violence against the demonstrators: "Many people were injured or lost their lives in People Power 3. Some were shot by snipers. To hang onto power, they'll even resort to violence." (Joji, 32, male, street vendor, April 4, 2008). The fact that demonstrators were shot—by snipers, not by stray bullets—was viewed by the poor as proof of the brutal nature of the "rich", who thought nothing of murdering the poor who opposed them.

To be sure, even in the mass sphere, there were those who criticized People Power 3 because they feared social breakdown or an adverse impact on their lives. They expressed such views as: "There would only be mayhem [if we tried to restore Erap to the presidency]. And if there's mayhem, prices of goods and gasoline will go up and people will suffer even more" (Samson, 52, male, housepainter, March 10, 2009).

Yet we should note that the same sense of powerlessness against the government and the "rich" is heard behind such comments. In the mass sphere, People Power 3 was perceived as a struggle for a great cause on which the poor staked their lives, but were tragically smashed by the blatant violence of the Arroyo government.

People Power 2 and 3 differed from People Power 1 in that no contact zone bridging the divisions in the dual public sphere was formed. This is because the middle class of the civic sphere did not treat the impoverished class from the mass sphere that supported populism as legitimate "adversaries" sharing the same democratic space, but rather regarded them as "enemies" to be eliminated. To oust a formally elected president necessitated appeals to a morality that superseded even the democratic legitimacy of election. This exacerbated the polarized moralization of politics and caused a breakdown in the democratic system's function of mediating conflicts among multiple values and interests in civil society.

CHAPTER 4

Moral Antagonism in Elections

Photo 13 A voter education poster reading "Accept money, [but] vote your conscience" (Pantranco, Quezon City, May 2004).

A majority of the Philippine electorate is made up of the poor, and thus politicians seek their votes without exception. Most studies of Philippine elections posit that the elite have traditionally employed clientelism and "political machines" to secure the votes of the poor, thereby monopolizing public office and obstructing initiatives by the poor to act on behalf of their own interests.[1] Rather than promote equality, they argue, Philippine electoral politics has actually reinforced elite rule.[2] It is also claimed that, in national elections since the late 1990s, populists emerging from the entertainment industry have manipulated the poor via the media.[3] These arguments assume that Filipino voters are mostly controlled or manipulated by competing elites.

However, morality-based appeals for political reform and the rejection of corrupt political practices have also played an important role in Philippine elections (Thompson 1995: 29–32). Moreover, despite a deep mistrust of the electoral process itself, voters have continued to enthusiastically go to the polls and invest hope in new leaders. Although Philippine elections are fraught with misrepresentation and coercion, they also provide voters with the opportunity to project their hopes for change and a better life, and this has contributed to the unexpected emergence of democratic forces (Kerkvliet 1996; Franco 2000). Therefore, when discussing elite rule, the ways in which ordinary voters perceive elections, and the roles they play in them, cannot be ignored.

The gap between the civic and mass spheres in how elections are perceived remains sizable. On the one hand, the civic-sphere middle class decries contemporary elections as morally corrupt, and seeks clean, fair and modern elections based on governance and policy issues. On the other hand, the mass-sphere poor support candidates who exhibit a spontaneous "kindness" toward the poor and needy, and criticize elections dominated by self-serving, insincere rich candidates. In this chapter, I intend to show how the hegemonic struggle between these two disparate moralities has fostered a moral antagonism in elections that undermines faith in the electoral system itself.

Getting Votes with Populism and Money

The Rise of Populism in National Elections

"National elections" as described here are elections held in districts nationwide for the president, the vice president and senators. Elections for representatives to the Lower House in single-seat electoral districts are not included. Due to factors such as increased social fluidity brought about by urbanization and the growing numbers of overseas contract workers, the decentralization of government, the dismantling of the two-party system and the spread of media, electoral machines in the national elections that followed democratization were less effective.[4] A political machine is a vertical chain of clientelist relations extending downward from a major presidential candidate through senators, representatives, provincial governors and mayors to individual voters, with an organized network that distributes benefits and gathers votes at each level. Before Marcos's declaration of martial law, there were two clearly defined electoral machines headed by the presidential candidates of the two dominant parties, the Nationalist Party and the Liberal Party. However, with the dismantling of the two-party system, the vote-getting networks linking the central and local elites became more fluid in post-democratization national elections.

One phenomenon that clearly demonstrates the decline of the electoral machines in national elections is the rise, at the expense of the traditional elite, of a counter-elite with inferior organizational and funding power. Members of the counter-elite are typically movie actors, newscasters, professional athletes who exploit the high visibility they enjoy in the media.[5] Faced with this competition, the traditional elite are forced to spend more money buying time for TV and radio campaign ads.[6] By appealing to the poor, presidential candidates in particular can boost their ranking in pre-election popularity polls and thereby increase not only donations from the business community that seeks influence over next president but also their organizational power. This is because many politicians will switch party affiliations to "join the bandwagon" of a front-running presidential candidate.

In elections in which the media plays a major role, candidates must present an idealized image while distinguishing themselves from the other candidates (Teehankee 2010). In this regard, cultivating an image of standing up to a specific social group identified as an "enemy" that threatens "us" is a particularly effective strategy. Therefore, for success in national elections, the creation of a "we/they" antagonism has become more crucial now than ever before.

As mentioned in the previous chapter, moral nationalism retained hegemony for some time after the democratization of 1986. In the senatorial election of 1987, the pro-Aquino ruling party coalition Lakas ng Bayan (People's Power), asserting that the "people" must renew their solidarity to prevent Marcos from returning to the Philippines, captured 22 of 24 seats in an overwhelming victory. The subsequent presidential election of 1992 was won by Fidel Ramos, who enjoyed nationwide name recognition as a leader of the democratization movement. Because he was not nominated as the unity candidate of the ruling party Laban ng Demokratikong Pilipino (Struggle of Democratic Filipinos) or LDP (also known as Laban), Ramos hastily formed a small party, Partido Lakas ng Tao (People Power Party), and ran as its candidate. As indicated by his campaign slogans "EDSA 1992" and "Empowerment of the People," Ramos highlighted his People Power background and thus sought to perpetuate the hegemony of moral nationalism.[7]

However, the presidential election of 1998 signified the decline of moral nationalism and the rise of populism. Although the party Puwersa ng Masang Pilipino (Force of the Filipino Masses), or PMP, was founded by Estrada, who stood as its candidate, it lacked organizing power.[8] Still, by wielding the populist discourse of *Erap para sa masa* (Erap for the masses), Estrada was able to gain the support of the poor and win in a landslide. This was an epochal development, because until then, the vote of the poor had been split under the clientelist politics of competing elite factions.[9]

In January 2001, the middle class's People Power 2 drove Estrada from office, and Arroyo was installed as president. However, two weeks before the midterm elections slated for May that same year, poor people seeking the reinstatement of Estrada besieged the Arroyo administration with People Power 3. An anxious Arroyo sought to allay the rage and discontent of the poor through such measures as distributing food to impoverished neighborhoods in Manila.[10] Despite these efforts, the poor continued to support Estrada. Of the 13 seats up for election in the Senate at the time, the pro-Arroyo People Power Coalition (PPC) took eight, but the pro-Estrada opposition coalition Puwersa ng Masa (Force of the Masses) won the remaining five. Among the winners of these seats were Estrada's wife Luisa and other politicians who had incited People Power 3.

Populism's deep-rooted support in the mass sphere was conspicuous once more in the presidential election of 2004. Action-film star Fernando Poe, Jr. launched the opposition alliance Koalisyon ng Nagkakaisang Pilipino (Coalition of United Filipinos), or KNP, and ran as its candidate in a close contest with Arroyo.[11] A popular actor known by the initials FPJ, Poe announced his candidacy in late November 2003 at the urging of his good friend Estrada, then under house arrest, and was instantly catapulted to the top of the polls. Declaring poverty his top-priority, Poe made his appeal to the mass sphere with a pledge to "provide food on the table for every Filipino." However, the country's neoliberal economic policy was taken for granted, and did not figure as a campaign issue. He sought to turn his unique resume as a high school dropout with no previous political experience into an asset, declaring that "unlike the elite, I am unaccustomed to politics and therefore unaccustomed to corruption."

However, Poe's campaign was poorly thought out.[12] He consistently refused to articulate any concrete policy or vision. His campaign speeches lasted about ten minutes, he failed to participate in television debates, and he otherwise made himself scarce in the media.[13] His support peaked at 25 per cent against Arroyo's 17 per cent in December 2003, but then steadily fell. As a result, he was unable to gain the cooperation of local elites, who wanted to back a winner, and thus could not expand his organizational base.[14]

Meanwhile, Arroyo ran as the incumbent candidate of the ruling alliance Koalisyon ng Katapatan at Karanasan sa Kinabukasan (Coalition of Truth and Experience for Tomorrow), or K4.[15] She stressed her experience and skills to secure middle-class support in the civic sphere while simultaneously currying favor with the mass sphere through pork-barrel spending and the promotion of an image of "care" for the poor.[16] To pay for the favors she dispensed, she exercised her incumbent's advantage by diverting government funds to her campaign and turning the entire administrative apparatus into one massive political machine. Furthermore, she did not reject any opportunities to boost her popularity via the media. In the hopes of increasing her own credibility with the poor, she asked a popular newscaster to be her vice-presidential running mate.[17] She also cultivated a more down-home image of herself by publicizing such nicknames as *Ate Glo* (Sister Glo), *Gloria labandera* (Gloria the Laundress), and *Ina ng bayan* (Mother of the Nation).[18]

Photo 14 A street sweeper hired by an Arroyo project said this: "My work is for Arroyo, my vote is for Poe." (Quezon City, April 2004).

In the end, Arroyo eked out a win by a narrow 3.5 per cent margin of victory.[19] A possible factor in this victory was the middle class vote, which was geared toward wanting "anybody but Poe" to win. However, an even more significant factor was Arroyo's massive pork-barrel largesse, which ate into Poe's populist appeal in the Visayas and Mindanao regions, garnering more than half of the poor's votes nationwide.[20] Poe's populism notwithstanding, the poor did not vote en bloc to the extent that they did in the 1998 election.[21] However, evidence of election rigging by Arroyo eventually surfaced, making it entirely possible that Poe was the actual winner.[22]

National elections during this period therefore saw the waning of clientelism and machine politics as a determining factor and the emergence of direct appeals to voters via the media in its stead. It was in the context of this new struggle for hegemony that populism came to the fore.

"Vote Buying" in Local Elections

Despite this change, in local elections, machine politics to gather the votes of the poor by dispensing favors is still crucial to success, although the role of image is undeniable.[23] Still, this does not mean that clientelism's stronghold has been maintained. Especially in local elections in Metro Manila, at least, the social changes of recent years have created conditions in which candidates can no longer control voting behavior as they wish, and the poor are able to vote more freely. Under these circumstances, how do candidates seek the support of the poor?

Schaffer (2007: 6) classifies the distributional strategies employed by candidates to gain voter support into "allocation policies," "pork-barrel spending," "patronage" and "vote buying," analyzing these in terms of the scope, timing and legality of distribution (see Table 18). First, let us look at "vote buying," in which candidates attempt to secure votes by making cash payouts just before an election. In local elections in the Philippines, these payouts are made, not by the candidate, but by vote gatherers known as *lider* or "leaders." Barangay captains and councilors may also serve as vote gatherers for higher-ranking candidates. On election day, poll watchers dispatched to polling places by the candidates employ a number of methods to check whether voters who accepted money vote as directed.[24] According to my informants, this practice is more thoroughly applied in the rural sector, where residents have virtually no anonymity and their voting behavior is easily monitored. In rural areas, vote gatherers may go from house to house dispersing cash in the wee hours before election day; some are said to buy votes by pointing a gun with bills inserted in the muzzle.

Table 18 Comparing Distributional Strategies of Electoral Mobilization

Distributive Strategy of Electoral Mobilization	Scope (How widely are material benefits distributed?)	Timing (When are material benefits distributed?)	Legality (Is the distribution of material benefits legal?)
Allocation policies	Whole classes of voters (elderly, unemployed, etc.)	Hard to time exactly; can occur at any time during electoral cycle	Legal
Pork-barrel spending	Local districts	Hard to time exactly; can occur at any time during electoral cycle	Legal
Patronage	Neighborhoods, villages, families, individuals	Ongoing throughout the electoral cycle	Gray legal status
Vote buying		Days or hours before election day, or on election day itself	Illegal

Source: Schaffer (2007: 6).

In the poor neighborhoods of Metro Manila, however, my informants maintain that while distribution of money from candidates is common, vote buying strictly controlled by threats of violence is less common and large resident populations enjoy relative anonymity in casting their votes. In this urban sector, there are more candidates in competition, and the *lider* adopt such tactics as inviting voters to their homes to hand over cash on the sly. Word quickly spreads that money is being doled out at so-and-so's house, and local residents descend on the place in droves. At candidate rallies, pamphlets are sometimes passed out with bills hidden inside. As many of my informants pointed out, however, it is impossible for candidates to maintain effective control over people's voting behavior, even if they have received money from them, so people can vote relatively freely in Manila's informal settlements, unlike in their home province.

Next, let us examine "patronage" and "pork-barrel spending," which candidates practice openly. Both constitute the selling of favors to the poor by providing resources of various types other than cash and asking for votes in return. According to Schaffer, "patronage" occurs just before an election and involves resources distributed to specific households or villages, while "pork-barrel spending" refers to more broad-ranging resource distribution that occurs on an ongoing basis. Naturally, the more ample a candidate's resources, the more pork-barrel spending there is to distribute across many districts.

The resources distributed via pork-barrel spending consist largely of public works such as roads, bridges, and waterworks. Patronage, on the other hand, takes such forms as free medical check-ups and medicine, free weddings, free food for children, free haircuts, student scholarships, and prizes for dance contests and bingo games. All sorts of people from squatter settlements line up at the city-hall offices of local politicians with requests: barangay officials petitioning for street paving and lighting, youth groups asking for donations toward the cost of basketball team uniforms, individual residents seeking help in covering medical or funeral expenses, and so on. Candidates for their part attend and make monetary offerings at voters' funerals,[25] and establish ritual kinships (*compadrazgo*) as godfather (*ninong*) or godmother (*ninang*) to voters' children at Catholic baptisms and weddings.

Photo 15 Resident asking for money from a mayoral candidate campaigning in a slum (Pasay City, February 2010).

When election season arrives, candidates' staff members prepare a campaign schedule in advance by marking up maps. Then, during election campaigns, candidates and their staff walk through squatter settlements on a near-daily basis over a period of months. In the squats, candidates and staff shake hands with residents and hand out cards with the candidate's name, picture and contact information. It is not unusual for them to also hand out a few hundred pesos in cash to residents who ask for money for drinks or for a child's medical treatment. Distribution of resources to the poor is crucial to winning a local election. In the words of a candidate who ran in a local election in Metro Manila in 2010:

> In the Philippines, it's how you help the people. That's the politics here. Not because you are bright, not because you are intelligent, as long as you help the people you'll do well. It's good if you are bright, but people do not look at that. You have to be *pang-masa* (pro-masses). If you are, you'll win. You have to go to birthday parties and hand out presents, attend funerals and give *damay* (condolence money), and always make an impression on the masses. (Candidate C for the Pasay City Council, 72, male, lawyer, February 11, 2010)[26]

> If you're a politician, people expect you to change their lives. They want to provide their children with an education, so you have to send them to school. They want to get work, so you have to give them work. Even if you have nothing to give, they come asking politicians to give them what they need for their daily life. It's very hard to change their minds from thinking that candidates help voters during election campaigns. If you refuse, they don't vote for you. (Candidate P for the Malabon City Council, 48, male, egg wholesaler, February 19, 2010)[27]

Local politicians insist that what they provide to the poor are no more than "services" (*serbisyo*) for residents, not favors for votes. When I explicitly asked a city council candidate whether dispensing favors to the poor was in fact an indirect form of vote buying, he scowled and replied:

> It's true that those accusations always come up. But I have always given aid to the poor, even at times other than elections, so it's not vote buying. I have also run free medical missions and free dental missions in poor districts since way back. These are services for the residents. (Candidate C for the Pasay City Council, 72, male, lawyer, February 11, 2010)

Granted, most local politicians are not happy with this mode of politics. First, they are burdened by the need for considerable funds to respond to the demands of the poor. During the era of the two-party system, party leaders provided campaign funds. With the post-democratization collapse of that system, however, candidates must increasingly procure funds on their own. Also, rather than engage in the direct distribution of resources, politicians find it cheaper to promote, for example, ordinances that encourage investment or policies that improve education; these practices also allow them to exercise their political skills. Yet, frustratingly enough, however excellent the policies they promote and implement may be, they do not translate into votes. Explaining that an ordinance he drafted had fostered the development of commercial districts with private capital, a council candidate had this to say:

> I prepared an ordinance setting up special an economic zone to encourage investment. But voters don't understand that kind of achievement; they vote based on the candidate's looks or popularity. The hardest to handle are the voters who pester you for money during campaigns. They pretend like it's a joke, but they mean it. If you turn them down, you get called a miser. (Candidate C for the Pasay City Council, 72, male, lawyer, February 11, 2010)

As previously discussed, in the electoral politics that prevail in Manila's local elections, candidates cannot fully control the voting behavior of the poor, and in turn, are compelled to provide them with a variety of resources in hopes of winning their votes.

The Votes of Citizens Beleaguered by the Masses

Seeking Honest, Intelligent Candidates

How do people in the civic sphere view the electoral politics of the Philippines? Here I would like to examine what the middle class envisions as "correct" voting.

First, the middle class considers "education" a crucial qualification for a candidate. Particularly in national elections, they are concerned with whether a candidate has received an adequate education. Describing the criteria by which he chooses a candidate, one of my interviewees said, "First is that they should be educated. What they took up should be related to political science or public administration. About managing people: If they have a master's or doctorate degree, it's a plus. Education is the number one." (Knox, 35, male, advertising agent, March 6, 2009). Another said, "For good government, they must meet educational requirements. An election should not be a popularity contest. How can the most powerful person in the Philippines be ignorant and stupid (*bobo*)? To achieve good government, they should make education a condition for eligibility as a presidential candidate." (Joji, 63, male, former business owner, April 20, 2008).

One reason for this emphasis on education is a concern with the international reputation of the Philippines. As the nation's representative, the president in particular is expected to measure up to other heads of state. As one interviewee put it, "The president must deal with global businesses and global people. He must have at least a modicum of intellectual capacity." (Alberto, 70, male, electrician, February 21, 2009). These people found it humiliating that someone like Estrada or Poe, who did not graduate from university and could not speak fluent English, could represent the Philippines on the global stage.

Among those in the civic sphere, Estrada's victory and Poe's candidacy were indeed catalysts for a renewed perception that education was an indispensable prerequisite for the presidency. However, their experience with the infamous Arroyo administration drove home the importance of such qualifications as "sincerity," "honesty" and "integrity," and a desire to serve the nation and resist corruption. This was because the corruption evinced by Arroyo, who held a doctorate in economics, was even more pernicious than that of Estrada. The period during which I conducted my interviews, between 2008 and 2009, was a time in which successive revelations about the venality and violence of the Arroyo administration were coming out, prompting the rueful realization that a good education by itself was no guarantee of good leadership. This inspired a renewed emphasis on presidential honesty. To quote one corporate executive: "Before, I looked for those with good leadership and management skills. Now, [after the experience with Arroyo] I just want an honest president who will jail corrupt people and tell the military to stop the killings." (Roland, 51, male, distributor, April 20, 2008)[28]

Needless to say, education was not ignored simply because of the increased emphasis on honesty and integrity. Honesty was viewed as a qualification ensuring that a candidate would utilize the intellectual skills acquired through education for the nation rather than for personal benefit. "All the politicians should have integrity and the right intentions. By integrity, you must do what you have sworn to do. By intention, they must be there to serve, not for power or glory. They must also have educational qualifications and the capacity to achieve these missions." (Rose, 53, female, foreign-owned insurance company employee, April 5, 2008). The notion of honesty often has nationalistic connotations, as expressed in such phrases as "service for the common good, not private gain" and "love for country." An employee working for the Asian Development Bank put it this way:

> I want to vote for candidates with integrity and a track record. It's also important that they have no history of corruption or graft. It's hard to prove, but someone with sincere love for country like Ninoy is good. But actually, there are not many candidates like that. Integrity means that person's intentions and character are above suspicion. For example, when they help strangers, they are doing it just for that, not some other purpose. (Ellen, 42, female, employee of Asian Development Bank, March 11, 2009)

However, it is difficult to discern solely from the information provided by election campaigns or the media whether a candidate is really someone who will perform honest public service. To help make that determination, members of the civic sphere place faith in a candidate's track record, which can be considered a reflection of honesty:

> I just go based on track record. Maybe this guy is an economist or a businessman. This guy would have good economic sense. Then he would be able to create policies that would, at least, help propel the economy. I always look at people who have track records for getting the job done. (Lawrence, 35, male, bank employee, February 8, 2009)

Conversely, candidates with a track record of corrupt dealings or pre-election handouts to the poor are shunned. "I don't support candidates who suddenly start putting up all kinds of buildings and structures when election time approaches. They engage in wasteful projects with money that comes from us taxpayers. Even the condolence money they give to the poor adds up to a lot." (Louie, 51, female, university clerk, February 21, 2009)

In short, voters in the civic sphere seek leaders who have the education and intellect required to run the country, as well as a solid record of honest service to the nation, devoid of self-aggrandizement.

Fear of the Votes of the Masses

Now let us look at how voting by the poor is viewed from the civic sphere. The poor vote came under scrutiny in the civic sphere with the presidential election of Estrada. Since then, each election has been accompanied by the voicing of apprehensions that the poor might cause the election of unqualified entertainers and corrupt politicians. Two columnists for English-language newspapers depicted the voting behavior of the poor as follows:

> The inscrutable poor masses out there have been publicized, lionized, satirized, analyzed, and wooed to death. Election time has a way of smoking them out of the woodwork, the cracks, and crevices where they dwell, as if candidates realize they exist for the first time. Suddenly the poor are on everyone's mind and lips, suddenly they rule, they poll. (Doyo 2004, April 29)

> Today, election day, is the day of the poor—the *masa*. Once every three years, the poor voter emerges from his *nipa* [palm] hut or cardboard hovel to flex his weary muscles. With unsteady hand, he casts his ballot in the neighborhood precinct. His vote is as good as that of the richest man in the land. (General 2004, May 10)

In certain contexts, the poor vote becomes a major issue. During the midterm election of May 2001, with residual passions from People Power 2 and 3 still alive, an issue was made of how many members of the opposition coalition, which included Estrada's wife, might win election to the Senate due to the poor vote. The fear was that the pro-Estrada faction would win a majority and be propelled back to power. Discourses such as the following circulated via the English-language dailies:

> The lesson here is that we should vote for candidates not because they are popular, but because their qualifications and backgrounds would make them good public officials. Let us not have another Erap. . . . I agree with the militant groups campaigning not for, but against candidates who helped Erap commit his sins against the people. Never again should the likes of Erap and his cronies darken Philippine society again. (N. Cruz 2001, February 14)

In the end, pro-Arroyo candidates took 8 of the 13 Senate seats up for grabs in the midterm elections, so the worst fears of those in the civic sphere were not realized. In the subsequent presidential election of 2004, however, Poe shot to the top of the opinion polls when he announced his candidacy, reigniting anxieties about populism. As a matter of fact, Poe's announcement triggered a plunge in the value of the peso, to 56.30 pesos to the US dollar, the lowest level in Philippine history.[29] This rekindled concerns about "showbiztocracy" (Esposo 2003, December 1) and the poor vote as fear grew in the civic sphere that a Poe victory would once again plunge the Philippines into chaos. To quote from one English-language newspaper column:

> [W]hen film superstars jump off the silver screen to extend their fantasy roles to sway unwitting idol-worshipping *masa* supporters for their political ambitions, we should all be concerned. This is no different from the case of a perverted father abusing his lovely little girl who idolizes him. (Esposo 2003, December 22)

The prominent columnist Amando Doronila also chastised Poe for shirking policy debates and other public forums for fear of revealing his ignorance and failing to articulate any clear economic policies at a time when the Philippines was facing severe economic problems:

> Popularity is neither policy nor program. Evading identification, for fear of losing popularity, is a travesty of elections as an exercise for the people to make informed choice in a democracy. To offer popularity as a cure to economic and political woes is a quick-fix solution. Worse, it is no less [than] criminal to inflict on the people a fraud—an illusion as a solution. (Doronila 2003, December 15)

> It takes programs and realistic economic policies to create jobs. . . . The main issue [is] the credentials and qualification of a presidential candidate to run the country competently and well. (Doronila 2004, January 26)

Many columnists expressed strong misgivings about Poe's English ability and education level, declaring that the poor must be rescued from their enthrallment to entertainer candidates if the populist threat was to be averted. One columnist from an English-language daily gave the following speech, which earned an ovation at a Rotary Club meeting:

> Requiring educational credentials for elective office may seem like intellectual snobbery, but it is a prudent requirement for the proper performance of important official duties. . . . Presumptuous candidates are trading on the mindless adulation of their fans to elevate them to elective positions, where they cannot function without director's cues to teach them how to act or idiot boards to tell them what to say. This is not mere paranoia, but rather an actual threat to our Republic. If this happens—and it will if we take no action to prevent it—we will have only ourselves to blame for our failure, as responsible citizens, to rescue our misguided countrymen from the illusions of the tinsel world. (I. Cruz 2004, April 4)

Indeed, fear of a Poe victory in the 2004 presidential election was so great that the National Citizens' Movement for Free Elections (NAMFREL), a citizens' organization that conducted poll-watching activities independent of the Commission on Elections (Comelec), improperly manipulated its early election return reports to Arroyo's advantage.[30] Moreover, in voting for Arroyo so as to prevent a victory by Poe, the middle class in effect facilitated the perpetuation of elite rule.[31] The antipathy within the civic sphere toward populism supported by the poor thus provoked reactionary voting behavior and misconduct that negated the democratic system.

Regarding local elections, those in the civic sphere expressed frustration with the entire political process, according to which candidates purchased the votes of the poor by showering them with benefits in the form of not only direct cash handouts but also various services. It was asserted that the poor lacked the requisite morality to participate in politics, and that as long as they were willing to sell their votes for a few hundred pesos, corrupt politicians would continue to win elections. Quoting again from some English-language newspaper columnists:

> These are the voters who are usually from the poor or squatter areas especially of the urban centers who are usually herded, fed and paid by politicians for their controlled votes. . . . these usually illiterate squatters are the politician's piggy bank controlled votes to win an election. The more squatters the better! (Espina 2001, May 20)

> It has been noticed by this sector that the greater mass of tax evaders and illegal residents of crowded communities usually dictate the outcome of popular elections. . . . [W]e see countless *barangays* [communities] being run not by the more responsible residents, but by the *tambays* [layabouts] who have all the time to do *ronda* [rounds] and strut around like minor officials puffed with illusions of grandeur." (Pascual 2000, August 3)

The middle class of the civic sphere was dismayed not only by the voting of the poor, but also by the electoral misconduct of the elite. One lawyer articulated her feelings of despair and powerlessness in the face of elections rigged by the elite as follows:

> The middle class is powerless. We are perfectly capable of choosing candidates. But the candidates all make the same campaign promises and don't offer us any real choices. Because of that, we can't make use of the skills we have to select the right candidate. Besides, it's too easy for Comelec to manipulate vote totals, and that has made the middle class apathetic. (Shelia, 35, female, lawyer, April 14, 2008)

As the above remarks demonstrate, a pervasive complaint in the civic sphere is that the Philippines suffers from malaise because the poor have exacerbated populist and vote-buying tendencies that enable corrupt politicians to win elections.

Reform Proposals for Voting Restrictions and Education

What efforts are being made to change this electoral behavior in and from the civic sphere? An election monitoring movement to prevent election rigging by the elite has existed since the 1950s. NAMFREL did important work in the snap election at the end of the Marcos era, and has continued to place monitors at polling places nationwide in post-democratization elections as well.[32] On the other hand, what sorts of proposals have been discussed or implemented regarding the poor vote? In the English-language press, it is not unusual to see "reform" proposals that would partially limit the voting rights of the poor (Schaffer 2008: 135–6). The aim is to deprive the right to vote to squatters, those who do not file a tax return and those who fail a prescribed competency test. The following is one description of such a proposal:

> One of the qualifications of voters is that they must be residents of the place where they intend to vote for at least six months. Proponents contend that squatters are not legal residents of the place where they are illegally squatting, and must therefore be disqualified. […] A disgruntled sector wants to limit voting rights only to those who file income tax returns. The basic idea is that those who do not pay taxes, or at least file ITRs, have no business dictating who should lead the country. (Pascual 2000, August 3)

Proposals to restrict the voting rights of the poor carry the implication that Philippine democracy would be healthier if the vote were limited to the middle class. The following exchange between an English-daily columnist and a reader makes this obvious. The columnist alludes to Estrada in bemoaning the quality of the electorate:

> [T]he Filipino people have "a genius for stupidity." It takes genius, for example, to elevate an inveterate drunkard, gambler, womanizer, liar and dropout with questionable intelligence to the highest position in the government and yet expect him to run the country well. (Licauco 2001, May 22)

A Philippine reader living abroad submitted this response by email:[33]

> In all the successful countries where democracy has worked, the middle class has become "the people". . . . Even in America, the mother of all democracies, the original voters were limited mostly to white, land-owning males. . . . What can be done to make democracy in the Philippines work, as shown by all practical history? Limit the democratic exercise to the middle class, either to those who pay taxes or to those who pass a certain competency test. (Quoted in Licauco 2001, June 5)

Behind proposals of this sort lies frustration that the middle class pays most of the country's taxes yet is ignored in the political process. Having pointed out that only the middle class has income tax withheld from its monthly salaries, while the rich evade taxes and the poor pay none, a bank employee goes on to say:

> This entire country is run by the middle class. The middle class is the one who provides the utilities, the hospitals and the educational structure for the poor. We pay taxes, and other people benefit. Would we send our children to public schools? You cannot send your own children to public school because the education system has really flopped. Government hospitals, we should be able to use them, but their services are lousy. We don't wanna use them. We would use a private one. Police are there to protect us, but no. Instead, they extort from us. We pay their wages, but they extort from us. You pay taxes to provide for these services, but we don't use them. So in effect, for what we're paying, we don't benefit at all. The whole system is really geared to protect the poor and the rich, and leave the middle class to die. He who pays the taxes should be the one allowed to vote, craft the policies and benefit from those policies. (Lawrence, 35, male, bank employee, February 8, 2009)

Proposals to restrict the vote attract attention in English-language newspaper columns at election time, but insofar as they run counter to the tenets of democracy, they do not necessarily enjoy broad support in the civic sphere. Most of those in the middle class that I interviewed cited education of the poor as a more realistic remedy than voting restrictions. Their belief was that the poor would also vote "correctly" if provided with a higher education. Some interviewees further asserted that the middle class must take the lead in making that happen:

> I'm sad to say that the *masa*, although they have the numbers, they may not have the foundation for good elections because they can be bought. It really involves the *masa* being educated of their rights under the democratic form of government. That is the job and responsibility of the middle class; they should be the ones educating the *masa*. It is not too late. They can change for the better. (Alberto, 70, male, electrician, February 21, 2009)

Based on this perception, churches, businesses, and members of the middle class initiated voter education programs for the poor. In the midterm election of 2001, voter education to persuade the poor not to support pro-Estrada candidates was particularly widespread. Organizations like NAMFREL and the Parish Pastoral Council for Responsible Voting (PPCRV) exhorted the poor to vote "morally" for "proper" candidates and to avoid being so quick to sell their votes or so dazzled by show business personalities. The Lopez conglomerate-owned ABS-CBN network broadcast TV commercials in which a poor street waif representing the "future of the Philippines" begged people to "vote for me." The ad urged voters to think not only of their own family but also of the greater good of the nation, to choose leaders carefully with a long-term perspective, to know their rights and responsibilities as voters, and to recognize that voting for the right leader could ensure that their children receive good governance, insurance and education.[34]

To educate voters, artists, intellectuals, businessmen, and professionals launched a foundation known as Pagbabago@Pilipinas (Reform@Philippines) and released a CD entitled *Pagbabago*, which they distributed through groups like NAMFREL and the PPCRV.[35] The CD featured such tunes as "*Hindi Mo Ako Mabibili*" ("You Can't Buy Me") by the popular band Aegis, with lyrics like "I'm poor, but I won't be bought. You've been fooling me all this time."[36] One English-daily columnist praised this burst of voter-education activity as follows:

> It must be the spirit of People Power 2. Never before have so many groups sprouted up for voter education. Politicized citizens, mostly students and young professionals, are banding together to teach slum dwellers and barrio folk about the evils of selling their votes or hopping onto celebrity bandwagons. Never again should voters take their ballots so lightly that they'd blindly go for any candidate who shakes their hand or builds them a bus stop or is seen to win anyway. It's a show of concern for democracy. (Bondoc 2001, February 26)

On the other hand, some columnists voiced concerns about voter education even as they acknowledged the need for it. For example, de Quiros (2001, May 15) critiqued the self-righteousness of voter education that attempted to inculcate the masses with answers "we" prepared in advance and then went on to say:

> If despite our efforts to do so, they still do not get it, then we have a right to think they are stupid. If they still vote for [pro-Estrada politicians], then we should start packing our bags for America. . . .You want to educate, listen to them first.

In the civic sphere, there is a strong sense of victimhood on the part of the middle class, which feels caught between the voting of the poor and the corruption of the elite, which they blame for exacerbating Philippine malaise. The victim mentality in turn reinforces a civic exclusivism that rejects the moral legitimacy of poor voters. Civic exclusivism obstructs the consolidation of democracy by undermining voters' willingness to accept even unfavorable election results as legitimate, an attitude indispensable to democracy. A clear demonstration of this was the extraconstitutional ouster of Estrada by People Power 2.

The Poor Vote Undermined by the Rich

Seeking Candidates Who Are "Kind" to the Poor

Turning now to the mass sphere, let us examine how the poor envision "correct" voting. According to a survey by the Institute of Philippine Culture, Ateneo de Manila University (2005), the poor recognize the importance of elections as a system for democratically selecting representatives, and take a candidate's track record, character and policies into account when voting. In light of their own socioeconomic circumstances, they also seek leaders who are pro-poor.[37] This is significant, because it clearly shows that the voting behavior of the poor is rational—in other words, modern. However, in focusing exclusively on the question of whether voting behavior is rational (modern) or irrational (traditional), the survey fails to adequately analyze the moral component.

Studies of social movements involving the poor also focus on their voting behavior, and explain support by the poor for specific politicians as a strategy to obtain various benefits such as improved living infrastructure, land acquisition, suspension of forced demolitions and so forth, and not because they are captive to clientelism (Karaos 2006; Velasco 2006; Kiba

2010; Kusaka 2010). However, this perspective explains voting behavior strictly in terms of benefit acquisition; once again, the moral component is not addressed.

Therefore, what I would like to do here is clarify what the poor actually view as "correct" voting, predicated on the finding that their voting behavior is indeed rational. First of all, the candidate attribute that takes highest priority in the mass sphere is being "pro-poor" (*maka-mahirap*) or "pro-masses" (*maka-masa*). A "pro-poor" candidate is one who does not seek immediate compensation in the form of votes, but is spontaneously concerned about the poor and extends them a helping hand due to a genuinely caring disposition.

> Candidates who pay attention to the *masa* are good. They should care about the masses, because the masses are the majority of the people. The rich keep getting richer, but they pay no attention to the poor. If politicians concern themselves only with the rich, the lives of the masses will only get harder. In every election I support candidates who show that they care about the poor, not only the rich. (Mely, 69, female, street vendor, March 12, 2009)

Likewise, weight is given to a "fair outlook" (*pantay-pantay ang pagtingin*) that treats everyone the same, rich and poor alike. This constitutes a moral judgment that a "correct" person should address the plight of the poor fairly or even prioritize it. One street vendor assigning equal weight to being "pro-poor" and "fair" had this to say:

> The candidate I want is someone who thinks about poor people, who cares about poor people. And they must be fair (*pantay-pantay*). Someone who's not corrupt, who's truly honest at heart. They must help the poor, not just look after the rich. (Gloria, 47, female, street vendor, April 4, 2008)

As indicated by this quote, corruption is also a target of criticism in the mass sphere. Politicians who engage in corruption are viewed as giving little attention to the poor and caring only about increasing their own wealth, however well off they may already be. Most people would agree with the following statement from this interviewee: "I support those who help the poor, not those who selfishly think only of their own profit." (Silveria, 30, female, factory worker, April 1, 2008) Conversely, the character of what is considered an upright politician is described by such expressions as "pious" (*maka-Diyos*), "God-fearing" (*may takot sa Diyos*), "having convictions" (*may paninindigan*), and "honest" (*matapat*).

In point of fact, however, plenty of politicians engage in corruption while also providing generous service (*serbisyo*) to the poor, so some overlap between the corrupt and the pro-poor is evident. Moreover, in an environment in which corruption extends from the highest to the lowest echelons of government, it is not easy to find candidates who are completely unsullied. For this reason, more than a few people take the pragmatic position of tacitly tolerating a bit of corruption in a candidate if they help the poor:

> If I hear a candidate is corrupt, I avoid him. If I hear someone is pretty good, that's who I vote for. But I don't care if they committed a crime. Everybody's the same. There's no such thing as a perfect person, and corruption is never going to disappear completely. (Delfina, 53, female, trash collector, February 7, 2009)

To the poor, the key to determining whether candidates are "pro-poor" lies in their "approachability" (*madaling lapitan*) and their "reliability" (*matakbuhan*) in a pinch. The poor carefully observe how a candidate interacts with them.[38] A candidate who "knows how to get along" (*marunong makisama*) with people, treating them as equal "neighbors" (*kapwa*), is regarded as "pro-poor." Conversely, a candidate who acts cold and arrogant, displaying false (*plastik*) sincerity, may become the target of whispered rumors that "he rubs his hands with alcohol [as a disinfectant] after shaking hands with poor people."

The lives of the poor are precarious; they are exposed to such risks as family illness and funerals, forced eviction from their homes and street stalls, fire and flood. When they get into trouble, they first call on relatives or networks of people from their home province for help, but often they are unable to obtain adequate assistance. In such crises, assistance from politicians provides an important safety net. They may personally visit the politician's office, or ask the *barangay* captain or one of the politician's vote gatherers (*lider*) to act as an intermediary. Election time presents by far the optimum opportunity to extract aid from a politician. Some of the poor tell stories such as this: "When an election nears, we can ask politicians for help. We went to the office of our representative and got the money for surgery for a family member" (May, 39, female, drugstore employee, February 10, 2009). However, such petitioning does not always bear fruit:

> When my father died, I was two months' pregnant and had no money. I went to the office of Congresswoman Annie Suzano in the *Batasang* [House of Representatives] to ask for help. I asked for some kind of work, any work—even street sweeping would be okay. The person in

the office told me to leave, saying they didn't know if she could find me a job. I couldn't get a direct meeting with her; I just kept getting passed from one staff person to another. So there's no way I could get the congresswoman to understand my situation. I'm sure that she's swamped with work, so her staffers wouldn't know for sure if she could help me or not. (Beng, 42, female, food vendor, February 7, 2009)

As in the above account, people wishing to meet with a politician must first speak to office staff and often come away empty-handed, without being able to meet with the politician directly or receive any assistance. For this very reason, "approachability" is considered a crucial requirement for a "pro-poor" politician.

The reason why so many poor people supported candidates from the entertainment industry was not only because of their celebrity status, but also because it was thought they might be more "approachable" than conventional politicians. "Politicians who are *artista* [performers] are better because they're close to the masses. Other politicians are only close to the rich" (Beng, 42, female, food vendor, February 7, 2009). However, there is no evidence that candidates from the entertainment industry actually help the poor. Most such candidates lost in the senatorial elections of 2007.[39] Underlying this result was a sense of disillusionment: "Many people regretted voting for entertainers in the last election. When they needed help, they couldn't approach the entertainer politicians either" (Pak, 54, female, newspaper vendor, April 1, 2008).

Profit vs. Morality

In view of the socioeconomic circumstances in which the poor find themselves, their voting behavior in favor of pro-poor candidates is eminently rational. However, particularly in local elections, where candidates and voters are in close proximity, voting behavior in which voters attempt to extract as many resources as possible from candidates carries the risk of embedding them more deeply in clientelist relations. Yet the poor do not necessarily feel compelled to acquiesce to candidates in exchange for resources. In practice, candidates are not guaranteed the support of the poor regardless of the amount of money and services they offer. Indeed, such largesse may cause them to be viewed as corrupt and in turn incur a moral backlash. Let us examine the moral lens through which the poor view the various forms of assistance dispensed by candidates.

According to Soon (2008; 2015), the poor support politicians not for the material aspect of their assistance but rather for its moral aspect:

the compassion, self-sacrifice and integrity it represents. They can discern whether a politician is extending a helping hand to the poor in a spirit of unstinting self-sacrifice born of an innate (*loob*) rectitude (*katuwiran*) and not for show (*kunwari*). My own surveys also support the finding that this moral perspective is broadly shared among the poor. In practice, however, the process of choosing a candidate may involve a conflict between profit and morality, and diverse opinions circulate within the mass sphere regarding morality in the context of voting.

First of all, the most prevailing view in the mass sphere is that you are not selling your vote if, even after taking money from a candidate, you vote for the candidate you originally supported.

> If someone offers me money I'll take it. There's nothing wrong with just accepting money, and no one is checking to see who I'll vote for. That's my business, not theirs. The money they toss around was ours to begin with, anyway. It's just going around and around. (Aying, 37, female, former department store clerk, February 16, 2009)

This point of view is not unrelated, it would seem, to the Catholic Church's voter education campaign slogan, "Accept money, but vote your conscious (*Tanggapin ang pera, iboto ang kursunada*)."[40] The logic that justifies the acceptance of money is also related to perceptions of injustice in the mass sphere. The thinking goes that Philippine politicians have unjustly lined their own pockets, preventing wealth from reaching the poor. Moreover, politicians get money from the value-added taxes that the poor pay on their daily purchases of cigarettes, liquor, gasoline and rice. Therefore, the money the candidates hand out belonged to the poor in the first place, and accepting it should not be a moral issue.

Yet, even in the mass sphere, taking cash from candidates does not meet with universal approval. In the interviews I conducted, more than a few people were critical of the practice of accepting cash handouts before elections. The primary reason given was a moral one. By accepting money, one person said, "you are selling yourself. Money is bad for your conscience" (Sobet, 39, female, housewife, April 2, 2008). A woman who said that she refuses to take money from candidates elaborated as follows:

> I may be this poor, but even when a candidate is going from house to house offering money, I never take any. I want to be honest. I hate the government for lying all the time, so the last thing I want to do is lie to myself. If I took their money, I'd feel like I was lying to myself. (Vicky, 46, female, handicraft maker, February 16, 2009)

Accepting money from candidates is not only criticized from a moral perspective, but also from a pragmatic, benefits-related one. Though the recipient may gain some short-term benefit, the argument goes, victory by corrupt candidates who throw money around before elections only breeds more government corruption, which works against the long-term interests of the poor:

> Wouldn't it be nice if they kept giving us money! (laughs) The masses have always taken money from candidates, saying that after all, it's not like we're stealing. But when [the candidates] win, they get into corruption right away to make back their expenses, and we don't benefit at all. All those people care about is lining their own pockets. (Ara, 46, female, laundress, April 7, 2008)

All too frequently, however, poverty drives people to accept money from candidates, despite feeling that it is morally wrong and against their long-term interests. As one street vendor put it: "Life is hard for me, so I can't turn down money. Money is a big help to poor people, so we have no choice but to accept it, even if we're being bought off. We know it's wrong, but our poverty wins out" (Janet, 38, female, fruit vendor March 17, 2009). Some people also say that they hesitate to refuse handouts because to do so would insult and embarrass the candidate:

> Sometimes a candidate asks for my vote, but I don't like him and actually want to vote for someone else. But it's hard to say, "I don't support you." If I don't want to embarrass him or let him see that I don't approve of what he's doing, I have no choice but to take what he offers. (Imelda, 43, female, snack-food factory worker, March 10, 2009)

It is understandably difficult to refuse cash offered by a candidate or *lider*. As a consequence, people find it necessary to take precautions to avoid such situations if one wishes not to get caught up in vote buying and selling. "During elections I go straight to the polling place and come straight home. One time there was a lunch counter where candidates were gathered, but I didn't stop by there. You have to listen to your conscience" (Mely, 69, female, street vendor, March 12, 2009). "If someone hands me cash straight out, I take it. But if I hear that people someplace are handing out money, I don't want to go there" (May Anne, 35, female, housewife, March 12, 2009). As these comments demonstrate, the poor do not simply sell their votes in exchange for cash received, and the morality of vote selling is an issue even in the mass sphere.

However, candidates hand out not only quantities of cash but also food, expenses for such occasions as weddings and funerals, free medical treatment and other services in abundance. How do people in the mass sphere view the acceptance of such services (*serbisyo*)? Unlike cash, services provided by candidates are often justified on moral grounds as behavior that helps the poor. Yet, not all services meet with approval, and not all candidates providing services earn support. What the poor positively evaluate are not services per se, but rather the moral component of assistance motivated by a spontaneous concern for the poor that is rooted in genuine compassion:

> Just receiving services doesn't make me feel obligated to vote a certain way. But if [the candidate] is providing services out of the goodness of his heart, I feel like returning the favor [by voting]. If he was helping people even before he ran for office, that's real kindness. What matters to me is whether someone does good things of his own accord, even if it doesn't help me personally. I check to see who is really helping out his fellowmen [*kapwa*] and deserves our vote—someone who comes to see us often and tries to help us as much as he can. (Ray, 39, male, lunch counter proprietor, March 1, 2010)

We should note here that, as the use of the word "neighbors" (*kapwa*) suggests, aid to the poor in the form of services is justified not by the morality of a vertical clientelism, but rather by that of a more horizontal solidarity. While the clientelism of trading votes for resources has not entirely disappeared from Manila's mass sphere, there is also evidence of a discourse that calls for politicians to distribute resources based on the morality of horizontal solidarity.

The next concern for the poor is how to determine which candidates to support. At election time, an extraordinarily large number of candidates actually vie with one another to dispense services in the squatters' settlements. In such circumstances, what criteria do residents use in choosing which candidates to vote for?

> They should help people, and not only at election time. Even when there are no elections they should think of us. There is a city council member who always comes here and helps out with funerals and such, even when the elections are way off—a politician who's easy to approach when youth groups [such as basketball teams] need assistance. (Alie, 28, female, gym employee, March 1, 2010)

> Gloria [Arroyo] helps people, but only her followers. If people like us who live in the squats and really need support ask her for help, she ignores us. (Ray, 39, male, lunch counter proprietor, March 1, 2010)

In short, the following two criteria serve as critical measures for determining whether candidates have genuine compassion and integrity: to what degree they distribute resources at times other than election time (that is, the period of providing services); and to how many people they distribute resources regardless of factional affiliation (in other words, the scope of service recipients).

Domination of Elections by the "Rich"

How do the poor perceive the power of their own vote? Are they confident that their majority status gives them considerable influence over election outcomes? Or do they feel powerless to change anything, no matter how many of them vote?

Most of the poor I talked feel as this person does: "It's the poor who make the most effort to go to the polls. The rich don't vote. They're the rich, after all" (Rosalinda, 24, female, housewife, March 1, 2010). It is certainly true that because the poor face so many problems that they cannot solve by themselves, many of them seek to build relationships with specific politicians who will provide them with assistance. On the other hand, quite a few members of the rich and the middle class do not participate in elections, particularly local elections, because they are not impressed by any of the candidates, or they feel generally powerless in terms of their affect on the results. In that respect, it is indeed the voting poor who determine election outcomes in the Philippines.

Despite this situation, the poor feel that no matter how much they vote, "the rich get richer and the poor get poorer". Even though the poor cast the majority of votes, it is a fact that their lives have remained hard over the years. How do the poor view this reality? Most believe that it persists because candidates favored by the "rich" buy the votes of the poor and otherwise rig elections:

> In elections, it's the rich who are stronger and decide the outcome. The poor really ought to be stronger, but the rich buy them off. Everybody should realize their own power. But the rich have money, while most of the poor are penniless and hungry—so even their hearts can be purchased with money. Not everyone, but just about. (Dig, 24, male, restaurant worker, February 7, 2009)

> I decide who to vote for by checking out the candidates' promises and campaign pledges, but those people never win. In the Philippines, it's always the people with money who win. The rich have tremendous influence. The government manipulates election results to its liking, and the elections are always rigged, so it's the same as if we didn't have any elections at all. (Gil, 42, male, tailor, March 12, 2009)

As the tailor suggests, election rigging by the Commission on Elections (Comelec), which answers to the president, is considered a major culprit.[41] Many people share this view: "Comelec raises or lowers the vote count to determine the winners. Even the presidential election is decided by them" (Loloy, 44, male, driver, March 31, 2008). This perception was reinforced by suspicions that Arroyo pressured Comelec to alter the vote count in the 2004 presidential election. At this time, many in Manila's mass sphere angrily asserted that Poe would have become president were it not for Arroyo's election rigging. In this way, a moral antagonism has been constructed in the mass sphere between the "poor" who seek a pro-poor leader and the "rich" who buy votes and manipulate election results. As far as the poor are concerned, it is the "rich" and the politicians rigging the elections who are responsible for the poverty and malaise of the Philippines.

This perception, that illegal manipulation renders one's vote meaningless, engenders a sense of powerlessness in relation to political participation: "The government controls everything by cheating. I don't feel like voting anymore. Even if I vote, they've rigged it so my vote doesn't mean anything" (Lina 40, female, general store proprietor, April 2, 2008); "Elections have no meaning for me. Things haven't gotten any better. I used to vote a long time ago, but now I just boycott" (Dol, 37, female, lunch-counter proprietor, April 4, 2008). Even so, among my interviewees, poor people who replied that they abstain from voting were in the minority. Philippine voter turnout is actually very high, 80 to 90 per cent, suggesting that most of the poor do vote.[42] Many of the poor are extremely diligent about going to the polls. At the Pechayan polling place I surveyed during the 2004 election, I witnessed a woman crying and stamping her feet in anger that her name did not appear on the list of registered voters.[43]

Why do the great majority of the poor continue to go to the polls with such fervor, despite feeling powerless to affect the outcome of elections? First, we may surmise that they are motivated by a desire to exercise

Photo 16 People crowding an outdoor polling place in Pechayan (May 2004).

their rights and obligations, as well as to demonstrate their convictions. As one woman put it: "The rich have the power, but the poor have the strength of their beliefs. That's all they've left us with, our beliefs. That's why most poor people care about their beliefs enough to vote" (Imelda, 43, female, snack-food factory worker, March 10, 2009). To lose the opportunity to act on one's convictions and exercise one's rights would be tantamount to losing one's dignity. No doubt this is why the woman I saw at the polling place was so angry that she could not vote.

A second reason is an abiding, albeit faint, hope that voting may help to change, however slightly, the harsh lives of the poor for the better. Even if there is no dramatic improvement in their lives, they can at least elect candidates who are less corrupt and who care for the poor a bit more. In that event, they may get to see a suspension of forced demolitions of their homes and less inflation in the price of goods. They may be able to ask for help when their family is faced with illness or other calamities. It appears that this slight hope amid general resignation is what drives poor people to the polls.

The Paradox of Voter Education

Education for "Correct" Voting

In both the civic and mass spheres, faith in the electoral process was shaken by the formation of moral antagonism over the question of "correct" voting, with those in each sphere believing that the other "they" unfairly control elections. The civic sphere in particular saw a rise in civic exclusivist sentiment, spurred by the gains of populism, which viewed the poor vote as evil and led to proposals to partially restrict voting rights. However, the fact that restrictions like this would violate the tenets of democracy has made them difficult to implement. Furthermore, because only a minority of voters belongs to the middle class and only a limited number of parties and candidates embrace their interests and moral stance, it is difficult for them to elect representatives to their liking who would pursue such electoral reforms.

Consequently, as described earlier, citizens' organizations engaged in election monitoring like NAMFREL and the PPCRV began to carry out voter education programs with the aim of getting the poor to vote "wisely" and "correctly."[44] Church and business leaders founded these organizations, with membership mostly from the middle class. To the Catholic Church, politics based on handouts to the poor or dominated by ambitious populists is objectionable on moral grounds. To the business community, such politics is nothing less than an obstacle to a sound business environment. By supporting voter education, both the Church and business leaders seek political reforms grounded in "clean" and "good" governance. Here, I will focus on the activities of the PPCRV, which engages in morality- and values-oriented voter education, and examine their possibilities and limitations.

The PPCRV is a movement of parish-based church groups that was formed in 1991 under the aegis of the Catholic Church. It was inspired by the Second Vatican Council (1962–65), which called for the Church to be more actively involved with social issues. The Philippine Catholic Church responded by seeking ways in which it could engage with the social problems of the country. Inevitably there was internal opposition to this new direction, and the Church did not immediately begin to exercise an impact on politics. However, due to the pivotal role the Philippine Catholic Church took in the democratization movement of 1986, it gained increased confidence in itself as a moral leader in social reform. The founding of the PPCRV at the Second Plenary Council of the Philippines in 1991 was based on the reasoning that, "In the Philippines today, given the general perception that politics has become an obstacle to integral development, the urgent necessity is for the lay faithful to participate more actively, with singular competence and integrity, in political affairs. It is through the laity that the Church is directly involved."[45]

As an official "citizens' arm" of Comelec, the PPCRV cites its objectives as election monitoring, voter education and election reform under the slogan "CHAMP"—which stands for "Clean, Honest, Accurate, Meaningful and Peaceful" elections.[46] PPCRV branches are set up in each diocese of the Catholic Church. Before an election, each branch serves as a venue for assembling local candidates and asking them to explain their policies and pledge to hold a clean election. At voter education seminars, the group teaches voters about the electoral system and the moral outlook it deems necessary for voting. On election day, it dispatches nearly 500,000 people nationwide to polling places to serve as volunteer poll watchers in an effort to prevent election fraud. After the election, they continue to monitor the winning candidates to see whether they are implementing policies as pledged.

Photo 17 A voter education program by PPCRV entitled "Understanding My Vote. Do You Already Understand?" (at a church in Caloocan City, February 2010).

The purpose of the PPCRV's voter education program is to achieve "a political order rooted in Truth, Justice and Peace" through "responsible voting as a faith response."[47] A "correct" vote as recommended by the PPCRV is one based on values such as truth, peace, love, justice, unity, equality, freedom, faith in God, respect for life, work, patriotism, promotion of the common good, order, and respect for law and government.

Let us now examine the actual voting behavior that these values call for, with reference to voter education materials prepared for the 2010 election by the Diocese of Cubao branch of the PPCRV. For example, "Love" is described as "caring for one another," which in practice means "we care for the welfare of everyone by voting for good people, even if they do not give us money, but because they will give us good government." "Freedom"-based voting means resisting coercion or manipulation in order to wisely choose candidates who always give priority to the public good. Applying "Truth" means to "make an effort to find out the true worth of all candidates, and do not easily fall for propaganda; do not engage in black propaganda." Voting that puts "Patriotism" into practice means "not accepting bribes of unworthy candidates who will bring the country to ruin and instead, exposing them and not voting for them," so that "only competent and honest officials will get elected" (Public Affairs Ministry, Diocese of Cubao 2010).

How do PPCRV members view the significance of this type of voter education? One member, a woman who graduated from a top-tier university and previously worked as a corporate secretary, said the following:

> The poor do not actually select a candidate, but merely jump on the winner's bandwagon. Also, they take whatever the politicians offer them. That is not the right behavior. When a politician offers condolence money at a funeral, that's certainly a gesture of kindness, which in the Philippines is perfectly normal. But does our politics or society get any better just because people hand out a lot of condolence money? (Teresita, 50s, female, Public and Political Affairs Ministry, Diocese of Kalookan, March 5, 2010)

A man who worked with the PPCRV at the Diocese of Malabon while employed by an airline company had the following to say:

> More poor people tend to have bad habits. It's because they didn't have the chance to get an education. We need to open their eyes to their social and economic responsibilities. We have to get them to vote for reasons other than because a candidate is famous or gives them money.

We have explained that it's the duty of politicians to help people, so it's not necessary to vote for them out of a sense of obligation. If they can't understand that such voting behavior is wrong, and change their ways, they are the ones who will suffer the most. We have to patiently explain to them, over and over, how to get themselves out of their present situation. (Arthur, 30, male, Public Affairs Ministry, Diocese of Malabon, airline company employee, February 14, 2010)

Difficulties with Voter Education

Voter education has the avowed objective of training the poor to choose able candidates who will serve the nation with integrity, instead of populists or corrupt politicians. This is none other than a practice of civic inclusivism that seeks to incorporate the poor into the "citizenry" by exercising hegemony from the civic sphere over the mass sphere via the contact zone. How successful, then, has this exercise of hegemony through voter education been in achieving its objective?

According to Schaffer (2008: 125–49), voter education has incurred a backlash from the poor, who view it as an attempt to impose on them the wealthy and middle classes' own notion of "what democracy ought to be." However, this diverges from my own survey findings. I showed materials used by the PPCRV for voter education to people in Pechayan and asked them their opinion. A minority of respondents did indeed express such views as: "It bothers me. Everybody has their own thoughts about what's right and their own beliefs, don't they?" (Boboy, 37, male, unemployed, April 1, 2008). Most, however, positively evaluated voter education as important: "Voter education is useful to people. Some people don't know who to vote for. Voter education helps get those people thinking. It can teach them something" (Dig, 24, male, restaurant worker, February 7, 2009). Therefore, voter education grounded in the morality of the civic sphere appears to be accepted, not rejected, in the mass sphere as well. Why is this so?

One reason is that the voter education conducted by the PPCRV does not mention specific candidates by name, but cites more abstract, universal values; in this way, it takes care not to invite a backlash from the poor. Another is that the moralities of the civic and mass spheres are not entirely opposed to one another, but share much in common; hence, there is room in the mass sphere for acceptance of the values espoused by voter education as legitimate. For example, the same deep-seated mistrust and anger over political corruption is found in the mass sphere, so the message "Don't vote for corrupt politicians" is acknowledged as important.

The moral view that people should not be directed or coerced to vote a certain way is also shared throughout the mass sphere.[48]

However, it also bears noting that the moral values of anti-corruption and voting freedom, although accepted, are not necessarily effective in changing the voting behavior of the poor. This is because various values espoused in voter education are interpreted or applied differently in the mass sphere. According to the PPCRV, for example, the values of "love," "freedom" and "truth" required for "correct" voting are equivalent to the value expressed in Tagalog as *maka-tao*, "kindness to people" (Public Affairs Ministry, Diocese of Cubao 2010). To the poor, there is no contradiction between supporting the value of "kindness to people" and supporting candidates who are populists or dispense cash and various services. This is because they see the quality of "kindness to people" in such candidates. One ardent Estrada supporter, affirming the need for voter education, elaborated the following: "Voters have to learn to vote for candidates because they have abilities and aren't greedy, rather than just because they look good. Candidates who are devoted to the poor, who are kind to people (Loloy, 44, male, driver, March 31, 2008).

Voter education also tries to get the poor to stop selling their votes. But as mentioned earlier, the moral view that "selling your vote is wrong" is already shared across the mass sphere, while the acceptance of cash is justified by such rationales as "You can take money and still vote for a different candidate" and "We're poor, so we have no choice but to accept money when it's offered." Voter education further criticizes the fact that the poor accept provision of various services by politicians as an indirect form of vote buying. But in the mass sphere, people scrutinize the large number of candidates who dole out services to determine who among them are truly "pro-poor." Therefore, when voter education calls for people to "stop selling your vote" or "vote for honest candidates who will work hard for the nation," they see nothing novel or that conflicts with the morality of the mass sphere; as a result, such exhortations are unlikely to alter actual voting behavior.

What causes this gap in perceptions? As I pointed out before, the moralities of the civic and mass spheres have elements that conflict and elements that are shared in common. When the civic sphere attempts to exercise civic inclusivist hegemony vis-à-vis the mass sphere by foregrounding moral values unique to the civic sphere, such as "entertainers are bad," they are likely to incur a backlash and fail in their effort. Consequently, they appeal instead to moral views shared by both spheres: "Let's avoid corrupt politicians", "Let's vote without being coerced by anyone", and so forth.

However, these more universal moral values are interpreted and applied differently due to differences in how the middle and impoverished classes go about seeking a "better life." That is to say, the middle class aspires to create a better Philippines over the long term by choosing the right leaders through an electoral process based on rational policy debate in line with the aforementioned moral values. On the other hand, the poor, due to their more precarious circumstances, support candidates who seem likely to solve the problems that press upon them in relation to land, residence and other necessities of life. As a result, even voter education that appeals to universal values cannot readily change the voting behavior of the poor.

Seeking Trans-boundary Communication

The civic inclusivism of the PPCRV has attempted to alter the political consciousness and voting behavior of the poor by exercising hegemony in the mass sphere, but this effort has reached an impasse. Nevertheless, it may be said that the voter education project has created a valuable discursive space—that is, a contact zone—where the moralities of the two spheres may encounter one another. This space is host to various measures aimed at improving communication between the civic and mass spheres. As mentioned earlier, attempts to impose moral values unique to the civic sphere upon the mass sphere provoke a backlash; yet, when an appeal is made to more universal moral values, they tend to be applied differently, preventing the achievement of the original objective. Let us examine how PPCRV members have sought to communicate with poor voters to resolve this impasse.

PPCRV members are aware of the difficulty of changing the voting behavior of the poor. They recognize that if a candidate enjoys the support of the poor, then the explicit rejection of that candidate, however corrupt and deficient in character they may be, will incur resentment, because it insults the dignity of the poor. Therefore, these members attempt as much as possible to devise and practice ways of communicating with the poor that do not challenge their dignity.

For example, one member conducts voter education not only in churches, but also in other day-to-day venues where the poor can relax.[49] Furthermore, he says he avoids explicitly stating his own opinion, instead "coming down to their level of thinking" as much as possible and attempting to make them aware of a new way of thinking through suggestions. He cites the following explanations as examples of his approach: "Candidates who hand out a lot of money during elections engage in corruption to make that money back once they get elected, right? So isn't it better not to vote for candidates who toss money around?" Or, "That politician suddenly launched a lot of projects just before his term was up. It seems like he must have had a lot of money left over to spend, because he didn't do a thing before then."

Middle-class staff members of most NGOs who deal with the poor, not only those at the PPCRV, communicate with them in this manner on a daily basis. One female staffer at an NGO says that she uses the following line of inquiry to get women who support Estrada to start thinking: "I was a big fan of Erap when I was young too. But would you think it was okay for your husband to womanize, drink and gamble just because he's handsome? No, right? Then why is it okay for the president to be a womanizer when it's not okay for your husband?" (Dedeng, 60s, female, NGO representative, February 14, 2010).

In this way, informal voter education venues are a site for communications that attempt to eventually bring the poor around to voting in the same "wise" manner as the communicators by interacting with them on a day-to-day basis and, based on an understanding of their circumstances and concerns, providing them with opportunities to think. This represents an effort to ultimately incorporate the poor into the "citizenry" while tolerating a certain degree of plurality between disparate moral values.

Yet, insofar as the practitioners have no intention of transforming their own moral values by listening to the words of the poor, this does not constitute an "agonistic" relationship (Mouffe 2000, 2005; Connolly 1991) in which both sides recognize one another's legitimacy. Nonetheless, unofficial voter education of this sort is significant in that it creates a deliberative space over electoral politics by establishing a conduit for a certain form of communication between disparate moralities while transcending the divisions of the dual public sphere.

CHAPTER 5

Moral Antagonism in Urban Governance

Photo 18 A resident of a squat (far right) watching his home being razed by the state (Pechayan, March 2008).

This chapter focuses on the moral division of the nation over issues pertaining to urban governance. Most members of the impoverished class in Manila secure a place to live by squatting illegally on public or private land and make their living in the informal sector through activities such as street vending. In a sense, they are living within "gaps" in the legal order of the state.

The prevalence of these illegal living conditions is, in the words of Migdal, a reflection of a "strong society, weak state" situation in which the state lacks the power to control society. According to Migdal (1988), the power of social control in most developing countries is shared by the state and local elites ("local strongmen") who vie for control of the populace through "rewards, punishments, and symbolic configurations"; and in this struggle, the state is unable to establish absolute dominance over the elite.[1] The Philippines may be thought of as a classic example of this situation, with the local elite maintaining strong influence over social control (Abinales and Amoroso 2005). However, in Manila, the presence of large numbers of poor people living outside the law indicates that this struggle extends beyond local elites to the poor, who also compete with the state in a fierce contest over the imposition of order on human behavior, that is, over governance.

Governance has traditionally been equated with the government and its monopoly of legitimate coercive power. The hierarchical mode of governance, however, has shifted to modes based on markets and networks against a background of privatization and decentralization. Stoker (1997: 17) points out that these newer forms of governance are based on coordination between the public and private sectors, and states that "governance is ultimately concerned with creating the conditions for ordered rule and collective action."[2] However, the process of governance, that is, of creating a social order to regulate human behavior, is anything but harmonious, and can grow belligerent in its imposition of disciplinary power. Particularly in Manila, where the state and diverse social forces vie with one another, it behooves us to examine the process of struggle over governance.

Friction between State Discipline and the Poor

An Urban Poor Living in the Gaps of the Legal Order

Many studies on Philippine politics share the assumption that the poor have been subordinated by the country's oligarchic local elite, and that civic organizations need to assist the poor in becoming independent of local elite control. In other words, state leaders, local elites and civic organizations are focused, as dominant actors, on the creation of social order, while the poor are relegated to a position in which they are subject to control by those actors or forces. However, this assumption is problematic because it ignores the agency of the poor in negotiating the dominant social order.

In fact, squatters and street vendors in developing countries have managed to acquire public land or elite-owned private land illegally and consequently exert a significant impact on the urban space and social order. Interestingly, unlike traditional social movements, these achievements have been made in spite of a lack of clear leadership, ideology and organization. Bayat (1997, 2000, 2010) refers to this phenomenon as "quiet encroachment"—a patient, persistent and penetrative assault on the state and the elite by poor people determined to weather any hardships to achieve a better life.[3] How then are the poor, who are supposed to be politically vulnerable, able to ignore the laws and power of the state as they engage in this quiet encroachment? As Bayat has observed, their payment of "protection money" to street-level bureaucrats and syndicates has ensured tacit acceptance of the illegal basis of their livelihoods.

Poor people moving from rural villages to Manila avoid the risk of forced eviction from land they squat on by paying protection money (*lagayan* or *kotongan*) to *barangay* (community) officials, security forces and syndicates. They usually need to bribe *barangay* officials or security forces only once, the amount they pay varying depending on the area of land they occupy. Although this is an informal system, it serves a function by imposing a certain order on land distribution in the squats. More specifically, this payment accords "ownership" status over land and housing to the families who initially occupied that land. They may then "sell" portions of it or rent out parts of their house for income.[4] However, people arriving later must rent housing because there is so little land left to occupy. In addition to rent, they must pay their landlords excessive electricity and water rates because they cannot contract directly with the power and water companies; this makes their lives even more difficult. Moreover, they are also ineligible for compensation in the event of a forced eviction. Thus, even among squatters, there exists an asymmetrical relationship between landlords and tenants.

The Filipino family I lived with in Pechayan moved to Manila from Bohol Island in 1998 and lived for some time as renters.[5] However, they were frustrated with the high rent and utility charges, so in April 2003 they began to build their own home. The land was owned by the University of the Philippines, whose campus security personnel ostensibly prohibited squatting on university property.[6] The family therefore paid protection money in the amount of 7,000 pesos to security personnel and 1,000 pesos to a *barangay* official. Attracting as little attention as possible, they gradually assembled a simple, unadorned structure out of used galvanized sheet iron and plywood. To build a house too quickly and ostentatiously would not only incur the envy of neighbors, but also risk its demolition while construction was still in progress, despite the payoffs. Later, the family added to the structure several times, building a second floor with four rooms in addition to their own, which they rented to other families for extra income.

Depending on the squat location, payoffs to a syndicate may also be necessary. According to Parnell, who conducted a survey for the National Government Center, a syndicate is a network of individuals, organizations or businesses that claims ownership of formal land titles, employs lawyers and enjoys close ties with government agencies and politicians.[7] In the process of allotting land, syndicates demand that the poor cover certain costs for land surveys, trials, lawyers' fees and the like. For the poor, this informal system guarantees them land and home "ownership" of a sort. In practice, syndicate vigilante groups composed of retired soldiers or police officers protect squatters from government agencies attempting to demolish their homes (Parnell 2003).

In 2003, a syndicate was involved in the large-scale illegal occupation of the Arboretum, a 54-hectare stretch of land owned by the University of the Philippines just behind Pechayan. First, someone claiming ownership of a title to the land dating from the Spanish colonial era sold the property to someone else. The purchaser subdivided the land and sold it to Muslims from the island of Mindanao; and in a very short time, about 500 homes and a mosque had been built.[8] However, the homes were eventually demolished because the people there had not paid sufficient "protection money."

Payment of protection money is also an integral part of the street vending trade. For people migrating from the countryside, street vending is one of the easiest means of livelihood in which to engage. The vendors occupy a spot on a sidewalk or street with a simple stall or cart from which they sell a variety of products, ranging from fresh produce—including fruit, vegetables, meat and fish—to clothing, toys, and bootleg CDs and DVDs. Numerous peddlers also walk around carrying wooden boxes with cigarettes and candy, or styrene foam containers with bottled water and other drinks, and hawk this merchandise to pedestrians, jeepney drivers, and so on. Fresh arrivals from the country find work at very low daily wages assisting established street vendors who have a certain amount of capital. Then, once they have learned the ropes of the business, they establish a livelihood for themselves as independent vendors by borrowing capital, typically from "Bombay" moneylenders (referred to as such due to their Indian origin),[9] in order to purchase goods in bulk at wholesale markets, which they sell on the street at retail prices.

The security forces of local governments and the Metropolitan Manila Development Authority (MMDA), a national administrative agency, have targeted street vendors in crackdowns for some time. The proliferation of street vendors is a cause of traffic congestion in and around major shopping districts. They also incur the resentment of commercial establishments and vendors in public markets who pay legitimate business taxes and tenant fees, and who demand that local governments impose restrictions on street vendors.

In reaction to this, street vendors organize themselves so that they can collectively respond to attacks by bureaucrats or other groups and negotiate with the government. They collect membership fees (*butaw*) that are used to pay protection money to local and central government agencies and the police to avert crackdowns, and obtain what is in effect tacit approval to do business. The weekly bribes paid by these vendors' associations range from several hundred to several thousand pesos, depending on the size of their membership and the negotiating skills of their leaders.[10] According to association leaders, they pay bribes not because they are coerced, but rather as a negotiating tool. Although it is difficult to ascertain the number of street vendors' associations, there are probably over 200 such groups in Quezon City, for example. If each association pays an average of 1,000 pesos per week, that adds up to 200,000 pesos in weekly off-the-books revenue for Quezon City.[11]

Photo 19 A street vendor mother and her child (Philcoa, February 2009).

In Philcoa, the district adjacent to Pechayan, the site of my survey, a vendors' association with 11 members was formed in 1974. As of 2002, there were three such associations, each with some 30 members. At that time, each association collected a membership fee of 20 pesos per day and paid 100 to 500 pesos per week to the *barangay* official, Quezon City's security and market management offices, local police precincts, the MMDA and neighboring commercial establishments. The official in charge of security visited the vending territory of each association on a certain day every week to collect the money. The police would frequently cadge fruit, pork, and other items from the vendors, which the association or its members would reimburse with "condolence" money (*damay*). It was also customary for the vendors' associations to send gifts of food and home appliances to local police chiefs on the occasion of their appointment or birthday. Thus, by joining an association, vendors are able to obtain safer and more favorable sales locations in exchange for paying a membership fee. However, the number of profitable sales locations is limited, so it is sometimes difficult to join an association without being introduced by a member to whom one is related by blood or birthplace. Because they are not able to join associations, or simply choose not to pay fees, some vendors, known as "flying street vendors," do business irregularly.

Though informal, the practice of securing, through bribery, tacit state approval of illegal bases of livelihood such as squats and street stalls is highly institutionalized; the poor refer to this as the "bribery system" (*lagayan system*). This system embodies a significant rebuttal to Philippine local political studies, which asserts the dominance of elite rule. According to these studies, the poor are nothing more than passive actors controlled by patron-client relations (Lande 1965), violence and coercion (Sidel 1999) or efficient political machinery (Kawanaka 2002).[12] However, the bribery system demonstrates that the poor do not unilaterally submit to the state ruled by the elite, but on the contrary, define the social order and urban space (Kusaka 2010). In the bribery system, the poor represent economic resources that influence local officials to tolerate their illegal bases of livelihood.[13] This is in contrast to conditions of clientelism or machine politics in which local elites offer economic resources to influence the voting behaviors of the poor.

Disciplinary Governance by the MMDA

However, the bribery system does not completely protect the livelihoods of the poor. State leaders have repeatedly ignored this system and pursued forced evictions of squatters and street vendors in the name of modernization. During the Arroyo administration, this role was primarily played by the MMDA under the chairmanship of Bayani Fernando.

Fernando was appointed chairman of the MMDA by Arroyo in June 2002, and held the post for eight years until the end of the Arroyo administration in June 2010. Initially, he was a businessman who founded companies involved in metal fabrication and sales. Later, however, he was led into politics by his father, the former mayor of Marikina City, and subsequently served as mayor of Marikina for three terms, from 1992 to 2001.[14] As Seki (2010) notes, Fernando sought to improve local security and sanitation by fostering the discipline and morality of each individual resident under the slogan "Fix our community" (*Ayusin natin ang komunidad*). Acquiring a reputation as the mayor who transformed Marikina into Metro Manila's cleanest and most orderly city, he was the recipient of numerous awards, both foreign and domestic.[15]

Fernando's crowning achievement was the "Save the Marikina River Project," which redeveloped the banks of the Marikina River, an environmentally degraded area of squatters' settlements prone to frequent flooding, into parkland and commercial property. To make room for this redevelopment, Fernando forced some 10,000 squatters to relocate to other parts of Marikina City.[16] He also built flood-containment spillways and added landfill. By adopting tough measures against waste runoff from factories and trash dumping by residents, he succeeded in cleaning up the Marikina River. The product of this redevelopment, Marikina River Park, attracted interest both at home and abroad as a shining example of "good governance" by a local government. Although the private sector has taken the lead in urban development in Manila in recent years, Marikina City was praised for the success of its redevelopment spurred by the political will of its mayor.

When Arroyo appointed Fernando to run the MMDA, she reportedly said to him, "What you did for Marikina, you must do for the whole of Metro Manila."[17] As MMDA chairman, Fernando announced an "urbanity" (*urbanidad*) program that would transform Manila into a sophisticated urban space through strict "discipline" and "enforcement of the law." This was a form of disciplinary governance that sought to impose state power as an absolute force on Manila's public space, requiring Manila residents, particularly the poor, to adapt their behavior to specific civic norms. The norms that Fernando had in mind are reflected in the slogans he promoted under a program known as *Metro Gwapo* ("Metro Handsome"). These slogans appeared on large posters throughout the city, carrying such exhortations to the citizenry as "No congestion" (*walang sagabal*), "No littering" (*walang kalat*), "No rotten communities" (*walang pook na bulok*), "No diseases" (*walang sakit*), "No bad smells" (*walang mabaho*) and "No rudeness" (*walang bastos*).

To beautify Manila, Fernando banned and fined such behavior as walking around half-naked or spitting in public places, saying that these actions were signs of moral and cultural degeneracy.[18] In his words, "Men walking the streets without shirts are penalized. . . . A person who goes out to the street naked has no sense of shame and is capable of doing the most horrible thing."[19] He also banned public urination by men and installed pink-colored public toilets throughout Manila,[20] declaring "If you can't stop men from pissing on the wall, in public, then at least teach them to do it in private, without anyone seeing them. If they get used to doing that, then they will eventually be reformed and realize that it's not cool to urinate with an audience."[21]

To convey the chairman's messages, the MMDA posted pink bulletin boards all over Manila, containing such warnings as "No crossing here, it's deadly!" (*Bawal Tumawid Dito, Nakakamatay*) and "There's always trash here. It's ugly!" (*Ang Lugar na Ito ay Laging May Basura. Pangit!*). These pithy admonitions attracted attention with their unique wording and color. In practice, however, it is difficult to control people's behavior through signage alone. Therefore, Fernando erected numerous pedestrian bridges and pink fences along the median strips of thoroughfares to prevent people from jaywalking. He also designated specific stops for public conveyances and put up fences to keep riders from getting on or off buses and jeepneys anywhere else.

Fernando's efforts at disciplinary governance included a number of practices that were perceived as extremely petty.[22] One English-language newspaper columnist said that Fernando's policies aligned with the "broken windows" theory,[23] according to which, a house with a broken window appears vulnerable to break-ins and therefore encourages theft and other more serious crimes. Fernando did in fact argue that cracking down on minor infractions and disorderly conduct that might at first glance seem trivial would eventually instill discipline in people, restore order in Manila and foster economic development.

Fernando also hoped to encourage investment from abroad by improving Manila's appearance. An example of this was his "Investor's Corridor Project," which beautified the roads around Manila International Airport to impart a good impression to foreign investors visiting the Philippines. Ultimately, Fernando's disciplinary governance was the embodiment of the notion that even a state lacking in financial resources could stimulate investment and achieve economic development in urban areas by imposing discipline on its residents, beautifying its cities, improving public safety, reducing traffic congestion and so forth. In this sense, it was a classic example of urban development in the age of neoliberalism.

Eliminating "Gaps" through Discipline

Fernando was nowhere more zealous than in his efforts to manage pedestrian sidewalks. As soon as he was appointed MMDA chairman, he announced that he would return the sidewalks to the public, declaring that it was imperative to Manila's development that all illegal vendors, stalls and other obstructions be removed from the sidewalks, and to this end, launched a "Sidewalk Clearing Operation."[24] He argued that restoring order to the city's sidewalks would bring economic prosperity to Manila, an effect that would extend rapidly to the poor as well.[25] In doing so, he insisted: "I am just enforcing the law. We need to follow the law. It is only right to force these vendors to do the right thing. Sidewalks are for pedestrians. Selling should be done in markets and properly designated vending zones."[26]

According to Fernando, the Sidewalk Clearing Operation was important for the following reasons. First, it would eliminate Manila's horrendous traffic jams. Because street vendors occupied the city's sidewalks, pedestrians were forced to court danger by walking in the roadways, thus narrowing the lanes available for traffic, exacerbating congestion and contributing to economic stagnation. Second, street vendors represented an absence of discipline and order that turned the streets into gathering places for pickpockets and drug dealers, making them a hotbed of crime; therefore, they must be removed for public safety reasons as well. Third, the goods sold by street vendors were contaminated by cockroaches and rats, and the health of consumers needed to be protected.[27] Finally, a ban on street vending was necessary to ensure the safety of the vendors themselves; in particular, peddlers who walked around hawking cigarettes, candy and newspapers put themselves at risk of being involved in traffic accidents.[28]

To provide a legal basis for removing obstructions from sidewalks, MMDA adopted MMDA Resolution 02-28, which authorized "the Metropolitan Manila Development Authority and the local government units to clear the sidewalks, streets, avenues, alleys, bridges, parks, and other public places in Metro Manila of all illegal structures and obstructions."

The resolution further states that "public places in Metro Manila are not properly utilized by the road users/public due to malpractices of some unscrupulous individuals who wantonly utilize these areas for displaying and vending their goods, as well as utilizing the same, in erecting some structures for commercial and advertising purposes," defining private uses of public space as "public nuisances."[29]

Fernando assembled an "MMDA Operations Team" of 700 to 1,000 personnel and assigned them the task of removing "obstructions." The team, which divided into crews of 20 or so, patrolled the streets of Manila in light-blue buses, their windows covered by wire screens to protect them from rocks or other projectiles. Street vendors made fun of these vehicles, calling them "prison buses" due to their appearance. The MMDA crews, armed with clubs, were accompanied by two or three gun-toting policemen as they engaged in obstruction removal and crackdowns on street vendors, destroying the vendors' stalls and confiscating their goods and carts. Sometimes they would even pour kerosene on the vendors' merchandise in order to render it unsalable.[30] In Philcoa, there were as many as three crackdowns per day. Whenever an MMDA bus arrived, the vendors would shout "Crackdown!" (*huli!*) or "Run!" (*takbo!*), grab their merchandise and flee *en masse*.

The objective of the MMDA was to deprive the vendors of all their capital. Street vendors borrow capital in increments of a few thousand pesos, generally from the "Bombay" moneylenders, use the money to purchase merchandise, and pay the loan back in daily installments. If their goods are confiscated or ruined, the vendors fall into arrears and are unable to borrow further capital to buy more goods. If there are frequent crackdowns between 5 and 9 p.m., when sales are especially brisk, the vendors are forced to hide their goods, which severely reduces their income. Moreover, the loss of business hours means that they are unable to sell all of their fruit, vegetables and other perishable produce, so they must then discard them, causing further losses.

The MMDA's crackdowns frequently escalated into violent confrontations with the street vendors. In September 2002, a street vendor in Makati attempted to resist MMDA personnel and police with a gun, and as a result, was shot and killed. Repeated crackdowns in front of the Baclaran Church in Parañaque City were particularly harsh, and in July 2003 a confrontation between vendors and the MMDA resulted in the death of a shopper from a stray bullet. The MMDA branch office at Baclaran was twice involved in fires caused by arson. The MMDA assigned 8 marines, 40 police officers

Photo 20 A family whose house was razed by the MMDA (Pechayan, March 2008).

and 15 Regional Special Action Unit troops to maintain order during the Baclaran crackdown. In Philcoa, there were frequent occurrences of street vendors throwing rocks and police firing warning shots. There were other instances of MMDA personnel or street vendors being stabbed or shot in various locations, adding up to over a dozen dead and many more injured. Although the actual circumstances remain unclear, in February 2009, a group describing itself as "leftists" attacked the vehicle of the commanding officer of a sidewalk clearing team with machine gun fire, killing the driver and seriously wounding the commander's son.

Fernando also initiated the forced evictions of squatters. His initial target was people living within ten meters of rivers or creeks. His argument was that flooding occurred throughout Metro Manila because the squatters threw trash into the waterways, which also endangered their own lives; hence, by evicting them, he was actually saving them.[31] Squatters alongside major thoroughfares were also targeted for removal in order to reduce traffic congestion.[32] Additionally, tens of thousands of households were forcibly removed from alongside train tracks to facilitate the redevelopment of the

Philippine National Railroad with foreign capital.[33] In Pechayan, where I lived, the MMDA destroyed over a dozen roadside homes as part of a road-widening project in March 2008.

According to a report by an international NGO, the MMDA evicted 14,468 households between January 2006 and September 2007.[34] In nearly all these cases, the procedures stipulated by the Urban Development and Housing Act for providing "adequate prior notice, consultation, and relocation" were not followed. About half of the evicted households were not offered a relocation site, and about 25 per cent were subjected to violence.[35] Fernando himself dismissed the idea of relocating squatters, saying, "It's like you are rewarded for squatting."[36]

One impetus for forced evictions was pressure from the private sector, which actively promotes urban redevelopment in order to profit from the thriving real estate business. As a consequence, the plight of squatters remains undiminished, even after the inauguration of the new Aquino administration in 2010 and a change in MMDA chairmen. Evictions associated with redevelopment have occurred repeatedly in numerous squatters' settlements, a prime example being the North Triangle of Quezon City, where the Ayala conglomerate is developing the city's Central Business District.[37]

The Aquino administration has also actively engaged the private sector in the construction of relocation sites for squatters. However, the availability of sites within Metro Manila is limited by high land prices, and most families are relocated to suburban sites some 30 to 50 kilometers from the city, where they struggle to secure a means of livelihood and pay the high commuting costs. Furthermore, although there are model "people's plan" projects in which NGOs have assisted in the construction of relocation sites with participation from residents, who enjoy better living conditions, the number of such sites is limited. Most sites lack adequate infrastructure and experience frequent interruptions in water and electricity supplies. Therefore, it is estimated that some 20 to 40 per cent of relocated families return to squatter settlements in the city as renters.

Criminalization of the Poor by the Citizenry

The Poor as Destroyers of Discipline and Order

How do people in the civic sphere view the urban spaces inhabited by the poor? To the middle class, squatters' settlements and the streets and alleys lined with vendors' stalls are lawless, dangerous places, hotbeds of depravity and corruption that reek with the stench from heaps of garbage and other foul odors, populated by pickpockets, muggers, drug dealers, addicts, pushy beggars, half-naked drunks and prostitutes. To the middle class, the poor symbolize the absence of discipline and order; they are seen as an evil presence that threatens public safety and impedes the modernization of the city. The following comment by the columnist Neal Cruz typifies this perception:

> The perennial traffic jams are the reason the government is widening Commonwealth Avenue and building flyovers and underpasses. The taxpayers are paying billions of pesos for these public works improvements. But a horde of sidewalk vendors is all that is necessary to spoil the best-laid plans of men. (Cruz 2002, May 15)

Another columnist decried the streets where vendors and their low-income customers mingle as "schools of anarchy" that corrupt public morals and integrity, where female shoppers think nothing of bumping their breasts amid the hustle and bustle, illegal vendors use rigged scales to cheat their customers, and the police collect bribes as a matter of course. To clean up such corruption, the columnist concludes, "we should support Chairman Fernando in ridding Metro Manila of these schools of anarchy" (Bas 2002, August 18).

Conversely, assertions by the poor of their rights have been met with explicit antipathy in the civic sphere. This was particularly the case in 2002, when a series of demonstrations against Fernando by street vendors resuscitated lingering fears from the previous year's People Power 3 in the civic sphere. Columns in the English-language press voiced some of the following opinions: "[S]idewalk vendors have taken over the sidewalks and their numbers and noise have made some of us afraid. . . . [N]ow the numbers and the noise of the illegals have drowned out the voices of the sane, the reasonable, and the law-abiding" (Amador 2002, August 28). "As a group, illegal vendors are a decisive factor in elections—just like politically formidable squatters. . . . Together they decide the quality of our leaders, the quality of life in our cities, and affect even the fate of the nation" (Zenarosa 2002, September 14). This exasperation with and fear of the poor is perhaps best summed up by the following lament: "Come to think of it: It sometimes seems that we have been long dominated by the undeserving poor that are startled when someone takes the cudgel for us to assert our rights as citizens" (Zenarosa 2002, August 28).

The viewpoint represented by these comments is loath to acknowledge any right of vendors to occupy the streets or of the poor to illegally occupy someone else's land. Prominent columnists like Doronila have repeatedly rejected poverty as a justification for illegal behavior.[38]

> The question . . . is when can a metropolitan authority begin clearing the streets of obstruction and returning them to the general public? Shall we wait until the poor are less poor before such a campaign can be undertaken? (Doronila 2002, September 4)

> If we are to follow the angry arguments of street vendors being driven out of the sidewalks that they are being deprived of their livelihood, that would be accepting the notion that the poor have the right to break the law because of their poverty. And if we consider that more than half of our population is poor, we can have an idea of the scale of lawlessness we are fostering. (Doronila 2002, August 26)

The same logic—that poverty is no excuse for illegal behavior—was also applied to squatters. The squats that abounded throughout Manila not only symbolized poverty, according to this view, but also signified a lack of law and order as well as obstacles to development.[39] It is particularly noteworthy that a discourse treating squatters as holders of vested interests enjoyed growing support in the civic sphere. In what sense were people living in the wretched environments of the squats thought to have vested interests? First of all, the squatters occupied prime downtown real estate, even as many members of the middle class commuted from the suburbs due to soaring land prices in the city center. Furthermore, the middle class, with its strong self-identity as taxpayers, had grown increasingly frustrated that politicians spent their hard-earned tax money on the poor in an effort to win votes. To those in the middle class, paying compensation and providing relocation sites to evicted squatters was like handing the taxes they paid over to criminals. Columnist Neal Cruz articulated this frustration as follows:

> These squatters are violating the law, but they are going to be paid and given new lots and houses by the government for doing so. Where does the money come from? From law-abiding taxpayers. Local governments periodically raise these realty taxes. . . . Yet these same local governments do not prevent squatters from invading private property. . . . [L]ocal officials coddle the squatters and even encourage them to settle in their territories because that means votes. . . . Remember, most of these squatters are not the deserving poor, but professional squatters, members of syndicates. (Cruz 2002, April 16)

A salient characteristic of this discourse is that it views squatters not as people structurally disadvantaged by an extremely stratified society, but rather as criminals who are profiting to the detriment of the public good. Consequently, they do not qualify as objects of empathy or pity, even when deprived of their homes through forced evictions. This attitude was evident in the reaction of viewers to a discussion on the ANC network's television program "The Rundown" (broadcast on September 23, 2010) about a large-scale eviction carried out that month in the North Triangle district of Quezon City. The program featured a debate between a senior official of the National Housing Authority, which owned the property, and a representative of the squatters. After watching this program, a columnist wrote that he was unable to feel any sympathy whatsoever for the squatters' representative, who loudly asserted the squatters' rights as if they were the actual landowners and rejected relocation to an alternate site out of hand. He also wrote that this view was shared by friends on Twitter (Esposo 2010, September 28).

The discourse of the poor as vested-interest holders leads to the logical conclusion that a solution to the squatter problem is to be found in depriving them of their voting rights, not in helping them acquire land or resettle elsewhere. Measures like the provision of relocation sites or the Community Mortgage Program, which helps squatters purchase land at low interest rates, only grant them special privileges that will encourage further squatting. If, instead, they are deprived of their vote, politicians will lose their incentive to coddle the squatters and penalties against their illegal behavior will be reinforced, the argument goes.[40]

In late September 2009, Tropical Storm Ondoy caused tremendous damage to riverside informal settlements in Metro Manila, and most survivors had to be evacuated. In the civic sphere, this prompted a surge of pronouncements that this was the perfect opportunity to rid Manila of its squatters.[41] One columnist wrote: "In a negative way, Ondoy actually prepared the ground for Metro Manila to rise again with less urban blight, minus the squatter colonies that have made a joke of our Torrens title system and concepts of public order and sanitation" (Pascual 2009, October 8). The government did in fact develop a plan for massive forced relocations for the avowed purposes of rescuing riverside households, said to number as many as 70,000, from the danger of floods, and preventing worse flooding due to the clogging of drainage channels with household trash.[42] However, this project did not move forward as planned, and after a while, the squatters began rebuilding their homes along the riverbanks.

The State and Right "Citizens" Who Won't Compromise with the Poor

In the civic sphere, where squatters and street vendors were overwhelmingly viewed as criminals who interfered with development, perpetuated moral decay and threatened public safety in Manila, it was argued that upright "citizens" ought to support Fernando. For example, journalist Teodoro Benigno (2002, August 26) likened Fernando to "a gust of fresh and wholesome air." In a letter published in an English-language daily, a professor at the University of the Philippines wrote: "He is God-sent, brave and courageous in his stand for the good of his fellow men."[43] The following comments appeared in various English-language newspaper columns: "The campaign by MMDA chair Bayani Fernando to rid Metro Manila of 'street anarchists' deserves the all-out support of right citizens" (Sinfuego 2002, September 4); "If we want a better quality of life in the urban jungle, we have to cooperate with Fernando" (Cruz 2002, June 19); "[I]t is a crusade against all forms of illegalities that people are so used to doing that they think it is alright" (Zenarosa 2002, September 14). Meanwhile, 90 per cent of the members of the Makati Business Club, a leading voice in the Philippine business community, expressed their support for Fernando.[44]

Fernando won praise in the civic sphere for his novel political style of taking strong measures to enforce the law and maintain order without yielding to social pressure, in effect declaring, "the government is not impotent in the face of disorder."[45] Out of concern for their election prospects, politicians generally do their best to avoid implementing policies that would incur the displeasure of the vast numbers of poor voters. Mayors in Metro Manila had heretofore given what amounted to tacit consent to street vending, and would even issue vending permits before the Christmas shopping rush. When election season arrived, politicians would all launch projects such as paving roads, installing street lighting, and repairing basketball courts in the squatters' settlements. Consequently, Fernando's stance of staunchly upholding law and order and ignoring protests from Manila's poor was daringly innovative in the context of conventional Philippine politics. Fernando himself recognized this, as indicated by the following quote:

> If being a bully would be a means to be effective, I'll remain a bully. It's a crime to compromise the interest of the people. . . . Fernando said it was wrong for his critics to call him a bully. "That's what's wrong with

this country. You should be called an angel when you implement the law. *Pero ditto* [But here], when you implement the law, *ikaw pa ang masama* [you are considered bad]."⁴⁶

It gives me a heavy heart to do things that offend some people. But being a public official, I cannot cry with them. Because if I cry, my eyes will be blind, and who else will guide them?⁴⁷

When NGOs and leftist organizations launched a flurry of protest demonstrations against Fernando in support of the poor, a fierce backlash in the civic sphere sparked such reactions as these: "[T]here are those who see Chairman Fernando's style insensitive and even arbitrary, and probably they are right, but only from the perspective of the underdog mentality and the weak ego structure" (Zenarosa 2002, August 28). "Those who loudly talk about championing the 'rights' of resentful 'sidewalk vendors' who're being cleared off the sidewalks are way off-base. They're snarling about the 'welfare' of a few score thousand so-called sidewalk vendors as against the rights and safety of 14 million Metro Manilans. Not just their arithmetic, but their logic is screwy" (Soliven 2002, August 28).

When some vote-seeking politicians postured about protecting the street vendors from the MMDA, they too became targets of criticism. For example, Joey Marquez, mayor of Parañaque City, ordered the arrest of MMDA personnel, declaring that they were violating the human rights of the Baclaran street vendors. One Parañaque citizen denounced this in a letter to the *Philippine Daily Inquirer*, writing that the mayor's protection of the vendors would only make them more brazen and "make the 'savior' more popular and . . . be able to gather more votes of the next election" (Ang 2003, August 23). Manila mayor Lito Atienza also banned crackdowns by the MMDA against street vendors in the city. This prompted *Philippine Star* columnist Max V. Soliven (2002, August 28) to write: "Atienza seems to be jealously guarding his fiefdom from Bayani's broom with the kind of zeal he ought to be demonstrating in cleaning up his fly-specked metropolis himself." In Manila, the columnist went on, "crowded and infested areas where not only the sidewalks have disappeared need Atienza's attention. If the mayor can't hack it, he should let the MMDA chairman do his job."⁴⁸

Similar criticisms were aimed at politicians angling for the squatter vote. For example, when President Arroyo issued lot titles to 150 squatter households in Cavite province in 2003, the *Manila Times* (2003, November 17) criticized the action in an editorial: "Lots are not cheap candy to be handed out for all and sundry. . . . [The] president's action is pre-election vote-buying." When anti-Fernando legislators began arguing in Congress for the abolishment of the MMDA, letters supporting Fernando poured in from English-language newspaper readers both at home and abroad. One reader asserted that the Philippines needed bureaucrats like Fernando who faithfully fulfilled their duties, not legislators and mayors concerned with getting votes.[49] Thus people in the civic sphere strongly supported Fernando and his strict application of law and order, and fiercely denounced efforts in support of the poor as a cause of the Philippines' long years of stagnation.

Law and Order as a Key to Growth

Fernando won widespread support in the civic sphere. After a columnist serving as moderator on a TV discussion program called for viewers to text-message their assessments of Fernando's policies, she reported that 80 per cent of the responses were favorable:[50]

> People, especially Metro Manilans, are sick and tired of the way rules and regulations are for the most part ignored, and the anarchy that this causes. . . . A heartening sign is that people have not bought the 'anti-poor' charges that have been hurled against Fernando to stir up anger against him. This indicates that more and more[,] poverty is no longer accepted as an excuse for breaking the law. . . . Which means that we might be beginning to have a discerning, rational public. (Collas-Monsod 2002, September 14)

That law and order became such a priority in the civic sphere has to do with the fact that they are viewed as a key to economic growth. Because those in power do not properly enforce the law in the Philippines, the thinking goes, order breaks down and the economy stagnates. Proper enforcement of the law would encourage Filipinos to exercise self-discipline and thereby foster economic development. As one economist put it, "I think we are capable of following rules if they are properly enforced. Filipinos abroad do follow the rules of a functional society" (Dennis, 39, male, economist at the Central Bank of the Philippines, April 5, 2008). Another bank employee cited Subic Bay, which was converted into a special economic zone after the closure of the US naval base there, as an example of how the economy would improve if people were made to understand the need for discipline:

You see Subic to be progressive, to be orderly. Nobody does anything stupid, because there is a strong hand managing itself.[51] People agree with that because they believe the vision 'We will transform Subic Bay port into the best moral city.' They believe in cleanliness and order of the place, and attracting business. They know that because of the belief, prosperity will come to them. If they believe the vision, they will gladly subject themselves to the discipline. If the people do not respect those policies, no matter how strict they are, they will violate it. If you write 'Do not piss' over here, they will piss over here! Here, we drive like crazy, but the moment we enter Subic, it becomes a disciplined zone, we become more disciplined because we are afraid of being apprehended, because everyone in the city believes in that discipline. (Lawrence, 35, male, bank employee, February 8, 2009)

To a middle class craving the rule of law and order, in the words of one columnist, "Fernando's most important contribution is proving that Filipinos can be law-abiding, that they are not congenitally corrupt, and that the common good can prevail over individual interests, given the proper incentives and leadership" (Collas-Monsod 2003, June 28).[52] Expectations of this sort reflected a nationalistic determination not to lag behind other Asian nations that were enjoying rapid economic growth. Lamenting that the Philippines lacked the order and discipline found in other Asian countries, journalist Benigno (2002, August 26) went so far as to declare: "[Fernando] cannot afford to fail. If he fails, we all fail. If anything so elementary as bumping off sidewalk vendors cannot be accomplished, and getting rid of them is allowed by law, then we fail dismally as a people." However, the longing for disciplinary governance also tends to reinforce the belief that democracy is not necessary as long as there is economic development. One business owner said as much: "I would rather have an authoritarian if the leader is the right one, concerned for the development of the country. I would not choose democracy that has a lot of clowns in the government" (Knox, 35, male, advertising agent, March 6, 2009). In short, the relatively minor issue of whether street vendors could be removed from Metro Manila drew intense interest and high expectations as a litmus test for the social and economic development of the Philippines.

Although few in number, comments also appeared in the English-language press that criticized Fernando's methods as "inhumane," even as sympathy was expressed for his objectives. In the *Inquirer*, a columnist and radio broadcaster Ramon Tulfo described how he had heard complaints on his radio program from a bus conductor and a blind masseur who both said they had been subjected to violence by the MMDA; when he asked Fernando about this, Fernando brusquely replied that the actions of the MMDA were justified (Tulfo 2004, May 22). In the same newspaper, a reader described witnessing the MMDA violently seize the merchandise of a peanut vendor, a young boy selling deep-fried foods scatter boiling oil as he fled and an old woman desperately try to protect her stock of cigarettes. The reader asked, "Is this what the MMDA chair claims as '*urbanidad*,' 'discipline' or 'peace and order in the streets'?" and argued that job creation should come first (Vargas 2005, July 19). In a column, Professor Michael Tan (2002, October 10) of the University of the Philippines asserted that the crackdowns by the MMDA were discriminatory:

> The upper classes are too quick to complain and too slow to give up the privileges that contribute to the problems. The measure of true grit for Bayani Fernando doesn't come with dousing the wares of sidewalk vendors with gasoline, but with the way he'll tackle the powers behind subdivisions, malls, and private schools [that increase traffic congestion as much as the street vendors do].[53]

Meanwhile, as Fernando's policies failed to achieve the expected results, even after some time had passed, his popularity gradually dwindled. In the interviews I conducted in 2008 and 2009, more than a few middle-class interviewees criticized his authoritarian methods, even while they continued to support his objectives. A corporate lawyer described his experience participating in meetings held by Fernando as follows:

> His methods are very backward and he doesn't listen to other people. I've been to his meetings, and they are actually more like lectures. He'll cut you off when you speak. It's a waste of time really. He insists on his own opinion. His very poor management style is altogether very disappointing. (Junji, 52, male, corporate lawyer, April 20, 2008)

Still, there is no question that during at least the first term of the Arroyo administration (2001–04), Fernando's discourse about restoring order through the enforcement of discipline and the law enjoyed widespread support in the civic sphere. Furthermore, the civic exclusivist discourse of a "citizenry" craving law and order conferred legitimacy upon the criminalization of street vendors and squatters, and upon policies expelling them from the city.[54]

Resistance by the Poor for Their Livelihood and Dignity

A Morality of Livelihood and Dignity Overriding Law and Discipline

In resisting the state's destruction of their homes and livelihoods, and in asserting their right to live in the city, the poor espoused two values supported in the mass sphere. The first was the value of "survival," that is, a belief that threatening people's way of life and depriving them of their means of livelihood was absolutely impermissible by any logic. This concept was articulated using such words as *kabuhayan* ("living" or "livelihood") and *hanapbuhay* ("means of livelihood" or "occupation"). In straightforward language, people decried the MMDA's destruction of their livelihoods as unjust: "People's livelihoods are being killed off little by little" (Jeffren, 43, male, unemployed, January 23, 2003). "They're killing the livelihoods of the poor by banning even the humblest of lifestyles" (Aying, 37, female, former department store clerk, February 16, 2009) Additionally, nearly all of them cited their responsibility to their families, particularly in terms of raising their children:

> They take away and burn the goods we sell at our stalls. Since we can't do business, we can't repay the money we borrowed [from moneylenders]. How are we supposed to feed our children? Should we steal? Who is it that's trying to kill us? The government, that's who. (Beng, 42, female, food vendor, February 7, 2009)

Such remarks reflect a palpable anger that the state would destroy even the modest livelihoods of people striving to improve, however slightly, the impoverished conditions they have been forced to endure for so long. Inspired by this perception of injustice, street vendors held demonstrations in which they carried signs with messages such as "Justice for the Livelihoods of Vendors!" (*Katarungan para sa Kabuhayan ng Vendors!*) and chanted slogans like "Fight for Our Livelihood!" (*Ipaglaban, Kabuhayan!*). A street vendors' organization in the Cubao district prepared a placard with the following message and raised it at demonstrations:

> Chairman Fernando, your service to the President is most impressive. But it is an attack on the right to existence [*karapatang upang mabuhay*] of us street vendors. You shouldn't be removing small vendors like us from the streets. You should set up a proper market. It's our right to earn an honorable living [*karapatan naming maghanapbuhay ng marangal*]. The solution to this problem is not kerosene, but a peaceful exchange of views. Vendors are honest. Filipinos want to live a decent life.[55]

As the above declarations suggest, another value espoused by the poor was human "honor" or "dignity" (*dangal, dignidad*), in the sense that everyone should be treated with equal respect regardless of the gap between the rich and the poor. Street vendors repeatedly spoke of "honorable work" (*marangal na hanapbuhay*). Dignity is important to the poor because the poorer one is, the more often they are treated with contempt by people of higher social standing. Street vendors endured scorn for their line of work; they were called "eyesores" (*sakit sa mata*) by neighborhood business owners and bureaucrats, or told by arrogant customers, "Who do you think you are? You're just a street vendor." One fruit seller described her response to an insulting look from a "rich woman" as follows:

> There was a rich woman clutching her bag like it was real valuable. She was on her guard because she thought I was a purse snatcher. That's why I picked a fight with her. I told her, "Ha! My merchandise is worth more than everything you've got in that bag." She didn't say a word, just grabbed a taxi and ran away. (Amy, 25, female, street vendor, April 4, 2008)

Another woman who went shopping at a department store said she got in a fight with a clerk who eyed her with contempt:

> I was hoping to buy a washing machine, but it was like they thought I was penniless. A clerk mistook me for a shoplifter. Rich people have smooth, pretty skin, right? There's a big difference between how they get treated as customers and how we do. If you look rich, you get treated completely different. They give you really nice service—"How do you like this one, Madam?" That clerk looked down on me even though she was just as poor. I didn't like acting all full of myself, but I took out my money and waved it in her face. (Beng, 42, female, food vendor, February 7, 2009)

Thus, the poor are extremely sensitive to the snobbish (*matapobre*) attitudes of the "rich," and their feelings of wounded dignity trigger an intense rage. As they see it, Fernando and the rich view the poor as a blot on the city and deny them respect as equal human beings. As one street vendor put it, "They look at poor people as if they're looking at garbage" (Maria, 28, female, street vendor, January 21, 2003). For this reason, slogans like "We are not garbage" and "We are not criminals" frequently appeared in anti-MMDA protests. A vendor in Philcoa highlighted his pride with a T-shirt printed with the message "I'm Proud to Be a Street Vendor" (*Street Vendor*

Photo 21 A T-shirt made by a Philcoa street vendor reads, "I'm Proud to Be a Street Vendor" (Philcoa, December 2002).

Ako May Dangal). Demonstrators also expressed their puzzlement and anger at being identified with criminals, carrying placards reading "Steal things or sell things, they'll arrest you either way" and "What do you think we're selling, drugs?"[56] Underpinning this pride was the conviction that they were doing nothing to be ashamed of, toward others or themselves. In explaining the meaning of "dignity" to me, one street vendor used the words *malinis* (clean, pure) and *matuwid* (right, straight).[57]

In the mass sphere, livelihood and dignity are regarded as values that transcend the law. In other words, squatting and street vending are essential to one's livelihood, and hence morally justified, even if they are illegal. Conversely, the impersonal, mechanical application of the law by someone like Fernando is wrong because it destroys livelihoods and denies dignity.

> It's the law that gives the MMDA its power. We obey the law in our own lives, but those MMDA guys are just blindly enforcing the law without thinking about whether what they're doing is right or wrong. (Henry, 22, male, unemployed, April 2, 2008)

Bayani's a dictator. Sure, he's right when he says it's illegal to live on the sidewalk. But what are people supposed to do when their houses are destroyed and they have no place to live? They have the right to fight against Bayani. (Abe, 62, male, former security guard, March 12, 2009)

Insofar as the rank-and-file MMDA employees assigned to the crackdowns were themselves poor, they might have been expected to share this moral outlook. For that very reason, street vendors and squatters were especially furious at the low-echelon personnel who doggedly followed Fernando's orders in carrying out the crackdowns. One elderly female street vendor, tussling with MMDA workers who were trying to seize her parasol and her boxes of cigarettes and coconut juice, yelled, "You people are poor, too, aren't you (*Parang hindi kayo mahihirap*)?!"

Additional pragmatic objections were also raised against this by-the-book enforcement of the law. If the poor were deprived of their means of livelihood, the logic went, they might be driven to commit even more serious crimes by their dire straits.

Rules that drive vendors from the streets and destroy squatters' homes are wrong. If they lose their way to make a living, they could become thieves or pickpockets. Better they should be street vendors than criminals, right? (Jonathan, 28, male, construction worker; April 4, 2008)

There was already a perception in the mass sphere that law enforcement was inherently unequal and favored the rich. As one housewife put it, "There's no law here for poor people. Everything is set up for the rich. If a hungry poor person steals just a little food, they throw him in jail. But when the rich steal a whole lot of money, they don't arrest them, do they?" (Emma, 49, female, housewife, March 12, 2009).[58] Or, "Poor people obey the law. But the rich can defy the law because they have [powerful] connections. That means justice isn't served" (Carlo, 43, male, gas mechanic, April 2, 2008). As a result, the prevailing opinion in the mass sphere was that the MMDA should go after politicians and wealthy people who had committed far more serious crimes instead of cracking down on street vendors and squatters. One unemployed man had this to say:

The MMDA has no pity for the poor people they drive from their homes or off the streets. Those guys don't give a damn about us, that's why they can treat us like they do. But what the MMDA really should be doing is cracking down on the really bad guys who break the principles (*patakaran*). (Boboy, 37, male, unemployed, April 1, 2008)

To poor people who think of themselves as living with pride despite their poverty, forced evictions in the name of law and order are thus patently unjust. This perception resulted in the formation of a moral antagonism in the mass sphere, according to which, the heartless "rich" deny the livelihoods and dignity of the "poor" and seek to expel them from the city.

Yet, even in the mass sphere, the necessity for urban development and discipline was not entirely dismissed; it drew limited support with the caveat that it should not hurt people's livelihoods or dignity. For example, one street vendor said: "I think [the discipline promoted by Fernando] is a wonderful thing for the nation. But we are being tossed out like so much garbage, without being given another place to go. His worst fault is that he refuses to consult with us, just pushes ahead without stopping" (Elma, 42, female, street vendor, January 19, 2003). Some squatters also expressed acceptance, to a point, of the propriety of forced demolitions by the MMDA:

> Houses in my neighborhood were demolished, but they didn't give anybody land to relocate to because they said they didn't meet the necessary requirements. The MMDA just showed up all of a sudden, without any warning, and on a rainy day no less. I do think demolitions are needed to make the main avenue look nicer. But even so, it's terrible that they didn't provide people with anyplace to move. (May, 39, female, drugstore employee, February 10, 2009)

Solidarity among the Urban Poor

How did Manila's poor stand up to the destruction of their bases of livelihood by the MMDA? According to Davis (2006), in the slums and informal sectors of cities in developing countries that constitute the bottom tier of global capitalism, fierce competition and the exploitation of labor by petty capitalists have broken up self-reliant networks and alliances among the poor and caused the outbreak of intense antagonisms and violence. It is true that social relations among Manila's poor are fraught with discord and feuding, and far from harmonious. Nevertheless, the ad-hoc social relations of the squats and streets have evolved toward solidarity in the face of threats from capitalists and the state, a solidarity grounded in the moral conviction that no one should be denied their livelihood or dignity.[59]

In March 2008, the MMDA destroyed over a dozen roadside squatters' homes in Pechayan as part of a street-widening project. A leftist students' organization went to the site and staged a protest for just one day, but most residents merely looked on with a fatalistic attitude. Those whose houses were destroyed did not put up any significant protest, concentrating instead on recovering household goods and reusable sheet iron and plywood. Pechayan residents did not close ranks in outright confrontation with the MMDA primarily because they wanted to avoid possible arrest or violence. Also, the incident involved the demolition of only a dozen houses, not the forced eviction of the entire community. The people who lost their dwellings had originally erected them along busy Commonwealth Avenue so that they could sell goods right in front of their homes. The closer a person's building lies to a major thoroughfare, the greater the danger of eviction grows. Precisely because these people had built their homes with full awareness of the risks involved, they did not garner much sympathy from other residents.

However, the families who lost their homes did gain the cooperation of the *barangay* and nearby residents in minimizing their losses and finding new places to live. Neighbors helped to rescue family possessions and reusable materials from the demolished houses and move them to a safe place. At the direction of the *barangay*, families made newly homeless took up temporary residence in the barangay hall and basketball court, where neighbors provided them with free food and water, loaned them money, hired them to work as carpenters or in shops, and otherwise helped sustain their livelihoods. Over time, some evacuated families moved into new rooms by bargaining with landlords for discounts on deposits. Other families slowly began rebuilding their homes and shops and paying protection money to the *barangay* and security forces. Thus, while Pechayan residents did not engage in organized resistance against the MMDA's forced demolitions, they did cooperate as neighbors to ensure the survival of the families who had lost their homes and helped them rebuild their lives.

Street vendors in Philcoa also cultivated solidarity with one another on the streets. They reduced the risk of forced eviction by the state by organizing themselves, paying off governing agencies and establishing a bribery system. Because securing capital was a life-and-death issue for vendors, they traded information about moneylenders and acted as each other's loan guarantors. If someone had their merchandise confiscated and lost their capital, others would help out by giving them "condolence" money (*damay*). To reinforce this practice of mutual assistance, street vendors cultivated the ritual kinships known as *compadrazgo*, serving as godparents to one another's children at baptisms, confirmation ceremonies and weddings. Although this was originally a religious practice, it has taken on a pronounced secular significance in terms of mutual social and economic aid. Despite not being a Catholic myself, I formed ritual family ties with several street vendors and loaned capital to these compadres (*kumpadre* or *pare* in short).[60] Once, one of my compadres had his fruit confiscated by Quezon City security personnel, and when he went to city hall to demand the return of his property, he was unexpectedly detained. His wife visited me with their baby and tearfully begged me to help, so I ended up posting bail for him.

However, relations among the street vendors were hardly harmonious; they also involved deep-seated mistrust, rivalries, and daily exchanges of insults and slander over such issues as payment of member fees, acquisition of good sales locations and street-sweeping duties. Even when their friends were serving as their loan guarantors, some vendors would skip town and return to their home province. Angry words sometimes escalated into fights in which knives were drawn. In Philcoa, intense hostilities erupted over member fees in one vendor organization. Fees collected by the leaders were basically earmarked for the payment of protection money. However, as the MMDA continued to carry out its crackdowns, members began to grow frustrated with paying fees that appeared to have no effect. The leaders explained that funds were needed for meetings and protests aimed at halting the crackdowns, but many members suspected them of pocketing the money. In response, the president of the organization threatened to have the authorities confiscate the merchandise of those who opposed them. Although this attitude incensed the members, quitting the association would increase vulnerability to a crackdown or eviction, and result in the loss of one's current selling location; therefore, most members gave up and suppressed their frustration.

As tensions grew in the association, one senior member openly criticized the president and demanded a vote of no confidence. This enraged the president, who in turn vilified this member, distributed disparaging leaflets, expelled him from the association and banned him from street vending. However, other vendors did not agree with his expulsion, and therefore proposed an election as a referendum on the association's leadership, to which the leaders agreed. Although there was support for new leadership in this election, the incumbent president was reelected thanks to her speechmaking talents and negotiating skills with the local government. However, the treasurer who had been suspected of pocketing member fees along with the president was replaced. As a result, the reelected president could no longer dip freely into the association's funds. In short, the group's members sought to address the problem by preventing the misappropriation of funds while still retaining access to the organizing and negotiating skills of the current leadership.

However, the woman who was elected as the new treasurer also diverted member fees for personal use. Because her family was about to move out of a rental unit and build a new house in Pechayan, she pocketed fees and used them to pay protection money to the local security force. Even as members harshly condemned her misconduct, they sought to settle the issue by having her resign as treasurer, not by expelling her from the association. Although she acknowledged that it was wrong to use the funds for personal purposes, she nonetheless justified it as follows:

> I have been paying the member fee every day for many years. All of our leaders up to now have used the fees we paid for their own purposes. But I have never used the fees at all. So what's wrong with my using them just this once? If I don't have a house I can't survive. (Anonymous, female, street vendor, August 5, 2004)

As the woman pointed out, some of the members who criticized her had themselves pocketed funds in the past, and this was common knowledge. Consequently, her own behavior was ultimately "forgiven," even as it drew strong reproach and dissatisfaction. Although the woman distanced herself from the group's activities for a while, she eventually began attending Christmas parties and other events as if nothing had happened. Originally a fruit vendor, she began to enjoy a thriving business when she switched to selling sausages, at which point, other vendors who had previously condemned her began to pester her for loans. Although she complained privately that they never repaid the money she had loaned them, she continued to accede to their requests.

In this way, poor people arriving from rural areas shared an impoverished, unstable livelihood and the threat of attacks by the state in the squats and streets of the city. Even as people repeatedly slandered, vilified and betrayed one another, they cultivated alliances for mutual assistance—albeit leavened by feuds and antagonisms—based on a morality that rejected threats to human survival for any reason. This solidarity provided the foundation for their resistance to the MMDA.

Resistance by the Street Vendors

Street vendors under attack by the MMDA felt compelled to respond in some way to preserve their means of livelihood. One option was to formally open shops in the public or private markets, as demanded by Fernando; however, no Philcoa street vendors did so. To rent such shops required the payment of exorbitant goodwill and rental fees, and the busy streets offered the potential of much higher sales than the markets. A second option was to look for other means of earning a living; however, few vendors were able to find a new line of work. For these reasons, most vendors continued to sell on the streets while employing a variety of strategies to deal with the harsh crackdowns by the MMDA.

This response began in July 2002, when three vendor organizations in Quezon City, Mandaluyong City and Makati City sought the assistance of Sanlakas, a left-wing political organization. That September, a "Metro Manila Vendors' Summit" was held in a chapel on the campus of the University of the Philippines under the leadership of Sanlakas and Father Robert Reyes. Attended by some 150 members of 8 vendors' organizations from various parts of Manila, the summit resulted in the founding of the Metro Manila Vendors Alliance (MMVA). The initials MMVA clearly suggested a stance in opposition to the "development" of the MMDA. The MMVA subsequently grew, and as of 2005 had been joined by 32 vendors' organizations.

Seeking a suspension of the crackdowns, the MMVA held a series of lively street demonstrations in front of the MMDA and the House of Representatives to call for negotiations; however, Fernando turned a deaf ear. Congressman Augusto Syjuco promised the MMVA that he would enact a law protecting street vendors, but quickly dropped the issue after he was criticized by English-language newspapers. A suit was brought

Photo 22 MMVA demonstration with a placard reading "Bayani, you're not a real bayani [hero]" (near the MMDA office on EDSA, October 2002).

Photo 23 Street vendors posing for a photo with a friendly MMDA employee (in front of Monumento Station, Caloocan City, August 2005).

before the judiciary, but due to the long time required to reach a court decision, this move held out little hope of rapid resolution. Therefore, in December 2002, the MMVA switched its negotiating target to local governments. They began staging demonstrations in front of various city halls and calling on mayors to ban crackdowns by the MMDA. However, none of the mayors responded to this demand.[61]

Although negotiations with the state did not go well, the street vendors enjoyed the unfamiliar experience of participating in demonstrations. Riding on jeepneys to the demonstration sites, they would laugh and exchange insults and jokes at Fernando's expense. Their protests frequently made the news, so when they saw themselves on TV or in the newspapers, they felt pride in their new visibility on the political stage. To them, the opportunity to yell "*Hayop kayo!* (You beasts!)" at the president or a cabinet member and loudly proclaim the rights of street vendors in public venues, and to have this broadcast around the country by the media, was also an occasion for salving their wounded dignity.[62] One MMVA leader proudly stated that she had gained a deeper understanding of the workings of society and politics through the process of leading these protests, and had also acquired the skills to negotiate with politicians and bureaucrats (Cion, 50s, female, MMVA leader, March 13, 2009).

However, as protests and negotiations continued with no results to show, the participants gradually lost their enthusiasm for demonstrations and increasingly came to view them as a waste of time. Walking and protesting for hours under the hot sun was exhausting, and it was negatively affecting their street vending work; therefore, they began to feel that time spent demonstrating to no effect would be better spent tending to their business. Moreover, when the street vendors were mobilized by Sanlakas to participate in demonstrations for other issues such as "against globalization," they felt as if they were being exploited while their own concerns were being ignored; this prompted feelings of alienation and antipathy.

Thus the majority of street vendors came to assign priority to "everyday forms of resistance" (Scott 1985)—that is, the routine pattern of evasion, stone throwing and bribery—over participation in the MMVA movement. When the MMDA demolished their stalls, they would continue selling their goods from carts or wooden boxes, a method that made it easier to escape the crackdowns. Although the large carts could not be moved quickly, it was feasible to haul merchandise to a safe place given sufficient prior warning. The use of wooden boxes limited the amount of merchandise one could sell at one time, but made it easy to flee quickly. Employing these tactics, the vendors engaged in a repeated cycle of running and hiding their wares whenever the MMDA made an appearance.

This evasion strategy worked much better if information about the MMDA's arrival could be obtained in advance. For this purpose, the vendors of Philcoa dispatched a teenager to the Quezon City Hall to serve as a lookout. The MMDA would clear the area in front of the city hall before moving on to Philcoa, so when the MMDA arrived at the city hall, the teenager would dash off on his bicycle to warn his comrades.

A more surefire warning system was bribing MMDA personnel or their police escorts to notify them by text message that "we're on our way now." The personnel and police assigned to the crackdowns were themselves poor people hired at very low wages, and were not at all averse to working with the street vendors, with whom they shared the same morality of survival. Besides, given that outraged vendors frequently responded by throwing rocks, it was far more sensible for the crackdown teams to take bribes and avoid a direct clash than to faithfully carry out their assigned duties. The result was the establishment of a bribery system in which money and information exchanged hands under a tacit consensus between the two sides that prioritized mutual survival.[63] As one vendor put it: "The people doing the crackdowns and the street vendors are both poor, so isn't it better for them to cooperate instead of hurting each other?" (Elma, 47, female, street vendor April 7, 2008).

Fernando finally suspended his crackdown on street vendors three months before the presidential election of 2004. Fernando reasoned that he had been unable to obtain the cooperation of mayors in Metro Manila, and that he wanted to avoid further casualties on the part of MMDA employees.[64] The general perception, however, was that Arroyo, who was seeking reelection, had ordered Fernando to suspend operations to prevent further erosion of her support among poor voters. When Arroyo was reelected, Fernando resumed the crackdown, but this time, it did not provoke the fierce clashes seen in the past. The reason for this was that MMDA personnel and the street vendors had already figured out how to "coexist." One crackdown team leader had this to say:

> At first, we behaved like new lovers, burning with passion and fighting all the time. Of course we couldn't allow street vending. But as our relationship gets longer and we get to know each other, we and the vendors have begun to avoid violence. (Anonymous, age unknown, male, MMDA Operations Team, August 26, 2005)

Thus, Fernando's ambition to rid Manila of street vendors floundered in the face of "everyday forms of resistance" by the vendors. Yet, while this resistance rescued the livelihoods of the vendors from danger, it also resulted in the reproduction of an informal basis of livelihood predicated on a bribery system, and did not contribute to the securing of legal protection for that livelihood.

Efforts to Legalize the Basis of the Poor's Livelihood

A Struggle between Conflicting Moralities

The civic and mass spheres were home to moralities with strong, mutually antagonistic perspectives on the urban governance of Manila, over which a fierce struggle ensued in the contact zone.

First, the poor who were targeted for expulsion by the MMDA sought to draw attention to their plight through demonstrations and the media. This constituted an attempt to exercise a counter-hegemonic move from the mass sphere toward the civic sphere, as well as to create a contact zone for addressing their problems. However, the moral appeal of the poor lacked sufficient power to persuade people in the civic sphere. As one NGO activist lamented, demonstrations criticizing the MMDA differed from the anti-government demonstrations of the past in that there was less participation by churchgoers, students, lawyers and other professionals (Morphy 2003, November 7, 2005, April 10).

This response, or lack of it, was a direct reflection of the effects of civic exclusivism in the civic sphere, in which the poor were not viewed as people needing help but rather as latent or actual criminals. Columnists in the English-language press portrayed residents of the squats as "professional squatters [and] members of syndicates" (Cruz 2002, April 15) and as "very enterprising and cunning fellows" (de la Rosa 2002, September 13). Likewise, Fernando himself described the street vendors as criminals in such declarations: "Most of street vendors . . . were not poor. They belong to a syndicate conducting money-making schemes"; he also claimed that a vendor shot to death by police because he fired a gun could not have been poor because he had bought a gun worth 15,000 pesos.[65] The counter-discourse of the poor was nullified by this civic exclusivist discourse, which criminalized the informal and illegal basis of their livelihood.

The experience of having earnest protestations over their plight fall on deaf ears in the civic sphere profoundly alienated the poor. Understanding from TV and other media that Fernando enjoyed powerful support from the "rich," the poor felt that "they and they alone (*sila sila lang*) can do as they please," and articulated this alienation through such remarks as: "The rich don't seem to want to see poor people on the street. They want to create a world where they can't see anyone but themselves" (Ningning, 34, female, street vendor, January 26, 2003). "The rich have cars, so they don't like it when we get in their way on the streets" (Elma, 42, female, street vendor, January 19, 2003). "The department stores will make more money if we're gone. The rich are in it together. They want to be the only ones making money; they don't like it that the poor exist" (Robina, 32, female, street vendor, January 25, 2003). "They talk about building a 'strong republic.' They want to build it all by themselves. They don't need us" (Melvin, 37, male, street vendor, January 25, 2003).

As their sense of alienation as objects of scorn denied treatment as equal human beings intensified, the poor grew disenchanted with Philippine democracy itself. In November 2002, street vendors held yet another demonstration in front of the MMDA demanding an audience with Fernando, and once again he rebuffed them. Suddenly, shouts of "We'll do EDSA [People Power] 4!" arose in the crowd and met with an uproarious response. Although this proved to be no more than a rallying cry and the vendors headed home in a mood of anger and despair, there is no doubt that the alienation they experienced when their appeals went unheard sowed the seeds for a politics of resentment.

Civic exclusivism shows a strong affinity for neoliberalism in its perception of a productive, autonomous "citizenry" as good, and its rejection of the notion that the poor are structurally disadvantaged people deserving of systemic aid. At the same time, civic exclusivism condemns self-reliant survival strategies such as illegal squatting and street vending as inappropriate for law-abiding "citizens." It demands greater self-discipline of the poor and urges them to become useful "citizens" who create wealth in the formal sector; however, this is extremely difficult to accomplish under the conditions of overwhelming inequality that extend to every corner of Philippine society. As a result, civic exclusivism exacerbates the exclusion of the poor and the fragmentation of society, and thereby risks igniting an explosion of resentment in the mass sphere.

Yet, the moralities of the civic and mass spheres are not mutually exclusive on every point, and share some common values over the issue of urban governance. First, they share a belief that everyone, whether rich or poor, should be equal before the law. Second, they are united in condemning politicians who skirt the law in order to enrich themselves. Furthermore, even though they are not in the majority, some in the civic sphere are concerned for the lives of the poor, and some in the mass sphere express sympathy with the goal of improving Manila through discipline. In these areas, one can see room to mediate the moral friction between the two spheres.

Mediating between Legalism and Squatting

Before Fernando initiated his attacks on the poor, there was in fact a practice of civic inclusivism in place with the potential to mediate between the discipline and legalism advocated in the civic sphere and the livelihoods of the poor supported in the mass sphere. Through their lobbying activities, several NGOs sought to legalize the poor's bases of livelihood. If this effort had succeeded, the poor, too, could have become law-abiding "citizens." In their appeals to the mass sphere, these NGOs attempted to persuade squatters and street vendors that legalizing their bases of livelihood was a more effective long-term solution than continuing to rely on the bribery system. To the civic sphere, they argued that legalizing the poor's bases of livelihood and getting them to buy into the legal system would solve a variety of urban problems.

Let us examine this effort first in the context of the movement associated with informal settlers.[66] Early in the Aquino administration, forces in the social movement that had spearheaded democratization succeeded in having sections promising "urban land reform" included in the 1987 Constitution (Article XIII, Social Justice and Human Rights).[67] However, these were not radical provisions for the redistribution of land, but rather a commitment to "make available at affordable cost decent housing and basic services to underprivileged and homeless citizens" (Article XIII Section 9) along with stipulations that "[u]rban or rural poor dwellers shall not be evicted nor their dwellings demolished, except in accordance with law," and that "[n]o resettlement of urban or rural dwellers shall be undertaken without adequate consultation" (Article XIII Section 10). Leaders from the Catholic Church, big business and academic institutions formed the Bishops-Businessmen's Conference (BBC) to push for legislation to implement these constitutional provisions, and launched a movement to make them law. In 1987, the BBC joined forces with the Presidential Commission for the Urban Poor to draft a bill and began lobbying to get the law passed. Many NGOs and people's organizations participated in this effort.[68] However, the bill failed to make headway as the issue of urban land reform got pushed aside by such crises as frequent *coup d'état* attempts and the closure of US military bases during the Aquino administration.[69]

What transformed this situation was the forced eviction of about 100 households in the Sitio Kumunoy squatters' settlement by the Quezon City government in September 1990. Cardinal Sin denounced the evictions as unjust and immoral and exerted intense pressure on members of Congress to pass urban land reform legislation.[70] In response, the House Committee on Housing and Urban Development drafted a bill. On March 9, 1991, representatives of government agencies, NGOs and peoples' organizations gathered at the Institute on Church and Social Issues at Ateneo de Manila University to deliberate on the draft. When the NGOs and peoples' organizations found flaws in the draft, they formed an Urban Land Reform Task Force and launched a more aggressive lobbying effort. In the House of Representatives, members of peoples' organizations packed the visitors' gallery and pressed members of Congress to pass the law. On March 24, 1992, President Aquino signed the Urban Development and Housing Act, making it law.[71]

Magadia (2003: 106–7, 110–1) cites the following factors as contributing to the passage of this bill: it was not perceived as a threat by congressmen with their power base in the provinces and senators elected by a national constituency; there were supporters of the bill in the Aquino administration; Cardinal Sin actively supported it; and there were few powerful opponents. Granted, the bill was not entirely without opponents, one being the Chamber of Real Estate and Builders' Associations, which represents developers. However, some BBC members were associated with the Chamber, and were able to broker a compromise (Carroll 1998: 128).

The Urban Development and Housing Act established legal procedures and a three-year grace period for forced evictions of informal settlers by the state. It stipulated that there were to be adequate consultations on relocation,[72] and also mandated a Community Mortgage Program through which informal settlers could obtain low-interest loans with which to formally purchase land.[73] However, those who were able to acquire land through this program amounted to fewer than five per cent of the informal settler families in Manila.[74] Moreover, as Manila land prices soared, local governments stood to collect more tax revenues by selling public land to private developers for commercial purposes. As a result, they took an uncooperative, even hostile stance toward squatters' movements seeking transfers of land (Shatkin 1999, 2000, 2002). Meanwhile the local governments and the MMDA repeatedly defied the provisions of the law, arbitrarily carrying out forced evictions without providing alternative relocation sites.

Peoples' organizations were expected to play a central role in the Community Mortgage Program under the guidance of NGOs and government agencies. As Shatkin has pointed out, this was a clear reflection of the neoliberal view that residents' services should be provided by the private sector and civil society as opposed to the state (Shatkin 1999: 35). As Berner and Seki have noted, the Community Mortgage Program created a division between those who repaid their loans in full and became landowners, and those who were unable to make the payments and remained squatters (Berner 1997: 175–9; Seki 2010). Seki analyzes this phenomenon as a consequence of neoliberal governance that foments a split between "citizens" who succeed at exercising self-discipline and "non-citizens" who fail to do so. While the Urban Development and Housing Act was an epochal experiment, it was unable to turn all squatters into "citizens."

Mediating between Legalism and Street Vending

Next, let us look at a movement that has attempted to resolve the conflict between legalism and street vending. This movement was initiated by the

Informal Sector Committee of the Bishops-Businessmen's Conference, which lobbied for the issuance of a street vendor protection order as part of the anti-poverty "Social Reform Agenda" of the Ramos administration.[75] The aim was to create a legal framework that would formally establish the rights of street vendors. To achieve this objective more quickly, the committee pursued the enactment of an Executive Order, which would take effect with the signatures of the president and cabinet, instead of a Republic Act, which would require passage by Congress.

In 1996, Ramos set up an Inter-Agency Task Force as proposed by the Informal Sector Committee of the BBC.[76] Based on the deliberations of the Task Force, Executive Order No. 452, "Providing for the guidelines that will ensure the security of registered vendors in the workplace," was issued in October 1997. The Executive Order mandated every local government to create an Inter-Agency Council in which vendors' organizations would be represented, to enact ordinances pursuant to the EO, designate workplaces, issue business permits and prohibit unwarranted demolitions. The order thus attempted to legalize street vending in designated areas by establishing a system under which vendors throughout the country would register with local governments.

Recognizing that a nationwide alliance of informal sector representatives was needed for negotiations with the government, in December 1997, the Informal Sector Committee established the Council of Workers in the Informal Sector (Kalipunan ng Maraming Tinig ng Manggagawang Impormal, or Ka-Tinig) with members from 48 vendors' organizations.[77] Ka-Tinig subsequently expanded its network to include organizations in provincial cities, not only Manila. One leader of a vendors' organization explained her incentive to join Ka-Tinig as stemming from a desire to improve the uncertain status quo, under which crackdowns continued despite the payment of bribes and new agreements had to be struck with each new mayor.[78]

The next objective for Ka-Tinig was to get the central government to establish "implementing rules and regulations" for Executive Order No. 452. Lobbying efforts to this end had reached an impasse due to poor relations with the Estrada administration, but resumed after Estrada's ouster in January 2001.[79] In late April 2001, President Arroyo, feeling threatened by People Power 3, saw the codification of these rules and regulations as a means of placating the poor, and thus convened an Inter-Agency Council to undertake this task immediately.[80] Actually, a draft of the rules and regulations had already been completed toward the end of the Ramos administration in March 1998. However, deliberations on the draft halted when the head of the MMDA Traffic Discipline Office at the time objected to the granting of permission to sell on streets and sidewalks and the temporary suspension of street vendor evictions. These two issues once again became points of contention between Ka-Tinig and the MMDA; however, this time, they worked out a compromise. First, vending would be prohibited along major thoroughfares, but permitted in all other designated areas. Second, forced evictions would be temporarily suspended while the selection of designated vending areas was still ongoing. These compromises paved the way for the establishment in June 2001 of rules and regulations for the implementation of Executive Order No. 452.

With these rules and regulations in hand, Ka-Tinig next approached various local governments and requested that they enact ordinances for the "designation of workplaces for vending, assignment of vending space, issuance of business permits, responsibilities of registered vendors, and security in the workplace." However, nearly all of the local governments ignored these requests.[81] The reason, one may surmise, is that these governments included vested interests, ranging from street-level officials in charge of markets and security to higher officials who enjoyed benefits from the bribery system. In other words, the bribery system that informally guaranteed the livelihoods of the street vendors also served, ironically, as a structural barrier to the formalization of street vending. As I have argued, the agency of the poor in establishing an informal order that encroaches upon the elite-dominated order simultaneously impedes their efforts to secure a stable income under the formal order (Kusaka 2010).

What is more, it was while this movement was at an impasse at the local level that the MMDA, under Fernando's chairmanship since 2002, asserted that Executive Order No. 452 was itself invalid and began carrying out severe crackdowns. In response, vendors' organizations in various locales withdrew from Ka-Tinig, which continued to lobby local governments, and shifted the focus of their activities to participation in the protest demonstrations led by Sanlakas. Meanwhile, as the vendors expanded and reinforced the bribery system by buying off low-ranking MMDA personnel, they abandoned the effort to formalize street vending, which reverted to its existence as part of the informal sector. Moreover, the informal situation encourages negative public discourse about street vendors, which can make demolitions appear entirely legitimate. Despite the attempts of Ka-Tinig to mediate the moral clash between legalism and the street vendors' livelihoods by institutionalizing street vending, that effort ultimately failed.

An informal order safeguards the lives of the poor, but their attempts to break away from that order have been stymied by civic exclusivism and disciplinary governance. Hence, the conflict between the legalism espoused in the civic sphere and the values of survival and dignity supported in the mass sphere remains unresolved to this day.

CHAPTER 6

The Revival of Moral Nationalism

Photo 24 Aquino supporters making the "L" sign (for laban, meaning "fight"), the symbol of People Power 1 with their fingers at Benigno Aquino III's final speech of the 2010 election campaign (Quezon Memorial Park, May 2010; photo by Saya Kiba).

As we have seen thus far in our examination of People Power, electoral politics, and urban governance, a pronounced moral division of the nation developed from 1998 on. This was one of the paradoxical consequences that counter-hegemonies unleashed from the desire for change against the traditional elite produced. In the mass sphere, the resonance of populism and a morality in support of livelihood and dignity led to the emergence of a moral antagonism between righteous, oppressed "poor people" and the heartless, self-serving "rich." In the civic sphere, on the other hand, the hegemony of civic exclusivism produced a moral antagonism between law-abiding "citizens" who participated in politics "correctly" and "masses" who support "bad" leaders and damage the rule of law due to lack in civic morals. Although various attempts were made in the contact zone to ameliorate this moral division of the nation, they cannot be said to have achieved substantive results. However, a significant easing of the division did occur during the period from the beginning of the second Arroyo administration in 2004 to Benigno Aquino III's administration via the 2010 presidential election.

This development has yet to be adequately explained. Quimpo (2010) conceptualized the Estrada and Arroyo administrations as "predatory regimes" that differed from the "clientelist regimes" of the past by highlighting their predatory character.[1] However, the only characteristics distinguishing a predatory from a clientelist regime appear to be the personal temperament and degree of corruption of the president, making the effectiveness of this distinction as an analytical concept questionable. If this new type of regime actually appeared, the changes in the power bases through which Estrada and Arroyo obtained legitimacy from society must be clarified.

On the other hand, Thompson (2010) explained changes in post-democratization Philippine politics in terms of its passage through a cycle of "reformism," "populism" and "neo-traditionalism."[2] First, Corazon Aquino practiced a reformism that opposed the corruption of Marcos and staked its appeal on moral grounds, and Ramos continued in this vein. However, this reformism was unable to solve the problems of poverty and inequality, setting the stage for the populism of Estrada, who pursued direct ties with the poor. In reaction to this populism, Arroyo employed money and violence to sever the ties between Estrada and the poor, practicing a form of neo-traditionalism that re-concentrated power in the hands of the previously loosened clientelist networks.[3] The extreme corruption that accompanied this neo-traditionalism then begat a revival of reformism under Aquino III.

However, some aspects of Thompson's argument remain problematic. First, the counter-hegemonic practices in the name of "reform" in the Philippines were far more diverse and contested than the reformism he describes. The hegemonic practices of moral nationalism, civic inclusivism and civic exclusivism I have discussed all compete in calling for "reform" of the existing political order, yet they vary widely in their influence on the political process, depending on which among them achieves hegemony. Second, Thompson treats change exclusively in terms of a predetermined cycle, ignoring how the political process has evolved in contingent ways due to unforeseen events. Therefore, in this chapter, I will focus on the occurrence of a contingent struggle for hegemony to explain the transformation in moral antagonism that occurred from the second Arroyo administration up to the 2010 election.

Corruption and Violence in the Arroyo Administration

Arroyo's Corruption and Maintenance of Power

Arroyo did not initially adopt the neo-traditionalist stance posited by Thompson, but she did attempt to garner support from civil society in a variety of ways. Because the middle-class-led People Power 2 had paved the way for Arroyo's assumption of the presidency, she first attempted to solidify the support of the civic sphere. In her inaugural speech as president, she pledged to achieve good governance by improving morality in government and society, putting an end to politics based on personality and patronage, and carrying out genuine reforms through a new politics based on party policy.[4] Her speech was peppered with such words as "new politics," "good governance," "ethic of effective implementation," "transparency," "entrepreneurial spirit" and "safety net." She also voiced intentions to tackle the poverty problem, appointing leaders from the NGO sector to key posts in her administration. Thus, Arroyo's initial appeals were generally in line with civic inclusivism.

Moreover, Arroyo started aggressively appealing to the mass sphere in May 2001 after People Power 3, which she took as a serious threat from the impoverished class, and adopted populism as a strategy for placating the angry poor. Utilizing the media to saturate the nation with images of herself interacting with the poor in urban slums and rural villages, she cultivated a new, poor-friendly identity as *Ate Glo* (Sister Gloria) or *Gloria labandera* (Gloria the laundress). At the same time, she doled out a variety of services to the poor, including Philippine Health Insurance (PhilHealth) cards, land transfers by presidential proclamation and employment opportunities. However, this "just folks" image did not jibe with Arroyo's elite background, and she was unable to take a truly confrontational stance against the elite or the wealthy class. As a result, she failed to win the support of the poor.

Arroyo next declared, in a State of the Nation Address (SONA) in July 2002, that she would strive to achieve a "strong republic," thus laying claim to a new image as a strong female leader. According to Arroyo, a "strong republic" was one that stood for the interests of the people over class and sectoral interests, that would execute good policy and deliver essential services through strong institutions and a strong bureaucracy, and that was indispensable to the achievement of economic development, social reform and victory over poverty. This represented an attempt to respond to the demands of both the civic sphere, which sought modern political reform, and the mass sphere, which sought a solution to poverty. However, the Arroyo administration became mired in political corruption without achieving any of these aims.

First, suspicions of misconduct by Arroyo in the 2004 presidential election surfaced in quick succession. She drew particularly strong condemnation for an incident involving a request to rig vote tallies that she allegedly made to the Commission on Elections (Comelec).[5] In June 2005, a tape of a wiretapped telephone conversation was made public, prompting ten cabinet members and top bureaucrats to resign in protest against Arroyo as elements of civic inclusivism cut their ties with the administration.[6] Although a motion for impeachment was filed in the House of Representatives, it was blocked by Arroyo's allies, who were in the majority.[7] This was followed by a series of revelations of corruption by Arroyo herself and by members of her family. Suspicions arose that her husband and her son, a congressman, had received payoffs of protection money from operators of *jueteng*, a form of illegal gambling popular with the poor.[8] There were also allegations of bid rigging on procurement of voting machines and public works projects such as Terminal 3 at the Manila Airport. Accusations that Arroyo's husband had improperly intervened in the bidding process for the National Broadband Network project and had received large bribes from the Chinese ZTE Corporation incurred a particularly vehement national backlash.[9]

The Arroyo administration was also marked by a period of extreme violence. Leaders of farmers' and workers' groups associated with Bayan Muna were assassinated one after the other. The involvement of the Philippine armed forces was suspected in the killings, which exceeded 1,000 victims. Since 2001, several Bayan Muna candidates were successfully elected to Congress under the party-list system. The armed forces perceived this as a threat, alleging that Bayan Muna is the legal wing of the CCP which continues to engage in armed struggle through the New People's Army and sought to destroy the organizational base of the CPP's legal arm through assassinations. Arroyo, who depended on the armed forces as her power base, essentially gave tacit approval to these human rights violations. Then, in November 2009, the public was shocked by a massacre in Maguindanao province, on the island of Mindanao, where the private army of one of the local elite families killed 57 rival family members and accompanying journalists. Behind this incident was a competition between these elites for control of the region's high concentration of development interests, which attracted foreign investment, official development assistance and public works money. Arroyo made a show of investigating the massacre, even going so far as to declare martial law in the province, but she herself had dispensed privileges to the perpetrating family and enlisted its help in rigging elections.

Economically, the Philippines generally appeared healthy under the Arroyo administration, posting a 7.3 per cent GDP growth rate in 2007; however, this positive trend was not felt in all corners of society. The nation's Gini coefficient, which indicates income disparity, increased from 0.4021 in 2003 to 0.4484 in 2009. A spike in the price of rice in 2008 made life more difficult for the poor. Because the Philippines relied on imports for some 10 to 20 per cent of the rice it consumed, an increase in international rice prices triggered a 50 to 100 per cent leap in domestic market retail prices. Poor people formed long lines in the hot sun at outlets selling less expensive government-subsidized rice. Most of the poor complained that prices of goods had risen under the Arroyo administration.

Yet, in spite of these incidents and her forfeiture of moral legitimacy, Arroyo managed to remain president for ten years—four as successor to the previous administration and six after being elected on her own. What sustained her presidency was her success in retaining the support of the top brass of the armed forces and members of the Lower House through her power over personnel management and the distribution of state resources. Arroyo secured the loyalty of officers who had helped put her in power by appointing them to important posts and suppressed elements attempting to undermine her administration. She also retained the support of a majority of members of the Lower House by exercising her authority over their pork barrel budgetary allocations, which required the president's signature. As a result, she was able to use her allies in the Lower House to block the motions for her impeachment submitted to Congress nearly every year by opposition-party legislators.[10] However, Arroyo's governance did salient damage to the democratic system and angered much of the country.[11]

The Failure of the Movement to Oust Arroyo

The Arroyo administration's loss of moral legitimacy could be seen in surveys of public satisfaction with the president. When suggestions of electoral fraud came to light in 2005, satisfaction with Arroyo plunged (see Figure 3). Her disapproval ratings stood out in comparison with those of every president since the advent of democratization. Even in the period just before Estrada was ousted over a scandal, his approval ratings exceeded his disapproval ratings. However, during the second term of the Arroyo administration, disapproval of Arroyo always exceeded approval. It might be said that Arroyo had become an "enemy of the nation" despised by people from every social class. Riding on this national sentiment, the left mounted demonstrations demanding Arroyo's resignation, and junior officers in the armed forces who were frustrated with the administration attempted a series of unsuccessful coups.

As early as 2003, toward the end of the first Arroyo administration, some 321 soldiers led by a group of junior officers known as the "Magdalo group" occupied a hotel in Makati, denounced the corruption of the Arroyo administration and senior officers in the armed forces, and called on the nation to launch a new People Power movement to oust Arroyo.[12] In the end, the rebels failed to mobilize significant support and were persuaded to surrender after one day. However, they were not entirely

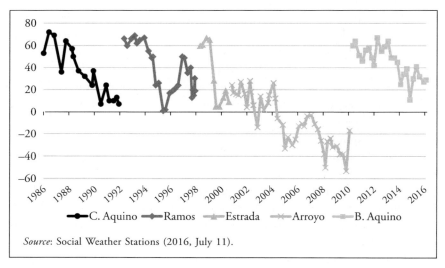

Figure 3 Net Satisfaction Ratings of Presidents of the Philippines

without public support. In the mid-term election of May 2007, Navy Lieutenant Antonio Trillanes IV, who had served as press spokesman for the rebels, won a seat in the Senate by campaigning from his prison cell. Former Senator Gregorio Honasan, who was suspected of involvement in the attempted coup, also won reelection. Thus, more than a few voters showed their support for rebels who had exposed the corruption of the Arroyo administration, but did so through the polls as opposed to street demonstrations.

In July 2005, a demonstration protesting election rigging took place in the Makati business district, with nearly 10,000 people calling on Arroyo to resign. Participants included former President Corazon Aquino and the Makati Business Club.[13] More large demonstrations demanding Arroyo's resignation followed. Although Arroyo attempted to quell these banned demonstrations without permits, they continued unabated in cities like Makati, where the mayor, Binay, belonged to the anti-Arroyo camp.

Tensions ran particularly high in February 2006, when a ceremony commemorating the "20th Anniversary of the People Power Revolution" was scheduled. Early on, anti-Arroyo forces had planned a large anti-government rally to coincide with the ceremony on February 25; several thousand people were expected to attend. A group of junior officers in the armed forces planned to use this opportunity to defect from the government in order to demonstrate their dissatisfaction with Arroyo. However, Arroyo learned of the plan in advance and, citing a "clear and present danger to our republic," declared a state of emergency a day before the scheduled rally, forcibly dispersed the protesters and arrested leftist legislators and activists. She also issued an arrest warrant for Senator Honasan, the former military man who was an influence on the junior officers. In response, a group of officers appealed to the public via the media at a protest on the night of February 26, calling once again for the ouster of Arroyo. However, as before, the government was able to exercise its powers of persuasion to quell the uprising before the night was over, and the state of emergency was lifted a week later.

Still, this did not put an end to the actions of anti-Arroyo forces. The following year, at the end of November 2007, Senator Trillanes, who was still under detention, walked out of the Makati Regional Trial Court, where he had been brought for a trial appearance, holed up in the Peninsula Hotel with some opposition politicians and left-wing activists, and demanded Arroyo's immediate resignation. Although the group called on the public to mount demonstrations, in the end, they were forced to surrender when a new People Power failed to rise up and the military stormed the hotel.

Photo 25 A left-wing demonstration calling for the ouster of Arroyo, along with slogans such as "Awaken the nation's conscience!" and "Replace the rotten system!" (España Boulevard, Manila, August 2005).

Then, in late February 2008, allegations of corruption in the National Broadband Network project sparked a rally in Makati attended by tens of thousands of people, including former presidents Corazon Aquino and Estrada. Once again, calls were issued for Arroyo's resignation, but once again, the protests failed to grow into a new People Power.

Considering their intense dissatisfaction with the Arroyo administration, why did people not respond to repeated exhortations to launch another People Power by taking to the streets to demand the president's resignation, as they had done before? As a possible explanation, Thompson (2010: 34) cites the lack of defections by the armed forces, whose top brass had been effectively co-opted by Arroyo, and the passive stance toward political involvement taken by the Catholic Church after the death of Cardinal Sin in 2005. Abinales (2008) cites the loss of mobilizing power by elements seeking moderate social reform since the 1990s as they became integrated into the governing establishment. However, these explanations focus only on the mobilizing side. Doronila (2007) asserts that "People Power fatigue" spread among the public as many began to question whether People Power was capable of transforming society, quipping that "EDSA (People Power) has become a national yawn."[14] Yet, Doronila also fails to explain why this "People Power fatigue" transcended sharp class divisions to be shared by the public at large. Let us now take a look at the discourses that prevailed at the time in the civic and mass spheres.

An "Enemy of the People" Transcending Class Divisions

Backlash in the Civic Sphere

The backlash against the corruption and violence of the Arroyo administration intensified a moral nationalism that viewed Arroyo as an "enemy of the people". It also enhanced a collective identity as "we = the people or nation" in opposition to the administration's corruption, an identity that ameliorated the moral division of the nation.

The middle class, which had placed Arroyo in the presidency via People Power 2, had expected her to put an end to political corruption and enact substantive political reforms. However, these expectations were thoroughly betrayed, triggering discontent and remorse over Arroyo in the civic sphere, which can be seen in the following comments: "The elite and the middle class hated Estrada's bad habits like drinking, gambling, ladies. They thought Erap was very sinful. But Arroyo was even more rotten" (Fred, 57, male, former bank manager, April 19, 2008). "GMA [Arroyo] exceeded Erap's corruption. Plus, she was more sophisticated than Erap." (Luie, 43, male, lawyer, April 16, 2008). A man who had actively participated in both the anti-Marcos student movement and People Power 2 discussed his regrets as follows:

> I played a major part [in People Power 2] actually. I introduced [the moderate left-wing party-list group] Akbayan to GMA. I raised funds and solicited for rallies, prepared food and brought it to EDSA. I even directed demonstrators near the Mendiola Bridge. I was active because I didn't like the Erap administration. At the time, corruption

was spreading because of Estrada, and Malacañang Palace was filthy. A president shouldn't be drunk all the time. But I lost my faith in the Arroyo administration. Arroyo is rotten to the core. She betrayed us. (Joji, 63, male, former business owner, April 20, 2008)

Yet, even as the middle class displayed a certain degree of sympathy with the coup attempts by officers of the armed forces, it was critical of coups as the means to an end due to the high risk of political instability that such actions incurred:

> The mutiny was a valid grievance of a dysfunctional system. They were forced to take extra-legal measures because the system was not working. But extra-legal measures are not a good way to improve the system. Extra-legal measures destroy things, and thus defeat the purpose of improving systems. (Edward, 50, male, employed at a foreign corporation, April 19, 2008)

Negative opinions were also expressed about calls for a renewal of People Power without solid future prospects, when there was no clear alternative to the president:

> Right now the middle class is in a situation that they are not supportive of efforts to remove the president through People Power. They see that there is no viable alternative, unlike EDSA 1 when there was a clear alternative. But now who is expected to lead? It is easy to bring down a president, but it's more difficult to let somebody succeed. It is not clear who will take over, and I think their feeling is "let's wait for the election". That's why many issues come out but people are not going in the streets. (Bert, 50, male, employed at a foreign corporation, February 15, 2009)

Behind this uncertainty about what sort of administration would replace Arroyo's was the fact that each of the diverse forces calling for Arroyo's resignation, ranging from army rebels to leftist groups, had their own agenda. In addition, if People Power succeeded and the president resigned, the next in line was supposed to be the vice president. However, Vice President Noli de Castro was a former newscaster whom Arroyo had picked as her running mate in the 2004 election to attract the votes of the poor. Although he enjoyed some support among the poor, the middle class had doubts about his ability to govern.

Furthermore, people had already lost faith in People Power as a means of effecting political and social change:

I have mixed feelings about changing Gloria. There is a question in my mind, who will be replacing her. It's already the third time to have People Power, but nothing's happening in the country. Maybe that's another reason why we didn't go there. We're all tired, every time something would happen in the government, we go to the streets. Nothing will happen. (Joey, 37, male, employed at a foreign corporation, February 15, 2009)

All the People Power was a big joke. People Power 1: economy go down; People Power 2: economy go down; [People Power] 3: go down. In the end, who suffers? The country and the people. Who benefits? The one who is in power. Every time there is a People Power anniversary, I think that's bullshit. If we don't have People Power, we might have been bigger than Malaysia or Thailand. (Knox, 35, male, advertising agent, March 6, 2009)

Judging from the experience of previous People Powers, it is true that forcing a change in presidents through street demonstrations has proven to be no guarantee of a better future for the Philippines: "People Power has happened so many times, but there hasn't been any improvement in the country. It has lost its meaning." (Ellen, 42, female, employee of Asian Development Bank, March 11, 2009).

For these reasons, the middle class of the civic sphere did not take to the streets, even as its antipathy toward Arroyo grew. By the time I conducted my interviews in 2008 and 2009, people were no longer talking about People Power, but rather about the need to wait for the opportunity offered by the upcoming election in 2010.

Backlash in the Mass Sphere

Meanwhile, the poor had felt an intense antipathy toward Arroyo from the outset because she had ousted Estrada, the president they supported. Although Arroyo tried different gambits to win the support of the poor, she failed. The poor found both her speech and behavior off-putting. In Pechayan, it was popular to make an insulting pun out of her middle name, Macapagal: *Ang kapal ni Arroyo* ("thick-faced Arroyo"). In Tagalog, *makapal* ("thick-faced") connotes "shameless"; to people in Pechayan, Arroyo's haughty, self-righteous demeanor in the face of countless scandals was "shameless," "thick-faced," and "arrogant."

The poor viewed the "rich" as having committed a grievous error by allowing themselves to be swept up in the mood of the moment, ousting Estrada and elevating Arroyo to the presidency without serious thought. Then, as more revelations of corruption in the Arroyo administration came to light, those who had faithfully supported Estrada became more convinced than ever that they were in the right. "The rich are opportunists (*balingbing*). They have no convictions. They used to support Arroyo, but now they're yelling against her" (Sobet, 39, female, housewife, April 2, 2008). "They're just opportunists. Look at what's happening now. They're sorry they installed Arroyo. She has made us suffer so much" (Pak, 54, female, newspaper vendor, April 1, 2008).

Unlike the civic sphere, the mass sphere was home to considerable support for the coup attempts by Trillanes and other young officers, viewing them as courageous acts in which the perpetrators risked their lives for the sake of the country: "I respect Trillanes. He really showed he was unafraid of anything, didn't he?" (Boboy, 37, male, unemployed, April 1, 2008). "I'm proud of what he did. He didn't act out of self-interest. He saw the evildoers in the government and the armed forces and it pained his conscience" (Niño, 28, male, unemployed, April 1, 2008). "Even though he worked for the government, he didn't care if he got fired. He's a hero" (Amy, 25, female, street vendor, April 4, 2008). "Trillanes did what he did for the good of the Philippine people. But Arroyo was afraid of him, so she threw him in jail" (Gloria, 47, female, street vendor, April 4, 2008). The extent of this support for the rebel officers was demonstrated by Trillanes's election to the Senate in 2007. One street vendor explained why she voted for him as follows:

> Trillanes is my idol. I voted for him and Honasan because I support people who fight for what is right. If we don't fight, those people in government will do whatever they please. (Villa, 57, female, street vendor, April 4, 2008)

Many people in the mass sphere similarly expressed active support for the ouster of Arroyo via People Power. "If only People Power would happen. Arroyo's government is rotten to the core. She should be doing all she can for the poor, but she's only in cahoots with the rich" (James, 22, male, unemployed, March 10, 2009). "Arroyo has to go. We should kick her out. The government is a mess" (Nelson, 43, male, janitor; March 17, 2008).

However, in actuality, these same people did not respond to calls for People Power. They believed that it would be difficult to remove Arroyo, since the armed forces had not withdrawn their support. "We can't get rid of Arroyo. The military is on Gloria's side. She keeps a tight rein on them and the police" (May Anne, 35, female, housewife, March 12, 2009). "Right now the government has everyone under its thumb, so People

Power is impossible. The military, the bureaucrats, everyone is eating out of Arroyo's hand. People Power can happen only when people inside the government switch sides" (Mely, 69, female, street vendor, March 12, 2009). People in the mass sphere also shared the concern articulated in the civic sphere that there was no viable alternative to Arroyo in sight. "I can understand why people are calling on Arroyo to quit, what with all the political scandals that have come to light. The only problem is, who will replace her?" (Taba, 40, female, general-store proprietor, April 9, 2008).

Thus, in the mass sphere as well, the majority of people I interviewed in 2008 and 2009 were of the view that it would be wiser to wait for the next presidential election in 2010 than to resort to People Power or a coup d'état:

> It's clear that there's corruption in the current administration. The president is tiny, but she's tough. Now that she's almost at the end of her term, it's better to wait for the election. But if she runs again, or the election is suspended, then it would be fine to have People Power. It would be for the good of the whole country. (Imelda, 43, female, snack-food factory worker, March 10, 2009)

In this way, despite some endorsements of regime change by extra-constitutional means such as People Power or a coup, doubts as to the feasibility of this approach led most people in the mass sphere to consider it preferable to wait for the 2010 election. Thus, with both the civic and mass spheres sharing this perception of Arroyo as an enemy of the nation transcending class divisions, the moral division of the nation grew less clear-cut and began to recede.

Morality versus Poverty as Issues in a Presidential Election

Electoral Issues

Although nine candidates ran in the presidential election of 2010, the race was essentially among the following four: Senator Benigno Aquino III of the Liberal Party, Senator Manuel Villar of the Nationalist Party, former President Joseph Estrada of Pwersa ng Masang Pilipino (Force of the Filipino Masses),[15] and former Defense Secretary Gilberto Teodoro of the ruling Lakas–Christian Muslim Democrats. Aquino and Villar engaged in a fierce campaign battle early on, but Aquino ultimately won in a landslide, with Estrada managing to come in second (see Table 19).

Table 19 2010 Presidential Election Results (Top Four Candidates Only)

Candidate	No. of votes	% of votes
Benigno Aquino III (Liberal Party)	15,208,678	41.87
Joseph Estrada (Pwersa ng Masang Pilipino)	9,487,837	26.12
Manuel Villar (Nationalist Party)	5,573,835	15.35
Gilberto Teodoro (Lakas)	4,095,839	11.28

Source: *Philippine Daily Inquirer* (2010, June 9).

Although the battle between Aquino and Villar might appear at first glance to signify a revival of the pre-martial law rivalry between their two parties, Liberal and Nationalist, in reality, this was not the case. It simply happened that the two candidates who belonged to the two oldest parties led in the opinion polls, prompting legislators to switch their party affiliations so as to jump on a winning bandwagon before the election. As Teodoro, the candidate of the incumbent party, languished far down in the polls, more legislators left Lakas to join either Aquino's Liberal Party or Villar's Nationalist Party. Thus, the campaign was a struggle, not between parties with strong organizations, but between factional networks affiliated with Aquino and Villar that had emerged under a party system in flux.

Consequently, it is difficult to discern any clear differences in ideology or policy among these parties. However, remarks by the respective candidates point to certain positions staked out during the campaign. Aquino espoused a moral nationalism that would fight corruption with "morality," while Villar and Estrada assumed the mantle of populism, promising to solve poverty by treating the poor with "compassion." Teodoro ran on a know-how platform, citing his resume of graduating from the University of the Philippines and Harvard University and taking first place in his bar exams as evidence that he had the "ability" to make the Philippines grow. Aquino's victory resulted from the hegemony attained by "morality" as an issue.

As mentioned earlier, Thompson (2010) explains the 2010 presidential elections in terms of an established political cycle according to which Arroyo's neo-traditionalism invited a moral backlash from the people, thereby setting up a victory for Aquino's reformism. However, in reality, it is more accurate to describe this process in terms of a competition between two different moralities raised in opposition to the corrupt politics of Arroyo: the moral nationalism of Aquino versus the populism of Villar and Estrada. The outcome of this battle between moral nationalism and populism was not predestined, but contingent. Let us now examine more closely the most intense point of contention in the election campaign: the hegemonic struggle between the moral nationalism of Aquino and the populism of Villar.

A Longing for Morality in the Face of Corruption

Aquino, also known by the nickname "Noynoy," had up to that point served as a congressman (1998 to 2007) and a senator (2007 to 2010). His father, Benigno "Ninoy" Aquino Jr., was the former senator who was assassinated during the Marcos regime, and his mother, Corazon "Cory" Aquino, was the former president who had been born into a major landowning family. Noynoy Aquino did not initially plan to run for president, but his mother's death on August 1, 2009, prompted a sudden surge of expectations and support for her son. According to a popularity poll of presidential candidates conducted by the Social Weather Stations (SWS) organization in September 2009, Aquino leapt to first place with a 60 per cent approval rating despite not having appeared in previous surveys (see Figure 5). Thus, a contingent occurrence just before the election campaign —the death of his mother, Corazon Aquino, who had been battling cancer—was a determining factor in both his candidacy and his victory.

When Corazon Aquino's casket was brought to Manila Cathedral on August 3, 2009, tens of thousands of people wearing yellow, the Aquino "family color," stood in line in the rain from dawn until late into the night. That day's edition of the *Inquirer* bore the headline, "Rich, Poor Come for Cory".[16] Her funeral, on August 5, was broadcast live throughout the country. Due to the throngs lining the route from the cathedral, the funeral procession took nine hours to reach the cemetery. The mourning of Corazon Aquino by so many people recalled the funeral of her assassinated husband during the Marcos regime, as well as the subsequent People Power movement for democratization. The conflation of the politics of Arroyo with that of Marcos further inspired people to invest the same hopes for reform they had previously held for People Power in the eldest son of the Aquinos, who were revered as pillars of moral virtue.[17]

Photo 26 Banners supporting Noynoy Aquino (EDSA, March 2010).

A patchwork of elements supported the Aquino campaign, among them, the elite Aquino-Cojuangco clan, moderate leftist groups like Akbayan, the Catholic Church and big business. This broad array of forces shared a sense of crisis about the politics of Arroyo as well as a fear of the populism of Villar and Estrada. That even Akbayan would actively support a scion of the oligarchic elite like Aquino reflected the hegemony of a moral nationalism calling for solidarity to encompass the elements of civic inclusivism.[18] Due to the hastiness of Aquino's declaration of candidacy, there was insufficient time for adequate preparation for the election campaign. Consequently, the Aquino camp relied not only on local Liberal Party elites, but also on networks of local NGOs and business groups to launch his campaign nationwide.

The Aquino campaign contrasted the Aquino family with Arroyo in dualistic terms of light versus dark, good versus evil, love versus hate, etc., framing the election as an opportunity for the world to emerge from darkness into light—that is, from the corrupt, self-aggrandizing politics of the Arroyo administration to a politics of moral virtue and service to others.[19] Moreover, the agent of this transformation would be a unified "people" transcending class, religion and all other divisions. The Aquino camp reintroduced the slogan *Hindi ka nag-iisa* ("You are not alone") that people had chanted after the assassination of Benigno Aquino Jr., and called on the nation to join together once again in a show of People Power to drive the bad elements out of the government, this time through votes instead of street demonstrations.

A music video of "You Are Not Alone," the Aquino campaign song, offered images of the "people" to whom the campaign appealed as the agent of change. In the video, the nation's people, led by Aquino, join together to retrieve the light and to free themselves from a dark, isolated state. It begins with a woman singing alone in the darkness. Another young girl then passes a single torch to Aquino, and the flames of the torch pass from Aquino's hand to one person after another, spreading the light. The people of the nation, each wearing a yellow shirt, join in a solidarity that overcomes differences in wealth, religion and age, and they hold torches up against the darkness. Led by Aquino, the people vanquish the darkness with light and a new day dawns. Reinforcing this imagery are the song lyrics (these below and others quoted in this chapter are translated from Tagalog), which call on people to follow the lead of the Aquino family in fighting corruption and serving the homeland in a moral solidarity of the nation:

> *We are with you*
> *When there is darkness all around, let us light the path to a beautiful future*
> *You will lead and we will follow; we will maintain our unity*
> *The Philippines is waiting for us to take action and support you*
> *You are not alone; the nation awakens*
> *We are with you; you are not alone*
> *Fill our hearts with pride in our country, with the help and blessing of God*
> *Let us unite; let us continue the struggle of Ninoy and Cory*
> *With the love of every citizen for our homeland*
> *Let us hide no longer; we will not give up*
> *With the help and blessing of God, let us join with all Filipinos*
> *In the past, the present, and forever more, you are not alone*[20]

A youth-oriented commercial song, "Pinoy," offering a perky melody and a rap by Aquino himself, was also used by the campaign. Again, the theme was a call for solidarity by the nation against injustice and in service to the Philippine people. *Pinoy*, originally a slang term for "Filipino," was transformed by this song into a nickname for Aquino. In effect, he adopted the name Pinoy as his own, thus purporting to represent every Filipino who sought a brighter future:

> *Pinoy (Noynoy), hope and peace of mind (Noynoy)*
> *That's what he will bring (Noynoy)*
> *He loves his fellow countrymen, and not just with words (Noynoy)*
> *He doesn't steal, you can trust him*
> *Hey, young people, the road is bright; he'll educate a new generation*
> *Guided by President Cory and Hero Ninoy, he won't do wrong*
> *[Rap-style speech by Aquino]: "Let's change our lives; I'll work hard for all of you.*
> *Let's show the world we're proud to be Filipinos."*
> *Noynoy, it's not just one man's battle*
> *Noynoy, everyone is together all the way*
> *Noynoy, Filipino people, this is our fight, Noynoy!*[21]

In this manner, the Aquino campaign made ample use of the discourse of moral nationalism. However, this appeal also contained elements not only of civic inclusivism, as shown by the support for Aquino among NGO communities, but also of civic exclusivism. The campaign repeatedly used phrases such as "cleanliness," "straightforwardness," "trustworthy," "I don't steal," "self-sacrifice," "volunteer spirit," and "we won't be bought." This discourse hinted at a civic-exclusivist portrayal of those who did not join in solidarity with Aquino as a "they" bought off by money, inferior to a "we" who feared for the future of the homeland and worked as volunteers. Indeed, campaign workers for Aquino disparaged Villar supporters as "paid for (*bayaran*)."[22] However, this civic exclusivism did not provoke a backlash from the poor or a serious moral division of the nation. Perhaps that is because the Aquino camp continued to make public appeals for national solidarity, while its civic-exclusivist discourse remained hidden and a subject of private discussion.

According to the SWS opinion polls, Aquino's approval rating, which had stood at 60 per cent in September 2009, was still holding up well at 49 per cent in December. These high ratings were indicative of widespread support across class lines for the morality he espoused. However, as the mood of mourning for Corazon Aquino began to dissipate, so did her son's approval ratings, sinking to 36 per cent in February 2010. Over the same period, Villar's ratings rose rapidly from 27 to 34 per cent, an improvement that can be attributed to the populist discourse he employed.

The Resurgence of Populism

Manuel Villar grew up in Tondo, said to be the largest slum in Asia, to become one of the new elite. He served three terms in the House of Representatives, from 1992 to 2001, before being elected to the Senate. After graduating from the University of the Philippines, his success in the land development business made him one of the wealthiest people in the country. Contributing to his financial success was a real estate development boom sparked by the globalization of the economy. Beginning in the 1980s, sales of subdivision residences and condominiums rose as growing numbers of overseas contract workers sent more money home and used it to purchase investment property or homes for their families or themselves after retirement. Viewed in terms of the respective economic bases of the competing elites, the presidential election of 2010 was a contest between Aquino, a member of the traditional elite whose power base lay in large landholdings and plantation management, and Villar, a member of the new elite who acquired their wealth through the new globalized economy.

Villar had been preparing for a presidential campaign from early on. As part of the new elite, he needed to build up a network of local elites from scratch. To this end, he served as speaker of the house and then president of the senate, reinforcing his organizational base while simultaneously working to resurrect the dormant Nationalist Party as a vehicle for his ambitions. Prior to the election, he secured the support of both the Marcos family and Bayan Muna.[23] He then propagated a "rags to riches" narrative of his life through the media, declaring that he was running for president in order to help Filipinos suffering from poverty as he once had.

Villar announced his candidacy in a speech at Macario Sakay Plaza in the Tondo district where he had lived as a child.[24] Macario Sakay was a hero of the Philippine independence movement who fought against American colonial rule but was subsequently stigmatized and executed as a "bandit." Because it is known as one of Asia's largest slums, the combined images of Tondo and Macario Sakay carry a symbolic significance, evoking both poverty and the aspirations of Filipinos seeking liberation from it. In his speech, Villar claimed that the purpose of his candidacy was to achieve "revolution against poverty" as he declared, "This election is about you. This is about Filipinos who have no voice in society." Moreover, because he had no interest in lining his own pockets, he promised that once he had made the poor wealthy, he would retire from politics and return to the private sector. At this point, the popular comedian Dolphy exhorted residents to support Villar, saying, "Don't you like that someone from Tondo could become president?"

Willie Revillame, host of the popular ABS-CBN TV show *Wowowee*, played an important part in Villar's campaign. *Wowowee* was a daytime entertainment program in which poor people could display their singing or dancing talents and win big cash prizes by participating in games or quizzes. The show and its host, Revillame, enjoyed immense popularity in the mass sphere. Villar appeared on *Wowowee* and promised houses and lots to game participants, as well as scholarships for poor children to attend school up through graduation from university. The recipients of these gifts wept for joy, hugged Villar, and thanked him exuberantly. Through these appearances, Villar attempted to impress TV audiences as someone who was close to Revillame and kindly disposed to the poor. In addition, on his campaign tours in the provinces, Villar was accompanied by entertainers, who performed songs and dances popular on TV in a format similar to *Wowowee*. For the poor in these localities, these events offered a welcome opportunity to see familiar TV celebrities up close.

However, the most instrumental facet in elevating Villar's name recognition and popularity was a television and radio advertising blitz surpassing those of the other candidates. During the course of the election campaign, TV and radio commercials for Villar came on every few minutes.[25] Through these ads, he drove home the message that he himself was born poor and that he would use the wealth and status he had achieved to help those in need. His hip-hop style campaign song *Naging Mahirap* ("Born Poor") did much to raise his recognition and popularity. In TV ads featuring the song, smiling slum children sang these words:

> *Did you ever swim in a sea of garbage?*
> *Did you ever celebrate Christmas in the middle of the street?*
> *This is our question: are you one of us?*
> *Did you know that he'll send us to school?*
> *He'll find us work and give us homes*
> *Villar is truly one of the poor, Villar is truly kind*
> *Villar is a man with abilities who created his own place in the world*
> *Villar will put an end to our poverty*

Another one of Villar's campaign songs was entitled *Hindi Bawal Mangarap ang Mahirap* ("It's Not Wrong to Dream When You're Poor"). This was a more stirring tune designed to appeal to the emotions of the listener. Again, slum children sang the song in TV ads:

You were born poor, yet you always held on to your dreams
Hard work and patience will be rewarded some day
It's not wrong to dream even when you're poor
Let us take the high road
Villar had a dream
Even if you're poor, believe in God and keep faith in your heart

Estrada, the pioneer of Philippine populism, also reentered the fray, asserting once again that he would launch a revolution as "one of the masses" against the ruling oligarchy, who he blamed for his ouster in 2001. In his candidacy announcement, he declared, "Bonifacio [the poverty-born hero who initiated armed struggle against the Spanish] was also born in Tondo. He was unable to finish his studies. I was also unable to finish my studies and I'm also for the masses."[26] In his 2010 campaign, he supplemented his familiar slogan *Erap para sa mahirap* ("Erap for the poor") with others like *Ibalik ang pwersa sa masa* ("Restore power to the masses") and *Kung may Erap may ginhawa* ("With Erap, life will be easier"). Meanwhile, he denounced Villar, who had taken up the same mantle of populism and adopted the same orange campaign color, as his imitator.[27]

However, there were some differences between the populism of Estrada and that of Villar. Estrada had previously used the words "class war" when denouncing the elite, the Catholic Church and big business, framing them as his enemies. Although Villar criticized Aquino and his vice-presidential candidate Mar Roxas, both members of the traditional elite, as *team haciendero* (the big landowner team), he also sought to maintain good relations with the business community, for example, by arguing that entrepreneurs could play an important role in combating poverty. In addition, Villar did not skimp in his efforts to appeal to the civic sphere, promoting the image of himself as a successful businessman. He also displayed a more neoliberal stance, emphasizing self-reliant "hard work and patience" (*sipag at tiyaga*). This was in contrast to Estrada, who stuck to promising the poor, "I will help you."

A Victory of "Morality" over "Poverty"

There is no question that Villar's surge in popularity reflected a certain degree of success with his populist position. In February and March 2010, however, Villar's approval ratings plunged from 34 to 28 per cent, and in the end, he received fewer votes than Estrada in the election, coming in third (see Figure 4). Most of the poor ultimately supported Aquino's appeal to "morality" over Villar's pledge to combat "poverty". Why was

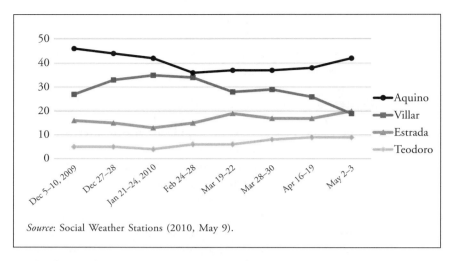

Figure 4 Pre-election Approval Ratings of the Presidential Candidates

this? To explain this development, let us examine the three issues that have played a pivotal role in presidential elections in the Philippines: "poverty," "morality," and "ability."

First, Villar sought to gain an advantage over Aquino by making "poverty" the key issue of the campaign. A focus on poverty was undesirable for Aquino because it would challenge his legitimacy. In contrast to Villar, whose birthplace of Tondo was a veritable symbol of poverty, Aquino's family owned the vast Hacienda Luisita, which was a symbol of entrenched elite rule. In November 2004, Luisita was the site of a massacre in which government forces opened fire on a gathering of protesters demanding the reinstatement of fired plantation workers. A total of 14 people were killed, including 2 children. Villar mentioned this in his criticisms of Aquino: "I will invite Noynoy [to Tondo] so that he would know how it is to be poor. I hope he will also bring me to Hacienda Luisita because I also want to see where the farmers were killed.. . . . I pity the farmers who were killed there."[28] Villar also described himself as one of the "real poor" (*tunay na mahirap*), emphasizing his birth into a poor family that made its living by selling fish, and telling of how his younger brother fell ill and died because the family could not afford medical treatment.[29]

However, Villar's poverty discourse failed to finesse the issue of morality, which had been brought to the fore by the corruption of Arroyo and the death of Corazon Aquino. The Aquino camp accused Villar of lying about his past, citing evidence that his mother was not a lowly fishmonger but a seafood wholesaler, and that his brother had been admitted to a private hospital.[30] Aquino's counterattack reduced the poverty question to one about the truth of Villar's background, effectively marginalizing poverty as a campaign issue.

Villar was the target of suspicions that he had engaged in considerable misconduct in the process of climbing to the top in the space of a single lifetime, first as an entrepreneur and then as a politician. Consequently, the emergence of morality as the central issue of the election campaign worked decisively to his disadvantage. Rival candidates were relentless in their attacks, accusing him of various forms of corruption.[31] As his image devolved into that of someone tainted by money, it further triggered fears that if elected, he might engage in corrupt practices to recoup his extravagant campaign expenses. In the end, all of these suspicions and allegations saw Villar's success story of rise from poverty through "hard work and patience" rewritten into a negative tale of someone in the pursuit of self-interest who was not averse to corrupt practices.

Moreover, Villar continually refused to appear at Senate hearings convened to investigate allegations of his misconduct. One rival candidate seized on this to accuse him of being a "coward" (*duwag*) in front of the media.[32] Most poor people related to Estrada's cultivated image as a Robin Hood-like macho "tough guy" (*siga*) who was unafraid to defy the law and the powerful, even at risk of his own life, for the sake of those who believed in him. Therefore, this "cowardly" image only exacerbated the poor's distrust of Villar.[33]

The Aquino camp also cast suspicion that Villar was secretly receiving support from the Arroyo family. Because of the many allegations of corruption aimed at Arroyo, she feared prosecution for plunder and other crimes at the moment her term as president would end. Consequently, the story went, Arroyo was providing under-the-table assistance to Villar, the likely winner, in hopes of gaining his support in return.[34] These allegations of covert collaboration between Villar and Arroyo (*Villarroyo*) gained traction, further sending Villar's ratings into a tailspin.

Yet, another potential campaign issue, "ability," could threaten to hurt Aquino. In the presidential elections of 1998 and 2004, the Church, the business community, and the elite harshly attacked Estrada and Poe, both former movie actors, as lacking the skills required of a president. In the 2010 election, rival candidates leveled the same criticism at Noynoy Aquino, claiming that he had not once drafted legislation during his 12 years in Congress and that he was merely riding on his parents' coattails without possessing the requisite skills to carry out reforms.[35] Aquino's rebuttal was that he was not interested in legislating just to score points, and that he had ample experience in such fields as financial management.

Ultimately, in the 2010 election, presidential ability was not the major issue it had been in previous campaigns; the theme of morality versus corruption had superceded it. Above all, Aquino, with his traditional elite background, did not incur serious opposition from the Church, big business or the elite—unlike Estrada or Poe, who caused these groups to fear that these two candidates would threaten the existing power structure. The conglomerate-owned mass media also followed up on its sweeping coverage of Aquino's mother's funeral with generally positive reporting on his candidacy, while also remaining persistently critical of Villar's alleged corruption.[36]

Moreover, the Aquino camp also incorporated poverty into its discourse of moral nationalism. At the end of 2009, Aquino's campaign slogan was *Hindi ako magnanakaw* ("I will not steal"); however, in January of the following year, he actively began using *Kung walang kurakot, walang mahirap* ("If there is no corruption, there will be no poverty"). Therefore, Aquino, too, began reaching out to the mass sphere by speaking of poverty.

As discussed, the decisive victory of Aquino's moral nationalism was the result of a contingent hegemonic struggle that cannot be understood in terms of a predetermined cycle per Thompson's argument. If an event like Corazon Aquino's death had not immediately preceded the election campaign, Noynoy Aquino would not have been one of its candidates, let alone its winner. Moreover, the sum of the votes for Estrada and Villar exceeded the tally for Aquino; thus, if the votes of the poor had not been split between these two candidates, it is highly likely that populism would have won the election.

The Reemergence of a Nation Longing for Morality

Class Differences in Voting Behavior

How was the struggle for hegemony in this presidential election articulated and fought in the dual public sphere? According to the pre-election surveys carried out by SWS, Aquino initially enjoyed high approval ratings among all classes; these gradually declined, but rallied in time to secure him a solid victory (see Figures 5, 6 and 7). Comparing Aquino's approval ratings from 2 to 3 May 2010, a week before the election, with those of the two populist candidates, Villar and Estrada, we see that Aquino was the clear

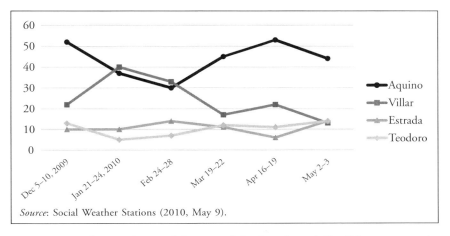

Figure 5 Pre-election Approval Ratings of the Presidential Candidates among the Wealthy and Middle Classes (classes A, B, and C)

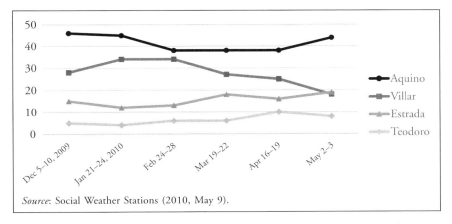

Figure 6 Pre-election Approval Ratings of the Presidential Candidates among the Poor (class D)

frontrunner, with 44 per cent versus 27 per cent among the wealthy and middle class, and the same disparity, 44 per cent versus 27 per cent, among the poor. This shows that Aquino's moral nationalism succeeded on the whole in winning support in both the civic and mass spheres. In the very poor class, however, the aggregate rating of the two populists exceeded that of Aquino, 44 per cent versus 35 per cent. The most impoverished

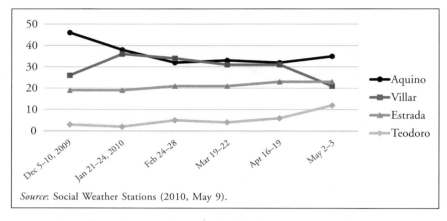

Figure 7 Pre-election Approval Ratings of the Presidential Candidates among the Very Poor (class E)

class exhibited a tendency to support the populism of Villar and Estrada, although this was considerably undermined by Aquino's moral nationalism.[37]

Discourses in the English-language press also demonstrate that moral nationalism met with support in the civic sphere. As mentioned earlier, many in the press were critical of Villar's populism and alleged corruption, and tended to support Aquino. For example, when Aquino first leapt to the top of the polls, Amando Doronila wrote the following in a column entitled, "Transparency Now a Defining Issue in Campaign":

> [T]he survey results reflect the deep and broad resonance of the issue of clean and honest governance that highlights Aquino's campaign theme. The ground swell of support for Aquino following the death of his mother, President Cory Aquino, flows from the public service record of his mother and his father, and the martyred former Sen. Benigno Aquino, whose honesty and transparency appear to have been accepted by the Filipino public.[38]

In other words, support for Aquino in the civic sphere reflected hopes, once invested in People Power, for the achievement of modern political reform that would put an end to corruption and lead to a healthier, wealthier Philippines.

However, in the mass sphere, how can we understand the tendency among the poor, who had until then provided the support base for populism, to support the moral nationalism of Aquino? Why did they support the morality espoused by Aquino despite pledges by Villar and Estrada to eradicate poverty? Let us examine this phenomenon in light of a survey I conducted in Pechayan from early February to early March 2010.

The Mass-Sphere Discourse on Aquino

Throughout the election campaign, intense political discussions took place continuously all over Pechayan. Even as residents remained fundamentally skeptical, believing that their lives would not significantly change regardless of who became president, they nonetheless spoke passionately about the need to elect a president who was truly kindhearted and would extend a helping hand to those in dire straits. During the survey period, Election Day was still two or more months away, so most people had yet to finalize their choice for president. Consequently, they were still closely scrutinizing the candidates and debating their merits with relatives and neighbors.

When asked for their assessment of Aquino, nearly everyone mentioned his parents, Ninoy and Corazon. Those who supported Noynoy Aquino spoke approvingly of the Aquino family as "kind (*mabait*)" and "proven (*subok na*)": "We already know that Noynoy's family are good people. His dead parents were kindhearted. If they did anything bad, I haven't heard about it" (Uta, 23, female, fruit vendor, March 8, 2010). They also spoke of expectations that if Aquino became president, he would follow in his parents' footsteps and, like them, devote himself to serving the Philippine nation and people:

> His father was a candidate we wholeheartedly supported, but he was killed before he could run for president. Now Noynoy is trying to make that come true. Filipinos support Noynoy. He's a kind person, so I think we can believe in him. Noynoy is popular with the masses. He seems to have sympathy in his heart for the poor. (Edgar, 54, male, coconut juice vendor, March 8, 2010)

These frequent mentions of Aquino's "kindness" can be attributed in part to the impression he cultivated of self-effacement and lack of ambition. Until his mother's death and the sudden surge of support for him that followed, Aquino had never displayed ambitions to run for president. Even as a senator, he maintained a low-key presence and seldom showed any inclination toward self-assertion. Those who detested Arroyo's aggressive, haughty attitude may have seen a contrasting "kindness" in Aquino's modesty.

However, those who expressed negative views of Aquino criticized him as someone who, unlike his parents, lacked the skills or experience to help the poor: "Noynoy is just famous because of his parents. What has he done for the country so far?" (Narge, 51, male, sidewalk watch repairman, March 8, 2010). "Noynoy hasn't done anything since becoming a senator, except collect his salary" (Rose, 24, female, housewife, March 1, 2010). "He says he'll get rid of corruption and poverty, but he should have been doing that long ago. He's been a senator for years, hasn't he? Too bad it's not his father running. Noynoy's nothing like Ninoy" (Babes, 47, female, food peddler, March 8, 2010).

Many were of the opinion that Noynoy lacked the skills and strong leadership required to make good on his pledge to eliminate corruption and poverty, and would merely be manipulated by "behind-the-scenes advisers" (*taong nasa likod*) without achieving anything substantial: "It's tough to wipe out corruption. Aquino will probably hire advisers smarter than he is, and when they become corrupt, he'll learn from them quick enough. Even if he becomes president, we won't benefit at all" (Narge, 51, male, sidewalk watch repairman, March 8, 2010).

Some people cynically remarked that since he was from the wealthy class himself, Aquino couldn't be expected to have any interest in eliminating poverty: "Look at Hacienda Luisita. He's not even helping the peasants on his own plantation. Do you think he's going to help us?" (Rose, 24, female, housewife, March 1, 2010). One young man ridiculed the vaunted "kindness" of the Aquino family and its service to the country as follows:

> Who owns Hacienda Luisita? Farmers there were shot and killed. They only get paid nine pesos a day. It's been over 20 years since democratization, but it's still the Aquino family's land. If Noynoy were a real human being, he'd have given the land to the farmers. And isn't he supposed to belong to the kindhearted Aquino family? There was no need for them to use violence. He says he's not a thief, but that's just a campaign slogan. (Jun, 26, male, pedicab driver, March 8, 2010)

Therefore, in Pechayan, although people who had a positive image of Aquino could be found, there were also many skeptics. Even so, Aquino obtained the votes of a sizable portion of the impoverished class. This can be attributed to the deep-seated distrust and suspicions of corruption aimed at Villar in the mass sphere, despite his claims to populism, at a time when people still felt an intense distaste for Arroyo's corruption.

The Mass-Sphere Discourse on Villar

Let us now take a look at assessments of Villar in the mass sphere. In Pechayan, young people in particular responded favorably to his campaign advertising. One student said, "His commercials are good. He says things that make you think. He makes you realize that, since he made it out of poverty and succeeded on his own, we should be able to do it, too" (Lopas, 20, female, college student, March 1, 2010). However, positive evaluations of Villar's ads did not always translate directly into support. Another young person praised the cleverness of Villar commercials that featured slum children, but at the same time, asserted the importance of thinking for oneself without taking input from the media at face value:

> The kids who appear in Villar's commercials are really cool. When children speak, adults believe them. These ads move anyone who watches them. But it's up to us to decide whether or not to believe what's in all these commercials. (Jun, 26, male, pedicab driver, March 8, 2010)

Nearly everyone expressed skepticism about Villar's promises to help the poor and end poverty. This was because of a disparity between rumors about him circulating in the mass sphere and what he said in the media. The mass sphere is a hotbed of rumors along the lines of "That councilor is easy to approach; I hear he gave someone funeral money when they went to his office" and "They say Erap gave land to squatters in that town". Such rumors spread quickly from sources unknown and circulate, with embellishments, throughout the mass sphere. Yet, despite Villar's frequent claims of a track record of helping the poor, I could find almost nothing in the mass sphere in the way of anecdotes about any of the poor receiving assistance from him. Consequently, he was the target of skepticism of this sort: "I wonder if he'd give scholarship money to my kids. There's nobody here who's gotten any help from him. He's only helped people who got on TV" (Babes, 47, female, food peddler, March 8, 2010).

Doubts were rife in the mass sphere as to whether Villar, in his heart of hearts, truly wanted to help the poor. My surveys were conducted at the same time suspicions were growing about Villar's corruption, and people were engaging in heated discussions over whether he was really "pro-poor," or merely pretending to be so in order to feather his own nest. Residents of Pechayan scrutinized Villar's speech and behavior in the media in an effort to discern his true intentions. The cook of a local lunch counter was critical of Villar's appearances on *Wowowee*, saying that he didn't display any initiative, which made his promises to help the poor open to doubt:

> I don't believe him. He only helps a few people, like the ones who appear on *Wowowee*. And that's because Willie Revillame, [the MC], says to him, "Senator Villar, won't you help these people?" He'd make a better impression on viewers if he first said to Willie, "I'm going to help them." When he said he'd give scholarships to poor kids so they could graduate from college, that's because Willie asked him to. (Rey, 39, female, lunch counter cook, March 1, 2010)

With near-daily reports of Villar's alleged corruption, concerns about his misconduct grew stronger in the mass sphere. These apprehensions revolved particularly around the huge sums he was spending on advertising. His campaign ads ran every few minutes on TV and radio, and it was obvious that his advertising outlays exceeded those of any other candidate. This gave rise to remarks such as the following: "If he becomes president, how is he going to make back the money he spent on his campaign? A lot of people are worried about that" (Ronald, 39, male, MMDA traffic monitor, March 8, 2010). Moreover, those with a negative opinion of Villar suggested that he was running for president not to help the poor, but rather to increase his own wealth:

> Villar just uses politics for his business; that's why he's rich. He makes money from politics. After he became a politician, he suddenly got rich, right? So those corruption rumors are probably true. (Jun, 26, male, pedicab driver, March 8, 2010)

People also argued that Villar's property development business threatened poor squatters: "He became a billionaire by developing subdivisions. But poor people can't live in subdivisions. If he becomes president, squatters like us will probably be evicted from our homes so he can build more houses for the rich" (Narge, 51, male, sidewalk watch repairman, March 8, 2010).

Rumors in the mass sphere also circulated that Villar was actually a puppet of Arroyo. A female street vendor who attended one of his campaign rallies acknowledged that she was impressed by his generosity in treating a large gathering of people to a meal but added that she could not believe what he said, and moreover, that he was under the influence of Arroyo and might very well engage in corrupt practices:

Villar is generous with his money. On February 9, I went to a rally for him in Laguna with about 20 friends. They gave us free transportation and food. He was really very generous and we ate our fill. It seems like he'll focus on the poor if he becomes president, and that would be great if it's true. But I don't know exactly what he'll do for poor people. After all, he's under Gloria's thumb, isn't he? They seem to be close pals, and Gloria looks after him. He may be a nice guy, but he's like Gloria's toy. If he becomes one of Arroyo's cronies, the corruption will only get worse. Actually, I feel closer to Erap. If only he were higher in the polls than Villar, I'd choose him (Uta, 23, female, fruit vendor, March 8, 2010).

Photo 27 A pro-Estrada banner hangs over the entrance to Pechayan (March 2010).

Though Villar promised to help the poor, many Pechayan residents questioned his sincerity and worried that he might be corrupt. A word frequently used by those speaking critically of Villar was *plastik* (literally "plastic," meaning "superficial, insincere"). Villar's cunning and shrewdness made people feel that he was not sufficiently trustworthy as a candidate. It was a common tendency in Pechayan to view Estrada more favorably than Villar. Even if the accusations of corruption leveled against Estrada were true, the sentiment was that at least his desire and ability to help the poor were "tried and tested" (*subok na*):[39]

> People have always said Erap is uneducated, that he didn't graduate from college. But I like him because he's helped so many people. His track record speaks for itself. I know he built lots of houses in Pasig and gave them to the poor for free. Out in the country, he gave each family a water buffalo. Even if he is criticized for being corrupt, we know he has done a lot for people. He's used the money he made from bribes to help the poor. That makes him different from other corrupt politicians. I really hope Erap wins. Many people's lives have gotten harder since he was forced out of office. (Weng, 27, female, general store salesperson, March 1, 2010)

In contrast with the active support in the civic sphere for the moral nationalism promoted by the Aquino camp, the discourse of the "people" in solidarity that transcended class differences was not so prevalent in the mass sphere. Residents of Pechayan exercised caution in their selection of a candidate, maintaining a skeptical attitude toward both Aquino and Villar. That Aquino ultimately won by a landslide may be attributed to the overwhelming revulsion that persisted in the mass sphere against Arroyo's corruption; this revulsion led most of the poor to shun the crafty-seeming Villar in favor of Aquino as the "lesser evil." Yet, the support base for populism in the mass sphere had by no means collapsed, as evidenced by Estrada's strong second-place showing.

The 2010 election result paradoxically meant that Aquino, a member of the traditional elite with its huge land ownership and plantation business base, perpetuated the tradition of elite democracy by winning support across class lines with a call for morality-based political reform. Another paradox was that Villar, who had succeeded as a new entrepreneur in the global economy, decided to gear his appeal to the mass sphere instead of to the civic sphere, even though the latter was more receptive to the morality of neoliberalism. Because middle-class voters are in the minority, populism is the only means the new elite currently has at its disposal to wrest power from the traditional elite. Consequently, the odds for the success of an electoral politics grounded in the civic inclusivism or exclusivism of the civic sphere remain low.

Elite Rule that Speaks of Morality

The Success of the Aquino Administration

The Noynoy Aquino administration, which made a watchword of morality-based reform, is regarded as a relative success. Initially it benefited from high expectations, with an approval rate of nearly 70 per cent. Although subsequent negatives, including a pork-barrel budget scandal, a poor response to the damage inflicted by Typhoon Haiyan and violence in Mindanao, caused temporary declines in these ratings, they quickly rebounded to a moderately high range, hovering around 40 per cent. Compared with other post-democratization administrations, all of which suffered late-term losses of support, this power of recovery was exceptional (see Figures 3). The economy also remained healthy, sustaining a GDP growth rate exceeding 6 per cent. With no *coup d'état* or People Power crises, the Aquino administration was unquestionably more stable and successful than the corruption- and strife-torn Estrada and Arroyo regimes.

According to Thompson (2014), presidential success or failure in the Philippines cannot be explained simply in terms of distributed patronage or personal temperament. Rather, it depends on whether the president is able to associate himself or herself with a reformist narrative and secure the support of strategic groups such as big business, the Church, civil society activists and the military. Because reformism in support of a discourse of democracy and good governance has taken root as legitimate since democratization, a president perceived as committed to the reformist narrative can maintain a stable administration. Although "reformism" as defined by Thompson would be more accurate if classified more specifically into moral nationalism, civic exclusivism and civic inclusivism, there is no doubt that a broadly-defined reformism established hegemony in the civic sphere and that the support this generated for Aquino contributed significantly to the stability of his administration.

On the other hand, how has Aquino approached the mass sphere, where populism continues to enjoy deep-rooted support? Aquino, by addressing the nation in Tagalog, employed two strategies to quash populist support among the poor. First, the administration sought to bring down its populist rivals through the moral nationalist practice of pursuing anti-corruption political reform. Second, it also engaged in the civic inclusivist practice of implementing morality-based anti-poverty policies that incorporated the poor into the "citizenry." NGO leaders and activists of Akbayan who made a salient contribution to the Aquino election campaign played a leading role in the civic inclusivist programs.

Hounding Political Rivals with Morality

In his 2010 State of the Nation Address, Aquino declared that there would be "no more influence-peddling, no more patronage politics, no more stealing, no more bribes", thereby pledging himself to the implementation of anti-corruption political reform. With the battle cry of "*ang matuwid na daan*" ("righteous path"), Aquino promised a political reform to eradicate corruption.

However, such reform would pose a dilemma. The Priority Development Assistance Fund (PDAF), whose disbursements took place at the discretion of legislators, was known as a "pork-barrel" fund and condemned as a source of corruption.[40] However, in the absence of a fixed and stable party system, the president cannot rely on party discipline to secure legislative support for reform and therefore feels compelled to disburse pork-barrel funds to legislators. Consequently, a radical reform like abolishing pork-barrel budgets is hard to carry out because it would destabilize legislative operations. However, the Aquino administration successfully skirted this dilemma between political stability and reform by attacking corruption of political opponents in the name of morality while introducing new forms of pork-barrel funds to maintain its influence over the majority in Congress.

The Aquino administration declared an investigation of the corrupt practices of the previous Arroyo administration as a top priority. Anticipating this move, Arroyo ran for Congress in 2010 and won a House seat in an effort to retain her influence as a legislator.[41] In addition, close associates that Arroyo had appointed to high positions in the judiciary blocked investigations of her misconduct through such actions as a ruling that a proposed Truth Commission was unconstitutional. Aquino responded by convening impeachment trials in Congress that forced the resignation of Ombudsman Merceditas Gutierrez in 2011 and removed Renato Corona from his post as Chief Justice of the Supreme Court the following year on the grounds that he had falsified a statement of assets and acquired illicit wealth.[42] Arroyo was then arrested for electoral sabotage committed in 2007, with charges later added for other corrupt practices during her term in office.[43] Opposition-party senators also joined forces with Aquino in the pursuit of Arroyo through impeachment trials and Senate Blue Ribbon Committee hearings.

However, in 2013, the Aquino administration shifted the target of its corruption investigations to political opponents in the Senate, including those who supported the impeachment of Corona. The impetus for this move was the revelation of the alleged plundering of some 10 billion pesos in pork-barrel funding for fictitious NGOs by over 100 senators and representatives between 2003 and 2013.[44] The Office of the Ombudsman filed charges against a total of 51 individuals, including incumbent senators and former representatives, for receiving kickbacks. Garnering the most attention was the arrest of three opposition senators, Bong Revilla, Jinggoy Estrada and Juan Ponce Enrile.

Vice President Jejomar Binay also became a target of corruption allegations. Since his appointment as mayor of Makati in 1986 by Corazon Aquino, he had turned the city into his clan's fiefdom. In 2010, he parlayed a populist strategy of providing free medical and educational services to the poor into his election to the vice-presidency. When he announced early on that he would make a bid for the presidency in 2016, his support among the poor made him the ruling party's top rival. Senators, civic groups, and the mainstream media joined with the Aquino camp to counter this threat with allegations that Binay had pocketed illicit gains from permits for public works projects and condominium construction in Makati City. Binay was able to block an impeachment motion in the House, but saw his support evaporate when he refused to attend hearings by the Senate Blue Ribbon Committee. Furthermore, his son, Makati Mayor Junjun, was dismissed and perpetually disqualified from public office for grave misconduct and dishonesty by an Ombudsman's suspension order in October 2015. In this instance, the moral politics practiced by the administration had clearly cornered its prey.

However, the anti-corruption reform agenda came back to bite the Aquino administration itself. With sentiment against the pork barrel rising across the nation, the Supreme Court ruled in 2013 that pork-barrel funding was unconstitutional because it was beyond the purview of the legislative branch to earmark new uses for funding after a budget had been passed. In response, the Aquino administration introduced a reform proposal under which the PDAF would be abolished, but budgetary allotments would still be disbursed to legislators, who would publicly disclose all projects and implement them through pertinent government agencies. Additionally, the Aquino administration appropriated the Disbursement Acceleration Program (DAP) in an effort to retain majority control of Congress. DAP had been introduced in 2011 as a system for stimulating economic growth by shifting funds to separate budgetary items for fast-track disbursement when there were delays in the implementation of the budget.[45] However, DAP also became a target of criticism when Jinggoy Estrada, one of the senators who had been arrested, alleged that senators had received 50 million pesos each from DAP as an incentive to vote for the impeachment of Corona. In 2014, the Supreme Court ruled that DAP, too, was unconstitutional because the alteration of budgetary items already approved by Congress exceeded the authority of the president. Arguing that DAP was constitutional, Aquino tried but failed to persuade the Court to reverse its decision. The result was a delay in the implementation of the entire annual budget, which lowered economic growth in the year.

Thus, the moral politics espoused by Aquino in the name of attacking corruption not only worked against his political opponents, but also imposed certain constraints on the Aquino administration itself via public opinion and the judiciary. In this respect, the scope of palpable "predatory politics" in the Philippines appears to be gradually shrinking. The degree of this change, and whether it has worked more to the advantage of Aquino's traditional elite or more to that of the populist counter-elite, remains a subject for future study.

Addressing Poverty with Morality

The Aquino administration actively developed social policies primarily aimed at reducing poverty and achieved the passage of several bills that had languished due to the influence of opposing forces.[46] According to Takagi (2015), these reforms could be pushed through because NGO activists, business leaders, and politicians with ample experience in policy legislation participated in the policymaking process of the Aquino administration, forming policy coalitions and assuming a leadership role vis-à-vis specific issues. Additionally, the high approval ratings of the administration enabled this political alliance to pursue reforms without fear of opposing forces, thus forming a "pocket of efficacy in the midst of a weak state." However, Takagi only examines the policymaking process and does not discuss how these social policies have been implemented or what effect they have had on the mass sphere. The anti-poverty policies of the Aquino administration have been aimed at poor people as designated by the National Household Targeting System for Poverty Reduction. Let us now examine their effect on the mass sphere while keeping in mind the characteristics of civic inclusivism embedded therein.

The primary anti-poverty strategy carried out by the Aquino administration consists of conditional cash transfers, a measure employed in various countries seeking to reduce poverty under tight fiscal constraints. The Philippines launched a pilot project in 2008, *Pantawid Pamilyang Pilipino Program* (Bridging Program for the Filipino Family), or "4Ps," with assistance from the World Bank and the Asian Development Bank. The Aquino administration expanded this into a full-scale program with the goal of applying it to 4.6 million households by 2016.[47] The beneficiaries were selected according to criteria such as assets, household possessions, employment, education and number of children from a pool consisting of mothers-to-be and mothers with children aged 14 and under living in areas designated as impoverished districts. Men were excluded from eligibility out of concern that they might squander the cash on liquor, gambling and other vices. The women were organized into groups of about 30 to attend family development sessions on topics such as regular prenatal check-ups, public hygiene and responsible parenthood under the tutelage of social workers from NGOs and the Department of Social Welfare and Development, who attempted to ensure that they sent their children to school every day and gave up vices such as bingo and other forms of gambling. Then, on the condition that they conformed to these moral requirements, they would receive a Health and Nutrition Grant of 500 pesos per month and an Education Grant of 300 pesos per month per child for up to three children.

According to Seki (2015), conditional cash transfers are not effective in directly reducing poverty. Although cash transfers provide the poor with some degree of livelihood support, the amounts are too small to enable recipients to actually extricate themselves from poverty.[48] The real purpose of such programs is "investment in human capital"—that is, the empowerment of the poor so that they become "good citizens" through a process, guided by social workers, of reflecting on their circumstances and cooperating with their neighbors. He points out that this is nothing more than a form of neoliberal governance that aspires to mold people's desires, hopes and beliefs by subjecting, monitoring, evaluating and controlling them as "responsible, free entities".

From another perspective, conditional cash transfers may also be understood as a policy that attempts to break through the impasse imposed by moral antagonism between the civic and mass spheres. Handouts by politicians to the poor are desired as "assistance" (*tulong*) in the mass sphere, but viewed as morally repugnant in the civic sphere. However, it could be possible to provide aid to the poor without incurring a major backlash from the civic sphere, if it were done on the condition that it would impart discipline to the poor by turning them into good, responsible "citizens". Nonetheless, the suspicion that cash transfers are a waste of taxpayers' money that only worsens the dependence of the poor is deeply ingrained in the civic sphere. Meanwhile, as Seki (ibid) demonstrates, discomfort and resentment persist in the mass sphere over the fact that the selection of recipients is an opaque process, that many people cannot receive cash transfers due to inadequate documentation, and that in exchange for receiving a small amount of money, one must submit to both criticism of their lifestyle as being immoral and pressure to correct it. It therefore appears no less difficult to incorporate everyone into the "citizenry" through conditional cash transfers than through any other civic-inclusivist practice that attempts to subsume the poor.

Next, the Aquino administration passed what is considered one of its most significant laws, the Responsible Parenthood and Reproductive Health Act of 2012 (RH Law). The impetus behind this legislation was a perception that the country's high population growth rate of 2 per cent per year was impeding economic growth and poverty reduction.[49] The purpose of the law was not to encourage birth control or abortion, but rather to support family planning through measures such as sex education and the distribution of free contraceptives at health centers throughout the nation by the Department of Health.

In declaring this bill to be a top-priority item, the Aquino administration won support from intellectuals, the business community and women's groups. However, the Catholic Church voiced strong objections on moral grounds. According to the Church, family planning through contraception was a coercive policy pushed by foreign countries and the United Nations that not only wrecked family ties by promoting hedonism and promiscuity but also was "pro-abortion" and "antilife" and therefore fundamentally immoral. Interestingly, though, the Church's opposition was not as vehement as when, for example, it took a leading role in the ouster of Estrada. When Congress passed the law in 2012, opponents petitioned the Supreme Court to declare it unconstitutional, but in 2014 the Court upheld its constitutionality (with the exception of eight provisions), and the law went into effect.

The RH law is viewed as part of the broader poverty reduction effort in that it assigns poor women priority in receiving health care services, information, contraceptives and "capacity building and monitoring." It also calls for "values formation" education that addresses such issues as underage pregnancy, the rights of women and children, codes of responsible underage conduct and responsible parenthood. These programs represent an attempt to provide poor women with sufficient information to transform them into responsible actors with freedom of choice. Both conditional cash transfers and RH law aim to discipline poor women into becoming moral agents of change in the mass sphere.

The opposition of the Catholic Church notwithstanding, the RH law drew broad support in the civic sphere. For example, 30 economists from the University of the Philippines published an article in the *Inquirer* that quoted numerous statistics to bolster the argument that because the poor lacked access to information about and means of contraception, many women had unplanned pregnancies during their teenage years, resulting in children who received inadequate education and the reproduction of the poverty cycle over successive generations. Unwanted births threatened the health and lives of mothers and children. Furthermore, the growth of the impoverished class required higher outlays for public education and health services, imposing a tremendous burden on taxpayers.[50] It was also argued that population growth-fueled increases in slums and migrants to Mindanao gave rise to social antagonism, and that affording the poor "real freedom of choice" in family planning was key to solving these problems.[51]

Where voluntary access to family planning is concerned, this support from the civic sphere of the moral intervention into the lives of the poor may well coincide with the wishes of the mass sphere. However, we must bear in mind that underlying the civic-sphere discourse of "rescuing the poor from poverty through family planning" is a tacit moral assumption that "the poor are poor because they irresponsibly produce too many children." Assumptions that blame poverty on the immorality of the poor have the effect of depoliticizing the phenomenon of structural inequality, and may result in the abandonment of poor people who do not adhere to the morality of the civic sphere as "undeserving of rescue." Supporters of the law also brandish surveys showing that most poor women repeatedly undergo unwanted births and that they endorse family planning. However, this civic-sphere discourse of poor mothers suffering from too many "unwanted children" does not correspond to the mass-sphere lifestyle, which values large families even amid poverty, and is problematic in its construction of the notion of "unwanted children."

The social policies of the Aquino administration exemplify a civic inclusivism of neo-liberal governance that attempts to address poverty with a limited welfare budget by educating the poor to become moral citizens. Granted, morality-based social reform can be evaluated as an anti-poverty strategy that avoids provoking interclass moral antagonism. Additionally, Aquino and his anti-corruption rhetoric may have succeeded in simultaneously vanquishing his populist adversaries and, to some degree, reducing support for populism in the mass sphere. However, morality does not rectify the unequal social structure per se, and moral intervention carries the risk of dividing people into "good" and "bad," thereby creating a new form of exclusion. With no clear prospects for the rapid amelioration of the deep inequalities within society, the danger that a future resurgence of populism will intensify the moral antagonism between the civic and mass spheres, and once again engender a pronounced moral division of the nation, remains.

CHAPTER 7

Beyond Moral Politics

Photo 28 View of sunset from the Philcoa overpass (January 2008).

Contributing to Philippine Political Theory

In this book, I have proposed a new theoretical perspective from which to analyze Philippine politics. Most previous studies of the subject have treated democratization in the Philippines as having achieved nothing more than the revival of elite democracy. However, the social changes following democratization have loosened the grip of clientelism and enabled the poor to participate in politics more freely. As a result, Philippine politics can no longer be explained simply in terms of elite democracy. At the same time, many studies of Philippine civil society assert that citizen participation in politics has contributed to democracy by opposing elite rule and promoting the interests of marginalized social groups. However, this argument does not explain why a middle class that self-identifies as a moral "citizenry" employed extra-constitutional means to oust a president supported by the poor, and why it has displayed an adamantly exclusionary stance toward the impoverished class.

In the Introduction, I addressed these issues by asking these questions: Why did a middle class styling itself as 'citizens' come to play this ambiguous role vis-à-vis the consolidation and deepening of democracy? What type of moral "we/they" relation would promote or advance democracy? Why is democracy in a stratified society easily destabilized? Regarding these issues, I criticized the prevailing assumption that democracy can be further consolidated and deepened if economic development increases the size of the middle class and the number of people participating in politics with an elevated "civic" consciousness. My critique was based on the fact that by definition, the concept of a moral "citizenry" inevitably constructs "non-citizens" equated with "the masses" as a constitutive outside. Therefore, the political characteristics of the middle class are not necessarily democratically inclined, and are largely dependent on their relations with other social groups. To be sure, a number of studies have discussed the dominance or exclusion of "the masses" by "citizens" in Philippine civil society from this perspective. However, these studies are limited by their assumption of a fixed antagonistic relationship between "citizens" and "masses" and their tendency to ignore roles of the ordinary people due to a bias for organized forces. In highlighting these moral aspects of class politics, I also criticize the dominant arguments that analyze class conflict strictly from the perspective of unequal distribution of resources.

In Chapter 1, I introduced hegemonic struggle in the dual public spheres as an analytical framework that surmounts these limitations. This approach examines struggles among the diverse hegemonic practices that appeal to different moralities in the dual public spheres and analyzes the role played in the political process by antagonistic "we/they" relations that are contingently constructed in the course of these struggles. In Chapter 2, I sought to flesh out this framework by showing how the dual public spheres derived from class disparities in language, media and living space that developed under colonialism, the building of the nation-state and the growth of capitalism. In Chapters 3 through 6, I employed this framework to analyze the vicissitudes of post-democratization Philippine politics while focusing on the contingent formation of antagonistic relations in civil society.

In 1986, with moral nationalism attaining hegemony against Marcos, an "enemy of the people", democratization was achieved by "the people" united in a solidarity that transcended class divisions. The continuation of elite rule and inequality, however, invited the rise of populism in the mass sphere beginning in 1998 and a civic-exclusivist backlash in the civic sphere created a pronounced moral division of the nation in which each side denied the legitimacy of the other "them," a development that seriously adversely impacted democracy. Civic-inclusivist social movements emerging in the contact zone showed the potential to alleviate this moral division, but were confronted with certain limitations. Then, in the presidential election of 2010, a backlash against the corruption of Arroyo brought moral nationalism to the fore once more, with the votes of "the people" desirous of a new politics, giving Aquino a landslide victory and serving to perpetuate the elite rule of the past.

This analysis supports my first thesis in response to the aforementioned question: that is, whether hegemonic struggles in civil society construct morally antagonistic "we/they" relations, including those between ordinary people not affiliated with particular organizations; and whether the dynamics of contingent changes in these relations are powerful determinants in the advancement or obstruction of democracy. This viewpoint of moral politics provides new insight into Philippine politics, which has been traditionally explained only from the perspective of "interest politics," which is defined by domination and the struggle over the distribution of resources. The dominant perspective regarding the struggle between elite rule and civil society over the allocation of resources cannot fully explain new developments in Philippine politics, which raises questions such as: Why do the middle and impoverished classes frequently antagonize each other, even though they share the common interests in challenging the elite? Why do counter-elites draw strong support from the poor even though they have made no improvements in the distribution of wealth? Why do reformative NGOs ally with the landed traditional elite who they have criticized? These contradictions in terms of interest politics can be understood from the contingent construction of moral "we/they" relations.

The above analysis also leads to my second thesis: the moralization of politics threatens democracy either by intensifying antagonistic "we/

they" relations to the extent that it advocates the exclusion and eradication of the other as "enemy," or by depoliticizing socioeconomic inequality to perpetuate elite rule in the name of the people's moral solidarity. This finding is original in that it counters previous studies on Philippine politics that condemn corrupt interest politics as evil and commend moral politics based on notions of what is "good." It also highlights the threat to democracy paradoxically posed by this moralization of politics, and newly explains why democracy in a stratified society is vulnerable to destabilization. Previous studies have argued that the rise of a middle class possessing elevated "civic" consciousness is crucial to averting the threat to democracy posed by intensified class antagonisms in a stratified society. Still, even their ascendance does not always contribute to democracy, if class politics becomes moralized.

Below I will summarize the risks associated with the moralization of politics and offer some theoretical proposals for solutions to the problem, with reference to the emergence of moral politics in the Philippines in the broader context of "macro" structural conditions.

The Rise and Paradox of Moral Politics

Moral Solidarity of the Nation

Moral nationalism is a hegemonic practice that calls for a "moral solidarity of the nation", overriding class divisions, in which both the civic and mass spheres oppose corrupt politicians as evil "enemies of the nation" and unite to create a better Philippines. Moral nationalism played a decisive role in the democratization brought about by People Power 1 in 1986, and in the victory of Aquino in the presidential election of 2010. In both cases, "the people" joined in solidarity against a corrupt president, and either ousted that president through street demonstrations or used the vote to demand an end to corruption.

In the process leading to democratization in 1986, the assassination of Senator Benigno Aquino Jr. was the catalyst for a surge of collective self-identity—transcending class as "we the people"—to oppose the dictator Marcos. Initially, the democratization movement arose in the civic sphere, where it was led by the Catholic Church, the business community and the urban middle class. However, as demonstrations in support of Corazon Aquino grew into a full-fledged protest movement, the poor also began to participate, albeit primarily out of curiosity. This turned the streets into a contact zone where people from the civic and mass spheres could interact. Together, unarmed demonstrators confronted armed troops in the streets, shared food and water, and generally looked out for one another. This created a horizontal solidarity in which class lines disappeared. In the elation of *communitas*, the poor recovered the dignity that they had been deprived of in the course of their daily lives. The result was the formation of "the people," which transcended the divisions of the dual public spheres and accomplished the democratization of the Philippines.

A national backlash against Arroyo, again transcending class divisions, played a significant part in the presidential election of 2010. In the mass sphere, Arroyo was already hated for usurping Estrada's presidency; rising rice prices and her haughty demeanor caused her reputation to sink even lower. In the civic sphere, successive allegations of misconduct destroyed trust in her altogether. As a result, the perception of Arroyo as the "enemy of the nation" took hold on both sides of the dual public spheres. Then, the contingent occurrence of the death of Corazon Aquino in 2009 evoked collective memories of the first People Power that had driven Marcos out of office. In the civic sphere in particular, this inspired a proliferation of the discourse of "the people" in solidarity against political corruption, and with it, a rise in support for the eldest scion of the Aquino family, Benigno Aquino III. Meanwhile, support for Aquino was by no means as strong in the mass sphere, but overwhelming distaste for Arroyo's corruption and deviousness spurred the majority of the poor to vote for the more self-effacing Aquino, perceiving themselves as one among "the people" seeking a new politics. As a result, Aquino drew support across class lines and won by a landslide.

Thus, moral nationalism twice gained hegemony in the dual public spheres, during and after democratization, constructing a moral solidarity of the nation and decisively affecting the political process. What, then, are the requisite conditions for the success of moral nationalism? First, there must be an "enemy of the nation" who is viewed as such, as Marcos and Arroyo were, across class lines in both the civic and mass spheres. Next, there must be a contingent event, such as the assassination of Benigno Aquino Jr. or the death of Corazon Aquino, which creates an object of empathy shared by most Filipinos, regardless of class. Finally, the discourse of moral nationalism, which tends to develop in the civic sphere, must also gain sufficient hegemony in the mass sphere. If populism establishes hegemony in the mass sphere, the success of moral nationalism is less likely.

Why did moral nationalism acquire a certain degree of hegemony in the mass sphere in 1986 and 2010, despite respective calls by the CPP and populists for solutions to poverty and inequality? The reason is that the poor, even as they continued to espouse the morality of the mass sphere and embrace different values from the middle class, collaborated in the effort initiated in the civic sphere to rid politics of rotten elements and build a better society. Poor people participated in People Power 1 not so much in the hope of reviving democratic electoral politics, but in the hope that post-democratization society would see the elimination of class hierarchies. The transformation of the streets where the protests took place into a contact zone where the middle and impoverished classes could interact with one another further reinforced this cooperative effort among classes with disparate values. By the same token, the poor who voted for Noynoy Aquino in 2010 sought a politics manifesting the "kindheartedness" they saw in the Aquinos, in contrast with the arrogance and shamelessness of Arroyo, more than they sought modern political reform represented by such notions as "good governance" and "accountability." It was in spite of this disparity in values that the poor participated in People Power or in voting behavior initiated in the civic sphere.

Moral solidarity of the nation has an ambiguous significance for democracy. On the one hand, it has served as the basis for movements and voting behavior that opposes corruption and abuse of power by politicians, even toppling an authoritarian regime and achieving democratization in its place. In that sense, it can contribute to democracy. However, at the same time, the discourse and practice of a moral solidarity of the nation that transcends schisms in society tends to depoliticize and marginalize the issue of reducing those severe inequalities. Although it brings the poor into the culture of "the people," they continue to be excluded both socially and economically. Therefore, moral solidarity of the nation tends to perpetuate elite rule.

In point of fact, democratization paved the way for the presidency of a member of an elite family, and the dominance of anti-corruption morality as a theme in the 2010 presidential election gave victory to the same clan. This is the paradox that moral nationalism as a counter-hegemony against corrupt traditional politics transformed the fortunate traditional elite with the national legacy into a moral agent of change. The paradox may be analyzed as what Gramsci called "transformism," through which a ruling class gradually conservatized and incorporated reformative and radical forces. It would be more precise, however, to say that the construction of a moral solidarity of the nation depended upon contingent resonance and intertwining of discourses, between those who saw hope in the moral nationalism and the traditional elite who tried to represent it.

Moreover, while moral solidarity of the nation may temporarily conceal divisions in "the people", it does not substantively heal them. The basis for this solidarity depends entirely on the existence of an evil "enemy of the nation," and does not include redistribution to rectify inequalities in the "nation" or deliberations to mediate "good versus evil" moral antagonisms. Consequently, when the "enemy of the nation" is gone, the class and moral divisions in the "nation," which have been left unaddressed, become even more salient. Indeed, the post-democratization Corazon Aquino administration was a composite of diverse forces whose power struggles inevitably destabilized the administration and prevented it from achieving any substantive land reform or other measures to reduce inequality in the Philippines.

Nonetheless, the moral solidarity of the nation is not entirely incapable of improving the status quo. By bringing in elements that support civic inclusivism under the umbrella of "the people," it can facilitate their rise to power. Numerous activists from NGOs and the moderate left played important roles not only in the democratization movement and election campaigns that supported Aquino family candidates, but also in the administrations that followed. If such forces are able to gain hegemony after the moral solidarity of the nation has completed its task of "exorcising the devil," they may be able to implement more sustainable measures to reduce inequality. However, pushing forward with civic-inclusivist reforms also incurs the risk of political destabilization due to backlash from such forces as the traditional elite, big business, and the military. Conversely, compromise with conservative forces to ensure stability poses a different dilemma, that of being unable to pursue reform. Also, as I mention later, civic inclusivism suffers from the contradiction that ultimately, it cannot fully include the poor.

In other words, the moral solidarity of the nation constructed by moral nationalism is effective in temporarily "exorcising" a corrupt political regime via People Power, elections, or the like, and in this respect, may contribute to democracy. Additionally, it can have a secondary effect of promoting forces that support civic inclusivism. However, moral solidarity of the nation neither promotes redistribution nor ameliorates the class or moral divisions of the nation, and hence fails to ensure the deepening of democracy. It must be acknowledged that, despite the calls for such "reforms," the moral solidarity of the nation has marginalized or coopted hegemonic practices that aim for equality, thereby perpetuating elite rule.

Moral Division of the Nation

The "moral division of the nation" is a condition in which moral antagonism has been created in and between the civic and mass spheres, with each "we" denying the legitimacy of the other "them." In the civic sphere, civic exclusivism resonates with a morality that seeks modern political reform, constructing a moral antagonism between "we citizens" who obey the law and participate in politics "correctly," and "those masses" who lack the skills and morals to do likewise. In the mass sphere, meanwhile, populism resonates with a morality that prioritizes the livelihoods and dignity of the poor, constructing a moral antagonism between an unfeeling "rich" who ignore the suffering of their countrymen, and "we poor" (that is, the masses), who the rich have deprived of dignity and wealth. The moral division of the nation represents the marginalization and radicalization of interclass antagonism from an issue of resource distribution into one of "good versus evil." Moral division of this sort came to play a pivotal role in the political process from the time of Estrada in particular, threatening Philippine democracy on a variety of levels.

The moral division of the nation first came into dramatic relief during the two People Powers of 2001. The impetus was Estrada's formulation of a populist hegemony in the mass sphere in 1998, exposing the class disparities and inequality that had been concealed by the moral solidarity of the nation and propelling him to the presidency. In the civic sphere, this provoked a powerful civic-exclusivist backlash against populism, intensifying the middle class's self-identity as a rational, moral "citizenry," and fomenting a moral antagonism that viewed the poor as irrational, immoral "masses." In 2001, the middle class-led People Power 2 ousted Estrada from the presidency. This sparked an intense backlash in the mass sphere by the poor, who believed that Estrada had been ousted by the self-righteous "rich" and thereby launched People Power 3 in an attempt to restore him to the presidency. These events posed a serious threat to the consolidation of democracy in the Philippines.

Subsequently, this moral division of the nation spread to electoral politics. The civic sphere saw the rise of a civic-exclusivist discourse in which the "citizens" of the middle class were held under the sway of the irrational votes of the poor "masses," which had rendered Philippine democracy dysfunctional. In order to improve electoral politics, it was therefore necessary to impose partial restrictions on the voting rights of the poor, or to educate them. In the mass sphere, on the other hand, people held out hopes for "pro-poor" politicians with an equitable outlook who would help the needy out of genuine concern; however, they also felt that society would remain stratified as long as the election-rigging "rich" continued to steal their votes. Thus, in both the civic and mass spheres, trust in electoral politics was eroded by a moral backlash against a "them" who unfairly controlled elections.

The moral division of the nation also became a destabilizing factor in democracy as it applied to urban governance. Bayani Fernando, the chairman of the Metropolitan Manila Development Authority (MMDA), instituted a form of disciplinary governance that strictly enforced the law against the illegal bases of livelihood of the poor through such measures as forced evictions of squatters and street vendors. These actions prompted a discourse in the civic sphere urging support for Fernando by "citizens" craving law and order, so as to rectify the current state of rampant anarchy caused by "masses" who used poverty as an excuse to break the law. In the mass sphere, however, the same actions reinforced perceptions that the intolerant "rich" were denying "poor people" of their humble livelihoods and dignity and attempting to drive them out of the city. Feelings of alienation and enmity grew as the poor found their attempts to draw attention to their suffering ignored by the government and falling on deaf ears in the civic sphere. In this way, the moral division of the nation affected urban governance by not only having a negative impact on reducing inequality, or on the deepening of democracy, but also incubating a politics of resentment that could have a destructive effect on the democratic system itself.

Why, then, did the civic exclusivism and populism, the two counter hegemonic-discursive practices against traditional politics, engender the moral division of a nation? There is no significant gap or antagonism between the civic and mass spheres in their critique of corrupt politics and their desire for a better Philippines. In this sense, there must be ample room for cooperation between the two spheres. However, the middle class and the impoverished class differ in how they pursue "betterment."

The poor are vulnerable to numerous risks, ranging from family illness to forced evictions, and are therefore under constant pressure to secure short-term benefits that ensure their day-to-day survival. The middle class, on the other hand, seeks more long-term benefits via modern political reform. Furthermore, as each class pursues its own interests, they come to perceive the other as an obstruction. To the impoverished class, political reform that calls for prohibitions on squatting and street vending, decries "services" rendered by politicians, and drives populists supported by the poor from office, is nothing less than a threat to their dignity and daily livelihood. To the middle class, the poor are nothing but a barrier to political reform because they use poverty to justify building an illegal base for their livelihood, perpetuate the practice of handouts by politicians, and elect populists to office. Thus, while both classes seek "betterment," they differ in their socioeconomic wherewithal to wait for it. This gap produces the moralization of politics that leads to the moral division of the nation.

In a welfare state typical of developed nations, the poor would have their survival guaranteed by a variety of welfare institutions, and this would give them the wherewithal to support more long-term reforms. However, the Philippines lacks such guarantees, compelling the poor to participate in politics and secure their means of livelihood through practices that may be despised in the civic sphere.

The fragmentation of discourse and living space also contributes to the moralization of class antagonisms. In moral politics, the poor are generally able to claim the moral high ground over groups with more resources by accusing them of unjust inequalities. For example, poor peasants deprived of their tenant rights or land by the commercialization of agriculture were able to parlay clientelist relations into appeals to landowners over the morality of survival and dignity to resist further impoverishment, thus imposing a certain degree of restraint on capitalist values.[1] However, in Manila today, the gap between the civic and mass spheres continues to widen, with increasing divergence in their economic activities as well as in the language of morality. As a result, people in the civic sphere can praise the morality of capitalism without feeling constrained by the morality of livelihood and dignity asserted by the poor in the mass sphere. In this manner, civic exclusivism and populism have reinforced hegemony in their respective spheres without engaging with one another, further exacerbating the moral division of the nation.

This phenomenon exposes the contradictions and limitations of civic exclusivism, according to which, a moral "citizenry" participates in politics so as to remedy various ills caused by the "masses" and achieve political reform. The "citizen" movement to oust a populist leader sparked a backlash from the "masses" and severely destabilized Philippine politics. The more harshly the "citizens" denounced populists in the name of cleaning up electoral politics, the more the "masses" sympathized with these populists who were being denied their dignity. The more the "citizens" supported attacks on squatters and street vendors in the name of bringing law and order to the city, the more the poor reinforced their illegal bases of livelihood through bribery, and the greater their enmity grew toward the "rich." The upshot was that civic exclusivism not only failed to achieve its objectives, but also drew a vehement backlash from the mass sphere, thus making the moral division of the nation more acute than ever.

In our studies of this new moral politics, we must take a more critical look at the effects of civic exclusivism, rather than merely critiquing populism. In the past, populism has been criticized for inciting enmity between classes by oversimplifying politics as a conflict between the "rich" and the "poor," as well as for inviting social chaos by granting power to irresponsible politicians. Yet, populism is at least capable of contributing to the deepening of democracy insofar as it gives prominence to the issue of socioeconomic inequality and demands its resolution. In contrast, civic exclusivism transforms interclass economic conflicts, which could in practice be mediated through redistribution, into a zero-sum moral antagonism based on a good versus evil. In so doing, it legitimizes the exclusion of the poor, and in this regard, is far more harmful to the deepening of democracy than populism. It may also threaten the consolidation of democracy by fostering the politics of resentment.

My argument about the moral division of the nation may invite criticism that the emphasis on a "we versus they" dichotomy overlooks the actual diversity and plurality of the real world. However, this argument is actually a critique of political moralization that itself reduces the complex and diverse social relations of the real world to a dualistic false image of a world divided into good and evil. There may also be criticism that the introduction of the dual public spheres as an analytical framework exaggerates this dichotomy. But in fact, this book addresses possibilities for destabilizing or deconstructing the civic-mass sphere dichotomy in its examination of the impact of a moral solidarity of the nation that transcends the boundaries of both the dual public spheres and the power exercised in the contact zone.

Practices that Mediate Moral Antagonism

Moral politics in the post-democratization Philippines has fluctuated between two types of antagonistic relations: moral solidarity of the nation and moral division of the nation. Meanwhile, the contact zone of the dual public spheres has been the site of civic-inclusivist practices by members of the middle class working through NGOs in an attempt to include the poor in the "citizenry." The activists involved in this effort include people born in the civic sphere who are concerned about the situation of the poor and people born in the mass sphere who received a higher education with the help of scholarships or remittances from relatives overseas; many are motivated by faith to try to build a better Philippines.

How can we evaluate these social movements? Tocquevillian civil society theory credits this kind of social movement as a contribution to democracy by "citizens." However, this is a one-sided viewpoint that turns a blind eye to the exclusivist hegemony of said "citizens." I argue that the true significance of social movements in the Philippines lies in their potential to mediate moral antagonisms via the divergent moralities of the civic sphere and mass sphere, not in their expansion of civic morality. Such mediation in social movements may serve to disturb the "citizens/masses" dichotomy, but never achieve its deconstruction. In fact, many of these activists identify themselves as belonging to the "masses" and employ the discourses of the mass sphere, despite being highly educated and speaking fluent English. The paradox is that when middle-class activists speak for the "masses," they risk depriving the actual "masses" of a voice and concealing the asymmetrical relationship in these social movements. Mediation in social movements also may contribute to inclusion of the poor in the "citizenry" as a practice of civic inclusivism, but it is not always successful. Rather, in my view, the full potential of mediation to transform moral antagonism into agonism would only be possible after the failure or impossibility of civic inclusion is exposed and realized, as I will argue.

One example of inter-class meditation through social movements is the voter education conducted by the Parish Pastoral Council for Responsible Voting (PPCRV), an organization composed of members of the Catholic Church. The PPCRV attempts to teach the morality of "correct" voting behavior to the poor so that they will not be manipulated by media images or cash handouts. This practice is predicated on the assumption that the poor are deceived by images and money because they lack an adequate education, and if properly educated, will vote in the same manner as responsible "citizens" and help to facilitate political reform.

This effort constitutes nothing less than an attempt to "enlighten" the poor with the morality of the civic sphere. The problem is that force-feeding civic-sphere morality to the mass sphere inevitably provokes a backlash from the poor. Therefore, the PPCRV has emphasized universal values that even the mass sphere will find palatable, along the lines of "Let's vote for good, honest candidates who will devote themselves to the country." To the poor, however, a "good, honest candidate" as championed by the PPCRV would be one who provides them with various services, or a populist who makes a point of displaying kindness. In the socioeconomic context of the mass sphere, even such universal values are interpreted differently, and are therefore not necessarily effective in altering the voting behavior of the poor.

To deal with this issue, some PPCRV members began to practice an unofficial form of voter education in which they sought to acquaint the poor with a new perspective through suggestions and the like. However, this practice also retained the character of unilateral "enlightenment," with little evidence of reciprocity in the sense of practitioners revising their own views as a result of deliberation with the poor. At the least, this practice played an important role in opening a conduit for communications between the civic and mass spheres that ensured a certain degree of plurality between their divergent moralities.

I have also examined social movements that attempt to formalize and legalize the bases for the livelihood of the urban poor. First, the Urban Land Reform Task Force collaborated on lobbying activities with peoples' organizations of informal settlers, and succeeded in passing the Urban Development and Housing Act. This law banned arbitrary forced demolitions of informal settlers' homes and set up a system through which they could formally purchase land. Similarly, Ka-Tinig worked with street vendors' associations to lobby the government, which eventually led to the implementation of Executive Order No. 452, which legalized and officially systematized street vending in designated areas. These movements achieved the incorporation of the interests of the urban poor into public policy and the legalization of their bases of livelihood, thereby mediating the moral antagonism between the legalism supported in the civic sphere and the survival of the poor supported in the mass sphere.

Despite these efforts, however, the moral friction between the two spheres remained. For example, squatters and street vendors had for many years protected their illegal livelihoods by paying protection money to syndicates and bureaucrats. Members of NGOs were morally opposed to these informal payments by the poor on the grounds that they perpetuated political corruption. The NGOs were also morally disapproving of informal settlers who fell into arrears on their payments to the Community Mortgage Program and of sidewalk vendors who obstructed traffic, drank liquor or littered in the streets. For their part, the poor resented the NGOs for recruiting them to demonstrate for causes such as anti-globalization, which had no direct bearing on their most urgent problems, and for failing to provide substantive assistance when their homes were demolished or their merchandise confiscated.

Still, even as the poor were not fully subsumed into the "citizenry" and remained at odds over moral values, the two sides avoided excessive confrontation as they slowly but steadily pursued their common objective of making the interests of the poor a part of public policy; by doing to, they achieved a certain degree of success in establishing new institutions. Granted, a lack of political will and skill on the part of politicians and bureaucrats hampered the effective implementation of these new institutions, making it difficult to claim that such movements achieved their initial aims. Despite the prohibition imposed on the forced eviction of informal settlers and street vendors by the Urban Development and Housing Act and Executive Order No. 452, the MMDA and local governments ignored them. Nonetheless, these social movements were highly significant for providing a model for mediating the moral antagonism between the civic and mass spheres and getting this approach reflected in public policy. A lesson from these cases is that attempts to mediate the moral division of the nation in the contact zone fail to achieve their objectives when they take the form of "enlightenment" bestowed upon the mass sphere by the civic sphere because of the moral friction between them, as in the case of voter education. If anywhere, the possibility of mediating moral antagonism between the two spheres may be realized in practices where members of the middle and impoverished classes engage purely on the level of interests—embracing but not excessively foregrounding their moral antagonism as they collaborate to make the interests of the poor a part of public policy, as in the social movements for legalization of the livelihood bases of the urban poor.

This suggests that the failure of civic inclusivism in establishing hegemony in the mass sphere actually opens a new possibility of interclass cooperation beyond morality. This "failure" also would mitigate the division of the poor community or the movement caused by organizing the activity of opposing NGOs with different ideologies or morality.[2] Moreover, unsuccessful civic inclusivism strengthens the poor's autonomy to flexibly cope with different problems in its changing political environment. My observation is that in a situation in which the poor have autonomy to decide whether they become members of NGOs, which NGOs they affiliate with, what repertoire they use to achieve their aim, and when they quit activities, they have the bigger bargaining power to make use of NGOs to address their own interest, avoiding the danger of being divided or manipulated by the ideology or morality of the NGOs.

For example, as the situation progressed, the street vendors' organizations not only switched their affiliation from Ka-Tinig to Sanlakas but also initiated their own informal everyday forms of resistance without being ordered by any NGO to do so. While their withdrawal from Ka-Tinig frustrated the advocacy to make the government implement the EO. 452, concentrating available resources into everyday forms of resistance was a reasonable decision when the government totally closed the political opportunity structure to the movement and helped them to survive the predicament. Besides switching of affiliation, many of the poor quit the activities of NGOs when they think it is not necessary. When the street clearing operation of the MMDA stopped after the change of its chairman, many of the vendors allied with Sanlakas became inactive. To keep them active, Sanlakas rewarded some loyal vendors with formal accommodations, by recommending them to a relocation and housing project of the city government.

In sum, civic inclusivism, which attempts to subsume the entire impoverished class into the "citizenry," is not necessarily effective in mediating the moral division of the nation. What is more, civic inclusivism can all too easily transmute into civic exclusivism when confrontations with the "intractability" of the poor reinforce judgments that they are, after all, "masses" lacking the skills or morals to become true "citizens." The limitation of civic inclusivism makes it all the more essential to seek ways of reducing inequality via the perpetual struggle among diverse forces at the level of interests—that is, the distribution of socioeconomic resources—while maintaining a watchful eye for excessive political moralization and operating on the assumption that moral antagonism between the civic and mass spheres is not likely to disappear. Because practices of this sort in the contact zone open a conduit for the articulation of mass-sphere interests without their marginalization by the morality of the civic sphere, they have the potential to contribute to the deepening of democracy.

Breaking Through an Impasse in Democracy
Moral Politics in the Neoliberal Era

The moral politics we have been discussing in this volume is a characteristic phenomenon of the Philippines, but at the same time, it is also a direct reflection of the worldwide rise of neoliberalism. Consequently, insofar as they have also had a profound impact on developed and other emergent nations, the structural conditions that led to the rise of moral politics in the Philippines must be discussed from a broader and more historical perspective.

At present, fundamental frictions between democracy and capitalism have grown conspicuous in a "post-welfare state" context in many developed countries, and in a "pre-welfare state" context in emergent and developing countries. With the end of the Cold War, a doctrine has taken hold that regards the adoption of democracy and capitalism by all states as imperative. However, there is a fundamental conflict between democracy and capitalism: democracy espouses the principle of equality, while capitalism continually generates inequalities. The inequalities created by capitalism carry with them the danger of eroding the legitimacy of democracy by exposing the fiction of democracy as self-government based on equal participation by an entire nation. In communist states that have introduced a capitalist economy, the growth of inequality poses a particularly serious dilemma, because socioeconomic equality is the basis for the system's legitimacy.

For many years, this conflict between democracy and capitalism was not apparent in Western nations. In the 16th and 17th centuries, bourgeois citizens of Western European countries obtained their political freedom through bourgeois revolutions, but in the 19th century, the working class created by the rise of capitalism also began to demand suffrage. This prompted fears among the bourgeois citizenry that political participation by uncultured laborers would ruin democracy.[3] Indeed, the rise of fascism in the early 20th century could be said to embody the realization of such fears. However, the class antagonisms engendered by the growth of capitalism were not so acute as to destroy the capitalist system per se, as had been anticipated by Marx. This is because the contradiction between capitalism and democracy as manifested in the form of antagonism between workers and the bourgeois was "resolved" by the postwar spread of Keynesianism and the welfare state. In other words, the political inclusion of workers into the universal suffrage system and institutions such as the Labor Party, as well as their socioeconomic inclusion through redistributive policies, enabled capitalism and democracy to coexist.[4]

Then, during the postwar economic boom enjoyed by most advanced nations, the demands of economic growth on the one hand and of the welfare state on the other were mutually supported. Socioeconomic guarantees for those who had dropped out of the "capitalism game" provided people with livelihood security and opportunities to take up new challenges, putting their economic capacity to work. In addition, the redistributive policies of the welfare state were sustained by a nationalism that perpetually constructed a single "nation." This era of high economic growth was characterized by the increased availability of resources and an expansion of social security systems, which reduced the likelihood of serious interclass antagonism.

However, starting with the "reforms" of Thatcher in the United Kingdom in the 1980s, developed countries began to dismantle their welfare-state systems under the influence of neoliberalism. Behind this shift were factors such as sluggish economic growth, government budget deficits, and increasingly fierce global economic competition. Today, states have lost the fiscal wherewithal to ensure the survival of those who have dropped out of the labor market, and people are compelled to engage in "self-governance" by taking responsibility for their own survival. This has accelerated the phenomenon of nations dividing into two sectors: a sector of people who have succeeded at active self-governance, are economically productive and pay their share of taxes; and a sector of those who have failed at self-governance, are unproductive and rely on welfare. Those in the sector that barely survives on welfare accumulate resentment against the society that has consigned them to this position vis-à-vis "winners," while those in the economically advantaged sector, who are constantly pressured to compete and hounded by fear of the consequences of failure, come to despise the "losers" who depend on welfare. As a result, recent years have seen a resurgence of visible class contradictions in most advanced nations, making it increasingly difficult to maintain the construct of a single "nation."

Furthermore, as Young argues, the transformation of modes of production from Fordist to post-Fordist has created economic insecurity, while the rise of individualism and the diversification of lifestyles has fostered "ontological insecurity," aggravating material and existential insecurities and fears. The result is a proliferation of moralism, as not only the poor but also the wealthy seek to assuage their anxieties by brandishing their personal values as moral absolutes, lashing out randomly at other groups they despise and attacking them for bringing calamity to their society and themselves (Young 1999: 2007).

What is more, the moral demarcation between "good" and "evil" becomes conflated with not only class lines but also by other lines such as ethnicity, religion and disease, such that those considered inferior are no longer treated as candidates for salvation but rather are condemned as evil presences harmful to society. For example, poor people and immigrants tend to be stigmatized as morally depraved welfare recipients and potential criminals. To avoid this exclusion on moral grounds, they must become upright "citizens" who have succeeded at self-governance. This way of thinking indicates that the prescription for solving inequality has shifted from a politics of recognition or redistributive interest politics to a moral politics that requires each individual to become an upright "citizen." However, this moral politics does not actually possess the power to rectify a stratified social structure, and is hence nothing more than a false prescription.

Meanwhile, the advance of social fragmentation and moral division of the nation has been a factor in the deepening of people's alienation from society and, however paradoxically, the boosting of a moral nationalism that calls loudly for national solidarity. Developed countries with increasingly stratified societies are also undergoing a deluge of discourses calling for the solidarity of "our" morally superior nation, concurrent with shrill warnings about the threat posed by foreigners, certain politicians, and others viewed as morally inferior "enemies of the nation." We have already seen how brittle and hollow the basis for this solidarity is, and efforts such as these to unify an entire nation are never successful. As evidenced by the search for "traitors" during wartime, the louder the calls for the moral solidarity of the "nation," the more the psychological impulse to expel those who fail to submit to this solidarity turns inward toward "us" and gains unstoppable momentum. Thus, while moral nationalism and the moral division of the nation are two different phenomena, they function as two sides of the same coin, that is, the rise to prominence of moral politics in the neoliberal era.

This situation provides a convenient opportunity for ambitious politicians who exploit accumulated resentment in society. In the time of the welfare state, the interest politics of distributing resources was a necessary strategy for politicians, but nowadays they can enjoy considerable support even without giving material benefits to their constituencies if they are successful in fermenting moral antagonism against the "enemy." Such politicians tend to appeal to "change" against the establishment. However, the Philippine case illustrates the danger that the very counter-hegemonic discursive practices that morally question and challenge the hegemonic elite can paradoxically help to perpetuate elite rule or escalate class conflict.

This ascendancy of moral politics embodies a significant paradox. A situation in which the welfare state is infeasible, stratification is growing and the value of limited resources is rising would appear to call for resource distribution based on more careful deliberations than ever before. However, the interest politics that would reduce socioeconomic inequalities is marginalized, and even threatened with extinction, because neoliberalism foregrounds a zero-sum moral politics that utterly denies the legitimacy of the other, treating "them" as evil enemies to be destroyed. The result is a buildup of bitterness and resentment in a broadly fragmented society, threatening the loss of the democratic underpinnings found in mutual engagement among diverse people.

The impact of neoliberalism described here is reflected by conditions specific to each country. The Philippines is characterized primarily by the fact that it suffers from not only profound inequalities but also a substantive division of the public sphere caused by class disparities in language, media and living space. Second, the country has experienced the challenges to democracy posed by a stratified society for over a century, dating back to the introduction of a democratic system in the early 20th century, as well as the adoption of neoliberal economic policies from the mid-1980s on. Finally, the Philippine democratic system lacks the capacity to respond to the demands of its society or a party system capable of mediating its social antagonisms, a condition that has encouraged the rise of a politics of resentment that bypasses the established system, fomenting repeated instances of People Power or attempted coup d'états. The Philippines has thus seen the growth of a politics of resentment grounded in the moral division of the nation and a consequent aligning of conditions that threaten its democracy.

In short, democracy in the neoliberal era finds itself torn by the contradiction between its inborn doctrine of equality and the reality of growing inequality; the Philippines has experienced a particularly severe version of this predicament. Yet, the Philippines has also given birth to numerous strategies for breaking through this impasse. One might even be so bold as to label the Philippines an "advanced nation" in terms of its pioneering experience with issues and challenges that many countries face today. In this respect, the findings about Philippine democracy and moral politics reported in this book may offer some value to other advanced or emergent nations.

What is the Basis for Social Solidarity?

Today, democracy under neoliberalism faces a crisis marked by the rise of a moral politics characterized by repeating cycles of moral division of the nation and a reactive moral solidarity of the nation. I would like to conclude by attempting a theoretical study, based on this book's findings, of measures for breaking through this impasse.

In discussing the possibilities offered by a multiplicity of publics in stratified class societies, Fraser (1992) argues that opposition to the civic public sphere by counterpublics can mitigate inequality and contribute to democracy. However, as I have argued in this book, when multiple publics formulate moral antagonism against their respective "others," opposition by counterpublics may not only fail to ameliorate inequalities but also exacerbate the moral division of the nation and pose a threat to democracy. Hence, the dilemma of democracy under neoliberalism cannot be resolved merely through resistance or opposition to the powers that be; rather, it requires a new basis for solidarity or mutuality that is capable of resisting social fragmentation.

One influential political theory with proposals for resisting social fragmentation is the liberal nationalism described by Miller et al. (1995). Liberal nationalism recognizes the preservation of individual "private cultures" on one hand, while demanding allegiance to the "public culture" by all members of a democratic system on the other. In this manner, it purports to restore national identity and foster both national solidarity and trust without suppressing cultural diversity. Proponents of liberal nationalism emphasize that democratic deliberation and redistribution are impossible without some level of solidarity consciousness. However, a national "public culture" that is meant to serve as a wellspring of unity tends to reflect culture of majority groups and cannot possibly be considered neutral by minority groups.

The examples provided in this book amply demonstrate the difficulty of creating a "public culture" that does not exclude certain people or cultures. In the Philippines, the morality of the civic sphere, which reflected a modern Western orientation and a capitalist ethos, claimed hegemony as a single public culture to which everyone should swear allegiance. However, this culture excluded the poor of the mass sphere and only amplified the moral division of the nation. Conversely, it might be possible to cultivate a new public culture grounded in vernacular language and the morality of the mass sphere. However, given that the nation-state of the Philippines was created under the aegis of colonialism, colonial vestiges like the English language are an intrinsic part of its national identity. Therefore, it simply is not feasible to eradicate such vestiges, and any such attempt would likely provoke severe exclusions and antagonisms within the nation.

Another idea that aims to achieve the unification of society without fomenting divisions or exclusion is the constitutional patriotism of Habermas (1996). This argument looks for the wellspring of social unity in spontaneous allegiance and attachment to constitutional principles formulated through participation in deliberations by every citizen. However, in virtually every nation-state today, there are linguistic divisions along class and ethnic lines, as well as minorities who lack a fluent command of the majority language. It would be difficult to hold free and equal deliberations over a constitution if the participants did not share a common language, and people who have effectively been excluded from constitutional deliberations for this reason are unlikely to feel a spontaneous attachment to that constitution. Moreover, deliberations over norms may only serve to make manifest the moral conflicts between participants; hence, there are no guarantees that the deliberative process would foster trust and solidarity with others, or keep from adding to the moral division of the nation.

Viewed in these terms, one must conclude that there are problems with the very concept of social unification through morality. Liberal nationalism advocates achieving social unity through a public culture, while constitutional patriotism calls for normative deliberation. These are, in effect, attempts to incorporate diverse people into "we, the citizenry," through a morality of public culture or normative deliberation. But insofar as a public culture cannot always be neutral toward all people, and normative deliberations over constitutional principles will inevitably preclude the participation of some, it is impossible to avoid the exclusion of people who for various reasons cannot or will not become "citizens." Hence, to the extent that fragmentation has already advanced in a society, attempts to resolve antagonisms through morality will always face daunting challenges.

Instead, is it not possible to shift the character of "we/they" antagonisms in a direction that is not destructive to democracy, even while accepting that such antagonisms and their underlying "lack of mutual understanding" will not be eliminated? What is crucial to this objective is the cultivation of what Mouffe and Connolly call "agonism," that is, an interdependent antagonistic relationship in which opposing forces exhibit consideration and respect for one another even as they continue to struggle (Mouffe 2000, 2005; Connolly 1991). However, Mouffe and Connolly do not precisely clarify how agonistic relations are to be fostered. Based on the findings discussed in this book, let us attempt to elucidate conditions that may be considered essential to the nurturing of agonistic relations.

Seeking a New Mutuality

First, expansion of the contact zones between multiple public spheres where diverse "others" encounter one another can help to suppress the moralization of politics.[5] The various forces that vie for hegemony in civil society spread discourses that dichotomize society into "good" and "evil" sides. Exposed to these discourses, we tend to amplify moral antagonisms by accepting and reproducing distorted collective representations of "them" through virtual worlds like the Internet that are devoid of real, substantive contact. However, in a life-world where we directly encounter actual "others" with their own names and identities, we come to understand that these collective representations of others are composed of individual human beings, some with whom we may be capable of establishing close friendships, and some with whom we may not. This experience helps us more readily recognize the fictitiousness of such dichotomies and begin to dismantle them.

It is true that life-world contact with "others" may actually reinforce existing prejudices, which could further fuel undisguised moral antagonism. However, such reinforcement of prejudices is usually based on limited, superficial contact, while more intimate, intense contact with others tends to dissolve prejudices. This is because closer acquaintance with the lives of others extricates them from collectively represented categories and brings them into relief as flesh-and-blood entities with their own identities. Close contact with others also works to disturb and dissolve existing hierarchical orders by, for example, inspiring respect, even awe, toward people once thought of as inferior.[6] As such experiences accumulate, they may contribute to the formation of agonistic relations by transforming the demarcation line of a collectively represented "we/they" dichotomy from a solid, fixed line into one that is broken and fluid.

Next, rather than strive for social unity based on certain designated moralities or normative deliberations, we need to reevaluate the role that interests can play in fostering human relations. We are more readily capable of building agonistic relationships at the level of interests associated with resource distribution, even with others whom we might find interacting at the level of moralities problematic. Whereas disputes over morality can all too easily lead to disapproval and denial of the legitimacy of others who embrace different worldviews, disputes over interests allow for the possibility of competition as "worthy opponents."

In criticizing moral politics and espousing interest politics, we may well invite criticism that the two cannot be separated, because people frequently cite moral arguments in claiming the legitimacy of their own interests. It may also be argued that whatever the dangers of moral politics, the removal of morality from politics would leave us with a politics of rampant, unbridled greed and self-interest. Yet another counterargument might be that the proliferation of interest politics within narrowly restricted groups that exclude certain people, with the strong continuing to exploit the weak, would merely serve to reproduce inequality anew. These critiques are all valid. In response, I would like to draw a distinction between a moral politics that merits criticism and one that merits support, and to propose some conditions under which interest politics can play a reformist role.

What I wish to criticize above all is moral politics that makes a non-issue of interest politics concerned with inequitable resource distribution by separating people into "good" and "evil," thus escalating fragmentation and exclusion. In contrast, I support an ethic of self-restraint according to which various competing actors seek to avoid harming others through excessive demands or assertions of a moral footing for their own particular interests. It is also imperative to foster an ethic of mutuality, that is, support for one another's lives, if interest politics is to provide a bulwark against social fragmentation and to contribute to the reduction of inequality. However, we must note that it is dangerous to claim a moral basis for this mutuality. Morality that asserts the correctness of its view of "what ought to be" may appear to bring people together in solidarity, but in fact, it merely separates them into "good" and "evil." Additionally, solidarity in the name of morality only papers over such problems as inequality and discrimination and may actually perpetuate them. For this reason, it is crucial that we recognize the violent character of an "ought to be" morality and, if anything, embrace the "evil" with the "good" in nurturing a mutuality of support for each other's lives.

The impetus for this mutuality is perhaps found in a spontaneous compassion for the vulnerabilities of life. Kusaka (2012) discussed the relationship between Filipino students who were studying in Japan on Japanese government scholarships after graduating from top Philippine universities and Filipino women who had traveled to Japan to earn money as entertainers. In the Philippines, class have separated these two groups, giving them little opportunity to encounter each other, but when they moved to Japan, they met in the contact zones provided by institutions such as churches and NGOs. Even there, many of the students reproduced discourses that treated these entertainers, including those who retired from the business, as morally and socially inferior.

However, some of these individuals overcame inter-class moral antagonism of this sort to develop an intimate mutuality. What brought the women and students together was an "ethics of care" that seeks to assuage the vulnerabilities of life. Though the students enjoyed advantages of class and education, they also bore such vulnerabilities as being gay or suffering from serious illnesses, while the entertainers dealt with troubles like domestic violence and divorce. Sharing smiles and Philippine-style meals gave all of them comfort and liberated them from the pain of being condemned as "bad" in the eyes of certain moral constructs for reasons of occupation or sexuality. These relationships also gave rise to a chain of connections through which people sought to share the healing they had experienced with others. The vulnerabilities of life provide a basis for mutuality precisely because no one enjoys advantages in every aspect of their life.[7]

This morality-transcending, mutual life support is a practice that constructs a new social order beyond the existing legal system of the state. The same can be said of the livelihood practices of the poor described in this book. In the slums and streets, people who were originally strangers created new interdependent relationships through which they ensured one another's basic survival, even if they were not on good terms. They would then join forces to negotiate with politicians and bureaucrats, forming clientelist relationships, *palakasan* (influence-peddling) and bribery systems to protect their livelihoods from the vagaries of illness, job loss, fire, flood and forced evictions. Unable to secure guarantees of their survival from the state, they created an autonomous order based on reciprocity with others, within which they sought to sustain their lives.

This informal system has been criticized as a form of political corruption that harms the interests of society as a whole by distorting the formal system of laws and elections. Yet, without their clientelist relations, the poor would be even further marginalized in electoral politics, and without their bribery system, the survival needs of the poor and the enforcement of the law by the state could generate severe violence. It is thanks to the existence of this informal system that the formal system is able to incorporate the poor and still function, however imperfectly. If the informal system were to be entirely eliminated, the formal system would also break down, and chaos would likely ensue.

Another problem with the informal system is that it impedes the ability of the poor to obtain guarantees for their survival through the formal system. Politicians and bureaucrats who profit from the bribery system try to restrict the lives of the poor to these informal conditions, while the influence-peddling system exacerbates the practice of handouts by politicians, thereby obstructing the institutionalization of more systematic redistribution policies. Nonetheless, the informal system is the result of the collaborative construction of a resilient order that enables people to survive while enduring contingent risks in a society where the state will not guarantee their survival. Particularly in an era of neoliberalism that eschews reliance on the state, it behooves us to reevaluate a practice through which people have created a life-sustaining social order with their own hands.

In summary, this book proposes the following prescriptions for resisting social fragmentation. First, an expansion of the contact zones between multiple public spheres that enables diverse people to interact with one another is needed. Second, while communication continues in these contact zones, conclusive definitions of "right" and "wrong" must be deferred in order to prevent further moralization of politics and maintain politics at the level of interests. Third, to construct an order of mutual life-support, a "soft" mutuality must be nurtured through care-based relationships and spontaneous compassion for the vulnerabilities of life. Admittedly, at this stage, these prescriptions are little more than suggestions, and their effectiveness will have to be determined through case studies and with further theoretical research. I hope to make the possibilities for a new post-fragmentation mutuality the subject of future research.

ADDENDUM

Duterte as a Drastic Medicine

Photo 29 Yoyoy (alias) talks about Duterte while holding a marijuana joint (Pechayan, March 2016).

I would like to briefly discuss how the argument of this book is applicable to the changing context of Philippine politics accompanied by the victory of Rodrigo Duterte in the 2016 presidential election.

Duterte employs another discourse of moral nationalism: that of "the people" who support "discipline" against the disorder of the state and society. In the election, his moral nationalism enjoyed nationwide support that has cut across social cleavages of religion, class and locality, which signifies the successful construction of a newer version of moral solidarity for the nation. While Aquino's moral nationalism was based on the call for "decent Filipinos," Duterte's version has been characterized by an "un-civic" or social-bandit-like form of morality that aims to destroy existing systems and their vested interests in order to save the people even if by resorting to extra-judicial means. Yet, as Aquino supporters once regarded non-supporters as paid and manipulated by corrupt politicians, this new form of moral nationalism still morally excludes others as enemies. Loyal Duterte supporters now patrol anti-Duterte discourses on websites and punish those who are critical of him. This moral exclusion of minority opposition, which must survive under the shadow of this new form of national moral solidarity, is alarming.

What, then, makes Duterte supporters so united and aggressive? It is not surprising that Duterte's moral discourse of discipline was hailed in the civic sphere, considering the educated middle class's longstanding desire for a strong state that could appropriately implement policy, laws and regulations without being compromised by strong social forces. However, it is interesting that his moral appeal to discipline has also enjoyed considerable support in the mass sphere, which has traditionally supported populist discourse coupled with various dole-outs, the strategy used by one of his opponents, Jejomar Binay.

Why did many of the poor prefer Duterte's discipline to Jejomar Binay's populist dole-out promise? Pointing out Binay's corruption scandal is not sufficient, because the poor believe that politicians are all corrupt to various degrees. Listening to the voices of the poor in Pechayan, they seem to have been bored with the same old discourse of "politics for the poor." A friend of mine said: "If you vote for Binay, it would perpetuate the corrupt system. Now we have to change the very system instead of trying to get a small share from a corrupt politician like a beggar." Behind such statements, there also may be a reason that the economic growth has uplifted some of the poor's life to be independent of dole outs from politicians.

Beyond immediate and direct benefits, what Duterte successfully appealed to in both the civic and mass spheres were the people's shared anger against their country's corrupt and inefficient institutions and their desire for a new Philippines as a respectable emerging nation. Despite high economic growth since the early 2000s, state laws and regulations have been ignored and exploited by the powerful and the affluent. While many people have benefitted from the corrupt system whenever they needed to avoid or distort the rule of law, an increasing number of people have realized the long-term negative impact of this corrupt system on public services. Those who are familiar with the Philippines can easily make a long list of the country's poor public services affecting functions in such areas

Photo 30 Teenagers play a coin gambling game all night long. Images of Duterte, marijuana and Christ are drawn on the game board (Pechayan, March 2016).

as infrastructure, bureaucratic procedure, monitoring economic activities, and peace and order.

To be sure, Aquino also appealed to moral politics against corruption. However, while his administration was aggressive in bringing down its political rivals, the bigger system of corruption remained almost untouched. At election time, Ron, a lawyer, told me: "I know Aquino and Roxas's reform is in the right direction but it's too slow to see any results. Their *matuwid na daan* (straight path) is so jammed up," implying the aggravatingly heavy traffic jams in Metro Manila. In other words, in seeking to cure the problems of the nation, impatient Filipinos saw Aquino as the kind of good medicine that requires considerable time to show its effect; so instead, they chose the drastic medicine of Duterte.

Behind this support for Duterte lies the people's reflection that the exploitation of laws and regulations through corrupt behavior has led to the breakdown of the public service system, and that it is imperative to reduce the degree of freedom to exploit through strict discipline in order to fix it. In particular, the desire of people for a more efficient system in the Philippines should be seen against the backdrop of the increase in the number of people who visit or live in foreign counties where rules and regulations are strictly implemented, which must have strengthened their desire. In fact, overseas Filipino workers are one of Duterte's strongest supporters. His determined anti-drug operation, despite human rights violations, gained popularity because the drug-trafficking business—operated by networks of syndicates and including police and other public officials—symbolizes the corrupt and inefficient system of the country.

While it is understandable that the civic and mass spheres share this discourse of fear regarding the crime and drug problems, I was surprised to find that many of my old friends in Pechayan who had the regular habit of using drugs also expressed support for Duterte. In the interviews I conducted during the election campaign period, I learned that they liked his rustic way of speaking, which is similar to the language of the mass sphere, and a unique aura that allows people to create various funny jokes. I asked Yoyoy (alias), "Are you serious? You may be killed," but he replied, "Surely not. If Duterte gets elected, everything will be free." I could not immediately understand what he meant, but a few more conversations made me realize that he had wanted change in his life but had failed because of friendships. He believed, however, that Duterte's presidency would emancipate him from his vicious habit.

When I revisited Yoyoy after the election in August, he had already quit the habit and had surrendered to the police along with some 30 other users and pushers, because the police threatened to kill them otherwise. The police were dispatched from a different station so that they could be more strict, having had no previous contact with the locals. They compiled a watch list of the surrendered and started patrolling houses in plain clothes at night. One night, when Yoyoy returned home, he found his wife and children crying because police had frightened them. The locals referred to this operation as "*oplan katok*" (operation knocking) with great fear. The ex-drug users and pushers complain that it is unjust and that even those who surrendered were extrajudicially killed. Their fear of being killed in order to to muzzle them is real, because they know the names of the police officers who had themselves been engaged in illegal business. Yoyoy regrets that he voted for Duterte, but he repeats his determination to "*magbago na ako*" (I change myself). While the words resonate with the Catholic narrative about the confession of sin and rebirth, they also overlap with Duterte's idea of "*pagbabago*" (change). Yoyoy's wife shared her sentiment with tears that thanks to Duterte, her husband was able to stop his bad habit and become more hard-working despite her bad experience with the police.

Duterte represents and justifies his violence as the "tough love" of a patriarch or social bandit exhibiting a morality beyond the rule of law in order to fix the system. His supporters regard this morality as justice, because they believe the law is nothing more than an instrument of the elites. Duterte has a dilemma, however: While he aims to establish a strong state with the full power to implement laws and regulations over society, he looks down on the existing judicial system and other state institutions as corrupt and inefficient, and so he tends to rely on extrajudicial means to achieve peace and order—which should further weaken state institutions.

This dilemma captures the predicament of contemporary democracy in the time of neoliberalism. Neoliberalism may promote economic growth but does not guarantee the improvement of public services and makes people's lives more precarious by expanding inequality and non-regular employment. However, democracy can neither promptly solve the discontent of the people nor prevent corruption, because it requires the reconciliation of conflicting interests among diverse actors. It seems that the democratic institution has lost much of its trust as an instrument for realizing equality and the improvement of life in many parts of the world. Considering this context, it would be precise to say that Filipinos who desire drastic and immediate change through "benign authoritarianism" have dared to take a risky gamble in order to break the paradox of neoliberalism and democracy.

AFTERWORD

This book is an extensively revised and expanded version of a doctoral dissertation submitted to the Graduate School of Social and Cultural Studies, Kyushu University, in March 2012. The original Japanese edition, which was published in April 2013 by Hosei University Press, received the 30th Ohira Masayoshi Memorial Award and the 35th Award for the Promotion of Studies on Developing Countries from the Institute of Developing Economies at the Japan External Trade Organization. It has also been reviewed in five newspapers and seven academic journals. On the occasion of the publication of this English edition, I have made a number of revisions in response to the critiques I have received regarding the Japanese edition. Also, because the Japanese edition only covered the period up to the presidential election of 2010, I have added a new section on the most recent Aquino administration to Chapter 6 and an Addendum in order to address the new development of the Philippine politics since then.

It never would have occurred to me to write this book had I not enjoyed close friendships with a great number of people. From my many friends in the slums and streets of Manila, I learned about the thoughts and philosophies of the mass sphere in the Philippines. Above all, the Luega and Juma-os family, with whom I lived, taught me by their example about the dignity of poor people. During my undergraduate days, my experience of work camp volunteer activities on Leyte Island, where I built waterworks and other community infrastructures with local villagers, made me fall in love with the Philippines. My friends in Leyte taught me so much—about the war, about rural poverty, about human kindness. More than the lectures I attended as a graduate school student in Manila, the political discussions I had while drinking, playing guitar, doing laundry or street vending with these poor but proud friends provided me with stimulation and inspiration. My conversations and experiences with these friends gave substance to my ideas. The opportunity to participate in the lifeworld and discursive space of these people, defiant in the face of marginalization, was a priceless experience. I hope to find some way to repay them for their kindnesses and to maintain these friendships in good faith for many years to come.

Sadly, there are people I will never be able to see again: my highly esteemed friends Nilo Jaballa and Selverio Rubillos from the town of Albuera, Leyte, and Peter Luega and Noella Ampuan, with whom I lived in Manila. Many other friends, poor but beloved by their families, have also lost their lives. If I had never met you, I would not be the person I am today. May you rest in peace.

Even as I was developing close ties with these impoverished friends, my poor English-language skills caused me to drop out of graduate school midway through my program at the University of the Philippines. Artists like Louie Cordero and Jun Sabayton, who engaged in art activities of great interest in Cubao after graduating from the College of Fine Arts at the University of the Philippines, provided me with renewed access to the civic sphere. Mercedes Ignacio-Nicolas of Ka-Tinig forced me to revise my thinking about NGO activists in light of her devoted and close-knit relationships with workers in the informal sector. My discussions with these individuals made me realize that in my one-sided criticisms of the "arrogance" of civic-sphere discourses and lifestyles, I was in fact the one guilty of such arrogance. After I returned to Japan, I had the good fortune to meet Marose Pereira and other Filipino lawyers studying at Kyushu University. From 2007 to 2008, I was admitted to the University of the Philippines' Third World Studies Center as a visiting researcher. This afforded me the opportunity to have discussions in English with the director, Teresa Tadem Encarnacion, and others on her staff. Without their acquaintance and assistance, I could not have surmounted my feelings of inferiority toward the English language and Philippine intellectuals and would not have been able to participate in the civic sphere. For this I am deeply grateful.

The opportunity to engage in comprehensive field research and make the acquaintance of so many people was made possible by research grants I received while in graduate school from the Fuji Xerox Setsutaro Kobayashi Memorial Fund, the Konosuke Matsushita Memorial Foundation and the Fukuoka Asian Urban Research Center. I wish to express anew my gratitude for these grants, which gave me tremendous support, not only financially, but also emotionally, at a time when I suffered from a lack of confidence in my endeavors.

I also received invaluable assistance from many scholars in the writing of this book. At the Graduate School of Social and Cultural Studies, Kyushu University, Professor Hiromu Shimizu graciously served as my first dissertation advisor. It was the admiration I acquired for Professor Shimizu's research while writing my senior thesis as an undergraduate in Tokyo that gave me the resolve to continue my studies in Kyushu. Professor Shimizu taught me the importance, from the perspective of cultural anthropology and Philippine studies, of alternating between the microscopic realities of life in the field and the general theory of political science. His guidance was distinguished by his provocative weaving of diverse narratives from the raw research of his students. The arguments in this book also took form in the course of many exchanges with Professor Shimizu over its "story." I owe him my deepest gratitude for his tireless encouragement through a decade of research.

After Professor Shimizu transferred to Kyoto University, Professor Seiki Okazaki, a specialist in political theory, kindly consented to be my dissertation advisor. Professor Okazaki reread my drafts many times over with a thoroughness and dedication that profoundly moved me. The process of revising these drafts, colorfully covered with the professor's handwriting, was extremely educational, adding depth to my thinking and teaching me how to write a treatise. As the very embodiment of a "citizen" who excludes no one while exercising impeccable self-restraint in both his public and private lives, Professor Okazaki was the subject of awe for a person like me, who tends to escape into idleness and self-indulgence with the excuse that I am an uncultured boor. I cannot thank him enough for cheerfully taking on the weighty responsibility of advising a student not only in a different field of study, but also remarkably different in temperament.

My fellow researchers and senior colleagues were always a source of great encouragement and stimulation through our intense, and sometimes alcohol-fueled, discussions. The Graduate School of Social and Cultural Studies at Kyushu University is highly interdisciplinary, and because of this, I was able to interact with colleagues from diverse fields, including cultural studies, cultural anthropology, normative political science, and history, on a daily basis. These discussions helped train me to convey my ideas to those outside of my own narrow field. I also had frequent conversations with other researchers of my generation in Philippine studies, including Yusuke Takagi, Saya Kiba, Atsumasa Nagata, Kentaro Azuma, Takamichi Serizawa, and Christopher Magno. The inspiration I received from these esteemed colleagues, both my contemporaries and my seniors, served as a powerful incentive for me to overcome my innate laziness and pursue my research with renewed dedication. I wish to express my thanks for the opportunity to work in such an ideal environment, one that allowed me to interact with people I hold in the highest regard.

The publication of this book was facilitated by a Grant-in-Aid for Publication of Scientific Research Results from the Japan Society for Promotion of Science. Leonardo A. Esclanda, who was introduced to me by Ima Ariate, readily provided a number of wonderful photographs. I could not have brought this book into the world without the encouragement and meticulous work of Nozomi Okuda of Hosei University Press, who handled the editing of the Japanese edition; Tetsuya Suzuki of Kyoto University Press; Yuko Hayami and Narumi Shitara of the Center for Southeast Asian Studies, Kyoto University; Paul Kratoska and Lena Qua of NUS Press sincerely and carefully coordinated the publication of the English edition; and last but not least, I would like to thank Danielle McClellan for her careful editing.

I offer my sincere gratitude to all of these individuals. Although this book owes its existence to the stern but loving support I received from a great many people, any errors or disorganization in its content are entirely my own responsibility; if nothing else, I hope they will serve as lessons for subsequent research.

As a researcher engaged in Philippine studies, I am often asked, "Why the Philippines?" The short answer is "because I dearly love the country." Although I currently work in Japan, I am always counting the days until I can return to the Philippines—just like an overseas Filipino worker. Since my birthday falls on Philippine Independence Day, I cannot keep from thinking that destiny may be involved. I became involved in research not because I wanted to be a scholar, but because I did not want to lose my ties to the Philippines, and if anything, I wished to deepen them. I felt like I somehow had to convey the complex emotions and experiences that I received from the Philippines in words.

When asked why I like the Philippines so much, I have to answer "because I like the people." The kindness I first experienced from people in the Philippines was unlike any I had experienced before. During every visit, I find myself seriously contemplating whether there is any way to import that kindness into Japanese society. To be certain, although the Philippines can seem like paradise to temporary visitors from abroad such as myself, it remains a deeply troubled homeland to those who live there. Many Filipinos, one in ten, work or live overseas because they are unable to fulfill their dreams in their own country. Even so, I believe that much can be learned from the Philippines for living well in these troubled times.

In this book, I may have overemphasized the negative aspects of the Philippines—the fragmentations, antagonisms, and hostilities of its

Afterword

society; these are certainly part of the reality of the Philippines and cannot be denied. However, what captivated me about the country was the kindness and powerful mutuality of the people. This, too, is a real aspect of Philippine society and not merely the romantic illusion of a temporary visitor. What are we to make of these contradictory qualities? Perhaps it is precisely because Philippine society is so torn by severe and deep-rooted divisions and antagonisms, etched by the violence of colonialism and capitalism, that it has also cultivated strategies for overcoming divisions and healing antagonisms. In the current era of neoliberalism, when the state can no longer be relied upon as a guarantor of survival, how might diverse people cooperate in supporting one another's lives, rather than accept the prescription of unbridled competition as a given? In its experience devising political practices to this end, with all the hardships and challenges the process entails, the Philippines is truly an "advanced nation."

While living in the slums, I heard more than my fill of the daily bickering that goes on among relatives and neighbors. Upon closer observation, however, I saw that even as people roundly bad-mouthed each other in private, they extended a helping hand to those in need and never ostracized anyone. Whether the target of criticism was a woman who embezzled funds from a street vendors' association, a young man who stole from his neighbors so that he could buy drugs or an idle, jobless man who spent every day drinking with someone else's money, he or she was accepted by family, friends, and local society, even as harsh words were said behind his or her back. Consequently, such individuals still had a place to call home and went on with their lives with their heads held high, as if they had done nothing wrong. Even as people fight and cast moral aspersions on one another, they continue to weave together a vernacular order of life-sustaining mutuality that transcends moral demarcation lines. I believe that our lives today, and democracy itself, are in need of such a practice.

It has been nearly 15 years since I began the research that produced this book. During that period, despite the support of numerous individuals, I committed a number of moral errors that I deeply regret. What has saved me is the presence of people close to me who remained unwavering in their support in spite of my transgressions. Finally, I wish to express my deepest gratitude to my parents and to my wife, Asuna Yoshizawa, for her caring support and inspiration.

Wataru Kusaka
Manila, March 2016

NOTES

Introduction

1. For a summation of research that analyzes democratization as a return to elite democracy, see Quimpo (2008: 35–40).
2. According to Quimpo (2008: 21–40), theories of elite rule in the Philippines can be classified into three categories. The first is "patron-client factional framework," which focuses on the vertical relationship between big landowners and the poor (Lande 1965; Agpalo 1972) and its modernized versions (Machado 1971, 1974, among others). Second, "neocolonial or dependency framework" focuses on collusion between the elite and the United States. Proponents of this type of theory, which emerged during the Marcos era, include Constantino (1978), who emphasizes the ongoing American domination of the Philippines, and Hawes (1987), who highlights control of the state by the capitalist class. Finally, after democratization, a "elite democracy or patrimonial framework" that focused on the plundering of national resources by the elite evolved. It includes "rent capitalism" (Hutchcroft 1998), in which the elite utilize "rent," that is, the regulatory power of the state over market competition, to amass capital; "bossism" (Sidel 1999), in which the elite monopolizes state resources and employs violence and coercion to control the masses; and the theory of "machine politics" (Kawanaka 2002), which efficiently organizes the masses from above. For accounts of the historical development of elite hegemony in the Philippines, see Simbulan (1965) and Anderson (1988).
3. "Class," as I have used it here, refers not so much to productive relations as it does to disparities in lifestyle, including education, language, accessed media, consumption patterns, place of residence, and so on.
4. Words employed in the Philippines to rally together for the "nation" include the English *people* and the Tagalog *bayan* (which can mean people, citizens, nation, homeland, or hometown).
5. However, in a previous work, Huntington (1968), in noting that political participation increased in developing countries in the late 1960s, argued that under an already fragile political system, politics became increasingly destabilized due to the excessive demands made by a middle class exploiting the weakening of traditional authority that accompanied modernization.
6. For an account of the middle class that supported de-democratization in Thailand, see Tamada (2008, 2014).

7. For representative sources, see Wui and Lopez (1997), Clarke (1998), Silliman and Noble (1998: 13), Magadia (2003), and Serrano (2003). As Ferrer (1997a) and Serrano (2003) point out, there are varying arguments and no consensus about the definition of civil society in the Philippine as elsewhere. However, discussions of Philippine civil society all share a paramount interest in the political participation of NGOs.
8. For example, NGOs have prioritized organizing the poor in places where there is a strong potential for mass mobilization due to a high likelihood of large-scale forced evictions (Pinches 2010: 303).
9. Granted, having been influenced by the theories of Freire (1968) on achieving social equality through "interactive education," members of Philippine NGOs pride themselves on emphasizing dialogue with the poor. In practice, however, many mobilizations are led by NGO strategies.
10. Laclau and Mouffe treat social phenomena as nonexistent outside of discourse. In this book, however, I treat discursive space as coexistent with social space and attempt to describe the relationship between discourses and social classes, social groups, social structures and so on.
11. See Ross (1977). Recent rational-choice theory in particular introduces the viewpoint that a preference for maximizing self-interest is not grounded in reality, and that an actor's identity and preferences are cultural constructs (Chai 1997; Torfing 2005: 4). Constructivism critiques previous studies that treat institutions as externally formed and static, introducing a perspective that analyzes the dynamic character of institutions transformed by ideas and culture (Hay 2006; Schmidt 2008).
12. See Mercer (2002: 11) and Hedman (2005: 5).
13. Magadia (2003) also points out that an alliance of NGOs and people's organizations played an important role in the passage of three laws related to agrarian reform, labor-management relations and urban land reform.
14. Although Hedman includes the US government in the dominant bloc, she describes it as having lost much of its influence in the wake of democratization.
15. Kerkvliet (2005: 18) also supports Quimpo, declaring: "We need, I submit, to devote more scholarly attention to understand the contested nature of democracy in the Philippines".
16. Linz and Stepan (1996: 7–8) also stress the importance to conceptualizations of civil society of the role played by ordinary citizens, unaffiliated with organizations, when they eventually do form large groups that transform power relations between the ruling establishment and the opposition.
17. Whereas "slum" is a concept that connotes wretched living conditions, "squatters' settlement" or "squat" connotes illegality vis-à-vis land ownership. In reality, however, both entities frequently overlap, so I have not made any strict differentiation between them.
18. Members of the impoverished classes tend to be hesitant to speak freely about politics in front of recording equipment. By interviewing close friends and their acquaintances, however, I was able to obtain relaxed responses.

19. I wish to thank Sandino Jose Manliclic, Galileo Garcia and Joseph dela Cruz for handling the transcription of these tapes.

Chapter 1
1. Ileto (1999) criticizes elite democracy theory in terms of a critique of Orientalism, arguing that American scholars have treated Philippine politics as a "negative other" contrasted with the ideal of American democracy, predicated on a binary opposition of "civilized citizens vs. uncivilized non-citizens." While this book does address the negative as well as positive aspects of Philippine politics, it shares Ileto's perspective in critically examining the effects of the "citizen vs. non-citizen" dichotomy.
2. See Constantino (1975) for an account of the formation of inequalities under Spanish rule.
3. See Simbulan (1965) and Anderson (1988) for accounts of the formation of the traditional elite.
4. See Constantino (1975).
5. One of the purposes of introducing an electoral system was to appease the elite and cut it off from the national independence movement.
6. Abinales and Amoroso argue that antagonism and cooperation between social forces and state leaders is the key perspective to understanding Philippine political history.
7. Another significant division in Philippine society is between Islam and Christianity. The Muslim local elite secured their interests on the local level by joining in a clientelist relationship with the Christian national elite, and did not seek to promote their religious agenda on the national level. As a consequence, Muslim discontent manifested itself outside the democratic system in the form of armed struggle.
8. The fact that the number or percentage of poor people is lower according to government statistics than to the findings of surveys by private polling organizations is attributed to the desire of the government to highlight the positive results of its poverty measures (Berner 1997: 21–8).
9. Here, five social classes are identified according to the characteristics of their residences (Bautista 2001: 1–2). A is the super-rich, primarily large plantation owners and business tycoons. B is the wealthy class, which includes government officials, successful doctors, lawyers and other professionals, mid-level landowners and successful entrepreneurs. A and B residences use quality building materials and are located in high-class subdivisions. C is the middle class, whose residences are well maintained, contain quality furniture, and tend to be located in subdivisions. D is the impoverished class, with residences made of cheap materials and located in shabby, crowded neighborhoods. Finally, E is the poorest class, with residences cobbled together of makeshift materials and located in cramped quarters in the worst areas of the urban slums.

10. Since many local and leftist NPOs do not register with the Securities and Exchange Commission, and defunct organizations may remain registered, the number of NPOs registered with the Commission provides a rough estimate at best (Igarashi 2011: 280).
11. See *Social Weather Stations* (2007, April 16).
12. Sidel asserted that under the structural conditions of "primitive accumulation of capital," according to which resources are monopolized by the state, local elites dominate the poor lacking resources of its own by gaining access to these state resources through electoral positions. In response to this argument, I pointed out that with the advance of economic globalization, some local elites do not always depend upon state resources, and instead reinforce their power base by recruiting private capital from Manila and abroad (Kusaka 2013).
13. In most cases, candidates attempt to appeal to voters through simple images suggesting that they will "oppose corruption" or "help the poor." rather than with specific economic policies promising redistribution or growth. This may be due to the fact that anyone aspiring to the presidency would be hard pressed to discard neoliberal economic policies in practice.
14. According to Kasuya (2008), prior to martial law, "presidential bandwagon" behavior by candidates for the Senate or the House centered on the party of the incumbent president. However, because the 1987 Constitution prohibited presidential re-elections, the number of presidential candidates with a chance of winning has grown, causing a dispersion of the bandwagon effect and giving birth to a fluid multiparty system.
15. Parties that found their support base among the poor and called for social and economic liberation, among them the Democratic Alliance and the Communist Party of the Philippines (CPP), were also formed. However, these parties were outlawed and their members resorted to armed struggle, and hence did not become part of the party system.
16. See Ateneo School of Governance and Konrad Adenauer Stiftung (2007).
17. As Kawanaka (2004) has noted, one of the structural conditions of the post-democratization political process is that policies cannot be formed or altered without a full consensus by three actors: the president, the Senate, and the House. Antagonistic relations among these actors are defined by the electoral system. The president and senators, who are elected by nationwide constituencies, vie for support from the entire spectrum of society, while members of the House, who are elected by local constituencies, are concerned with funneling benefits to their home districts.
18. Fraser (1992: 125–6) evaluates the public sphere as an arena for the formation and enactment of identities, and stresses the significance of the opportunity to participate in the public sphere, speak in one's own voice, and construct and express one's own cultural identity.

19. In his preface of the second edition of *The Structural Transformation of the Public Sphere*, Habermas (1990), too, states that to prevent complete exclusion from the civic sphere, it is important for marginalized social groups to form their own "plebian public spheres," which allows communication to be practiced among multiple public spheres. However, he also views compromise between civic and plebian spheres as possible and assumes that serious issues of dominance, subordination or exclusion will not arise between them. The preface of the second edition is not translated into English and I refer to the Japanese translation.
20. Fraser (1992: 124) mentions the danger that social divisions may be exacerbated through contestation among multiple public spheres, yet optimistically argues that there is no long-term danger of this because counter-publics possess the publicity to disseminate their own discourses in order to gain support from outside.
21. There are also nationalists, albeit few in number, who use Tagalog for speech and writing on abstract subjects.
22. Such criticism is often expressed in Tagalog by slang words like *jologs, masa, bakya, promdi* and *badoy*. For definitions of these words see Garrido (2008: 449–52).
23. The mass sphere is characterized as a public sphere with its foundation in the numerous intimate spheres.
24. The impression made on the listener varies depending on whether one expresses a concept with a word derived from English, Spanish or a vernacular. For example, the concept "teacher" may be expressed by the English *teacher*, the English-derived *titser*, the Spanish *maestro,* or the Tagalog *gulo*. The English word imparts an impression of urban sophistication; the Spanish, that of a country hick. On the other hand, using Tagalog for a word such as "teacher" that is normally expressed in English or Spanish sounds stuffy and stridently nationalistic.
25. Other joking remarks include "I used up all my English" and "My English is a water buffalo [i.e., very slow-paced]."
26. See Pinches (1996, 2010: 287–8). Behind the middle class's aspirations of modernity is national pride, manifested in the desire not to see the Philippines fall even further behind other Asian countries that have achieved substantial economic growth.
27. As Seki (2012) argues, the middle class is fearful of "falling," i.e., losing social status and the ability to secure its children's future, under the current system. Consequently, many members of the middle class feel deeply disillusioned by Philippine politics, and have come to pin their hopes on emigration overseas.
28. See Pinches (1999), according to whom, ethnic-Chinese Filipinos have long been dismissed with contempt as "money-grubbing penny-pinchers." At least in the civic sphere, however, the entrepreneurial ethos of ethnic-Chinese Filipinos has recently come to be praised as contributing to Philippine growth.

29. Moral economy has also served to legitimize clientelism as a means by which people of high social status guarantee the survival of those of low social status.
30. For example, education, well-built housing, sanitation and regular incomes have also become elements of the demand for a right to a decent livelihood (Kerkvliet 1990: 265–73).
31. For example, in poor rural or urban areas, it is common to observe such situations in which poorer people ask a help for wealthier relatives or neighbors appealing morality of mutual help but such request meet with a bitter remark based on the idea that attributes the needy circumstance to the lack of self-reliance and entrepreneurship.
32. In the mass sphere, one often hears people relate such personal experiences as "Rich people never greet you when you pass them on the street" and "When I went shopping, I was treated like a thief."
33. Hollnsteiner (1970) posited that "shame" is something one is made conscious of in the context of being unable to repay a favor bestowed, and that it sustains the attitude and practice of repaying favors. However, as Pinches points out, this understanding of shame is not appropriate in ignoring its function as an impetus for resistance.
34. They are extremely sensitive to the way in which they are viewed by those with high social status. As a foreigner living in a squatters' settlement, I took the utmost care to ensure I would not be considered "arrogant" (*mayaban*).
35. See Pinches (1991, 1992). For the poor, the worst type of humiliation is to be treated not as a human equal, but like a "beast" (*hayop*), particularly by those of high social status. This arouses intense anger. Conversely, the insult "You're a beast" (*hayop ka*) serves as a forceful expression of objection to someone who denies the dignity of another.
36. Objects of intense empathy of this sort include Jose Rizal, who was executed by the Spanish colonial government, Benigno Aquino Jr., who was assassinated under the Marcos regime, and Flor Contemplacion, a housemaid working overseas who, despite indications that the charges against her were false, was executed in Singapore.
37. See Scott (1985) and Kerkvliet (1990) for discussions of the moral politics of landowners and tenants in rural villages.
38. The concept of the contact zone was introduced by Pratt (1992) in her rejection of the view of colonial rule as unilaterally dominating its periphery. According to Pratt (ibid: 7–8), contact zone is "social spaces where disparate cultures meet, clash, and grapple with each other, often in highly asymmetrical relations of domination and subordination" or "the space in which peoples geographically and historically separated come into contact with each other and establish ongoing relations, usually involving conditions of coercion, radical inequality, and intractable conflict." Furthermore, "it invokes the space and time where subjects previously separated by geography and history are

co-present, the point at which their trajectories now intersect. . . . A 'contact' perspective emphasizes how subjects get constituted in and by their relations to each other."

39. This book focuses on social movements as a representative of contact zone because they have the most significant influence on the political process. In fact, however, there is a broader diversity of deliberative practices taking place in contact zones. For example, the taxis that ply the streets of Manila serve as spaces where drivers from the impoverished class and passengers from the middle class frequently engage in political discussions. Another example is that, as I have argued elsewhere (Kusaka 2012), overseas Filipino workers in Japan have fostered a new sense of intimate community through their daily encounters and a practice of mutual help with people of other classes who they would not have the opportunity to meet at home.

40. See Spivak (1988).

41. For example, Japan's former Prime Minister Jun'ichiro Koizumi enjoyed high approval ratings when he constructed a pro-reform "we" by criticizing bureaucrats as "obstructive forces" who clung to their vested interests. Prime Minister Shinzo Abe also garnered support during his first cabinet when he promoted a "we Japanese" identity by taking a hardline stance against North Korea.

42. According to Butler (1990), "subjection" by "interpellation" does not necessarily succeed in creating a "subordinate subject," and may instead give birth to an agent with the power, however unstable, to speak out at the same time. The interpellated subject is not unilaterally implanted with an identity that fully conforms to the ruling hegemony, but retains the counter-hegemony to negotiate with it.

43. Connolly (1991) criticizes fixed identities as suppressing the abundance of human life and inviting the subordination or exclusion of the self or the other. He further argues that living with contingency and "conflicts" in identity generates agonistic respect—in other words, struggle with opponents accompanied by respect. Recognizing that the opponent's identity is also characterized by contingency and conflicts makes it possible to respect them and, the thinking goes, to construct a mutually dependent agonism in which individuals interact with, resist and challenge their opponents while maintaining that sense of respect.

44. According to Dryzek (2010: 15), "[m]eta-consensus can refer to agreement on the legitimacy of contested values, on the validity of disputed judgments, on the acceptability and structure of competing preferences, and on the applicability of contested discourses."

45. If we broadly define populism as politics based on antagonistic "we/they" relations, then the four hegemonic discursive practices described in this book could all be said to be variants of populism. To avoid confusion, however, I will employ the concept of populism in the limited sense described here.

46. The civic sphere is dominated by a ternary antagonism among "the elite," "the citizenry" or the middle class, and "the masses," while the mass sphere is dominated by a binary antagonism between "the rich" and "the poor." Moral nationalism attempts to create a common enemy by encouraging antagonism toward "the elite" in the civic sphere and toward "the rich" in the mass sphere, thereby constructing the "people" that transcends class lines.
47. In this book, I adopt the discursive approaches of Laclau and Canovan on populism. Laclau (1977: 172–3) states that "populism consists in the presentation of popular-democratic interpellations as a synthetic-antagonistic complex with respect to the dominant ideology." More forthrightly, he defines populism as none other than a construction of "the people" based on a chain of "equivalence" made of "empty signifiers" (Laclau 2005). According to Canovan (1993: 3), "populism is "an appeal to 'the people' against both the established structure of power and the dominant ideas and values of the society."
48. The concept of "the masses" as it applies to the mass sphere refers to the poor people that make up the majority of the population; however, due to its usage in the Communist movement, the term also has a confrontational image. On the other hand, terms describing objects of mass enmity include "big people" (*malalaking tao*), "bourgeois" (*burgis*), "elites" (*elitista*) and so on. To keep terms simple in this book, I have used "the rich" (*mayayaman*) as shorthand for all of these concepts.
49. Although communism is also an important hegemonic practice, I have not addressed it in this book because there has been a noticeable decline in the importance of its pure discourse. While the Communist Party of the Philippines continued armed struggle after democratization, it allegedly also founded legal party-list groups such as Bayan Muna, and NGOs under their umbrella employ a discourse resembling civic inclusivism as they organize the poor and place their priority on parliamentary struggle.
50. I did not consider the unlikely scenarios that civic exclusivism would colonize the mass sphere or that populism would establish hegemony in the civic sphere.

Chapter 2

1. See Abinales and Amoroso (2005: 92–4).
2. See Agoncillo (1990: 93). The Philippine experience was different from that of Mexico and other colonies in Latin America, where Spanish became the *lingua franca* due to the large number of immigrants arriving from Spain and their intermarriage with indigenous peoples. One reason for this difference was that the greater distance from Spain and the relative lack of resources made it infeasible for Spain to send large numbers of administrators and military personnel to the Philippines.
3. As summarized by Rafael (2000: 21), quoting the *Report of the Philippine Commission* (vol. 1, pp. 3–4), "benevolent assimilation" was motivated by the

rhetoric of "win[ning] the confidence, respect and affection of the colonized," according to which, "colonization entailed the cultivation of the 'felicity and perfection of the Philippine people' through 'uninterrupted devotion' to those 'noble ideals which constitute the higher civilization of mankind.'"
4. Initially, American troops serving in the Philippine-American War who had teaching credentials were enlisted to work as teachers in the Philippines. In 1901, 540 American teachers arrived in Manila aboard the USS *Thomas*. The following year, their numbers were augmented, until a total of 1,074 Americans were teaching in the Philippines.
5. Some 500 students went to the United States under a US government-sponsored scholarship program that lasted from 1903 to 1910. From 1910 to 1938, another 14,000 students went to the US under private funding.
6. See Constantino (1966) for a vigorous critique of English-language education, which he argues caused Filipinos to lose the nationalist desire for independence, uprooted them from their native culture, deprived them of the opportunity for creative thinking in their vernacular language, and led them to tolerate economic exploitation by other countries.
7. See Sibayan and Gonzalez (1996: 139).
8. See Uchiyama (2000) for an account of the discussion over national language in the Constitutional Convention.
9. The Japanese government banned the use of English and approved Japanese and Tagalog as official languages. It also adopted Tagalog as the language for education other than in Japanese language classes, and encouraged the use of Tagalog by government agencies.
10. One measure adopted to improve bilingual education is the experimental use of "*lingua franca* education," which incorporates the use of local common languages into regional curriculums. However, this approach faces problems such as a lack of instructors and materials.
11. According to Tupas (2007), those assigning priority to English asserted that students' English skills were on the decline, that Filipino workers needed to be more competitive in the global labor market, and that Filipinos could become nationalists without speaking the Filipino language. In fact, most Filipinos do not strongly identify learning Filipino with nationalism, and believe that one can fully identify as a Filipino without using the language. Meanwhile, those assigning priority to Filipino asserted that failure to do so was a violation of the 1987 Constitution's stipulation of Filipino as a primary "language of instruction in the educational system," that English was already being used in the classroom and did not need to be re-stipulated as a language of education, and that people who had thoroughly mastered a first language would find it easy to master a second. Bernardo (2007: 14–9) criticizes this either-or "English vs. Filipino" dispute as overly simplistic and advocates the active introduction of "*Taglish*," a mix of the two languages.

12. See Sibayan and Gonzalez (1996), Kobari (1999), and Nical, Smolicz and Secombe (2004).
13. Sibayan and Gonzalez (1996: 163) classify Philippine English into the following five categories: (1) English by individuals who are barely literate; (2) English by overseas contract workers; (3) English by white-collar workers; (4) English by the wealthy and middle classes; and (5) English by intellectuals. Categories (1) through (3) constitute the vast majority of the total.
14. From the *Philippine Statistical Year Book* for various years. In the 2000s, the Philippine literacy rate and the primary education enrollment rate were both about 95 per cent, and the secondary education enrollment rate was about 65 per cent; these are not considered to be low rates.
15. English is the primary language of instruction and research in higher education, with the exception of a few fields such as Philippine literature. Nearly all high-level intellectual activities rely on English.
16. Even those born into poor families can improve their social status by going overseas to work. Educational background, however, is an important factor in getting contract work abroad, with six out of ten overseas contract workers having at least some university education (Suzuki 2007: 22).
17. For similar arguments, see Tollefson (1991), Sibayan and Gonzalez (1996), and Hau and Tinio (2003).
18. According to Lippmann (1922), human beings are incapable of recognizing complex real environments, but do recognize the "pseudo-environments" created by the media and act accordingly. The information transmitted by the media does not directly control people's thoughts and actions, as the erstwhile "bullet theory" would have it. Rather than rely entirely upon the media, people form political views based on their own personal experiences and exchanges of information through interpersonal networks, sometimes adopting a critical interpretation of the media.
19. The "alternative press" as described here is the equivalent of a "watchdog" that guards the interests of the general public against the powerful, while the "dominant press" is equivalent to a "lapdog" of the powerful. See Frago (2006) for a table that lists major print media since the Spanish colonial period based on Teodoro's categories.
20. See Rosario-Braid and Tuazon (1999: 294–5) and Ables (2003: 3–15) for accounts of the media under Spanish rule.
21. An example would be *Kalayaan*, the newspaper of the secret society Katipunan. For discussions of the discourses of revolutionary leaders of lower-class origin, see, Ileto (1979: 75–114) and Ables (2003: 16–22).
22. See Coronel (1999: 7). To attract as many readers as possible, newspapers in the 1920s often used a combination of Spanish, English, Tagalog and other indigenous languages.

23. One underlying factor was that, for their international news coverage, these media depended almost entirely on American wire services or the US Information Agency, which provided information free of charge (Abaya 1968).
24. See Ofreneo (1984: 22–4, 41–52, 64–9).
25. See Frago (2006: 170–1) and Ofreneo (1984: 25).
26. See Ofreneo (1984: 73–5, 113–5).
27. One objective of the family-owned business groups in owning media was "rent seeking" through which they influence trade and economic policies and other business-regulating powers of the state to their advantage. Competition among these groups was clearly reflected in editorials by the media they owned.
28. In 1968, newspapers published in Manila were four to six times more expensive than those published in New York, even after taking price differentials into account, and the average Filipino had to work for 20 to 22 days to earn enough to buy one (Chowdhury 1968).
29. Articles in English-language newspapers were mostly written by journalists who had received US-oriented education and training and could not write in a native language (Ofreneo 1984: 133, 203).
30. In 1967, Metro Manila comprised about one-eighth of the nation's population, but consumed two-thirds of all newspapers and magazines published in the Philippines. Whereas 11 newspapers and magazines per 100 people were distributed in Metro Manila and environs, the ratio was only one per 1,000 people in rural areas (Abaya 1968). Also, the great majority of regional newspapers were written in English or in a mixture of English and native languages, a clear indication that they were only circulated among the local elite (Ofreneo 1984: 129–33). The most successful of the native-language magazines was the Tagalog weekly *Liwayway*, which was published by the Roces family. The circulation of *Liwayway* grew from 20,000 in 1930 to 85,000 in the 1950s (Ables 2003: 26; Ofreneo 1984: 58–60).
31. See Robles and Tuazon (2007: 240–8).
32. See Rosario-Braid and Tuazon (1999: 301).
33. According to Coronel (1999), a relaxation of obstacles to citizenship and the abolition of laws restricting certain economic activities to Filipinos paved the way for the attainment of social legitimacy by ethnic-Chinese entrepreneurs, who acquired newspapers in hopes of influencing politics.
34. According to Coronel (1999: 10–13), the *Manila Bulletin* represents the most salient example of owner intervention; it is characterized by conservative content that prioritizes relations with the administration in power at any given time. Meanwhile, the *Philippine Daily Inquirer*, which originally earned popularity as an anti-Marcos newspaper, is the most independent from the government due to the editors' adamant rejection of owner intervention, as well as recognition by the executive team that the newspaper's critical stance toward the government contributes to sales. The *Philippine Star* avoids criticizing either business or government and tends to support the interests of the ethnic-Chinese entrepreneur Lucio Tan, said to be an indirect shareholder in the paper.

35. See D. Smith (2000: 121–2). As of 2002, English-language newspapers cost 15 pesos, while most tabloids cost 5 pesos.
36. Radio stations also continue to proliferate, growing from 539 stations in 1998 to 695 in 2005 (Robles and Tuazon 2007: 252).
37. After democratization, GMA began broadcasting talk shows in English that hosted serious discussions on political and social problems. However, because ABS-CBN's Tagalog news programs had seized such a large viewer share, GMA also switched to mass-oriented Tagalog programming (Rimban 1999: 50). Since self-production is far more costly than the purchase of syndicated foreign programs, not all TV stations are capable of producing their own programming.
38. In February 2006, an incident occurred in which 30,000 poor people waiting to appear on the first-anniversary show of *Wowowee* were crushed or trampled in a stampede, leaving 78 dead and over 400 seriously or slightly injured.
39. ABS-CBN intentionally arranges for the participation of the poor in its programs. One executive said in an interview, "Everybody wanted to speak out, to be heard. *Pagkakataon nang magsalita* (It was time to talk) and feel free." (quoted in Rimban 1999: 49).
40. Legazpi initially sought to establish Cebu or Panay as the center of colonial government, but ultimately chose Manila due to its vitality as a commercial hub.
41. The designated *arrabales* were Binondo, Santa Cruz, Quiapo, San Miguel, Sanpaloc, Tondo, Paco de Dilao, and Ermita.
42. Burnham was a leading architect of the "City Beautiful Movement," part of the urban renewal trend that gained prestige in the US in the latter half of the 19th century. He was active in developing plans for Chicago, Washington and other cities.
43. In 1950, this commission was reorganized as the National Planning Commission to take on regional development projects.
44. In 1972, the Metropolitan Mayors Coordinating Committee was established to foster cooperation among local governments in dealing with urban problems such as crime, traffic, flooding, fires and water shortages. However, this effort failed to yield substantial results due to local government disputes over jurisdiction and financial resources (Caoili 1988: 127–9).
45. One impetus for this move was the 1974 integration of local police departments into a Metropolitan Police Force, which proved effective in improving public safety and made the case for an integrated administrative structure more persuasive (Caoili 1988: 142–52).
46. From 1960 to 1970, Manila's population grew at an extremely high rate of 4.8 per cent. An annual natural increase of 100,000 was augmented by a comparable number of migrants. Between 1960 and 2007, the population of Manila grew from 2,462,488 to 11,553,427.

47. The formal sector of the city consists of the public sector and economic entities that have established themselves as modern businesses. The informal sector, broadly defined, consists of everything else.
48. See Culibao (1997). Bhowmik (2005: 2260) roughly estimates that there are approximately 50,000 street vendors in Metro Manila.
49. Economic liberalization has been accompanied by a shift from regular to contract employment that lasts for periods of six months or less. Because most contract workers find their jobs through employment agents, they must pay 10 to 15 per cent of their wages to the agent, reducing their income to minimum-wage levels. The result is more low-level formal sector work for low wages and under bad working conditions, with the distinction between that and informal-sector work increasingly ambiguous.
50. See Velasco (2006: 112–3) for a description of this process.
51. For example, the Ayala Group contracted to build MRT-3, an elevated rail line running through Makati along the EDSA highway.
52. For a description of the government's policy toward squatters, see Karaos (1993, 1995).
53. For the Miss Universe Pageant in 1974, 100,000 people were forcibly evicted; for the IMF/World Bank annual meeting in 1976, 60,000 were evicted. In a "Last Campaign" against squatters in 1982, 46,000 households were forcibly relocated to Payatas, Quezon City and Bagong Silang, Caloocan City.
54. See Karaos (1993, 1995) for an account of the activities of ZOTO.
55. See Karaos et al. (1995) and Magadia (2003) for descriptions of the process by which this was accomplished.
56. See Shatkin (2004: 2480). Problems associated with this program included difficulty acquiring sites due to soaring land prices, problems finding sites for relocation, difficulties in organizing residents, delays in repayment by peoples' organizations, and opposition to the program by local governments (Berner 2000: 562).
57. Shatkin (2004) argues that under the influence of neoliberalism, which treats the city as a space for maximizing profits through the circulation of capital rather than as a space for residents, politicians and bureaucrats are intentionally "forgetting" about the housing problems of squatters.
58. The name "Philcoa" is an acronym for the nearby Philippine Coconut Authority.
59. See Barangay Operations Center, Quezon City (n.d.), "Barangay Profile: Old Capitol Site."
60. In the 1980s, there were frequent conflicts between migrants from the Ilocos region and those from the island of Samar, but inter-ethnic antagonism of this sort has gradually subsided. With each succeeding generation in the slums, intermarriage and ritual kinship expand networks of trust that supersede ethnic origins.
61. A peoples' organization, the Barangay Old Capitol Site Neighborhood Association, Inc. (BOCSNAI), was formed in Pechayan in 2003 with the

support of a church-related NGO, the Claret Urban Poor Apostolate (CUPA). However, few residents are aware of the existence of the organization, and its activities are far from conspicuous.

62. According to a 2008 survey conducted by the private market research firm Synovate, newspaper circulations were 660,221 for the *Philippine Daily Inquirer*, 570,559 for the *Philippine Star*, and 518,184 for *Manila Bulletin*. See *Philippine Daily Inquirer* (May 30, 2008).

Chapter 3

1. For accounts of People Power 1, see Lane (1990), Thompson (1995), and Franco (2000: 199–254). For accounts of People Power 2 and 3, see Doronila (2001), Doronila ed. (2001), Lande (2001) and Hedman (2005: 167–86).
2. Marcos stood out among politicians with his resume as someone who was not from the traditional landowning elite, but rather, was a part of the new elite who participated in guerrilla activities during World War II and obtained a higher education after the war, as well as scoring at the top of the national bar examination.
3. For descriptions of the process by which the authoritarian Marcos regime collapsed and was succeeded by democratization, see Fujiwara (1988) and Thompson (1995). There are also numerous accounts by journalists, as in M. Mercado, ed. (1986).
4. Among the factors that enabled Marcos to declare martial law were his control of the armed forces, which he had dramatically expanded while stacking the command with associates from his home province, and the tacit approval of the United States, which was concerned with containing Communism as part of the Cold War and protecting its economic interests.
5. Business circles welcomed martial law because it gave them the opportunity to freely bring in foreign capital without interference by the legislature, while the middle class supported Marcos's slogans of "national development" and "economic development" (Fujiwara 1988: 50–5).
6. Marcos did in fact achieve successes in land reform and nationwide improvement of the infrastructure. His objectives in land reform were to deprive rival elites of their power base and to nip communism in the bud. However, landowners employed various tactics to impede the implementation of land reform. Meanwhile, many peasants who acquired land went into debt purchasing the large quantities of fertilizer and pesticides required to grow high-yield varieties of rice and had to relinquish their land. Moreover, this reform applied only to cropland for rice and corn, not to the sugarcane and coconut plantations owned by business cronies of Marcos.
7. The economic collapse occurred because Marcos not only lavished special business privileges on his cronies, but also raided the national treasury to cover their losses. Another contributing factor to the deterioration of public finances was the continuous spending of huge sums of money on unproductive

public works projects by the Ministry of Human Settlements and the Metro Manila Commission headed by Imelda Marcos.
8. As Fujiwara (1988: 48–56) points out, the CPP, which had engaged in struggle against the dictatorship from the outset, had won over students and workers in the cities and was expanding liberated zones in rural areas through armed struggle. Non-communist social movements were also pursuing activities aimed at restoring elections and a parliamentary system. After the second oil crisis of 1979, the business community also began to raise objections to the favorable treatment received by Marcos's business cronies. When Marcos reinstituted the legislature in 1978 in an effort to legitimize his regime both domestically and abroad, the elite demanded the powers they had enjoyed before martial law.
9. This indicates that the urban middle class led the protests. There were also leftist-led demonstrations around the Mendiola Bridge near Malacañang Palace.
10. Yellow became the symbolic color of the Aquino family in reference to the American hit song *Tie a Yellow Ribbon*. In the song, a man released from prison after many years is returning home, but first writes to his wife to ask her to let him know if she is still waiting for him by tying a yellow ribbon around "the old oak tree." For the first year after her husband's assassination, Corazon Aquino wore black mourning clothes, but during the subsequent election campaign she always wore yellow to symbolize her love for and fidelity to her husband.
11. NAMFREL is a group that was organized by church and business leaders and the US government to ensure the victory of Ramon Magsaysay in the 1953 presidential election over incumbent President Elpidio Quirino and to defeat the Hukbalahap Rebellion (Hedman 2005: 44–87). It then went dormant for some time, but was reorganized with the reinstitution of congressional elections in 1984 by the business community and the church, which viewed Marcos's abuse of power and the rapid advance of the CPP as threats to be addressed through "free and fair elections" (Ibid.: 88–115).
12. The Catholic Church had adopted an ambiguous position of "critical collaboration" with the Marcos regime. Behind this stance was a schism over what direction to take in response to calls for reform of the church's role in Philippine society in accordance with the Second Vatican Council of 1962–5. Under the leadership of Cardinal Sin in the wake of the Aquino assassination, moderates consolidated their power at the expense of radicals and pushed for a policy of moderate reform that was both anti-Communist and anti-Marcos (Miyawaki 2005: 29–31).
13. However, Brillantes (1992) notes that not all residents of the impoverished Smokey Mountain district participated enthusiastically in People Power. This disparity may originate in the difference between those who took to the streets out of curiosity or because they were swept up in the festive atmosphere, and

those who stayed home because they feared for their own safety or could not afford the transport cost.
14. For example, in campaign leaflets distributed by the Aquino campaign, Benigno Aquino and residents of the squats were held in the same light as martyrs killed by the Marcos regime (Pinches 1991: 184).
15. Fujiwara (1988: 69–72) posits that while People Power represented the formation of a community of "civil society" or "the people" (*bayan*) that transcended previous political forces, it simultaneously concealed class antagonisms. Shimizu (1991: 217–8) further argues that the Catholic narrative made possible a movement that swept up the poor as well as the middle class, but paradoxically also made that movement politically flimsy. Citing field research at the Luisita plantation and the memories inscribed in the monument of People Power, Claudio (2013) substantiates his thesis that the People Power narrative obscured class politics and exacerbated elite rule. In contrast, Igarashi (2011: 126–201) asserts that a counter-hegemony formed by "cause-oriented groups" during the democratization process exercised a certain degree of influence on democratic institutions, and therefore that democratization did not end up reflecting the inclinations of ruling class conservatives exclusively.
16. Tolentino points out that in Estrada's movies, "the masses do not speak or they speak only in unison."
17. "Erap" spelled backwards is *pare*, a term of familiarity meaning "buddy" or "pal."
18. Estrada's father was an engineer who graduated from the University of the Philippines and had studied for a time in the US. His mother was a pianist who once won a beauty contest. All nine of his siblings graduated from university.
19. According to a biography of Estrada, he was expelled from Ateneo de Manila High School for getting in a fight to protect a Filipino friend who was being bullied by an American exchange student (Crisostomo 1999: 74–5). Tolentino (2010: 75) suggests that this anecdote represents Estrada as a hero who sacrificed his opportunity for higher education in order to defend Filipino honor.
20. In 1939, the Philippines was already fifth in the world in movie production (Rosario-Braid and Tuazon 1999: 294). In the 1960s, increased advertising revenues further invigorated the film industry, and even the poor flocked to cinemas to see Tagalog films.
21. Quiapo, the scene of the story, is a working-class commercial district that developed around the Quiapo Church. It is crowded with street vendors and shoppers, and the air is full of the odors of fresh produce, human bodies, sweat and raw garbage.
22. Quoted from a magazine of the period by Hedman (2001: 30).
23. Folklore regarding social bandits is not a product of tradition, but rather of such modern upheavals as nation-state formation, colonialism and the expansion

of capitalism. The tale of the liberation of the mythological hero Bernardo Caprio from his bonds had a significant impact on the worldview of people who committed themselves to the Philippine Revolution (Ileto 1998: 1–27). Makario Sakay, who was active in the Philippine Revolution and continued to fight as a guerrilla against the Americans, was also viewed as a social bandit (Ileto 1979: 161–208). In the chaotic period following World War II, Nardong Putik (real name: Leonardo Manecio) survived frequent ambushes by the police and US forces and was worshiped as a hero by farmers in Cavite (Gealogo 2000). The movie actor Ramon Revilla Sr. played the role in 1972 and 1984 in two films titled *Nardong Putik*, and the appeal of his "bandit" image helped him win election to the Senate in 1992.

24. Hedman (2001) also introduces *Diligin Mo ng Hamog ang Uhaw na Lupa* ("Water the Thirsty Earth with Dew"), screened in 1975 while martial law was in effect, in which Estrada played David, a savior of poor farmers. A landowner who plans to develop the farmland into subdivisions orders his private army to kill the leader of the protesting farmers. David becomes their new leader, resisting the landowner's harassment while leading the impoverished farmers to new land. At the same time, David does not condone the revolutionary guerrillas led by his older brother, but instead seeks land reform through negotiation with the government. Tolentino (2010: 76–8) suggests that the film is a form of collusion with the Marcos regime, which professed to save the peasantry through land reform while cracking down on communism.

25. For accounts of the Estrada presidential campaign, see Crisostomo (1999: 174–208), Laquian and Laquian (1998: 83–184), and Salazar (2006: 145–58).

26. This campaign afforded young people the opportunity to view Estrada's films with people of their parents' generation (Bautista 2001). Spearheading the effort was Horacio Morales, who had launched the anti-Marcos movement as a leader of the CPP-affiliated National Democratic Front (NDF), and after democratization, headed the NGO Philippine Rural Reconstruction Movement. Other leftist/nationalist intellectuals such as Francisco Nemenzo and Randy David also supported Estrada because they viewed him as a means of breaking away from elite rule.

27. See the *Philippine Star* (1998, May 30) and Almario (1998, June 15).

28. According to exit polls by SWS, 48 per cent of the poorest class (E) and 38 per cent of the poor class (D) voted for Estrada (Mangahas 1998: 124; Bautista 2001: 4).

29. *Government of the Philippines Official Gazette*, "Inaugural Address of President Estrada (English Translation), June 30, 1998." For the original Tagalog version, see *Government of the Philippines Official Gazette*, "Inaugural Address of President Estrada, June 30, 1998." and Malaya and Malaya (2004: 283–95).

30. Not only in the Philippines, but also elsewhere, populism since 2000s has diverged from the 1960s Latin American experience in its affinity for economic liberalism over distributive policy (Weyland 2003).
31. For detailed accounts of the inner workings of the Estrada administration, see Doronila (2001: 27–46) and Constantino-David (2001).
32. Singson was a member of the provincial elite with a reputation for shady connections to the underworld. His explosive allegations are thought to have been prompted by a falling out with Estrada over the distribution of profits from *jueteng*.
33. See Social Weather Stations (1999). During the same period, support for Estrada also fell from 27 per cent to 5 per cent among the poor (class D), and from 43 per cent to 18 per cent among the very poor (class E); however, his approval ratings still remained higher than his disapproval ratings.
34. In 1992, the CPP split into two factions: the "Re-Affirmed" (RA) faction, which reaffirmed its commitment to the path of revolution and the "Rejected" (RJ) faction, which rejected traditional Maoism and instead prioritized parliamentary struggle. The RA faction continues to call itself the Communist Party, with Bayan Muna participating in legislative politics as its alleged legal arm. Sanlakas and Akbayan constitute the RJ faction. For a discussion of Bayan Muna's position regarding calls for Estrada's resignation, see Casino (2001). For a discussion of the stance of the business community, see Luz (2001).
35. Behind the efforts to oust Estrada in the House of Representatives was resistance to Estrada's attempt to abolish "pork-barrel" budget allocations by the representatives.
36. According to surveys by SWS, 47 per cent of those polled nationwide said they followed the impeachment trial "all of the time" and 40 per cent "some of the time." In Manila, a total of 98 per cent followed the trials (Bautista 2001: 11–3).
37. Pro-Estrada Senator Teresa Aquino-Oreta was caught by TV cameras dancing for joy in the Senate chambers, earning her the derisive nickname "dancing queen" in the civic sphere.
38. The EDSA Shrine and its statue of "Mary, Queen of Peace" were erected on EDSA in the Ortigas district of Manila by the Catholic Church to commemorate the triumph of People Power 1. The shrine subsequently came to be viewed as a symbolic space bestowing moral legitimacy on anti-government demonstrations.
39. See Velasco (2004) for a description of the activities of Kompil II.
40. Arugay seems to treat "civil society" not as a domain, but as a physical entity identified with a specific social movement. This conceptualization is also frequently employed by leftists and NGO activists in the Philippines.
41. The text message "Wear black to mourn the death of democracy" circulated via cell phones at this time.

42. See Bautista (2001: 14–5).
43. *Iglesia ni Cristo* cultivated a close relationship with Marcos so that the group's freedom of worship would not be threatened; after democratization, it supported Estrada through mass voting. Meanwhile, Mike Velarde, leader of *El Shaddai*, which boasted eight million members, served as Estrada's spiritual advisor.
44. See the *Philippine Star* (2000, December 22).
45. See Bautista (2001: 26).
46. For a discussion of the role played by the military in this regime-change drama, see Hernandez (2001).
47. For detailed accounts of the political process culminating in Estrada's resignation, see Doronila (2001), Lande (2001), San Juan (2001) and Coronel (2001).
48. See Malaya and Malaya (2004: 305–8).
49. Bautista (2001: 7–14) argues that the poor who participated in People Power 2 may not have had the opportunity to obtain a public school education but did receive an informal education through their activities as leftists or members of Catholic lay groups, through which they acquired an awareness that motivated them to seek social reform.
50. See Henderson (2001, 21 January). The essay is also quoted by (Bautista 2001: 26–7).
51. In response to demands from the Catholic Church, among others, the Arroyo administration repealed the death penalty in June 2006.
52. According to an opinion survey by SWS, immediately after the change of administrations, 60 per cent of the poor accepted the installation of Arroyo as president (Bautista 2001: 28–30). This suggests that the subsequent arrest of Estrada came as a tremendous shock to the poor and triggered People Power 3. See Doronila (2001: 220–46) and Tordesillas and Hutchinson (2001: 245–52) for accounts of how People Power 3 unfolded.
53. These opposition leaders included Miriam Defensor-Santiago, Juan Ponce Enrile, Gringo Honasan and Panfilo Lacson.
54. See Pinches (2010: 300).
55. Notwithstanding the Catholic Church's presentation of a new vision of itself as the "church of the poor" at the Second Plenary Council of the Philippines in 1991, it was unable to acquire hegemony in the mass sphere.
56. The failure of the major TV stations to cover People Power 3 was said to be due to fear that coverage would make the demonstrations grow larger. In rebuttal, the TV stations claimed that they had been unable to provide coverage because the demonstrators harassed their reporters and cameramen.
57. One observer said, "People Power 3 was bigger than People Power 2. People Power 2 extended to White Plains Avenue, but in People Power 3, the crowds spread all the way to Camp Aguinaldo." (Joey, 37, male, employed at a foreign corporation, February 15, 2009).

58. Estrada's rise and fall was partly a reflection of rifts in the elite, business, and religious sectors. First, many members of the counter-elite supported Estrada, while the traditional elite tended to support Arroyo. Second, mainstream business circles, including the Ayala conglomerate and the Makati Business Club, supported both People Power 1 and 2, while business magnates such as Eduardo Cojuangco and Lucio Tan, who had thrived under the Marcos regime, provided financial support to Estrada in an effort to regain the privileges they had lost under democratization. Finally, whereas the Catholic Church had played an important role in People Power 1 and 2, the new religious groups *Iglesia ni Cristo* and *El Shaddai* supported Estrada through prayer rallies and mass voting by their adherents among the poor.
59. See the *Philippine Daily Inquirer* (1998, May 11).
60. See Laquian and Laquian (2001: 249).
61. See Laquian and Laquian (1998: 220–2).
62. According to Carroll (2001: 247), Cardinal Sin believed that it was imperative to directly and resolutely challenge a massive evil at the heart of Philippine society, and that he must therefore use his social and moral capital to demand the resignation of the president.
63. See the *Philippine Daily Inquirer* (2001, January 18). For a discussion of the involvement of the Catholic Church in People Power 2, see Moreno (2006: 122–31).
64. See Miyawaki (2005). For example, pastoral letters by the Catholic Bishops' Conference of the Philippines used the word "moral" twice as often in the 1990s as in the 1970s or 1980s (Miyawaki 2006: 100, note 35).
65. The Erap jokes provided here were quoted by the Philippine Center for Investigative Journalism (2001). Note, however, that Erap jokes were originally used by Estrada during his election campaign to foster a sense of solidarity with the poor through self-effacing humor. While he was a senator, Estrada self-published *ERAPtioin* (Jurado and German 1994).
66. See the *Philippine Daily Inquirer* (2001, January 21).
67. Such assessments were to some degree a rebuttal to negative reactions from overseas. As Abueva (2001: 84–5) reports, publications like *Time*, *Newsweek* and the *Far Eastern Economic Review* gave negative coverage to People Power 2, describing it as a "lynching" or a form of "mob rule" that ignored democratic institutions.
68. For example, at a political science lecture I attended at the graduate school of the University of the Philippines in 2002, the instructor and students praised the fact that former presidents of South Korea had been put on trial for corruption.
69. The word "toothless" is used to ridicule the poor because few of them visit a dentist regularly and hence many are missing a number of teeth.
70. Quoted by Schaffer (2008: 134).

71. Quoted by Schaffer (2008: 134) and by Tordesillas and Hutchinson (2001: 250). The original Tagalog text is as follows: "*Tinatawagan lahat na dugyot at mangmang, mga bungal at walang salawal. Patunayan nating wala tayong utak—Pumunta tayo sa Edsa*, please pass
72. Quoted by de Quiros (2001, April 30), who also cites the following jokes: "All those who believe that Erap is innocent, please light a candle—and burn your house down." "[At EDSA] you can make a killing there if you put up booths that offer dental and facial services." "The rally at EDSA is not going to grow as fast as EDSA 2 because the people there don't know how to 'text.'"
73. Quoted by Doronila (2001: 240).
74. See the *Philippine Daily Inquirer* (2001, April 30).
75. Quoted by de Quiros (2001, April 30).
76. Quoted by Schaffer (2008: 134).
77. See the *Philippine Daily Inquirer* (2001, May 28).
78. See also de Quiros (2000, November 14).
79. See Balisacan (2001). Estrada's lowering of fees for agricultural water use by poor farmers also caused a funds shortage that disrupted agricultural policy (Nozawa 2001). In addition, his promotion of cronies to important posts and prioritizing of the interests of private developers threw his housing policies for the urban poor into disarray (Constantino-David 2001).
80. Residents of Pechayan heard much about Estrada's aid to the poor via gossip and the media, but did not actually receive any goods themselves. Nevertheless, they continued to support Estrada.
81. See Gutierrez (2001, May 2) and David (2001, July 29).
82. It must be noted that the *Pasyon* is interpreted differently in the civic and mass spheres and hence defines the political process in different ways. In People Power 1, the *Pasyon* worldview was exclusively linked to democratization in the civic sphere, obscuring the issue of resolving inequalities. On the other hand, the Philippine Revolution and People Power 3 initiated by the mass sphere were accompanied by more destructive impulses against the current ruling power structure itself.
83. *Jueteng* operations are informally systematized, and the job of bet collector (*kubrador*) provides a valuable source of income to poor people without steady employment.
84. However, there were some cases of spontaneous participation by unemployed youth who had also participated in People Power 2 at the urging of activists from *Anak Bayan*, a leftist youth group. They described the difference between the two People Powers as follows: "I joined People Power 3 so that my house wouldn't be torn down. It was fun, but it was totally crazy and I couldn't avoid getting hurt. I supported People Power 3, but the people who came to People Power 2 were nicer" (Boboy, 26, male, waterworks construction worker, April 1, 2008).

Chapter 4

1. Among the cited means by which the elite controls the votes of the poor are patron-client relations (Lande 1965), violence and coercion (Sidel 1999) and organization and profit-sharing from above (Kawanaka 2002).
2. In 1998, a party-list election system was introduced whereby one-fifth of the seats in the House of Representatives would be proportionally allotted to representatives of marginalized social groups such as peasants, women and indigenous communities. However, there is no indication that marginalized social groups have gained any substantial benefit from this system.
3. See, for example, Aquino (1998).
4. See Chapter 1.
5. In 1955, movie actor Rogelio de la Rosa was elected to the Senate. Aspiring to the presidency in the 1961 election, he starred in the film *Dugo at Luha* (Blood and Tears), which portrayed poor people whose needs are ignored by the government, but ultimately threw his support behind another presidential candidate, Diosdado Macapagal (Hedman 2001: 20–1). This precedent notwithstanding, entertainers seeking office during that period had to be nominated by either the Nationalist or Liberal Party, and were not in a position to run on their own. The present-day phenomenon of populism threatening traditional politicians had yet to arrive.
6. According to Gloria (2004a), the traditional elite's sense of crisis over celebrity politicians spurred the passage of a law that banned political advertising, the "Act Introducing Reforms in the Electoral System by Amending Certain Sections of the Omnibus Election Code and for Other Purposes," in 1987. This law took effect in 1992, but failed to halt the entry of celebrities into politics. In 2001, the traditional elite switched to a strategy of utilizing the media, and the law was subsequently repealed. As a result, campaign advertising surged from the 2004 election on, and candidates began spending over half their war chests on ads.
7. However, Ramos did not win on image alone; as Aquino's designated successor, he also utilized the state's organizational and financial resources in his campaign (Teehankee 2010: 126–7). Coming in second was Miriam Defensor Santiago, who ran on an "anti-corruption" platform and won support among the youth and urban middle class with her tough image. Ramon Mitra, who ran as the unity candidate of the ruling Laban party, finished a disappointing fourth despite the overwhelming advantage in organization and funding he enjoyed through the support of most local elites.
8. Estrada's PMP joined forces with the Nationalist People's Coalition (NPC) and Laban ng Demokratikong Pilipino (LDP or Laban) to form the coalition Laban ng Makabayang Masang Pilipino (Struggle of the Patriotic Filipino Masses), or LAMMP.
9. Jose de Venecia Jr., the candidate of the ruling Lakas party, came in a distant second despite having access to abundant organizational and funding power

as Ramos's designated heir apparent. In third place was Raul Roco, who had an image of intellect and ability and earned support from the urban middle class and youth, but lacked organizational strength and lost everywhere except for in his home region of Bicol. These results demonstrate the difficulty of winning elections solely on the basis of organizational and financial strength on the one hand, or image and policy positions on the other.

10. When distributing food, Arroyo sought to ingratiate herself to the poor by bringing social workers, doctors, dentists, comedians and action film stars with her. She also tried to impress the poor by showing respect for Estrada through such measures as building a home for him on the grounds of a hospital for his house arrest.

11. KNP was composed of Estrada's PMP, Laban (headed by Edgardo Angara), and Partido ng Demokratiko Pilipino–Lakas ng Bayan (the Philippine Democratic Party– People's Power; PDP-Laban).

12. Poe's relations with the media were soured by such incidents as his harsh scolding of a female TV reporter, which drove her to tears, in front of a large audience on his campaign tour. Also, despite the fierce attacks by the Arroyo camp over his lack of skills, intellect and experience, Poe avoided negative campaigning against Arroyo (Fonbuena 2004: 64).

13. According to results from an SWS survey, only 25 per cent of those surveyed had actually heard Poe speak on TV, on radio or at rallies, while less than the 32 per cent had heard Arroyo. See de Castro (2004, Mar. 29).

14. KNP was only able to back 26 of its own candidates for 211 incumbent seats in the House of Representatives, and only 12 candidates for 76 provincial governorships (Teehankee 2010: 141).

15. Although the 1987 Constitution prohibited elected presidents from serving more than one term, reelection of an incumbent was permitted if it took place within four years of succession to the post to fill a vacancy left by the previous president's resignation, impeachment or death. Arroyo had been promoted to president from vice president in 2001, and was therefore allowed to run as an incumbent. K4 included the ruling Lakas-Christian Muslim Democrats (Lakas-CMD), the Liberal Party, the Nationalist Party, and the Nationalist People's Coalition (NPC).

16. Arroyo randomly issued presidential "promulgations" to transfer public lands to their occupants, who were largely pro-Estrada squatters (Kiba 2010: 55–60). She also initiated a project providing employment and low-cost food to the poor, known as *Ginintuang Masaganang Ani* ("Golden Harvest for the People")–Countrywide Assistance for Rural Employment and Services, which forms the acronym GMA-CARES (GMA being Arroyo's initials). The phrase "GMA CARES" and Arroyo's picture were painted on mobile stores, known as *Tindaha ni Gloria Labandera* (Gloria the Laundress Shops), that sold everyday necessities and food at low prices. Arroyo also allocated a budget of six billion pesos to provide the poor with "Philhealth

cards" issued by the Philippine Health Insurance Corporation (Philhealth) that guaranteed free treatment at public hospitals, and announced that the cards, which bore Arroyo's photo, would be distributed to five million poor people by April 6, Arroyo's birthday. Beginning in late 2003, Arroyo created a large number of short-term jobs by hiring 250,000 people nationwide through the Department of Public Works and Highways to work as street sweepers. The sweepers wore blue shirts printed with the words *Programang Pangtrabaho ni Pangulong Gloria* (Jobs Program of President Gloria), and similarly worded billboards sprang up along roads throughout the country. For an account of these activities, see Go (2004, Apr. 26) and Mable (2004, Mar. 27).

17. Arroyo's vice presidential candidate was Senator Noli de Castro, a former newscaster also known by the nickname "Kabayan" (Countryman). His folksy manner of speaking played a valuable role in Arroyo's campaign.
18. See Velasquez (2002, Oct.–Dec.) for a description of Arroyo's image strategy. When she ran for the Senate in 1995, her campaign slogan was *Nora Aunor sa Senado* (Nora Aunor for Senator), playing on her superficial resemblance to the popular actress Nora Aunor (Crisostomo 2002: 18–9).
19. The presidential candidates were Arroyo, Poe, Senators Panfilo Lacson and Raul Roco, and Eddie Villanueva, leader of the religious group Jesus Is Lord Church.
20. See de Castro (2004, June 7).
21. According to exit polls by SWS, 40 per cent of the "poor" voted for Arroyo and 32 per cent for Poe, while 43 per cent of the "very poor" voted for Arroyo and 35 per cent for Poe. What the SWS data does not show, however, is that support for Poe far surpassed support for Arroyo in Manila's mass sphere. At one polling place I observed in Pechayan, for example, Poe received approximately three times as many votes as Arroyo.
22. One reason for Poe's loss was the split of the poor vote between him and Lacson, who earned support from the poor by spearheading criticism of Arroyo. Though known for his aggressiveness as director-general of the Philippine National Police under the Estrada administration, including allegations of extrajudicial killings of gang members, he won the support of taxi and jeepney drivers by cracking down on police who extorted bribes from drivers.
23. Flaviano (2013) analyzed Manila's 2013 mayoral election, in which incumbent Alfred Lim was defeated by Estrada, from the perspective of image construction and contestation: "The Cop vs. the Hoodlum."
24. It is an accepted practice for candidates to send their own poll watchers to polling places to prevent election rigging by rival candidates.
25. Vote gatherers also convey information about funerals, requests for assistance and the like from poor voters to politicians. One vote gatherer described her role as that of a "bridge" between residents and politicians and a "gatekeeper"

selecting residents to receive aid from the politicians (Cora, 50s, female, housewife, Mar. 7, 2010). The larger a politician's campaign war chest, the more vote gatherers they can hire.

26. Pasay City Council candidate C, a former lawyer, served in the city council for three consecutive terms, from 1992 to 2001. His father also served as a Pasay City councilor during the Commonwealth era, from 1937 to 1945. Candidate C's son succeeded him in the Pasay City Council, serving three consecutive terms from 2001. Because the 1987 Constitution prohibits election to more than three consecutive terms, the son was unable to run for city councilor in 2010, so candidate C stood for election again.
27. Malabon City Council candidate P ran for the city council after serving three terms as a barangay councilor.
28. As I will discuss in Chapter 6, Arroyo's second term (from 2004 to 2010) saw a succession of assassinations of peasant leaders and others affiliated with the Bayan Muna. These were referred to as "political killings."
29. To assuage the fears of the business community, of foreign investors, and of the middle class, the Poe camp announced the recruitment of 11 economists who supported economic liberalization as "brains", but this gesture appeared to have no effect. See Carandang (2004, Mar. 15).
30. According to Calimbahin (2010: 182–5), Jose S. Concepcion Jr., the businessman who revived NAMFREL in 1983, donated large sums of money to Arroyo. His son had also been appointed as a presidential advisor to Arroyo.
31. Arroyo enjoyed the largest support, 31 per cent, among the rich and middle class, while Roco won 19 per cent (Social Weather Stations 2004, 5 Apr.). Roco was known as a reformist politician, but his bout with cancer decreased his support. Considering this, it can be estimated that Arroyo received around 50 per cent of the rich and middle class vote.
32. However, as I mention in endnote 46, NAMFREL did not engage in election monitoring activities in the 2010 election.
33. Some columnists publish their email address in the newspaper, enabling readers to send in their views and reactions.
34. See Torre (2001, Apr. 11).
35. See the *Philippine Star* (2001, Apr. 26).
36. Details about this CD can be found on the Pagbabago@Pilipinas website (Pagbabago@Pilipinas 2002).
37. See Institute of Philippine Culture, Ateneo de Manila University (2005). Based on this data, Aguilar (2005) argued that the poor treat elections as a form of gambling like cockfighting and participate actively with the expectation that they will get some share of the winnings if the candidate they bet on wins, with the understanding that some electoral misconduct is inevitable and that the social structure cannot be changed.

38. In national elections, it is impossible to make close contact with presidential or senatorial candidates, so the poor base their judgments on the media. Local elections, on the other hand, permit more direct interaction with the candidates, so people evaluate them based on personal encounters, either directly or indirectly through acquaintances or relatives.
39. In the elections for 12 open Senate seats, movie actor Cesar Montano came in 18th, popular TV program host Vicente Sotto placed 19th, and another movie actor, Richard Gomez, came in 25th; all lost. Then again, the popular newscaster Loren Legarda won.
40. This was the sort of discourse employed by opposition parties to combat the money and vote-getting machinery of the ruling party in elections prior to martial law. In the presidential election of 1986, the Aquino camp used this slogan to urge voters not to let themselves be co-opted by the powerful Marcos machine: "*Tanggapin ang pera, ilagay sa bulsa, pero Oposisyon ang balota*" (Take the money, put it in your pocket, but vote for the Opposition) (Thompson 1995: 32).
41. Vote counting has been computerized since the 2010 general election in order to prevent election rigging and improve efficiency.
42. According to a joint exit poll by SWS and ABS-CBN, voter turnout was 89 per cent for the 2001 synchronized election (which included posts at all levels from president to city council) and 81 per cent for the 2004 election (Social Weather Stations 2001, May 14; 2004, May 18). These are considerably high turnouts compared to those for Lower House elections in Japan, which have ranged between 60 and 70 per cent since the 1990s.
43. Names missing from voter lists prepared by Comelec are an issue in every election. For example, in the 2004 election, about 2 per cent of voter names were reportedly missing (Social Weather Stations 2004, May 18).
44. According to Ramon Casiple, director of the Institute for Political and Electoral Reform, voter education began to be implemented after democratization. He classifies voter education methods and content according to the groups carrying it out as follows: morality-focused education by Catholic Church-related lay groups such as the PPCRV; education of their members by NGOs; education of students by existing educational institutions; and education via TV commercials by media-owning conglomerates (from an interview on February 19, 2010).
45. See Catholic Bishops' Conference of the Philippines (1992: Article 348).
46. In addition to the PPCRV, NAMFREL was also originally accredited as an official "citizens' arm" of Comelec. However, NAMFREL lost much of its credibility when it was alleged to have manipulated early return reports to Arroyo's advantage in the 2004 presidential election (Calimbahin 2010: 182–5). Then, in the 2010 elections, Comelec revoked NAMFREL's official accreditation, citing questions about its neutrality and fairness.

47. See Public and Political Affairs Ministry, Diocese of Kalookan (2010). The PPCRV offers two types of voter education: "technical education," which explains the electoral system and the voting process, and "moral education," which discusses the criteria for choosing "correct" candidates. Here I have focused on the latter.
48. There is also a moral precept, particularly in the mass sphere, that members of the same family should vote in solidarity for the same candidate; hence, people do not necessarily consider it a virtue for individuals to vote autonomously. Even so, they agree that the vote of the family unit should be free from external coercion.
49. This is because most of the poor do not attend church every Sunday (Arthur, 30, male, Public Affairs Ministry, Diocese of Malabon, airline company employee, February 14, 2010).

Chapter 5

1. Whereas this framework places the state and society in contraposition, Migdal (2001) later proposes a "state in society" approach that focuses on the process by which the state and society transform one another.
2. One characteristic of newer forms of governance is service delivery through networks upheld by trust and mutual adjustment between interdependent public and private sectors (Rhodes 1996).
3. Bayat (2000: 56–7) argues that where Scott's "everyday forms of resistance" is defensive, "quiet encroachment" by the urban poor is offensive. However, he does not restrict his view of the practices of the urban poor to quiet encroachment. If the benefits obtained through quiet encroachment are attacked by the state, the poor will respond with organized resistance. Moreover, Bayat asserts that if the political opportunity structure is more democratic, they may then seek to have their rights guaranteed by the state through organized action.
4. Someone who "owns" a large plot of land and profits handsomely from renting it out is referred to as a "professional squatter."
5. They originally came from Bohol and lived in a squatter settlement in Cebu but moved to Manila because their house was demolished while they were visiting relatives in another city.
6. Because the Philippine National Police and local government security personnel are not permitted to engage in policing activities on university campuses, the University of the Philippines has its own security force.
7. According to Parnell, these networks came to be called syndicates after democratization. In August 1987, President Aquino issued Proclamation No. 137, which stipulated the transfer of 137 out of 440 hectares set aside for the National Government Center to households that had been living on the land since before democratization. At that time, only certain designated peoples' organizations were recognized as local representatives, in reaction

to which, a network of non-designated peoples' organizations, accompanied by associated state agencies and powerful individuals, launched a protest movement. The Presidential Commission for the Urban Poor responded by applying the label "syndicate" to networks opposed to the proclamation, thus equating them with criminal groups. The residents themselves did not use the term "syndicate," but referred to a network by its leader's or organization's name, or sometimes by the term "recalcitrant."

8. See David (2003, July 6), Tandoc Jr. (2003, June 15), and Cruz (2003, June 17).
9. This loan system is referred to as "5-6" because vendors must typically repay 6,000 pesos for every 5,000 borrowed from a Bombay moneylender. The repayment period is negotiable, but usually around one month. The lenders make daily rounds on motorbikes collecting several hundred pesos from each borrower. When vendors complete their repayment, they can renew the 5-6. For more detailed account of the Bombay credit system, see Kondo (2003).
10. According a survey I conducted in August 2003, Association A in Quezon City was paying 500 pesos per week to the market management office, the security office and the MMDA; they were also making occasional payments of 100 to 200 pesos to the police. Association B in Caloocan City made weekly payments of 2,500 pesos to the security office, 500 pesos to the traffic office, and 500 pesos to the police.
11. It is not easy to determine how this money actually flows. However, in local governments where mayors enjoy extensive authority over personnel management, it is difficult to imagine the offices involved concealing such amounts from the mayor. Street vendors and NGOs perceive that mayors at least tacitly approve this practice.
12. Illy (1986) cites the example of Manila and Cross (1998), who defined the relationship between street vendors and local officials in Mexico City as reciprocal clientelism. However, they ignore the oppositional nature of the bribery system in its encroachment upon the power of both the state and the elite.
13. Scott (1969b: 325–9) discusses how bribery in the process of implementing the law is an alternative means of interest representation by marginalized people, who are constrained from wielding influence legislative processes.
14. Fernando majored in mechanical engineering at the Mapúa Institute of Technology, which makes him a rarity among Philippine politicians, most of whom attended law school.
15. He received awards from the Asian Institute of Management and the Konrad Adenauer Foundation of Germany, among others.
16. See R. Mercado (1998: 14). To get squatters to relocate, Fernando pressed them to form peoples' organizations and participate in the Community Mortgage Program, which enabled such organizations to purchase land with

low-interest loans. The designated relocation sites were the districts of Malanday and Tumana in Marikina City.
17. See the *Philippine Star* (2002, June 14).
18. See the *Philippine Star* (2004, Sept. 7).
19. Quoted in Cagurangan (2003: 4). According to the *Philippine Star* (2004, Sept. 7), the chief director of the National Capital Region (NCR) Police Office also said, "If there are many shirtless men roaming around in a certain community, there are also many criminals such as thieves, snatchers, and robbers in that area."
20. Fernando favored the color pink in all these projects, explaining that it "stood for the aspiration of every Metro Manilan 'to be in the pink of health'," according to the *Philippine Star* (2004, Jan. 1).
21. Quoted in Cagurangan (2003: 4).
22. Also banned was the practice of hitching a ride (*sabit*) on the back of a jeepney.
23. See Jimenez-David (2002, Aug. 22). The "broken windows" theory is associated with former New York City mayor Rudolph Giuliani III, who said he subscribed to it.
24. Fernando's targets for removal also included illegally parked vehicles, roadside trees and *barangay* halls that occupied sidewalks. However, he aimed his most persistent crackdown efforts at street vendors.
25. See the *Philippine Daily Inquirer* (2002, Oct. 13).
26. See the *Manila Times* (2003, Sept. 25).
27. See the *Manila Bulletin* (2003, May 24) and the *Philippine Daily Inquirer* (2003, May 24). The Philippine Department of Health also frequently issued warnings that the food sold by street vendors was unsanitary because it was exposed to garbage and bacteria, and could cause food poisoning and diarrhea. See the *Philippine Daily Inquirer* (2003, Oct. 31).
28. See *Philippine Headline News Online* (2003, May 10).
29. See MMDA Resolution 02-28.
30. Fernando explained that the tactic of pouring kerosene was a way to avoid confrontation with the street vendors by making it unnecessary to confiscate the merchandise and to negate rumors that the MMDA was selling confiscated merchandise on the black market. See the *Philippine Star* (2002, Aug. 20; 2002, Nov. 12).
31. See the *Philippine Star* (2002, July 9).
32. The thoroughfares in question included C-5, which runs between Quezon City and Parañaque City, and R-10 in the Tondo district of Manila.
33. The Arroyo administration implemented the Northrail Project linking Manila and the Clark Special Economic Zone with capital from the Chinese government, later from the Japanese ODA, and the Southrail Project linking Manila and Laguna province with capital from the South Korean government. For details on the activities of railside peoples' organizations, see Velasco (2006).

34. See Centre on Housing Rights and Evictions (2007: 4).
35. See Philippine NGO Coalition (n.d.: 81).
36. See the *Philippine Daily Inquirer* (2007, Sept. 5).
37. The site of this redevelopment project was 29.1 hectares of public land owned by the National Housing Authority. Due to the large size of the project and the presence of an active peoples' organization in the district, it met with stubborn resistance. Residents erected barricades and threw rocks at the police and demolition teams. The National Housing Authority attempted to relocate the residents to Rodriguez, a suburb in Rizal province, but few of them obliged. In fact, residents destroyed the relocation office set up by the Authority.
38. One reader responded to Doronila's column by writing: "Old folks like me who need to walk to exercise have no more sidewalks to walk safely on. I have paid taxes all my life. Why not give me back the sidewalks which I helped pay for?" See Sison (2002, Sept. 12).
39. The Chamber of Real Estate and Builders' Associations, a powerful interest group, declared that the removal of squatters was a crucial element of social reform (Shatkin 2008: 398).
40. See, for example, the *Manila Times* (2003, Nov. 17) and Cruz (2002, Apr. 15).
41. Ondoy caused severe flooding in Manila, resulting in at least 464 deaths and some 100 million USD in physical damage.
42. At that time, the *Philippine Star* asked for readers' views on whether the government would remove riverside squatters to distant relocation sites. The majority of respondents were of the opinion that the relocation of squatters to other districts was absolutely imperative, but due to limited funds as well as a lack of will by politicians seeking squatters' votes, they thought it was unlikely. However, there were expectations that if anyone could effect a change, it would be Fernando, who was praised for his staunch political will: "If Bayani Fernando becomes president, relocation will happen almost immediately. Political will is direly needed and nobody comes close to BF." See the *Philippine Star* (2009, Nov. 3).
43. Quoted by Zenarosa (2002, Sept. 22).
44. See Cagurangan (2003: 4)
45. Cruz 2002, June 26.
46. See opinion letters section of the *Philippine Star* (2004, Jan. 1).
47. Quoted in Cagurangan (2003: 2).
48. When Congressman Augusto Syjuco expressed his support for street vendors opposing the MMDA, the columnist Belinda Olivares-Cunanan (2002, Sept. 14) wrote, "[politicians like Syjuco are] grandstanding when they take the side of the vendors against the rest of the citizens who have been greatly inconvenienced by the loss of the sidewalks."
49. See the *Philippine Daily Inquirer* (2005, May 20).

50. In 2002, when this occurred, cell phone use had not yet spread widely among the poor, so it can be surmised that most people sending text messages to the program were from the middle class.
51. Richard Gordon, who was chairman of the Subic Bay Metropolitan Authority during the Ramos administration, introduced disciplinary governance to Subic. Gordon served as senator from 2004 and ran for president in the 2010 election, with Fernando as his vice-presidential running mate, but lost badly.
52. However, not all members of the middle class supported strict observance of the law at all times. For example, one middle-class male acknowledged that he had been stopped for traffic violations several times but was always able to avoid punishment by paying a small bribe to street-level officials, who expected it (Joey, 37, male, employed at a foreign corporation, 2009, Feb. 15).
53. Fernando did attempt to open subdivision streets for general use in order to reduce traffic congestion. However, he was unable to carry out this plan due to the opposition of residents who feared losing the expensive security they enjoyed in the subdivisions should the streets be opened.
54. However, the influence of this civic-sphere discourse on electoral politics was limited. Fernando ran for vice president twice, in 2004 and 2010, but lost badly both times. This was because his name recognition was low outside the Manila area, and even in Manila, poor people who viewed him unfavorably constituted the majority of the electorate.
55. The leftist organization Sanlakas provided numerous slogans for use in demonstrations, but street vendors rarely employed them verbatim. For example, Sanlakas used such epithets as "fascist," "Hitler" and "human rights violator" to criticize Fernando, but the street vendors tended to yell and write slogans of their own choice that resonated with their lives.
56. These words were used in a demonstration held in January 2003 in front of Quezon City Hall.
57. See Soon (2008) for a discussion of the concept of *matuwid*, connoting righteousness and honesty, as it relates to the Catholic notion of purity within the human heart (*loob*).
58. In the Philippines, the higher one's social status, the easier it is to secure a trial outcome to one's advantage. As reasons for this, Lopez (1999) cites difficulties for the poor in obtaining witnesses, the inability to communicate their concerns to their attorneys due to insufficient legal knowledge, overworked public attorneys, and the absence of judicial investigators in public attorneys' offices.
59. See Bayat (1997, 2010: 19–26) for an account of the formation of informal networks by the urban poor and the political significance of these networks, citing the example of Tehran. For an account related to squatters' settlements in Manila, see Berner (1997), who asserts that a local "we" identity forms the

60. I told my compadres that I did not need to charge any lending interest (*tubo*), but they demanded otherwise. Thus, I lent them capital of thousands of pesos at the rate of 5–5.5, cheaper than 5–6 they would get from the Bombay moneylenders. However, I subsequently learned that charging interest was reasonable because one compadre abruptly returned his province before he finished repayment.
61. Actually, Manila Mayor Lito Atienza and Makati Mayor Jejomar Binay had already banned crackdowns by the MMDA in their cities, not because of the MMVA's petition, but rather because of a political rivalry with Fernando. Atienza provided vendors with sales tables and permitted them to operate in the Quiapo district on the condition that they paid 20 pesos a day to the City of Manila and 20 pesos a day to a cooperative. Binay permitted night vending along parts of Jupiter Street.
62. Fr. Robert Reyes conducted street masses in Philcoa on Christmas and New Year's Eve in 2002. When he sprinkled holy water on the street and vendors, it was taken as a symbolic cleansing of the "impurities" that had been unjustly attributed to the vendors and a restoration of their wounded dignity.
63. According to an MMDA Operations Team member who spoke on condition of anonymity at a fast food outlet in Monumento, Caloocan City, they recognized that some of their colleagues were taking money from the vendors and tacitly allowing street vending (2005, Aug. 26). However, MMDA Undersecretary Cesar Lacuna stated that Fernando had attempted to prevent bribery of personnel by prohibiting them from carrying cell phones and informing them about crackdown sites only at the last minute (interview, 2009, July 3).
64. See the *Philippine Daily Inquirer* (2004, Mar. 18, 19).
65. See the *Manila Times* (2002, Oct. 1).
66. For details on the process of legislating the Urban Development and Housing Act, see Gatpatan (1992), Tabora (1992), de Leon and Chaves (1994), Karaos (1993), Karaos et al. (1995), Karaos (1998), Carroll (1998), Van Naerssen (2003) and Magadia (2003).
67. The concept of urban land reform was first addressed in Presidential Decree No. 1517, issued by Marcos in 1978. This decree prescribed the optimization of urban land use for public welfare, but this went largely unrealized (Magadia 2003: 110).
68. The leading organizations were the Foundation for Development Alternatives, the Institute on Church and Social Issues and PAKSA-LUPA.
69. When President Aquino set an order of priority for 20 bills, urban land reform ranked 15th (Karaos et al. 1995: 37).
70. See Magadia (2003: 107).

71. In 1997, lobbying by NGOs led to the abolition of Marcos's Presidential Decree No. 772, which had criminalized squatters and legitimized forced evictions. According to Karaos (1998), after democratization, the urban poor found it easier to win concessions from the government through policy proposals on specific issues submitted by a loose alliance of fragmented social movements, rather than through confrontations with the government by a more solid alliance.
72. See Chapter 2, "Friction between Two Urban Spaces," for details on the content of the Urban Development and Housing Act.
73. To expedite passage of the bill, the NGOs and peoples' organizations lobbied for items that would readily gain the endorsement of Congress, and therefore shelved such items as restrictions on land ownership in cities and the introduction of an innovative taxation system for land ownership.
74. See Shatkin (2004: 2480). For a discussion of problems with the Community Mortgage Program, see Chapter 2, "Friction between Two Urban Spaces."
75. The Social Reform Agenda was an anti-poverty agenda formulated by the Ramos administration in 1994. It is noteworthy that the state institutionalized the participation of NGOs and peoples' organizations to improve the framing and implementation of public policy through cooperation (Magadia 2003: 156–75).
76. This committee was composed of representatives from the Department of the Interior, the Philippine National Police, the Department of Trade and Industry, the Department of Labor and Employment and the Informal Sector Section of the Social Reform Council.
77. The leader of Ka-Tinig was Mercedes Ignacio-Nicolas. She had also worked as an organizer of street vendors and pedicab drivers for the Parish Based Labor Organization (PaBLO), and as representative of the informal sector on the Social Reform Council. As a social activist, she is known by the name Ka Dedeng.
78. From an interview with Celia (50s, female, leader of LRT-Monumento street vendors' organization; 2004, May 15).
79. The reason for this falling out was a confrontation with Estrada over appointments to the National Anti-Poverty Commission, which was established as a successor to the Social Reform Council. Commission members were to consist of representatives elected from 11 basic sectors, including farmers, fishermen, indigenous people, women and informal sector workers. However, Estrada directly appointed his allies to the commission. Ka-Tinig and other groups responded by filing a complaint against Estrada and others with the Supreme Court (Katinig et al. v. President Joseph Estrada et al. 1999). From this point on, relations between Ka-Tinig and the Estrada administration were severed (from an interview with Ignacio Nicolas, 50s, female, Ka-Tinig leader, 2005, Aug. 17).

80. At a meeting of the Inter-Agency Council convened on May 2, the day after People Power 3, the chair, who was Secretary of the Department of the Interior, conveyed President Arroyo's wish to sign the implementing rules and regulations within 15 days, and asked that they be finalized as quickly as possible. At a meeting on May 8, the chair once again pressed for finalization, declaring that issuing these rules and regulations was crucial to the stability of the government. For details on the involvement of the Arroyo administration in the rules and regulations for Executive Order No. 452, see Inter-Agency Council 2001.
81. The sole exception was Quezon City, where the incumbent mayor, Mel Mathay, enacted an ordinance in hopes of securing the street vendor vote just before the mayoral election of 2000, when he was trailing former congressman Feliciano Belmonte (from an interview with Evelyn, 60s, female, former leader of a street vendors' organization in Quezon City, 2005, Sept. 28).

Chapter 6

1. According to Quimpo, a predatory regime is created by the conjunction of two corrupt institutions: a presidency with broad powers over discretionary spending and appointments and patrimonialistic political parties. Under a predatory regime, the government's system of checks and balances breaks down, leading to the spread of corruption, the systematic plundering of state resources and the conversion of public institutions into mechanisms for plunder.
2. Thompson treats all of these political styles as forms of elite democracy.
3. Marcos had earlier constructed a pyramid that extended from himself at the top to voters at the bottom, via local elites as intermediaries. Through this pyramid, he controlled politics by distributing resources and imposing punishments. According to Thompson, Arroyo successfully revived this system, and for this reason, he categorizes her governance as "neo-traditionalist."
4. See Malaya and Malaya (2004: 3058).
5. A recording of a telephone conversation between Arroyo and Comelec official Virgilio Garcillano was divulged. Because Arroyo could be heard saying "Hello, Garci" on the tape, this became known as the "Hello Garci" scandal. Yet another scandal involved the alleged diversion of 728 million pesos that had been earmarked for fertilizer purchases by the Department of Agriculture to Arroyo's campaign coffers.
6. Because the press conference where these resignations were announced took place at the Hyatt Hotel, the 10 resigning officials were referred to as the "Hyatt 10."
7. The motion to impeach was rejected in a full session of the Lower House by a vote of 173 to 32. Another impeachment motion was filed in 2007 in the wake of the ZTE scandal, but this was also rejected.

8. Arroyo had become president in the first place due to allegations that Estrada had taken protection money from *jueteng* operators. Consequently, she lost what remained of her legitimacy when the same accusations were leveled against members of her immediate family.
9. As a possible explanation for this rampant corruption at the presidential level, Kawanaka (2006) cited an institutional change that enhanced the president's authority over resource distribution following democratization. Previously, resources had been concentrated in the hands of the state, where they were fought over by elite legislators. However, after democratization, with the privatization of government enterprises and the growth of foreign investment, private corporations that wished to get a share of this business were compelled to compete with one another in cultivating close relations with the president, who had the power to issue permits and licenses for private capital. Kawanaka sees this as a factor in the increased occurrence of presidential bribery.
10. Up until the end of July 2006, eight motions for impeachment were filed; however, the House Judiciary Committee rejected them all.
11. David (2008, Feb. 23) wrote that under the Arroyo administration, "the justice system has become a weapon to intimidate those who stand up to power, the military and the police have become the private army of a gangster regime, the Commission on Elections has become a haven for fixers who deliver fictitious votes to the moneyed and the powerful, the government bureaucracy has been turned into a halfway house for political lackeys, misfits, and the corrupt, and the House of Representatives has become its hired cheering squad."
12. The Magdalo group was led primarily by Philippine Military Academy graduates of the class of 1995 who were members of elite units such as the Scout Rangers of the Army and the Naval Special Operations Group. The group accused top military commanders of taking bribes from equipment vendors and smuggling weapons to anti-government Muslim forces and Arroyo of ordering terrorist bombings in Mindanao to foment fear and prop up her regime, as well as failing to pay wages to frontline troops.
13. However, the Catholic Church, which had lost a powerful leader with the death of Cardinal Sin a month earlier, only asked for clarification of the allegations without actively calling for Arroyo's resignation.
14. See Doronila (2007, Feb. 23).
15. The 1987 Constitution prohibited the reelection of anyone who had served as president for four years or more. Since Estrada had only served as president for two and a half years, Comelec allowed him to run.
16. See the *Philippine Daily Inquirer* (2009, Aug. 8).
17. Of course, the Aquino family was not always a paragon of virtue. Before his assassination, Benigno Aquino Jr. was seen as an exceedingly ambitious elite politician. In addition, as Arillo (2000) points out, Corazon Aquino's administration was not entirely devoid of corruption. Noting that the Aquino

presidency was a period of excessive hiring of civil servants, Fujiwara (1990: 55–8) sees this as an indication that corruption had also been "democratized."
18. This process can be referred to by the Gramscian concept "*transformismo.*"
19. For a detailed account of the Aquino campaign, see Rocamora (2010).
20. Translated from Tagalog.
21. Translated from Tagalog.
22. To be sure, Aquino campaign workers did not come away empty-handed. I personally observed that they received items such as the latest cell phones (in yellow) imprinted with a picture of the Aquino family.
23. This resulted in the peculiar phenomenon of the Marcos family and associates of the Bayan Muna, which had suffered persecution as CPP under Marcos's martial law, collaborating to secure the election of Villar.
24. See the *Philippine Daily Inquirer* (2009, Nov. 30; 2009, Dec. 1) for a description of Villar's candidacy announcement and the circumstances in which it took place.
25. According to a survey by AGB Nielsen, Villar's radio and TV advertising expenditures from February 9 to March 2, 2010 came to 120 million pesos, compared with 88 million spent by Estrada and 87 million by Aquino. See the *Philippine Star* (2010, Mar. 10).
26. See the *Philippine Daily Inquirer* (2009, Dec., 1a).
27. Villar also adopted orange as his campaign color, despite the fact that Estrada had always used orange for that purpose. See the *Philippine Daily Inquirer* (2009, Dec. 1b).
28. See the *Philippine Daily Inquirer* (2010, Mar. 31). In response, Aquino announced a plan to redistribute the Luisita land among its tenants, and declared that he would continue to live in his Manila residence instead of moving into the presidential palace, thus making a point of his frugality. For details on Aquino's rejoinder, see the *Philippine Daily Inquirer* (2010, Feb. 10; 2010, Apr. 15).
29. See the *Philippine Daily Inquirer* (2010, Mar. 29).
30. See the *Philippine Daily Inquirer* (2010, Mar. 30).
31. Among the allegations made public against Villar were that he got the construction routes of major thoroughfares changed to inflate the price of real estate he owned, and that he improperly pressured the Philippine Stock Exchange into allowing him to sell stock he owned before the end of its lock-up period in order to free up funds for his election campaign.
32. Senator Consuelo "Jamby" Madrigal criticized Villar at a forum held at De La Salle University in remarks that were broadcast nationwide on the ABS-CBN news.
33. See de Quiros (2010, Apr. 7).
34. On Mar. 30, 2010, Teodoro, the candidate of the ruling Lakas party, resigned from his position as party chairman, complaining that President Arroyo was not providing him with sufficient monetary and organizational assistance.

Local elites associated with Lakas also expressed frustration that they were not receiving adequate campaign funds. These claims, that Arroyo was not dispensing campaign money to her own party, fueled suspicions that she was providing financial assistance to Villar.

35. Seizing on rumors that Aquino had suffered from severe depression as a university student, Villar criticized him as lacking the stamina to serve as president. Aquino responded by saying although he suffered a bout of depression after his father had been murdered, he never sought any type of medical attention. For details on Aquino's rebuttal, see the *Philippine Daily Inquirer* (2010, Jan. 11; 2010, Apr. 29).

36. Pro-Aquino bias was particularly apparent in ABS-CBN's reportage. One reason may be that the network's owners, the Lopez family, shared similar hardships with the Aquino family under the Marcos regime.

37. Although data on approval ratings by class in different regions of the country could not be obtained, an examination of the elections since democratization suggests the following trends. The urban sector civic sphere tends to abhor populism and support moral nationalism. The urban middle class also tends to support candidates espousing civic inclusivism or exclusivism as an appealing alternative, but due to constraints on fiscal and organizational power and limited name recognition, there are rarely any promising candidates. The poor in the rural sector mass sphere, where clientelism holds more sway, tend to vote for presidential candidates supported by the local power elite. On the other hand, the poor in the urban sector mass sphere enjoy greater voting freedom, and therefore tend to respond favorably to populism.

38. See Doronila (2009, Sep. 16).

39. It was also frequently argued that even the island of Mindanao was peaceful during the Estrada era. This impression was no doubt influenced by the Estrada campaign's condemnation of the massacre in Maguindanao province, which occurred during the Arroyo administration. However, Estrada had in fact launched a massive military operation against Muslim anti-government forces on the island.

40. Senators and representatives were allowed to disburse 200 and 70 million pesos, respectively, at their discretion.

41. Although Arroyo's eligibility to run again was challenged, Benjamin Abalos, an associate of Arroyo who was chairman of the Commission on Elections, accepted her candidacy application, and the Supreme Court approved it under the aegis of Chief Justice Corona. Arroyo also ran and won in the 2013 election, declaring her candidacy while under hospital arrest.

42. Gutierrez, a college classmate of Arroyo's husband, served in several important posts in the Arroyo administration. Corona was appointed Chief Justice of the Supreme Court just one month before Arroyo stepped down from the presidency. Under Corona, the Court issued a series of decisions unfavorable

to the Aquino family, notably one involving the agrarian reform of their Luisita plantation.
43. Other charges included graft related to bidding by the Chinese ZTE Corporation, misuse of Philippine Charity Sweepstakes Office funds and corruption associated with ODA-funded bridge construction projects.
44. According to the Commission on Audit, pork-barrel expenditures under the Arroyo administration from 2007 to 2009 came to 116 billion pesos, well over the budgeted amount of 79.8 billion. Most of this funding was released to congressmen in the Arroyo camp, with two-thirds of the expenditures unaccounted for.
45. From 2011 to 2013, DAP disbursed 144.4 billion pesos out of a total allocation of 167.1 billion.
46. Among these were the Sin Tax Reform Act, which raised cigarette and liquor taxes, the Enhanced Basic Education Act of 2013, which extended the basic education period by two years to conform to international standards, and the National Health Insurance Act of 2013, which expanded the ranks of those eligible for health insurance.
47. The program was allocated 12 billion pesos in the fiscal 2010 budget and 29 billion in fiscal 2011.
48. According to a 2011 report by the World Bank and the Australian Agency for International Development, the annual income of beneficiaries rose 12.6 per cent and their poverty rate declined 6.2 per cent. However, there has been no perceptible change in the nationwide poverty rate (Thompson 2013: 261–2).
49. In 2014, the population of the Philippines passed the 100 million mark.
50. Thirty University of the Philippines Economists (2012) Population, Poverty, Politics and RH Bill, *Philippine Daily Inquirer*, July 28, 2012.
51. Kaka Bag-ao (2012), "Overwhelming Case for the RH Bill," *Philippine Daily Inquirer*, Oct. 13, 2012.

Chapter 7
1. See Scott (1985) and Kerkvliet (1990).
2. See Karos (1998) and Kiba (2010) for fragmentation of the urban poor caused by organizing the activities of opposing social movements. Another outcome of civic inclusivism I witnessed several times and think as negative is that the poor chose the seemingly disadvantageous option of refusing any benefits presented by the government as compromise and thus adhered to a hard-liner struggle to get nothing.
3. For example, Mill (1865) advocated the introduction of proportional representation to ensure that educated intellectuals retained a certain degree of influence in election politics. Mass society theory, which saw the irrationality of the masses as a threat, came to be vigorously debated in the 20th century.

4. I referred to Fujiwara (1994) for this argument.
5. Although this book has focused on social movements as examples of contact zones, opportunities for direct contact are by no means limited to social movements, as I point out in Chapter 1.
6. In Nishio, Kusaka, and Yamaguchi (2015), we described how Japanese student volunteers in work camps encountered Hansen's Disease survivors in China and rural villagers in the Philippines, developing strong emotional relationships and admiration that dismantled collective categories and hierarchical orders based on medical histories, nationality, and so on.
7. As for those who go to work overseas—as many as one Philippine citizen out of ten—the new mutualities they cultivate while abroad may have the potential to overcome the moral divisions between classes discussed in this book.

BIBLIOGRAPHY

Abinales, Patricio N. and Donna J. Amoroso. 2005. *State and Society in the Philippines*. Lanham, MD: Rowman & Littlefield.

Abinales, Patricio N. 2008. "Notes on the Disappearing 'Middle' in Post-Authoritarian Philippine Politics," in *The Rise of Middle Classes in Southeast Asia*, ed. Shiraishi Takashi and Pasuk Phongpaichit. Kyoto: Kyoto University Press; Melbourne: Trans Pacific Press.

Ables, Higino A. 2003. *Mass Communication and Philippine Society*. Quezon City: University of the Philippine Press.

Abueva, Jose. V. 2001. "A Crisis of Political Leadership: From 'Electoral Democracy' to 'Substantive Democracy'," in *Between Fires: Fifteen Perspective on the Estrada Crisis*, ed. Amando Doronila.

Agoncillo, Teodoro A. 1990. *History of the Filipino People,* 8th ed. Quezon City: Garothech Publishing.

Agpalo, Remigio E. 1972. *The Political Elite and the People: A Study of Politics in Occidental Mindoro*. Quezon City: College of Public Administration, University of the Philippines.

Aguilar, Filomeno V. 2005. "Betting on Democracy: Electoral Ritual in the Philippine Presidential Campaign," *Philippine Studies* 53, 1: 91–118.

Alibutud, J.R. 1999. "Dear Xerex," in *From Loren to Marimar: The Philippine Media in the 1990s*, ed. Shelia S. Coronel. Quezon City: Philippine Center for Investigative Journalism.

Almond, Gabriel A. and Sidney Verba, eds. 1963. *The Civic Culture: Political Attitudes and Democracy in Five Nations*. Princeton: Princeton University Press.

Alsayyad, Nezar and Ananya Roy. 2004. "Urban Informalities: Crossing Borders," in *Urban Informality: Transnational Perspectives from the Middle East, Latin America, and South Asia*, ed. Ananya Roy and Nezar Alsayyad. London: Lexington Books.

Anderson, Benedict. 1983. *Imagined Communities: Reflections on the Origin and Spread of Nationalism*, rev. ed. London: Verso, 1991.

———. 1988. "Cacique Democracy in the Philippines: Origins and Dreams," *New Left Review* 169: 3–31.

Aquino, Belinda. 1998. "Filipino Elections and 'Illiberal' Democracy," *Public Policy* 2, 3: 1–26.

Arillo, Cecilio. 2000. *Greed & Betrayal: The Sequel to the 1986 EDSA Revolution*. Makati City: IAME Design Studio.
Arugay, Aries. A. 2004. "Mobilizing for Accountability: Contentious Politics in the Anti-Estrada Campaign," *Philippine Sociological Review* 52: 75–96.
Balisacan, Arsenio M. 2001. "Did the Estrada Administration Benefit the Poor?" in *Between Fires: Fifteen Perspectives on the Estrada Crisis*, ed. Amando Doronila.
Bautista, Maria Cynthia Rose Banzon. 1998. "Culture and Urbanization: The Philippine Case," *Philippine Sociological Review* 46, 3/4: 21–45.
———. 1999. "Images of the Middle Class in Metro Manila," *Public Policy* 3, 4: 1–37.
———. 2001. "People Power 2: 'Revenge of the Elite on the Masses'?" in *Between the Fires: Fifteen Perspectives on the Estrada Crisis*, ed. Amando Doronila.
Barangay Old Capitol Site, Dilliman, Quezon City. n.d. "Mahikling Kasaysayang ng Barangay Old Capitol Site, Dilliman-Lunsod ng Quezon." Dilliman, Quezon City.
Barangay Operation Center, Quezon City. n.d. "Barangay Profile: Old Capitol Site." Barangay Operation Center, Quezon City.
Bayat, Asef. 1997. "Un-Civil Society: The Politics of the 'Informal People'," *Third World Quarterly* 18, 1: 53–72.
———. 2000. "From 'Dangerous Classes' to 'Quiet Rebels': Politics of the Urban Subaltern in the Global South," *International Sociology* 15, 3: 533–77.
———. 2010. *Life as Politics: How Ordinary People Change the Middle East*. Stanford: Stanford University Press.
Bernardo, Allan B.I. 2007. "Language in Philippine Education: Rethinking Old Fallacies, Exploring New Alternatives amidst Globalization," in *(Re)Making Society: The Politics of Language and Identity in the Philippines*, ed. T. Ruanni F. Tupas. Quezon City: University of the Philippine Press.
Berner, Erhard. 1997. *Defending a Place in the City: Localities and the Struggle for Urban Land in Metro Manila*. Quezon City: Ateneo de Manila University Press.
———. 2000. "Poverty Alleviation and Eviction of the Poorest: Towards Urban Land Reform in the Philippines," *International Journal of Urban and Regional Research* 24, 3: 554–66.
Bhowmik, Sharit. 2005. "Street Vendors in Asia: A Review." *Economic and Political Weekly*, May 28–June 4: 2256–64.
Boudreau, Vincent. 2001. *Grass Roots and Cadre in the Protest Movement*. Quezon City: Ateneo de Manila University Press.
Bourdieu, Pierre. 1979. *Distinction: A Social Critique of the Judgement of Taste* (A translation of *La Distinction: Critique Sociale du Jugement* [Paris: Éditions de Minuit, 1984]). Cambridge: Harvard University Press.
Brillantes, Alex Bello, Jr. 1992. "National Politics Viewed from Smokey Mountain," in *From Marcos to Aquino: Local Perspectives on Political Transition in the Philippines*, ed. Benedict J. Tria Kerkvliet and Resil B. Mojares. Honolulu: University Hawai'i Press.

Burton, Sandra. 1989. *Impossible Dream: The Marcoses, the Aquinos, and the Unfinished Revolution.* New York: Warner Books.
Butler, Judith. 1990. *Gender Trouble: Feminism and the Subversion of Identity.* London: Routledge.
Calimbahin, Cleo. 2010. "Capacity and Compromise: COMELEC, NAMFREL and Election Fraud," in *Politics of Change in the Philippines*, ed. Yuko Kasuya and Nathan Gilbert Quimpo.
Canovan, Margaret. 1999. "Trust the People!: Populism and the Two Faces of Democracy," *Political Studies* 47, 1: 2–16.
———. 2002. "Taking Politics to the People: Populism as the Ideology of Democracy," *Democracies and the Populist Challenge,* ed. Yves Mény and Yves Surel. New York: Palgrave.
Carroll, S.J., John. 1998. "Philippine NGOs Confront Urban Poverty," in *Organizing for Democracy: NGOs, Civil Society and the Philippine State,* ed. Sidney Silliman and Lela Noble. Manila: Ateneo de Manila University Press.
———. 2001. "Civil Society, the Churches, and the Ouster of Erap," in *Between the Fires: Fifteen Perspectives on the Estrada Crisis*, ed. Amando Doronila.
Castells, Manuel. 2002. *The Information Age: Economy, Society and Culture,* vol. 1, *The Rise of the Network Society*, 2nd ed. Oxford: Blackwell Publishing.
Caoili, Manuel A. 1988. *The Origin of Metropolitan Manila: A Political and Social Analysis.* Quezon City: University of the Philippines Press.
Casino, Teodoro A. 2001. "View from the Streets: Different Folks, Different Strokes," in *Between Fires: Fifteen Perspective on the Estrada Crisis*, ed. Amando Doronila.
Catholic Bishops' Conference of the Philippines. 1991. Second Plenary Council of the Philippines, Jan.–Feb., Manila.
Chai, Sun-Ki. 1997. "Rational Choice and Culture," in *Culture Matters: Essays In Honor Of Aaron Wildavsky*, ed. Richard J. Ellis and Michael Thompson. Boulder: Westview Press.
Chowdhury, Amitabha. 1968. "An Asian Press Perspective," in *Asian Newspapers' Reluctant Revolution,* ed. John A. Lent. Ames: Iowa University Press.
Clarke, Gerard. 1998. *The Politics of NGOs in South-East Asia: Participation and Protest in the Philippines.* London: Routledge.
Claudio, Lisandro. 2013. *Taming People Power: The EDSA Revolutions and Their Contradictions.* Quezon City: Ateneo de Manila University Press.
Connolly, William E. 1991. *Identity/Difference: Democratic Negotiations of Political Paradox.* Ithaca: Cornell University Press.
Constantino-David, Karina. 2001. "Surviving Erap," in *Between the Fires: Fifteen Perspectives on the Estrada Crisis*, ed. Amando Doronila.
Constantino, Renato. 1966. "The Miseducation of the Filipino," *Graphic*, June 8. Reprinted in Renato Constantino (1966), *The Filipinos in the Philippines: And Other Essays* (Quezon City: Filipino Signatures).
———. 1975. *The Philippines: A Past Revisited.* Quezon City: Tala Publishing Services.
———. 1978. *The Philippines: Continuing Past.* Quezon City: Tala Publishing Services.

Coronel, Shelia S. 1999 "Lords of the Press," in *From Loren to Marimar: The Philippine Media in the 1990s*, ed. Shelia S. Coronel. Quezon City: Philippine Center for Investigative Journalism.

———. 2001. "The Unmaking of a President," in *EDSA 2: A Nation in Revolt*. Pasig City: Anvil Publishing.

Crisostomo, Isabelo T. 1999. *President Joseph Estrada: From Stardom to History*. Quezon City: J. Kriz Publishing.

———. 2002. *The Power and the Gloria: Gloria Macapagal Arroyo and Her Presidency*. Quezon City: J. Kriz Publishing.

Cross, John C. 1998. *Informal Politics: Street Vendors and the State in Mexico City*. Stanford: Stanford University Press.

Culibao, Mayet. 1997. "Fast Facts on Metro Manila's Informal Sector," *Intersect* 12, 8: 4.

David, Randy. 2002. *Nation, Self and Citizenship*. Quezon City: University of the Philippines Press.

Davis, Mike. 1990. *City of Quartz: Excavating the Future in Los Angeles*. London: Verso.

———. 2006. *Planet of Slums*. London: Verso.

de Leon, Annie and Percival Chaves. 1994. "Urban Poor Coalition, in *Studies on Coalition Experiences in the Philippines*, ed. Cesar P. Cala and Jose Z. Grageda. Makati City: Bookmark.

del Rosario, Tess. 2004. "Pasyon, Pelikula at Telenovela: The Hidden Transcript of Edsa Masa," *Philippine Studies* 52, 1: 43–77.

Diamond, Larry. 1999. *Developing Democracy toward Consolidation*. Baltimore: Johns Hopkins University Press.

Doronila, Amando. 2001a. *The Fall of Joseph Estrada: The Inside Story*. Pasig City: Anvil Publishing; Makati City: Philippine Daily Inquirer.

———, ed. 2001b. *Between Fires: Fifteen Perspectives on the Estrada Crisis*. Pasig City: Anvil Publishing; Makati City: Philippine Daily Inquirer.

Dryzek, John. 2000. *Deliberative Democracy and Beyond: Liberals, Critics, and Contestations*. Oxford: Oxford University Press.

Ferrer, Miriam Coronel. 1997a. "Civil Society: An Operational Agenda," in *Democracy and Citizenship in Filipino Political Culture*, ed. Maria Serena I. Diokno. Quezon City: Third World Studies Center.

———. 1997b. "Civil Society Making Civil Society," in *Civil Society Making Civil Society*, ed. Miriam Coronel Ferrer. Quezon City: Third World Studies Center.

Fisher, Julie. 1998. *Nongovernments: NGOs and the Political Development of the Third World*. West Hartford: Kumarin Press.

Flaviano, Emerald. 2013. "The Cops vs. the Hoodlum: Implicating Myths of Criminality and Justice in Manila's 2013 Mayoral Campaign," Paper presented at the International Convention Asia Scholars.

Flores, Patrick. 1998. "The Illusions of a Cinematic President," *Public Policy* 2, 4: 101–19.
Fonbuena, Carmela S. 2004. "The Fallen King," in *Spin and Sell: How Political Ads Shaped the 2004 Elections*, ed. Glenda M. Gloria, Ana Maria L. Tabunda and Carmela S. Fonbuena. Makati City: Foundation for Communication Initiatives and Konrad Adenauer Foundation.
Frago, Perlita M. 2006. "The Media and Philippine Politics," in *Philippine Politics and Governance: Challenges to Democratization and Development*, ed. Teresa S. Encarnasion Tadem and Noel M. Morada. Quezon City: Department of Political Science, University of Philippines Dilliman.
Franco, Jennifer Conroy. 2000. *Campaigning for Democracy: Grassroots Citizenship Movements, Less-Than-Democratic Elections, and Regime Transition in the Philippines*. Quezon City: Institute for Popular Democracy.
Fraser, Nancy. 1992. "Rethinking the Public Sphere: A Contribution to the Critique of Actual Existing Democracy," in *Habermas and the Public Sphere*, ed. Craig Calhoun. Cambridge: MIT Press.
Freire, Paulo. 1968. *Pedagogia do Oprimido*. São Paulo: Paz e Terra. English translation (1970), *Pedagogy of the Oppressed*. New York: Continuum.
Friedmann, John. 1986. "The World City Hypothesis," *Development and Change* 17, 1: 69–83.
Fujiwara, Kiichi. 1988. "Filipin ni okeru 'Minshushugi' no Seido to Undou ['Democrasy' as Institution and Movement in the Philippines], *Shakai Kagaku Kenkyu* 40, 1: 1–94.
———. 1990. "Filipin Seiji to Kaihatsu Gyousei [Philippine Politics and Developmental Administration]", in *Filipin no Kougyoka: Saiken heno Mosaku* [*Industrialization of the Philippines: Seeking Reconstruction*], ed. Mitsuo Fukuoka. Tokyo: Ajia Keizai Kenkyujo.
———. 1994 "Kougyouka to Seiji Hendou [Industrialization and Political Changes]," in *Sekai Seiji no Kouzou Hendou 3* [*Structural Change of Global Politics 3*], ed. Yoshikazu Sakamoto. Tokyo: Iwanami Shoten.
Garrido, Marco. 2008. "Civil and Uncivil Society: Symbolic Boundaries and Civic Exclusion in Metro Manila," *Philippine Studies* 56, 4: 443–65.
Gatpatan, Marlane V. 1992. "The Making of a Law for the Urban Poor," in *Pulso Monograph No.11: The Urban Development and Housing Act of 1992: Issues and Challenges*. Quezon City: Institute on Church and Social Issues.
Gealogo, Francis A. 2000. "Nardong Putik in the Genealogy of Tagalog Folk Heroes," in *Geopolitics of the Visible: Essays on Philippine Film Cultures*, ed. Roland B. Tolentino. Quezon City: Ateneo de Manila University Press.
Global Call to Action against Poverty Philippines. 2001. "Kwentuhang Bayan: Pagbabalik-Tanaw sa Martsa ng Maralita [Kwentuhang Town: Reflections on the March of the Poor]."

Gloria, Glenda. 1995. "Makati: One City, Two Worlds," in *Boss: 5 Case Studies of Local Politics in the Philippines*, ed. Jose Lacaba. Quezon City: Philippine Center for Investigative Journalism.

———. 2004a. "Selling a Candidate," in *Spin and Sell: How Political Ads Shaped the 2004 Elections,* ed. Glenda M. Gloria, Ana Maria L. Tabunda and Carmela S. Fonbuena. Makati City: Foundation for Communication Initiatives and Konrad Adenauer Foundation.

———. 2004b. "No to Makeovers," in *Spin and Sell: How Political Ads Shaped the 2004 Elections,* ed. Glenda M. Gloria, Ana Maria L. Tabunda and Carmela S. Fonbuena. Makati City: Foundation for Communication Initiatives and Konrad Adenauer Foundation.

Habermas, Jürgen. 1968. *Strukturwandel der Öffentlichkeit: Untersuchungen zu einer Kategorie der bürgerlichen Gesellschaft.* Frankfurt am Main: Suhrkamp. 2nd edition, 1990. English translation (1989), *The Structural Transformation of the Public Sphere: An Inquiry into a Category of Bourgeois Society* (Cambridge: MIT Press).

———. 1996. *Die Einbeziehung des Anderen: Studien zur politischen Theorie.* Frankfurt am Main: Suhrkamp. English translation (2000), *The Inclusion of the Other.* Cambridge: MIT Press.

Harvey, David. 2012. *Rebel Cities.* London: Verso.

Hau, Caroline S. and Victoria L. Tinio. 2003. "Language Policy and Ethnic Relations in the Philippines," in *Fighting Words: Language Policy and Ethnic Relations in Asia,* ed. Michael E. Brown and Sumit Ganguly. Cambridge: MIT Press.

Hawes, Gary. 1987. *The Philippine State and the Marcos Regime: The Politics of Export.* Ithaca: Cornell University Press.

Hay, Colin. 2006. "Constructivist Institutionalism*,*" in *The Oxford Handbook of Political Institutions,* ed. R.A.W. Rhodes, Sarah A. Binder and Bert A. Rochman. Oxford: Oxford University Press.

Hedman, Eva-Lotta E. 2001. "The Specter of Populism in Philippine Politics and Society: Artista, Masa, Eraption," *South East Asia Research* 9, 1: 5–44.

———. 2005. *In the Name of Civil Society: From Free Election Movements to People Power in the Philippines.* Honolulu: University of Hawai'i Press.

Hernandez, Carolina G. 2001. "Reflection on the Role of the Military in People Power 2," in *Between Fires: Fifteen Perspectives on the Estrada Crisis,* ed. Amando Doronila.

Hollnsteiner, Mary Racelis. 1970. "Reciprocity in the Lowland Philippines," *Four Readings on Philippine Values,* ed. Frank Lynch and Alfonso de Guzman II. Quezon City: Institute of Philippine Culture, Ateneo de Manila University.

Hsiao, Hsin-Huang M. and Hagen Koo. 1997. "The Middle Classes and Democratization," in *Consolidating the Third Wave Democracy: Themes and Perspective,* ed. Larry Diamond et al. Baltimore: Johns Hopkins University Press.

Huntington, Samuel. 1968. *Political Order in Changing Societies*. New Haven: Yale University Press.
———. 1991. *The Third Wave: Democratization in the Late Twentieth Century*. Norman: University of Oklahoma Press.
Hutchcroft, Paul D. 1998. *Booty Capitalism: The Politics of Banking in the Philippines*. Ithaca: Cornell University Press.
Igarashi Seiichi. 2011. *Minshuka to Shimin Shakai no Shin Chihei: Filipin Seiji no Dainamizumu* [*New Horizons of Democratization and Civil Society: The Dynamism of Philippine Politics*]. Tokyo: Waseda University Press.
Ileto, Reynaldo C. 1979. *Pasyon and Revolution: Popular Movement in the Philippines, 1840–1910*. Quezon City: Ateneo de Manila University Press.
———. 1998. *Filipinos and Revolution: Event, Discourse, and Historiography*. Quezon City: Ateneo de Manila University Press.
———. 1999. "Lecture 3: Orientalism and the Study of Philippine Politics," in *Knowing America's Colony: A Hundred Years from the Philippine War*, Philippine Studies Occasional Paper Series No.13, Center for Philippine Studies, University of Hawai'i at Manoa. Revised and reprinted in *Philippine Political Science Journal* 22, 45 (2001):1–32.
Illy, Hans. F. 1986. "Regulation and Evasion: Street Vendors in Manila", *Policy Science* 19: 61–81.
Ionescu, Ghita and Ernest Gellner, eds. 1969. *Populism: Its Meaning and National Characteristic*. London: Weidenfeld and Nicolson.
Jurado, Emil P. and Reli L. German. 1994. *ERAPtion: How to Speak English without Really Trial*. Manila: Emil P. Jurado and Reli L. German.
Karaos, Anna Marie. 1993. "Manila's Squatter Movement: A Struggle for Place and Identity," *Philippine Sociological Review* 41, 1: 71–91.
———. 1995. "Manila's Urban Poor Movement: The Social Construction of Collective Identities," PhD thesis, New School for Social Research.
———. 1998 "Fragmentations in the Urban Movement: Shift from Resistance to Policy Advocacy," *Philippine Sociological Review* 46, 3/4: 143–57.
———. 1999. "Perceptions and Practices of Democracy and Citizenship among Urban Middle Class Families", in *Democracy and Citizenship in Filipino Political Culture*, ed. Maria Serena L. Diokno. Quezon City: Third World Studies Center, University of the Philippines.
———. 2006. "Populist Mobilization and Manila's Urban Poor: the Case of SANAPA in the NGC East Side," in *Social Movements in the Philippines*, ed. Aya Fabros, Joel Rocamora and Djorina Velasco. Quezon City: Institute for Popular Democracy.
Karaos, Anna Marie, Marlene V. Gatpatan and Robert V. Hotz. 1995. *Making a Difference: NGO and PO Policy Influence in Urban Land Reform Advocacy*. Quezon City: Institute on Church and Social Issues.
Kasuya, Yuko. 2008. *Presidential Bandwagon: Parties and Party System in the Philippines*. Tokyo: Keio University Press.

Kasuya, Yuko and Nathan Quimpo, eds. 2010. *The Politics of Change in the Philippines*. Pasig City: Anvil.
Kawanaka, Takeshi. 2002. "Power in a Philippine City," IDE Occasional Papers Series No. 38. Institute for Developing Economies, Chiba, Japan.
———. 2004. "Filipin Seiji to Minshushugi [Philippine Politics and Democracy]," in *Gendai Higashi Ajia to Nihon 4: Kaiiki Ajia [Comtemporary East Asia and Japan 4: Maritime Asia]*, ed. Sekine Masami and Yamamoto Nobuto. Tokyo: Keio University Press.
———. 2006. "Filipin: Tokken wo Meguru Seiji to Keizai [The Philippines: Politics and Economy over Privileges]," in *Ajia no Seiji Keizai Nyumon [Introduction to Asian Political Economy]*, ed. Katayama Yutaka; and Oonishi Yutaka. Tokyo: Yuuhikaku.
———. 2010. "The Urban Middle Class in the Instability of New Democracies," IDE Discussion Paper No. 260, Institute of Developing Economies, Chiba. Available at http://www.ide.go.jp/English/Publish/Download/Dp/pdf/260.pdf [accessed Aug. 10, 2011].
Kerkvliet, Benedict J. Tria. 1990. *Everyday Politics in the Philippines: Class and Status Relations in a Central Luzon Village*. Berkeley: University of California Press.
———. 1995. "Toward a More Comprehensive Analysis of Philippine Politics: Beyond the Patron-Client, Factional Framework," *Journal of Southeast Asian Studies* 26, 2: 401–19.
———. 1996. "Contested Meaning of Elections in the Philippines", in *The Politics of Elections in Southeast Asia*, ed. R.H. Taylor. Washington, DC: Woodrow Wilson Center Press; Cambridge: Cambridge University Press.
———. 2005. "Political Expectations and Democracy in the Philippines and Vietnam," *Philippine Political Science Journal* 26, 49: 1–26.
Kiba, Saya. 2010. "Sramu no Jumin Undou to Gaibusha: Filipin Manila Shutoken no Jirei kara [Social Movement and Outsiders in Slum Communities in Metro Manila, Philippines]." PhD dissertation, Kobe University. Available at http://www.lib.kobe-u.ac.jp/repository/thesis/d1/D1004820.pdf [accessed Apr. 20, 2011].
———. 2012. "'Sentaku to Kyosou' no Sramu niokeru Seizon Senryaku: Manila no Jumin Soshiki no 25 nen [Strategy of Survival in the Slums in Metro Manila: Between Competition and Selection]", *Rekishigaku Kenkyu* 888: 24–39.
Kimura, Masataka. 2002. "Filipin Chukansou Seisei to Seiji Henyou [Emergence and Political Change of the Filipino Middle Class]," in *Ajia Chukansou no Seisei to Tokushitsu [Emergence and Characteristics of the Asian Middle Class]*, ed. Hattori Tamio, Torii Takashi and Funatsu Tsuruyo. Tokyo: Ajia Keizai Kenkyujo.
Kobari, Yoshihiro. 1999. "Reassessment after 15 Years: Attitudes of the Students of Cebu Institute of Technology toward Filipino in Tertiary Education," in *The Filipino Bilingual: A Multidisciplinary Perspective,* ed. M.L.S. Bautista and G.O. Tan. Manila: De La Salle University Press.

Kondo, Mari. 2003. The "Bombay 5-6": Last Resource Informal Financiers for Philippine Micro-Enterprises, *Kyoto Review of Southeast Asia* 4. Available at https://kyotoreview.org/issue-4/the-bombay-5-6-last-resource-informal-financiers-for-philippine-micro-enterprises/ [Mar. 20, 2015].

Kusaka, Wataru. 2010. "Governing Informalities of the Urban Poor: Street Vendors and Social Order Making in Metro Manila," in *The Politics of Change in the Philippines*, ed. Yuko Kasuya and Nathan Quimpo.

———. 2012. "Kyokaisen wo Shinshoku suru 'Iyashi no Kyodosei': Sesshoku Ryoiki toshiteno Zainichi Filipinjin Shakai [Encroaching Boundries from Contact Zone: 'Care and Mutuality' of the Filipino Communities in Japan]," *Contact Zone* 5: 124–43.

———. 2013. "'Business Friendly' na Elite Shihai: Global Ka to Filipin Chihou Seiji no Henyou ['Business-Friendly' Rule of Local Elites: Capital Investments and Local Politics under Globalization in Ilocos Norte, Philippines]," in *Higashi Ajia "Chihou teki Sekai" no Shakaigaku [The Sociology of "Local World" in East Asia]*, ed. Masaru Fujii, Takai Yasuhiro and Kobayashi Kazumi. Kyoto: Koyo Shobou.

Kymlicka, Will. 2002. *Contemporary Political Philosophy: An Introduction*, 2nd ed. Oxford: Oxford University Press.

Laclau, Ernesto. 1977. *Politics and Ideology in Marxist Theory: Capitalism-Fascism-Populism*, London: Verso.

———. 2005. *On Populist Reason*. London: Verso.

Laclau, Ernesto and Chantal Mouffe. 1985. *Hegemony and Socialist Strategy: Towards a Radical Democratic Politics*. London: Velso.

Lande, Carl. H. 1965. *Leaders, Factions and Parties: The Structure of Philippine Politics*. New Haven: Yale University Southeast Asia Studies.

———. 2001. "The Return of 'People Power' in the Philippines," *Journal of Democracy* 12, 2: 88–102.

Lane, Max R. 1990. *The Mass Urban Movement in the Philippines, 1983–87*. Canberra: Department of Political and Social Change, Research School of Pacific Studies, Australian National University.

Laquian, Aprodicio A. and Eleanor R. Laquian. 1998. *Joseph "Erap" Estrada: The Centennial President*. Vancouver: Institute of Asian Research, University of British Columbia.

———. 2001. *The Erap Tragedy: Tales from the Snake Pit*, Pasig City: Anvil Publishing.

Linz, Juan and Alfred Stepan. 1996. *Problems of Democratic Transition and Consolidation: Southern Europe, South America, and Post-Communist Europe*. Baltimore: John Hopkins University Press.

Lippmann, Walter. 1922. *Public Opinion*, London: Allen & Unwin.

Lipset, Seymour Martin. 1959. *Political Man: The Social Bases of Politics*, New York: Doubleday.

Lopez, Maria Glenda S. 1999. "The Poor on Trail in the Philippine Justice System," *Kasarinlan* 3, 4: 69–90.

Lumbera, Bienvenido. 2000. "James Dean at U.S.T.," *Pelikula: A Journal of Philippine Cinema*, Mar.–Aug.: 11–14.
Luz, Guillermo M. 2001. "People Power 2: A Business Perspective," in *Between Fires: Fifteen Perspectives on the Estrada Crisis*, ed. Amando Doronila.
Lynch, Frank. 1975. "Big and Little People: Social Class in the Rural Philippines," in *Society, Culture, and the Filipino: Introductory Readings in Sociology and Anthropology*, ed. Mary Racelis Hollnsteiner, Maria Elena B. Chiong, Anicia Paglinauan-Castillo and Nora S. Villauneva. Quezon City: Institute of Philippine Culture, Ateneo de Manila University.
Macapagal-Arroyo, Gloria. 2002. Second State of the Nation Address, July 22. Available at http://www.gov.ph/2002/07/22/gloria-macapagal-arroyo-second-state-of-the-nation-address-july-22-2002/ [accessed Dec. 6, 2011].
Machado, Kit G. 1971. "Changing Aspects of Factionalism in Philippine Local Politics," *Asian Survey* 11, 1: 1119–32.
———. 1974. "From Traditional Faction to Machine," *Journal of Asian Studies* 33, 4: 1182–99.
Magadia, Jose. 2003. *State-Society Dynamics: Policy Making in a Restored Democracy*. Manila: Ateneo de Manila University Press.
Magno, Alexander R. 1994. "Filipino Politics in the Electronic Age," *Kasarinlan* 10, 1: 31–5.
———. 1998. "Between Populism and Reform: Facing the Test of May 1998," *Southeast Asian Affairs* 1998: 199–212.
Magno, Christopher N. 2003. "Si Erap at ang Samahan ng Maralitang Tagalunsod [Erap and the Association of Urban Poor]", unpublished Master Thesis, Department of Sociology, University of the Philippines.
Magno, Francisco A. 1993. "Politics, Elites and Transformation in Malabon," *Philippine Studies* 41, 2: 204–16.
Malaya, J. Eduardo and Jonathan E. Malaya. 2004. *So Help Us God: The Presidents of the Philippines and Their Inaugural Addresses*. Manila: Anvil Publishing.
Maslog, Crispin C. 2007. "The Metro Manila Press: Profile and Analysis of Metropolitan Newspaper, Magazines and Journals," in *Philippine Communication Today*, ed. Crispin Maslog. Quezon City: New Day Publishers.
Mangahas, Mahar. 1998. *SWS Surveys on the 1998 National Elections*. Quezon City: Social Weather Stations.
———. 2004. "The SWS Survey Time Series on Philippine Poverty and Hunger, 1983–Present". Available at http://www.nscb.gov.ph/ncs/9thncs/papers/poverty_sws.pdf [accessed July 23, 2011].
Mercado, Monia, ed. 1986. *People Power: The Philippine Revolution of 1986*. Manila: Veritas Publications and Communications Foundation.
Mercado, Ruben G. 1998 "Environment and Natural Resources Management: Lessons from City Program Innovations," Discussion Paper Series No. 98-32, Philippine Institute for Development Studies. Available at http://dirp3.pids.gov.ph/ris/dps/pidsdps9832.pdf [accessed Dec. 22, 2010].

Migdal, Joel S. 1988. *Strong Societies and Weak States: State-Society Relations and State Capability in the Third World*. Princeton: Princeton University Press.

———. 2001. *State in Society: Studying How States and Societies Transform and Constitute One Another*. Cambridge: Cambridge University Press.

Mill, John Stuart. 1865. *Representative Government*, 3rd ed. London: Longman, Green, Longman, Robert & Green.

Miller, David. 1995. *On Nationality*. Oxford: Oxford University Press.

Miyawaki Satoshi. 2005. "Filipin Catholic Kyokai nitotteno 'EDSA': Kyoukai teki Bunmyaku, Kokumin Level deno Senryaku, Seiji Shakai teki Shogeki [The Catholic Church on 'EDSA': Ecclesial Context, National Strategy and Socio-Political Impact]," *Toyo Bunka Kenkyujo Kiyo* 148: 27–55.

———. 2006. "Filipin Catholic Kyokai no Miru 'Filipin': Sono Rekishi to Bunka no Mikata ['Philippines' from the View of Philippine Catholic Church: Its Historical and Cultural Perspective]," *Christ to Sekai* 16: 81–105.

Moore, Barrington. 1966. *Social Origins of Dictatorship and Democracy: Lord and Peasant in the Making of the Modern World*. Boston: Beacon Press.

Moreno, Antonio F. 2006. *Church, State, and Civil Society in Postoauthoritarian Philippines: Narratives of Engaged Citizenship*. Quezon City: Ateneo de Manila University Press.

Mouffe, Chantal. 2000. *The Democratic Paradox*. London: Verso.

———. 2005. *On the Political*. London: Routledge.

Nical, Iluminado, Jerzy J. Smolicz and Margaret J. Secombe. 2004. "Rural Students and the Philippine Bilingual Education Program on the Island of Leyte," in *Medium of Instruction Policies: Which Agenda? Whose Agenda?*, ed. James W. Tollefson and Amy B.M. Tsui. Mahwah, NJ: Lawrence Erlbaum Associates.

Nishio Takeshi, Wataru Kusaka and Kenichi Yamaguchi. 2015. *Shounin Yokubou no Shakai Henkaku: Workcamp nimiru Wakamono no Rentai Gihou* [*Social Movements and Desire for Recognition: Forging Solidarity though the Work Camp*]. Kyoto: Kyoto University Press.

Nowak, Tomas; and Kay Snyder. 1970. "Urbanization and Clientelist Systems in the Philippines," *Philippine Journal of Public Administration* 14, 3: 259–79.

Nozawa Katsumi. 2001. "Estrada Seikenki Filipin no Nougyo Kaihatsu to Kangai Seisaku [Agricultural Development and Irrigation Policy of the Estrada Administraion], *Asia Daigaku Kokusai Kankei Kiyou* 10, 3: 1–39.

Ofreneo, Rosalinda Pineda. 1984. *The Manipulated Press: A History of Philippine Journalism since 1945*. Mandaluyong City: Cacho Hermanos.

Pagbabago@Pilipinas. 2002. "Pagbabago the CD". Available at http://www.pagbabago.com.ph/past-projects/pagbabago-the-cd/ [accessed Aug. 15, 2011].

Parnell, Philip C. 2003. "Criminalizing Colonialism: Democracy Meets Law in Manila," in *Crime's Power: Anthropologists and the Ethnology of Crime,* ed. Philip Parnell and Stephanie Kane. New York: Palgrave Macmillan.

Persson, Torsten and Guido Tabellini. 2000. *Political Economics: Explaining Economic Policy*. Cambridge: MIT Press.
Pertierra, Raul et al. 2002. *Text-ing Selves: Cellphones and Philippine Modernity*. Manila: De La Salle University Press.
———. 2006. *Transforming Technologies: Altered Selves — Mobile Phone and Internet Use in the Philippines*. Manila: De La Salle University Press.
Philippine Center for Investigative Journalism. 1999. *Joke ni Erap: A Jokebook to Support Serious Journalism*. Quezon City: Raintree Publishing.
———. 2001. *A Scrapbook about EDSA 2: People Power Uli! with Jokes, Text Messages, Photos, Digital Images and More*. Quezon City: Raintree Publishing.
Philippine NGO Coalition. n.d. "Philippine NGO Network Report on the Implementation of the International Covenant on Economic, Social, and Cultural Rights 1995 to Present." Available at http://www2.ohchr.org/english/bodies/cescr/docs/info-ngos/PhilippinesNGOCoalition41.pdf [accessed Dec. 26, 2010].
Pinches, Michael. 1991. "The Working Class Experience of Shame, Inequality and People Power in Tatalon, Manila," in *From Marcos to Aquino: Local Perspectives on Political Transition in the Philippines*, ed. Benedict J. Tria Kerkvliet and Resil B Mojares. Honolulu: University Hawai'i Press.
———. 1992. "Proletarian Ritual: Class Degradation and the Dialectics of Resistance in Manila," *Pilipinas* 19: 67–92.
———. 1994. "Modernization and the Quest for Modernity: Architectural Form, Squatter Settlements and the New Society in Manila," in *Cultural Identity and Urban Change in Southeast Asia: Interpretative Essays*, ed. Marc Askew and William Logan. Geelong, Victoria: Deakin University Press.
———. 1996. "The Philippines' New Rich: Capitalist Transformation amidst Economic Gloom," in *The New Rich in Asia: Mobile Phones, McDonalds and Middle Class Revolution*, ed. Richard Robison and Davis S.G. Goodman. London: Routledge.
———. 1999. "Entrepreneurship, Consumption, Ethnicity and National Identity in the Making of the Philippines' New Rich," in *Culture and Privilege in Capitalist Asia*, ed. Michael Pinches. London: Routledge.
———. 2010. "The Making of Middle Class Civil Society in the Philippines," in *The Politics of Change in the Philippines*, ed. Yuko Kasuya and Nathan Quimpo.
Pratt, Mary Louise. 1992. *Imperial Eyes: Travel Writings and Transculturation*. London: Routledge.
Public Affairs Ministry, Diocese of Cubao, Parish Pastoral Council for Responsible Voting. 2010. "Values Related to Election: Kabanalan at Kabayanihan." Manila.
Public and Political Affairs Ministry, Diocese of Kalookan, Parish Pastoral Council for Responsible Voting. 2010. "Orientation-Seminar, St. Joseph the Workman Parish." Manila.
Putnam, Robert D. 1993. *Making Democracy Work: Civic Traditions in Modern Italy*. New Jersey: Princeton University Press.

———. 2000. *Bowling Alone: The Collapse and Revival of American Community*. New York: Simon & Schuster.
Quimpo, Nathan Gilbert. 2005. "Oligarchic Patrimonialism, Bossism, Electoral Clientelism, and Contested Democracy in the Philippines," *Comparative Politics* 37, 2: 229–50.
———. 2008. *Contested Democracy and the Left in the Philippines after Marcos*. New Haven: Yale University Southeast Asia Studies.
———. 2010. "The Presidency, Political Parties and Predatory Politics in the Philippines," in *The Politics of Change in Philippines*, ed. Yuko Kasuya and Nathan Gilbert Quimpo.
Rafael, Vicente. 2000. *White Love and Other Events in Filipino History*. Durham: Duke University Press.
———. 2003. "The Cell Phone and the Crowd: Messianic Politics in the Contemporary Philippines," *Philippine Political Science Journal* 24, 47: 3–36.
Rhodes, Roderick Arthur William. 1996. "The New Governance: Governing without Government," *Political Studies* 44: 652–67.
Rimban, Luz. 1999. "The Empire Strikes Back," in *From Loren to Marimar: The Philippine Media in the 1990s*, ed. Shelia S. Coronel. Quezon City: Philippine Center for Investigative Journalism.
Rivera, Temario. 2000. "Middle Class Politics: The Philippine Experience," *Journal of Social Science* 45: 1–22.
———. 2007. "The Middle Class in Philippine Politics," *Philippine Politics and Governance: Challenges to Democratization & Development*, ed. Teresa S. Encarnasion Tadem and Noel M. Morada. Quezon City: Department of Political Science, University of Philippines Dilliman.
Robison, Richard; and David S.G. Goodman. 1996. "The New Rich in Asia: Economic Development, Social Status and Political Consciousness," in *The New Rich in Asia: Mobile-Phones, McDonalds and Middle Class Revolution*, ed. Richard Robison and Davis S.G. Goodman. London: Routledge.
Robles, Chi-Chi F. and Ramon R. Tuazon. 2007. "Philippine Broadcasting: Profile and Analysis of Philippine Broadcasting Industry," in *Philippine Communication Today*, ed. Crispin Maslog. Quezon City: New Day Publishers.
Rocamura, Joel. 2010. "Partisanship and Reform: The Making of a Presidential Campaign," in *The Politics of Change in the Philippines*, ed. Yuko Kasuya and Nathan Gilbert Quimpo. Pasig City: Anvil Publishing.
Rosario-Braid, Florangel and Ramon R. Tuazon. 1999. "Communication Media in the Philippines: 1521–1986," *Philippine Studies* 46, 3: 291–318.
———. 2000. "Post-EDSA Communication Media," *Philippine Studies* 48, 1: 3–25.
Rosendorff, B. P. 2001. "Choosing Democracy," *Economics and Politics* 13: 1–29.
Ross, Marc Howard. 1997. "Culture and Identity in Comparative Political Analysis," in *Comparative Politics: Rationality, Culture, and Structure*, ed. Mark Irving Lichbach and Alan S. Zuckerman. New York: Cambridge University Press.

Rueschemeyer, Dietrich et al. 1992. *Capitalist Development and Democracy*. Chicago: University of Chicago Press.
Salazar, Zeus A. and Sylvia Mendez Ventura. 2006. *President Erap: A Sociopolitical and Cultural Biography of Joseph Ejercito Estrada (1)*. San Juan: PRG Foundation.
San Juan, Thelma Sioson, ed. 2001. *People Power 2: Lessons and Hopes*. Pasig City: ABS-CBN Publishing.
Sankalas. 2003. "Press Release: Sanlakas Solon Brings Vendors' Issues to Congress," Oct. 8. Available at http://www.geocities.ws/sanlakasonline/pr/03/oc/pr/kong.html [no access date].
Sassen, Saskia. 2001. *The Global City: New York, London, Tokyo*, 2nd ed. Princeton: Princeton University Press.
Schaffer, Frederic C. 1998. *Democracy in Translation: Understanding Politics in an Unfamiliar Culture*. Ithaca: Cornell University Press.
———. 2007. "Why Study Vote Buying?" in *Election for Sale: The Causes and Consequences of Vote Buying*, ed. Frederic C. Schaffer. Quezon City: Ateneo de Manila University Press.
———. 2008. *The Hidden Costs of Clean Election Reform*. Ithaca: Cornell University Press.
Schmidt, Vivien. A. 2008. "Discursive Institutionalism: The Explanatory Power of Ideas and Discourse," *Annual Review of Political Science* 11: 303–26.
Scott, James C. 1969a. "The Analysis of Corruption in Developing Nations," *Comparative Studies in Society and History* 11, 3: 315–41.
———. 1969b. "Corruption, Machine Politics, and Political Change," *American Political Science Review* 63, 4: 1142–58.
———. 1972a. "Patron-Client Politics and Political Change in Southeast Asia," *The American Political Science Review* 66, 1: 91–113.
———. 1972b. "The Erosion of Patron-Client Bonds and Social Change in Rural Southeast Asia," *Journal of Asian Studies* 32, 1: 5–37.
———. 1977. *The Moral Economy of the Peasant: Rebellion and Subsistence in Southeast Asia*. New Haven: Yale University Press.
———. 1985. *Weapons of the Weak: Everyday Forms of Peasant Resistance*. New Haven: Yale University Press.
———. 1990. *Domination and the Arts of Resistance: Hidden Transcripts*. New Haven: Yale University Press.
Seki, Koki. 2010. "Governing Through Exclusion: The Un/Making of the 'Citizen' and 'Community' through Neoliberal Urban Development in Metro Manila, Philippines," *Japanese Review of Cultural Anthropology* 11: 67–101.
———. 2012. "Difference and Alliance in Transnational Social Fields: The Pendular Identity of the Filipino Middle Class," *Philippine Studies* 60, 2: 187–222.
———. 2015. "Capitalizing on Desire: Reconfiguring 'the Social' and the Government of Poverty in the Philippines," *Development and Change* 46, 6: 1253–76.

Serrano, Isagani. 2003. "Civil Society in the Philippines: Struggle for Sustainability," in *Civil Society in Asia*, ed. David Schak and Wayne Hudson. Aldershot: Ashgate Publishing Limited.

Shatkin, Gavin. 1999. "Community Based Organizations, Local Politics, and Shelter Delivery in Manila," *Kasarinlan* 3, 4: 31–50.

———. 2000. "Obstacles to Empowerment: Local Politics and Civil Society in Metropolitan Manila, the Philippines," *Urban Studies* 37, 12: 2357–75.

———. 2002. "Working with the Community: Dilemmas in Radical Planning in Metro Manila, the Philippines," *Planning Theory & Practice* 3, 3: 301–17.

———. 2004. "Planning to Forget: Informal Settlements as 'Forgotten Places' in Globalizing Metro Manila," *Urban Studies* 41, 12: 2469–84.

———. 2006. "Global Cities of the South: Emerging Perspectives on Growth and Inequality," *Cities* 24, 1: 1–15.

———. 2008. "The City and the Bottom Line: Urban Megaproject and the Privatization of Planning in South East Asia," *Environment and Planning A* 40: 383–401.

Shimizu Hiromu. 1991. *Bunka no Naka no Seiji: Filipin "Nigatsu Kakumei" no Monogatari* [*Politics in Culture: Stories of "February Revolution" in the Philippines*]. Tokyo: Kobundo.

———. 1995. "Songen to Wakai, soshite Fuzai no Seigi: Filipin Shakai no Chitsujo [Dignity, Reconciliation and Absence of Justice: Social Order of the Philippine]," in *Senren to Soya: Shakai wo Rissuru Kachi* [*Sophistication and Rudeness: Values that Order Society*], ed. Shimizu Akitoshi. Tokyo: Tokyo University Press.

Shiraishi, Takashi. 2008. "The Rise of Middle Classes in Southeast Asia," in *The Rise of Middle Classes in Southeast Asia*, ed. Shiraishi Takashi and Pasuk Phongpaichit. Kyoto: Kyoto University Press; and Melbourne: Trans Pacific Press.

Sibayan, Bonifacio P. and Andrew Gonzalez. 1996. "Post-Imperial English in the Philippines," in *Post-Imperial English: Status Change in Former British and American Colonies, 1940–1990*, ed. Joshua A Fishman, Andre W. Conrad and Alma Rubal-Lopez. Berlin: Mouton de Gruyter.

Sidel, John T. 1998. "Take the Money and Run?: Post-Marcos 'Personality' Politics," *Public Policy* 2, 3: 27–38.

———. 1999. *Capital, Coercion and Crime: Bossism in the Philippines*. Stanford: Stanford University Press.

———. 2008. "Social Origins of Dictatorship and Democracy Revisited: Colonial State and Chinese Immigrant in the Making of Modern Southeast Asia," *Comparative Politics* 40, 2: 127–47.

Silliman, Sidney; and Noble, Lela, eds. 1998. *Organizing for Democracy: NGOs, Civil Society and the Philippine State*. Manila: Ateneo de Manila University Press.

Simbulan, Dante C. 1965. *The Modern Principalia: The Historical Evolution of the Philippine Ruling Oligarchy*. Quezon City: University of the Philippine Press.

Smith, Desmond. 2000. *Democracy and the Philippine Media, 1983–1993*. New York: Edwin Mellen Press.
Smith, Neil. 1996. *The New Urban Frontier: Gentrification and the Revanchist City*. London: Routledge.
Smolicz, Jerzy J. and Illuminado Nical. 1997. "Exporting the European Idea of a National Language: Some Education Implications of the Use of English and Indigenous Languages in the Philippines," *International Review of Education* 43, 5/6: 507–26.
Soon, Chuan Yean. 2008. "Politics from Below: Culture, Religion, and Popular Politics in Tanauan City, Batangas," *Philippine Studies* 56, 4: 413–42.
———. 2015. *Tulong: An Articulation of Politics in the Christian Philippines*. Manila: University of Santo Tomas Publishing House.
Spivak, Gayatri Chakravorty. 1988 "Can the Subaltern Speak?" in *Marxism and the Interpretation of Culture*, ed. Cary Nelson and Lawrence Grossberg. Urbana: University of Illinois Press.
Stoker, Gerry. 1998. "Governance as Theory: Five Propositions," *International Social Science Journal* 155: 17–28.
Suzuki Yurika. 2007. "Filipin: Kakusa wo Jochou suru Kakusa Shakai [Philippines: Unequal Society that Worsens Inequality]," *Ajiken World Trends* 132: 20–24.
Tsabora, Joel. 1992. "The UDHA: A Step Forward for the Urban Poor," in *Pulso Monograph No.11: The Urban Development and Housing Act of 1992: Issues and Challenges*. Quezon City: Institute on Church and Social Issues.
Tadem, Teresa Encarnacion. 2008. "Situating NGO Advocacy Work in Middle Class Politics in the Philippines," in *The Rise of Middle Classes in Southeast Asia*, ed. Shiraishi Takashi and Pasuk Phongpaichit. Kyoto: Kyoto University Press; Melbourne: Trans Pacific Press.
Takagi, Yusuke. 2008 "Politics of the Great Debate in the 1950s: Revisiting Economic Decolonization in the Philippines," *Kasarinlan* 23, 1: 91–114.
———. 2015 "Changing Civil Society, Policy Coalitions, and Politicians: Philippines Social Policy Reform," Paper presented at the GRIPs ESP Tsunekawa Group Second Workshop, Nov. 11, 2015, Kyoto.
———. 2016. *Central Banking as State Building: Policymakers and Their Nationalism in the Philippines, 1933–64*, Kyoto CSEAS Series on Asian Studies. Singapore: National University of Singapore Press.
Tamada, Yoshifumi. 2008. *Myths and Realities: The Democratization of Thai Politics*. Kyoto: Kyoto University Press; Melbourne: Trans Pacific Press.
Tanate, Kenneth and Omura Kenjiro. 2004. "Perceived Living Condition in the Gated Communities in Metro Manila," *City Planning Review* 39: 379–84.
Teehankee, Julio C. 2010. "Image, Issues, and Machinery: Presidential Campaigns in Post-1986 Philippines," in *The Politics of Change in the Philippines*, ed. Yuko Kasuya and Nathan Quimpo.
Teodoro, Luis V. 1998. "Re-examining the Fundamentals," *Philippine Journalism Review* 11, 2: 22–26.

Thompson, Mark R. 1995 *The Anti-Marcos Struggle: Personalistic Rule and Democratic Transition in the Philippines*. New Haven: Yale University Press.

———. 2007. "*Presidentas* and People Power in Comparative Asian Perspectives," *Philippine Political Science Journal* 28, 51: 1–32.

———. 2010. "After Populism: Winning the 'War' for Bourgeois Democracy in the Philippines," in *The Politics of Change in the Philippines*, ed. Yuko Kasuya and Nathan Quimpo.

———. 2013. "Revising Reformism in Philippines," in *Democracy in East Asia: A New Century*, ed. Larry Diamond, Marc F. Plattner and Yun-Han Chu. Johns Hopkins University Press.

———. 2014. "The Politics Philippine presidents Make: Presidential-style, Patronage-based, or Regime Relational?," *Critical Asian Studies* 46, 3: 433–60.

Tolentino, Roland B. 2010. "Masses, Power, and Gangsterism in the Films of Joseph 'Erap' Estrada," *Kasarinlan* 25, 1/2: 67–94.

Tollefson, James W. 1991. *Planning Language, Planning Inequality: Language Policy in the Community*. London: Longman.

Torfing, Jacob. 2005. "Discourse Theory: Achievements, Arguments, and Challenges," in *Discourse Theory in European Politics*, ed. David Howarth and Jacob Torfing. Basingstoke: Palgrave Macmillan.

Tupas, T. Ruanni F. 2004. "The Politics of Philippine English: Neocolonialism, Global Politics, and the Problem of Postcolonialism," *World English* 23, 1: 47–58.

———. 2007. "Back to Class: The Ideological Structure of the Medium of Instruction Debate in the Philippines," in *(Re)making Society: The Politics of Language, Discourse, and Identity in the Philippines*, ed. T. Ruanni F. Tupas. Quezon City: University of the Philippine Press.

Turner, Victor. 1974. *Dramas, Fields, and Metaphors: Symbolic Action in Human Society*. Ithaca: Cornell University Press.

Uchiyama, Fumiko. 2000. "Filipin Kokumin Keisei nitsuiteno Ichi Kousatsu: 1934 nen Kenpou Seitei Kaigi niokeru Kokugo Seitei Giron [The Creation of a Philippine National Language: Discussions during the Philippine Constitutional Convention of 1934]," *Tounan Ajia: Rekishi to Bunka* [Southeast Asia: History and Culture] 29: 81–104.

Van Naerssen, Ton. 2003. "Globalization and Urban Social Action in Metro Manila," *Philippine Studies* 51, 3: 435–50.

Velasco, Djorina. 2004. "Kompil II: A Study of Civil Society's Political Engagements," *Philippine Sociological Review* 52: 97–118.

———. 2006. "Life on the Fast Track: Mobilizing the Urban Poor for Change," in *Social Movements in the Philippines*, ed. Aya Fabros, Joel Rocamora and Djorina Velasco. Quezon City: Institute for Popular Democracy.

Yamaguchi, Kiyoko. 2006. "The New 'American' Houses in the Colonial Philippines and the Rise of the Urban Filipino Elite," *Philippine Studies* 54, 3: 412–51.

Young, Jock. 1999. *The Exclusive Society: Social Exclusion, Crime and Difference in Late Modernity*. London: Sage Publications.
———. 2007. *The Vertigo of Late Modernity*. London: Sage Publications.
Weyland, Kurt. 2003. "Neopopulism and Neoliberalism in Latin America: How Much Affinity?" *Third World Quarterly* 24 , 6: 1095–15.
Wui, Marlon A. and Glenda S. Lopez, eds. 1997. *State Civil Society: Relations in Policy-Making*. Quezon City: Third World Studies Center.

Periodicals

30 University of the Philippines Economists. 2012, Jul. 28. "Population, Poverty, Politics and RH Bill," *Philippine Daily Inquirer*.
Abaya, Hernando J. 1968. "Our Vaunted Press: A Critique," *Philippine Graphic* 35, 16. Reprinted in Luis V. Teodoro and Melinda Q. de Jesus, eds. (2001), *The Philippine Press and Media, Democracy and Development* (Quezon City: University of the Philippine Press).
Almario, Manuel F. 1998, June 15. "Estrada and the Unfinished Revolution," *Philippine Graphic* 9, 2.
Amador, Zenaida. 2002, Aug. 28. "Hostage to Numbers and Noise?" *Manila Bulletin*.
Bas, Rene Q. 2002, Aug. 18. "Anarchist Street Vendors," *Manila Times*.
Benigno, Teodoro C. 2002, Aug. 26. "Ticking of the Bomb/ Kudos to Bayani Fernando," *Philippine Star*.
Bondoc, Jarius. 2001, Feb. 26. "Voter Education Is Not Enough," *Philippine Star*.
Cagurangan, Mar-Vic. 2003, Aug. 16. "The Metro Chief: After Bringing Sanity to the Streets of Metro Manila, MMDA Chairman Bayani Fernando Sets His Eyes on the Vice-Presidency," *Philippine Free Press*, pp. 1–4.
Carandang, Ricky. 2004, Mar. 15. "Borrowed Brains," *Newsbreak*, p. 15.
Collas-Monsod, Solita. 2002, Sept. 14. "Overwhelming Approval for BF's Campaign," *Philippine Daily Inquirer*.
———. 2003, June 28. "Doing What is Right," *Philippine Daily Inquirer*.
———. 2002, Sept. 14. "Overwhelming Approval for BF's Campaign," *Philippine Daily Inquirer*.
Coronel, Leandro V. 2001, May 19. "Discovering the Poor," *Philippine Daily Inquirer*.
Cruz, Neal H. 2000, July 31. "Stop Politicians from Coddling Squatters," *Philippine Daily Inquirer*.
———. 2001, Feb. 14. "Being Popular is Not the Same as Being a Good Senator," *Philippine Daily Inquirer*.
———. 2002, Apr. 16. "Make Joey Lina Implement Lina Law Completely," *Philippine Daily Inquirer*.
———. 2002, May 15. "Anarchy in the Streets," *Philippine Daily Inquirer*.
———. 2002, June 19. "Return the Sidewalks to the Pedestrians," *Philippine Daily Inquirer*.
———. 2002, June 26. "Comelec, MMDA Chiefs Reveal Their Plans," *Philippine Daily Inquirer*.

———. 2003, June 17. "Squatting Syndicates Invade Campus of State University," *Philippine Daily Inquirer*.
Cruz, Isagani. 2004, Apr. 4. "Intellectual Snobbery?", *Philippine Daily Inquirer*.
Cueto, Donna S. and Christian V. Esguerra. 2001, May 28. "Sin Laments Desecration of Edsa Shrine," *Philippine Daily Inquirer*.
David, Randy. 1997, Dec. 14. "What is a Trapo?" Reprinted in *Nation, Self and Citizenship: An Invitation to Philippine Sociology* (Quezon City: Department of Sociology, College of Social Science and Philosophy, University of the Philippines, 2002).
———. 2001, July 29. "The Hidden Injuries of the Poor," *Philippine Daily Inquirer*.
———. 2003, July 6. "Land Invasion," *Philippine Daily Inquirer*.
———. 2003, Sept. 28. "The Presidency in Our Time," *Philippine Daily Inquirer*.
———. 2004, Feb. 8. "The Making of the 'Masa' Vote," *Philippine Daily Inquirer*.
———. 2008, Feb. 2. "Thoughts on New Politics," *Philippine Daily Inquirer*.
———. 2008, Feb. 23. "Bonfire of Institutions," *Philippine Daily Inquirer*.
de Castro, Isagani Jr. 2004, Mar. 29. "Memo for Poe," *Newsbreak*, p. 6.
———. 2004, June 7. "Gloria's Classic Win," *Newsbreak*, p. 19.
de Quiros, Conrado. 2001, Apr. 30. "Again, the 'Dumb' Masa," *Philippine Daily Inquirer*.
———. 2001, May 5. "Voter Education Starts Now, And Humbly," *Philippine Daily Inquirer*.
———. 2010, Apr. 7. "Phenomena," *Philippine Daily Inquirer*.
dela Rosa, Fred. 2002, Sept. 13. "Going, Going: Sidewalks, Beaches, Esteros," *Manila Times*.
Doronila, Amando. 1998, May 18. "1998 Polls Did Away with Old Nations," *Philippine Daily Inquirer*.
———. 2001, Apr. 30. "Philippines Sitting on Edge of Civil War," *Philippine Daily Inquirer*.
———. 2001, May 2. "The State Defends Itself," *Philippine Daily Inquirer*.
———. 2002, Sept. 4. "Manila's Street Should Return to the Public," *Philippine Daily Inquirer*.
———. 2002, Aug. 26. "MMDA Faces Daunting Task amid Street Action Politics," *Philippine Daily Inquirer*.
———. 2003, Dec. 15. "Popularity Neither Policy Nor Program," *Philippine Daily Inquirer*.
———. 2004, Jan. 26. "Main Issue Is Who Is Best Qualified to Lead the Nation," *Philippine Daily Inquirer*.
———. 2007, Feb. 23. "Edsa People Power Fatigue: A Revisionist View," *Philippine Daily Inquirer*.
———. 2009, Sept. 16. "Transparency Now A Defining Issue in Campaign," *Philippine Daily Inquirer*.
Doyo, Ma. Ceres P. 2004, Apr. 29. "The Metaphors and Vote of the Poor (1)," *Philippine Daily Inquirer*.

Espina, Rene. 2001, May 20. "Minding Other People's Business," *Manila Bulletin*.
Esposo, William. 2003, Dec. 1. "Know the People Promoting Poe and Showbiztocracy," *Philippine Daily Inquirer*.
———. 2003, Dec. 21. "Philippine Elections: Garbage In and Garbage Out," *Philippine Daily Inquirer*.
———. 2010, Sept. 28. "An Impossible Haves and Have-Nots Dialogue," *Philippine Star*.
General, Honesto C. 2004, May 10. "Close Encounter with a Masa Voter," *Philippine Daily Inquirer*.
Go, Miriam Grace. 2004, 26 Apr. "Selling the Future," *Newsbreak*, 16–19.
Gutierrez, Eric. 2001, May 2. "Gloria Should Talk To Estrada Loyalists," *Philippine Daily Inquirer*.
Jimenez-David, Rina. 2002, Aug. 22. "BF's War of Attrition," *Philippine Daily Inquirer*.
Kaka Bag-ao. 2012, Oct. 13. "Overwhelming Case for the RH Bill," *Philippine Daily Inquirer*.
Licauco, Jaime T. 2001, May 22. "Erap Mirrors the Filipino Consciousness," *Philippine Daily Inquirer*.
———. 2001, June 5. "Concerned Filipinos abroad Write on What's Happening to the Country," *Philippine Daily Inquirer*.
Mable, Jing A. 2004, Mar. 27. "Kalsada Natin, Alagaan Natin: A Project Worth Paying For", *Philippine Free Press*, pp. 17–24.
Manila Bulletin. 2003, May 24. "Many Sidewalk Vendors Sell Dirty Goods, Says MMDA."
Manila Times. 2002, Oct. 1. "Illegal Vendors' Syndicate Sowing Anarchy, Says MMDA Chairman."
———. 2003, Nov. 17. "Editorial: How Government Abets Mendicancy."
———. 2003, Sept. 25. "MMDA Adds More Muscle to Antistreet-Peddling Drive."
Morphy, Dennis. 2003. Nov. 7. "The Seamless Robe of Human Rights," *Philippine Daily Inquirer*.
———. 2005, Apr. 10. "Tough Love," *Philippine Daily Inquirer*.
Olivares-Cunanan, Belinda. 2001, May 1. "Rift Between Opposition Moderates and Militants," *Philippine Daily Inquirer*.
———. 2002, Sept. 14. "Support for Bayani Fernando," *Philippine Daily Inquirer*.
Pascual, Federico D. 2000, Aug. 3. "If We Deny Voting Rights to Squatters," *Philippine Star*.
———. 2009, Oct. 8. "Don't Allow Squatters' Return to Old Locations," *Philippine Star*.
Philippine Daily Inquirer. 1998, 11 May. "Bishops Tell Voters: Anybody but Erap."
———. 2001, Jan. 18. "Stay on Edsa until Evil Is Conquered by Good."
———. 2001, Jan. 21. "Triumph of the People."
———. 2001, Apr. 30. "Appeal to the More Sensible Demonstrators."
———. 2001, May 2. "Estrada Royalists Overwhelm Cops on Way to Palace."

———. 2001, May 28. "Sin Laments Desecration of Edsa Shrine."
———. 2002, June. "Ease Traffic, Take Sidewalks back from Vendors: MMDA."
———. 2002, Oct. 13. "Fernando Unfazed by Calls for His Ouster."
———. 2003, May. "Many Sidewalk Vendors Sell Dirty Goods, Says MMDA."
———. 2003, Aug. 23. "Good Project Put in Wrong Hangs."
———. 2003, Oct. 31. "People Urged Not to Buy Food Sold in Cemeteries."
———. 2004, Mar. 18. "MMDA Chair Keeps off Vendors."
———. 2004, Mar. 19. "Mayors Failed to Support Our Drive Says MMDA."
———. 2005, May 20. "On Abolishing the MMDA."
———. 2007, Sept. 5. "MMDA Chief Vows Relocation of Squatters, Clearing of Streets." Available at http://newsinfo.inquirer.net/breakingnews/metro/view/20070905-86871/MMDA_chief_vows_relocation_of_squatters,_clearing_of_streets [Jan. 19 2012].
———. 2008, May 30. "Inquirer Still No.1 in Readership."
———. 2009, Aug. 8. "Rich, Poor, Come for Cory."
———. 2009, Nov. 30. "Villar Vows to Lead Revolution vs Poverty; Ebdane Quits Race."
———. 2009, Dec. 1a. "Estrada, Villar, Villanueva File CoCs amid Fanfare."
———. 2009, Dec. 1b. "Clash of Colors: Estrada Says He Used It First."
———. 2010, Jan. 11. "Aquino Hits Back at Villar."
———. 2010, Feb. 10. "Aquino: I Will Redistribute Hacienda Luisita in 5 Years."
———. 2010, Mar. 29. "My Brother Died Poor, Villar Insists." Available at http://newsinfo.inquirer.net/breakingnews/nation/view/20100329-261478/My-brother-died-poor-Villar-insists [accessed Jan. 19, 2012].
———. 2010, Mar. 30. "Villar Was Never Poor, Says Aquino." Available at http://newsinfo.inquirer.net/breakingnews/nation/view/20100330-261649/Villar-was-never-poor-says-Aquino [accessed Jan. 19, 2012].
———. 2010, Mar. 31. "Villar to Aquino: I'll Take You to Tondo, Take Me to Luisita." Available at http://newsinfo.inquirer.net/breakingnews/nation/view/20100331-261780/Ill-take-you-to-Tondo-take-me-to-Luisita [accessed Jan. 19, 2012].
———. 2010, Apr. 15. "Aquino's Dream: To Stay in His QC House Even as President." Available at http://newsinfo.inquirer.net/breakingnews/nation/view/20100415-264411/Aquinos-dream-To-stay-in-his-QC-home-even-as-president [accessed Jan. 19, 2012].
———. 2010, Apr. 29. "Aquino: I Got Depressed over Dad's Death but Did Not Seek Medical Help." Available at http://newsinfo.inquirer.net/breakingnews/nation/view/20100429-267145/Aquino-admits-to-depression-but-not-to-being-out-of-control [accessed Jan. 19, 2012].
———. 2010, June 9. "Aquino, 15th President of the Philippines."
Philippine Headline News Online. 2003, May 10. "Get Cigarette Vendors off The Streets—Fernando." Available at http://www.newsflash.org/2003/05/ht/ht003377.htm [accessed Mar. 16, 2003].

Philippine Star. 1998, May 30. "'Centennial President' Likens Self to Andres Bonifacio."
———. 2000, Dec. 22. "Impeach Trial Just Like in the Movies."
———. 2001, Apr. 26. "Name Musicians Record Voter Education Songs."
———. 2002, June 14. "Fernando Named MMDA Chairman."
———. 2002, July 9. "MMDA Chief Eyes Dikes to Prevent Metro Floods."
———. 2002, Aug. 20. "After Kerosene on Food, MMDA Eyes Dye on Goods."
———. 2002, Nov. 12. "Prepare the Kerosene."
———. 2004, Jan. 1. "The Year the MMDA Flexed Its Muscles."
———. 2004, Sept. 7. "MMDA to Fine Topless Men."
———. 2009, Oct. 11. "Editorial: Resettlement."
———. 2009, Nov. 3. "Inbox World: Do You Believe That Squatters Living in River Bankments Will Ever Be Relocated?"
———. 2010, Mar. 10. "Noynoy, Villar Statistically Tied in SWS Poll."
Romano III, Vincente. 2001, May 2. "Poor People Power," *Philippine Daily Inquirer*.
Sinfuego, Roy. 2002, Sept. 4. "Fernando Deserves Support," *Manila Bulletin*.
Sison, Consuelo. 2002, Sept. 12. "Give Us Back the Sidewalks," *Philippine Daily Inquirer*.
Siytangco, Deedee A. 2003, Aug. 8. "Angel Thought of the Day," *Manila Bulletin*.
Soliven de Guzman, Sara. 2002, Sept. 19. "Talk about Human Rights," *Philippine Star*.
Soliven, V. Max. 2002, Aug. 28. "Waste No Tears on Marohombasar: There Are More Thugs Around," *Philippine Star*.
Tan, Michael. 2002, Oct. 10. "True Grit," *Philippine Daily Inquirer*.
Tandoc Jr., Edson. 2003, June 15. "500 Squatter Families Invade UP Prime Land," *Philippine Daily Inquirer*.
Torre, Nestor U. 2001, April 11. "Voter Education Campaign on TV," *Philippine Daily Inquirer*.
Tulfo, Ramon. 2004, May 22. "MMDA's Fernando Condones Abuses by Men," *Philippine Daily Inquirer*.
Vargas, May. 2005, July 19. "Anti-People Practice of the MMDA," *Philippine Daily Inquirer*.
Velasquez, Tony. 2002, Oct.–Dec. "Picture Imperfect," *The Investigative Journalism Magazine*, pp. 20–3.
Zenarosa, Hern P. 2002, Aug. 28. "MMDA's Fernando Needs Public Support," *Manila Bulletin*.
———. 2002, Sept. 14. "What Happens Then If Fernando Quits," *Manila Bulletin*.
———. 2002, Sept. 22. "MMDA Sets Trend on Street Clearance," *Manila Bulletin*.
———. 2002, Dec. 11. "MMDA 'Wish List' for Positive Reforms," *Manila Bulletin*.

Government Materials
Katinig et al. v. President Joseph Estrada et al. 1999. Synopsis.
The Philippine Constitution Law of 1987.
The Local Government Code of 1991, Republic Act No. 7160.

Urban Development and Housing Act of 1992, Republic Act No. 7279.
Executive Order No. 452 of 1997, "Providing for the Guidelines That Will Ensure the Security of Registered Vendors in the Workplace," Oct. 24. Office of the President of the Philippines, Manila.
Rules and Regulations Implementing Executive Order No. 452 of 2001, June 25. Office of the President of the Philippines, Manila.
Inter-Agency Council. 2001. "Minutes of Special Meeting of the Inter-Agency Council on E.O. 452, Providing for the Guidelines That Will Ensure the Security of Registered Vendors in the Workplace (May 2, May 4 and May 8)." Manila.

Statistics

Asian Development Bank, *Key Indicators*.
Central Intelligence Agency. *World Factbook* online. Available at https://www.cia.gov/library/publications/the-world-factbook/fields/2172.html [accessed July 7, 2016].
National Statistics Coordination Board. *Philippine Statistical Yearbook*.
Philippine Information Agency. *Philippine Media Factbook*.
Social Weather Stations. 1999. "October 1999 Ratings of Government." Available at http://www.sws.org.ph/pr102699.htm [accessed Aug. 15, 2011].
———. 2001, May 14. "Voter Turnout is 89%: ABS-CBN / SWS Exit Poll, Social Weather Stations." Available at http://www.sws.org.ph/exit01/ex01rpts.htm [accessed Aug. 15, 2011].
———. 2002. Survey Sourcebook.
———. 2004, May 18. "The SWS 2004 Day of Election Survey: 81%, or 35.4 Million, Went to Vote; 75% Voted for President, 72% for VP, 71% for Senators, 35% for Party List; 2.1% Said Their Names Were Missing." Available at http://www.sws.org.ph/pr051804.htm [accessed Aug. 15, 2011].
———. 2010, May 9. "BW-SWS May 2-3, 2010 Pre-Election Survey: Aquino Leads by 22 Points; Binay Ties Roxas at 37%; Revilla and Jinggoy Estrada Ahead; AKB Leads 13 with Guaranteed Party-List Seats." Available at http://www.sws.org.ph/pr20100509.htm [accessed May 7, 2011].
———. 2016, July 11. "Second Quarter 2016 Social Weather Survey: PNoy's Final Net Satisfaction Rating at 'Moderate' +29." Available at http://www.sws.org.ph/pr20160711.htm [accessed July 14, 2016].
World Bank GINI Index. Available at http://data.worldbank.org/indicator/SI.POV.GINI [accessed July 7, 2016].

INDEX

Abante, 64–5
ABS-CBN, 61, 65, 78, 116, 138, 214, 281, 295, 305, 306
advocacy, 249
agency/agent, 11, 157, 193
agonism, 44–5, 49, 246, 256, 276
Akbayan, 14, 98, 203, 210, 227, 287
American
    capital, 60–1, 63
    colonial period, 23, 79
    democratic values, 69
    democracy, 272
    rule, 52–3, 59
Americans, 23–4, 53, 55, 60–1, 278, 286
Anak Bayan, 290
Ang Bayan, 62
Angara, Edgardo, 292
Aquino, Benigno III, vii, 19, 195, 196, 207, 208, 239
Aquino, Benigno Jr., 62, 82, 211, 238, 239, 275, 304
Aquino, Corazon, 82–3, 86–7, 196, 201, 202, 209, 212, 216, 218, 229, 238–9, 241, 284, 304
Aquino-Oreta, Teresa, 287
Arroyo, Gloria-Macapagal, 18–9, 56, 82, 101, 104, 108, 114–6, 119–20, 124–6, 131, 133, 135, 146–7, 162, 172, 175, 187, 192, 196–210, 216–7, 221–2, 224–5, 227, 239–40, 288–9, 292–5, 298, 303–7
Ateneo de Manila: High School, 94, 285
    University, 99, 139, 190, 294

Atienza, Lito, 172, 301
authoritarianism, 39, 84, 264
Ayala Conglomerate (Group), 73, 78–9, 282

Baclaran, 165–6, 172
Bagong buhay, 60
Barangay, 72, 76, 84, 90, 126, 135, 141, 158, 161, 181, 282, 294, 298
    captain, 126, 141
    officials, 128, 158, 161
Bayan Muna, 98, 198, 213, 277, 287, 305
Bell Trade Act, 60
Belmonte, Feliciano, 303
benevolent assimilation, 52, 277
Binay, Jejomar, 201, 229, 261, 301
Binondo, 64, 69, 281
Bishops-Businessmen's Conference (BBC), 190, 192
Bonifacio, Andres, 59, 97
bossism, 270
bribery system, 161, 181, 186–7, 189, 193, 258–9, 297
broken window theory, 163, 298
Bulgar, 64
Burnham, Daniel H., 69

Caloocan City, 150, 185, 282, 297, 301
Catholic Bishops' Conference of the Philippines, 106, 289, 295
Catholicism, 41–2, 47
cause-oriented group, 30, 285

Cavite, 64, 172, 286
celebrity, xiii, 65, 138, 142, 291
cellphone, 66, 78, 99, 287, 301, 305
Chamber of Real Estate and Builders'
    Association, 191, 299
Chinese, 23–4, 40, 52, 63–4, 73, 76,
    198, 274, 280, 298, 307
  elites, 23
  entrepreneurs, 20, 40, 63, 73, 280
  mestizos, 23, 52, 69
Christ, vii, 36, 41–2, 87, 105, 112,
    262
Christianity, 52, 59, 272
Church, 9, 11–3, 18, 41, 43, 47, 52,
    58–9, 62–3, 69, 79–80, 82, 84,
    85, 87, 103, 106, 110, 113, 138,
    143, 149–50, 154, 165, 188, 190,
    203, 210, 215, 217–8, 227, 232–3,
    238, 246, 258, 283–5, 287–9, 293,
    295–6, 301, 304
city
  inner, 67
  private, 73, 254
  public, 73–4
  revanchist, 67
civic
  culture, 9–10
  exclusivism, 46–8, 139, 188–9, 194,
    196, 212, 227, 242–5, 249,
    277
  inclusivism, 46–9, 92, 152, 154,
    189, 196–8, 210, 212, 226–7,
    230, 233, 241, 246, 249, 277,
    306–7
  organization, 14, 157
civil society, 8–15, 17, 22, 33–5, 44,
    50, 66, 92, 99, 107, 120, 191, 197,
    227, 236–7, 246, 256, 271, 285,
    287
  Gramscian, 11, 22
  Tocquevillian, 10, 12, 22, 44, 246
class
  demarcation line, 6

disparity, 4, 21, 55, 91, 236, 242,
    253
division/divide, 5, 7, 57–8, 66, 203,
    207, 237–9
  line, 6, 17, 34, 50, 57, 212, 226,
    239, 252, 277
clientelism (patron-client relation), 31,
    32, 39, 42, 93, 121, 126, 139, 145,
    161, 225, 275, 297, 307
Coalition of Truth and Experience for
    Tomorrow (K4), 125, 294
colonial
  anti struggle, 53, 113
  era, 32, 95, 159
  government, 23, 52–3, 59, 69, 275,
    281
  rule, 22, 52, 57, 59, 213, 275
  system, 17, 23
colonialism, 51, 59, 236, 255, 269, 285
colony, 108
Commission on Elections (Comelec),
    135, 147, 150, 198, 295, 303–4
common enemy, 47–8, 277
Commonwealth Avenue, 78, 168, 181
Commonwealth Government, 54
communication, 18, 34–5, 51, 57, 62,
    66–7, 105, 154–5, 247, 259, 274
communism, 40, 47–8, 277, 283, 286
Communist Party of the Philippines
    (CPP), 62–3, 84, 91, 98, 198, 240,
    273, 277, 284, 286–7, 294, 305
community mortgage program, 75–6,
    78, 170, 191, 248, 297, 302
compadrazgo, 128, 181
communitas, 89–90, 104, 239
Conception, Jose S., 294
Congress, 2, 33, 54, 84, 91, 141–2,
    173, 184, 190, 192, 198–9, 217,
    228–30, 232, 302
Congressional Commission on
    Education, 56
Constantino-David, Karina, 98, 287,
    290

Constitution
   1935, 54, 84
   1973, 84
   1987, 190, 273, 278, 292, 294
   Biak-na-Bato, 52
Constitutional
   Convention, 54–5, 60, 278
   patriotism, 225
constructivism, 3, 11, 271
contact zone, 5–6, 18–20, 35, 38, 42–3, 46–9, 90, 120, 152, 154, 187, 196, 237–8, 240, 245–6, 248–9, 258–9, 275–6, 308
counter-hegemony, 2, 4, 12–3, 20, 43–4, 276, 285
coup d'etat, 85, 103, 109, 190, 207, 227, 253
Couples for Christ, 36, 105
criminalization, 16, 167, 175
crony, 62, 70, 133, 225, 283–4, 290
cronyism, 39–40
Cubao, 151, 153, 176, 266

De Castro, Noli, 204, 293
De la Rosa, Rogelio, 291
De La Salle University, 305
De Venecia, Jose, 291
decentralization, 31, 75, 122, 157
democracy
   consolidation of, 3, 7, 18, 139, 242, 245
   contested, 14
   deepening of, 2–3, 236, 242–3, 245, 250
   deliberative, 45, 51
   elite, 2, 10, 13–4, 17, 20, 22, 44, 226, 235–6, 270, 272, 303
democratization, 2, 6, 8, 10, 18, 20, 30, 32–4, 38–9, 46, 48, 56, 63, 65–6, 70, 73, 75–6, 83, 86, 89–92, 95, 122–3, 130, 136, 149, 190, 196, 200, 209, 222, 227, 235, 237–41, 246, 270–1, 273, 277, 281, 283, 285–6, 288–90, 295–6, 302, 304, 306
   movement, 10, 30, 39, 48, 63, 86, 89, 123, 149, 238, 241
Defensor-Santiago, Miriam, 288, 291
deliberation, 7, 34, 43–7, 51, 114, 192–3, 241, 247, 253–5, 257
deliberative
   democracy, 45, 51
   space, 44, 155
Department of Agrarian Reform, 76
developers, 72–5, 91, 290
dignity, 18, 40–3, 48, 97, 101, 111–2, 118, 148, 154, 176–8, 180, 185, 194–5, 239, 242–5, 265, 275, 301
disciplinary governance, 161–3, 174, 194, 243, 300
discipline, 11, 157, 162–4, 167–8, 174–6, 180, 189, 252, 233, 260, 263
discursive
   arena, 34–5
   practice, 46, 48, 60, 243, 253, 276
Dolphy, 214
dominant bloc, 13, 271

economic reform, 39, 73, 94, 97
EDSA, 82, 85–6, 88, 90, 92, 102, 105, 107–10, 116, 184, 203, 210, 282, 287, 290
   Shrine, vi, 81, 99–103, 108, 110, 116, 287
education, viii, 5, 20, 24, 26–7, 34–5, 41, 47, 50–7, 59, 95, 110, 118, 129–32, 134, 136–8, 149, 151, 231–3, 246–8, 258, 270–1, 275, 278–80, 283, 285, 288, 295–6, 307
   bilingual, 54–7, 278
   higher, 26, 44, 52–3, 57, 59, 137, 246, 279, 283, 285
   institution, 69
   interactive, 271

policy, 56
system, 52, 137

El Shaddai 100, 103, 288–9
election monitoring, 13, 30, 136, 149–50, 294
elite, 2, 4, 6, 19, 22, 43, 83–4, 94, 96
    democracy, 2, 10, 13–4, 17, 20, 22, 44, 226, 235–6, 270, 272, 303
    new, 213, 226, 283
    rule, 121–2, 135, 161, 216, 227, 236–8, 240, 242, 253, 285–6
enemy of the nation, 17, 200, 207, 239, 241
English, xii, 16–7, 35–6, 38–9, 44, 51–8, 60–6, 77–9, 87, 98–9, 106, 108, 117–8, 131, 133–8, 168, 171, 173–4, 184, 188, 220, 246, 255, 270, 274, 278–81, 286
    ability, 36, 38, 53, 57, 134
    language education, 51–3, 55–6, 278
    language magazine, 61–2, 87
    language newspaper, 16, 36, 60–3, 66, 87, 98, 106, 108, 133–5, 137, 163, 171, 173, 184, 280–1
    program, 66
Enrile, Juan Ponce, 229, 288
Erap jokes, 106–7, 289
Estrada, Joseph, vi, vii, xi, 3, 12, 14, 18, 66, 82–3, 92–116, 118–9, 124, 131, 133, 136, 138–9, 153, 155, 192, 196, 200, 202–10, 215–21, 225–7, 229–30, 232, 239, 242, 285–93, 302, 304–6
    corruption, 18, 115
    film (movie), 96, 285–6
    populism, 18, 92
    wife, 124, 133
everyday forms of resistance, 186–7, 249, 296

Executive Order 452, 192–3, 247–8, 303

fairness, 40, 295
Far Eastern Economic Review, 289
Fernando, Bayani, 162–8, 171–81, 183–5, 187–90, 193, 243, 297–301
film (movies), 65, 70, 78, 79, 93–6, 101, 111–2, 124, 134, 285–6, 291, 292
    festival, 70
    star, 94, 101, 124, 292
    Tagalog, 93, 285
forced eviction (demolition), 19, 75–6, 78, 89, 139, 141, 148, 158, 162, 166–7, 170, 180–1, 190–3, 243–4, 247–8, 258, 271, 302
formal sector, 24, 39, 43, 68, 71–2, 77, 156, 180, 189, 192–3, 266, 282, 302

Garcia, Carlos, 60
gated communities 35, 57, 72–3, 79
gentrification, 67
global
    business, 131
    capitalism, 68, 180
    competition, 68, 251
    economy, 213, 226
    labor market, 278
    market, 56
    megacities, 67
    population, 67
    South, 68
globalization, 56, 186, 213, 248, 273
GMA, 65, 78, 281
good governance, 138, 149, 162, 197, 227, 240
Gordon, Richard, 300
Gramsci, 11, 13, 22, 43, 240, 305
    civil society, 11, 22
    perspective, 13

Hacienda Luisita, 216, 222, 285, 305 307
Hegemonic
    practice, vii, 11, 45–6, 196, 236, 238, 242, 277
    struggle, 1, 3, 5, 11, 13–5, 17, 22, 34–5, 46, 50, 57–8, 122, 209, 218, 236–7
    struggle in the dual public spheres, 17, 22, 34, 236
hierarchy, 43, 90
Honasan, Gregorio, 201, 206, 288
Hukbalahap, 284

Iglesia Ni Cristo, 100, 103, 116, 288–9
Ignacio-Nicolas, Mercedes, 266, 302
Ilocos, 98, 282
Ilustrado, 52, 59
imagined community, 58
IMF, 68, 73, 282
impeachment, 99, 107, 114, 198–9, 228–30, 287, 292, 303–4
informal sector, 68, 71–2, 77, 156, 180, 192–3, 266, 282, 302
Institute for Political and Electoral Reform, 295
Institute on Church and Social Issues, 190, 301
Institute of National Language, 54
integrity, 48, 106, 131–2, 143, 146, 150, 152, 168
interest politics, xiii, 1, 4–5, 7, 9, 20, 237–8, 252–3, 257
internet, 66, 78–9, 256
intimate sphere, 274
Intramuros, 69

jueteng, 98, 115, 198, 287, 290, 304

Kalayaan, 40, 279
Ka-Tinig, 192–3, 247, 249, 266, 302

Katipunan, 279
Koalisyon ng Nagkakaisang Pilipino, 124, 292
Kongreso ng Mamamayang Pilipino Kompil II, 99

Laban ng Demokratikong Pilipino, 123, 291
Laban ng Makabayang Masang Pilipino, 96, 291
Lacson, Panfilo, 288, 293
Lakas ng Tao, 92, 123
Lakas-Christian Muslim Democrats, 207, 292
land reform, 40, 90–1, 190, 241, 247, 271, 283, 286, 301
language, xii, 5, 1, 23–4, 35–6, 38, 41, 50–9, 176, 236, 253, 255, 263, 270, 278–9
    education, 57
    Filipino, 55–7, 278
    national, 54–5, 278
    official, 52, 54–5, 278
    vernacular, 36, 61, 255, 278
lay group (organization), 36, 101, 288, 295
leftist, xi, xiii, 12, 14, 32, 43, 49, 75, 78, 97, 166, 172, 180, 201, 204, 210, 273, 284, 286–8
Legarda, Loren, 295
Liberal Nationalism, 254–5
Liberal party, 123, 207–8, 210, 291–2
liberalism, 58
lider, 33, 126–7, 141, 144
lifeworld, 35–7, 265
lingua franca, 38, 57, 277–8
livelihood, x, xii, 5, 19, 40–3, 47–8, 72, 77, 84, 158, 159, 161, 167, 169, 176, 178–81, 183, 187–9, 193–5, 231, 242–5, 247–8, 251, 258, 275
Liwayway, 280
local elite, 23, 30, 33, 51, 84, 123, 157,

161, 199, 213, 272–3, 280, 291, 303, 306
Local Government Code, 31, 91
Lopez de Legazpi, Miguel, 69
Lopez Family, 61, 65, 306
Luneta Park, 69, 85, 100

MacArthur, Douglas, 60
Magdalo Group, 200, 304
Magsaysay, Ramon, 60, 284
Makati Business Club, 98, 106, 171, 201, 289
Makati City, 184, 229
Malabon City, 129, 151–2, 294, 296
Malacañang Palace, vi, 101, 103–4, 114, 117–8, 204, 284
Malaya, 62–3, 87, 92, 286, 288
Mandaluyong City, 184
Manila Bulletin, 63, 78, 280, 283, 298
Manila Cathedral, 209
Manila Daily Bulletin, 60
Manila Times, 60–1, 63, 98, 172, 298–9, 301
Marcos
  anti-, 63, 84–5, 203, 280, 284, 286
  family, 213, 305
  regime, 2, 62, 75, 82–5, 91, 95, 209, 275, 283–6, 289, 306
Marcos, Ferdinand, 2, 17, 33, 55, 62–3, 65, 70–1, 75–6, 82–91, 95–6, 104–5, 122–3, 136, 196, 203, 209, 213, 237–9, 270, 275, 280, 283–6, 288–9, 295, 301–3, 305–6
Marcos, Imelda, 62, 70, 75
Marikina City, 79, 162, 298
Marquez, Joey, 172
martial law, 2, 30, 33, 39, 55, 62, 70, 84, 86
media
  alternative, 58–60, 62–3
  dominant, 58–60, 62–3

English, 17
new, 66
Mendiola bridge, 101, 116, 203, 284
Metropolitan Mayors' Coordinating Committee, 281
Metro Manila Authority (MMA), 70
Metro Manila Commission (MMC), 70
Metro Manila Vendors' Alliance (MMVA), vii, 184–6, 301
military, 19, 32, 60, 69, 85, 119, 131, 190, 201, 206–7, 227, 241, 277, 288, 304, 306
Mindanao, 61, 126, 159, 199, 227, 233, 304, 306
Mitra, Ramon, 291
MMDA resolution, 164, 298
modernization, 8, 38, 42, 74–5, 162, 168, 270
moneylender, 37, 159, 165, 176, 181, 297, 301
moral
  antagonism, v, 4–6, 18, 20, 45–8, 81, 121–2, 147, 149, 156, 180, 196–7, 231, 234, 241–2, 245–9, 253, 256, 258
  division of the nation, 6–7, 17–20, 48, 83, 156, 195–6, 203, 207, 212, 234, 237, 242–6, 248–9, 252, 255
  economy, 40, 275
  nationalism, v, 17, 19, 46–8, 91–2, 123–4, 195–6, 203, 208–10, 212, 218–20, 226–7, 237–41, 252, 260–1, 277, 306
  politics, vi, xiii, 1, 4–5, 7, 19, 82, 229–30, 238, 244–6, 250, 252–4, 257, 262, 275
  solidarity of the nation, 6, 18–20, 48, 211, 238–9, 240–2, 245–6, 252–4
moralization of politics, vii 4, 7, 29, 20, 105, 120, 122, 171, 178, 182,

186–9, 191–4, 199, 208, 237–8, 244, 247, 256, 259, 265, 273, 283–2, 286, 295, 301, 305
Morales, Horacio, 97, 286
Muslims, 159, 207, 272, 292, 304, 306
mutuality (mutual help), 254, 256–9, 269, 275–6

National Citizens' Movement for Free Elections (NAMFREL), 85, 135–6, 138, 149, 248, 294–5
nation state, 236, 255, 285
National Anti-Poverty Commission, 302
National Government Center, 70–1, 159, 296
National Housing Authority, 17, 170, 299
nationalism, v, 7, 19, 46–8, 52, 82, 91–2, 123–4, 195–7, 199, 201, 203, 205, 207–13, 215, 217, 221, 223, 225–7, 229, 231, 233, 237–41, 251–2, 254–5, 260–1, 277–8, 306
Nationalist party, 123, 207–8, 213, 292
Nationalist People's Coalition (NPC), 291–2
Nemenzo, Francisco, 286
neo-colonolialism/dependence theory, 274
neoliberalism, xiii, 7, 20, 164, 189, 226, 250–1, 253–4, 259, 264, 269, 282
neo-traditionalism, 196, 208
new politics, 6, 38, 96, 197, 237, 239
new rich, 24
NGO, viii, xi, xii, xiii, 2, 9–13, 18, 30–2, 43, 49, 75–6, 78, 80, 91, 97–8, 116, 155, 167, 172, 187, 189–91, 193, 197, 210, 212, 227, 229–31, 237, 241, 246, 248–9, 258, 266, 271, 277, 283, 286–7, 295, 297, 299, 302
North Triangle, 117, 167, 170

Old Capitol Site, 76, 90, 296, 282
Ondoy (Typhoon) 170, 299
overseas contract worker, viii, 24, 28, 30, 73, 122, 213, 279

Pagbabago@Pilipinas, 138, 294
Parañaque City, 165, 172, 298
Parish Based Labor Organization (PaBLO), 302
party-list election, 291
Pasig City, 226
Passion of Christ, 59, 83, 112–3, 290
patronage, 39, 126–8, 197, 227–8
patron-client relations, 32, 161, 270, 291
Pechayan, vi, vii, 21, 37, 76–8, 118, 147–8, 152, 156, 158–9, 161, 166–7, 180–1, 183, 205, 221–3, 225–6, 261, 263, 282, 290, 293
People Power Coalition, 124
People Power 1, vi, vii, 18, 82–3, 86–7, 98–9, 105–6, 109, 113, 117, 120, 195, 205, 238, 240, 283, 287, 289–90
People Power 2, vi, xi, 3, 18, 66, 81–3, 97, 99–108, 110–1, 113–5, 120, 124, 133, 138–9, 197, 203, 205, 242, 283, 288–90
People Power 3, xi, 13, 18, 82–3, 101, 103–4, 108–12, 116–20, 124, 168, 192, 197, 205, 242, 288, 290, 303
People Power 4, 188
People's Movement Against Poverty, 103
people's organization, 12–3, 75–6, 91, 190, 271
Philcoa, vii, 50, 76–8, 160–1, 165–6, 177–8, 181–3, 186, 235, 282, 301
Philippine Coconut Authority, 76, 282
Philippine Daily Inquirer, 36, 62–3, 78, 87, 106, 109, 208, 283, 289–90, 298–9, 301, 304–7

Philippine Health Insurance Corporation, 293
Philippine Herald, 60–1
Philippine Rural Reconstruction Movement, 286
Philippine Star, 36, 63, 78, 172, 283, 286, 288, 294, 298–9
Poe, Fernando Jr., 101, 124
political
　participation, 4, 6, 8, 10, 17, 22, 28, 33, 34, 47, 51, 91, 147, 250, 270–1
political party, 11, 33–4, 92, 303
political reform, 9, 12, 19, 39, 93–4, 122, 149, 198, 203, 220, 226–8, 240, 242, 244–5, 247
population growth, 55, 71, 232–3
populism, 18, 40–8, 83, 92–4, 97, 120, 122, 124, 126, 133, 135, 149, 195–7, 208–10, 213, 215, 218, 220, 222, 226–7, 234, 237, 239, 242–5, 276–7, 287, 291, 306
pork-barrel, 94, 97, 125–8, 227–9, 287, 307
Parish Pastoral Council for Responsible Voting (PPCRV), vii, 138, 149–53, 246–7, 295–6
predatory regime, 196, 303
Presidential Anti-organized Crime Commission, 96
Presidential Commission for the Urban Poor, 190, 297
Propaganda movement, 59
public space, 163, 165
public sphere, vi, vii, 5–6, 19, 22, 34–5, 42, 46, 48, 50–3, 57–9, 61, 63, 65–7, 69, 71, 73, 75, 77, 79, 81, 83, 120, 155, 218, 236, 239, 245–6, 253–4, 256, 259, 273–4
　counterpublics, 34–5, 254, 274
　plebian, 274
　subaltern counterpublics, 34

Puwersa ng Masang Pilipino, 103, 207–8

Quezon City, 15, 50, 69–71, 76, 79, 81, 89, 117–8, 121, 125, 160–1, 167, 170, 182, 184, 186, 190, 282, 297, 300, 303
Quezon, Manuel, 54, 69, 76
Quiapo, 95, 281, 285, 301
quiet encroachment, 158, 296
Quirino, Elpidio, 284

radio, 37, 60–1, 63, 65–6, 69, 85, 96, 103, 123, 175, 214, 224, 281, 292, 305
Ramos, Fidel, 70, 91–2, 96, 123, 192–3, 196, 200, 291–2, 300
rational choice theory, 271
Recto, Claro, 60
redistribution, 8, 40, 47, 111, 190, 241, 245, 254, 259, 273
reformism 196, 208, 227
Remate, 64
rent, 23
　capitalism, 270
　seeking, 280
Revillame, Willie, 214, 224
revolution, x, 2, 48, 59, 83–4, 90–1, 94, 97, 111, 201, 213, 215, 250, 286–7, 290
　armed, 84
　Philippine, 286, 290
　unfinished, 97
revolutionary
　leaders, 59, 279
　movement, 54, 59
Reyes, Robert Fr., 184, 301
Rizal, Jose, 59, 87, 275
Roces family, 61, 280
Roco, Raul, 292–3
Rotary Club, 134
Roxas, Manuel, 60, 215, 262

rule of law, 19, 38, 174, 196, 261, 264

Sakay, Makario, 213
San Juan Town, 94–5, 116
Sanlakas, 98, 184, 186, 193, 249, 287, 300
Second Plenary Council of the Philippines, 149, 288
Second Vatican Council, 149, 284
shame, 41, 83, 89, 163, 275
Sidewalk Clearing Operation, 164, 166
Sin, Jaime, 85, 88, 98–9, 106, 110, 113, 190–1, 203, 284, 289, 304
Singson, "Chavit" Luis, 98, 112, 287
social capital, 9
social control, 23, 84, 157
social movement, 6, 8, 13, 20, 44, 47–9, 84, 91, 139, 158, 190, 237, 246–8, 284, 287, 302, 307–8
Social Reform Agenda, 91, 192, 302
Social Reform Council, 302
Sotto, Vicente, 295
Spain, 23, 52, 58–9, 69, 97, 277
Spanish
  citizen, 52, 59
  colonial government, 52, 59, 275
  language, 17, 38, 52–4, 58, 274, 277
  newspaper, 51
  religious order, 23, 52
  rule, 51–2, 59, 87, 159, 272, 279
strong republic, 188, 198
strong societies and weak states, 23
structural adjustment programs, 68
Subic, 173–4, 300
Social Weather Station (SWS), viii, 25–7, 31, 98, 209, 212, 218, 286–8, 292–3, 295
Syjuco, Augusto, 184, 299
syndicate, 72, 95, 158–9, 169, 188, 248, 263, 281, 296, 297

tabloids, 35, 37, 63–5, 78, 281
Tagalog, xi, xii, 16, 35–9, 52, 54–5, 57, 59–66, 77–8, 93, 96–7, 153, 205, 211, 227, 270, 274, 278–81, 285–6, 290, 305
  films, 93, 285
  newspaper, 60
  programming, 35, 66, 78, 281
Taglish, 36, 278
Tan, Lucio, 280, 289
television, 33, 37, 65, 78, 99, 124, 170, 214
Teodoro, Gilberto, 207–8
Tondo, 75, 94, 100, 213–6, 281, 298
traditional elites, 2, 18, 20, 23–4, 43, 47–8, 123, 195, 213, 215, 218, 226, 230, 237, 240–1, 242, 289, 291
Trillanes, Antonio IV, 201
TV, 60–2, 65–6, 79, 96, 101–3, 112–3, 123, 138, 173, 185, 188, 214, 223–4, 281, 287–8, 292, 295, 305
two-party system, 33, 122–3, 130
Tydings-McDuffie Act, 54

University of the Philippines, x, xii, 76, 78, 97, 158–9, 171, 175, 184, 208, 213, 233, 266, 285, 289, 296, 307
UP-Ayala Land Techno Hub, 78
urban
  development, 68–70, 72–6, 162, 164, 167, 180, 190–1, 247–8, 301–2
  land reform, 190, 271, 301
  planning, 69, 73
  space 17, 67, 69, 72–4, 76, 158, 161–2, 167
Urban Land Reform Task Force, 190, 247
Urban Development and Housing Act, 167, 190–1, 247–8, 301–2

urbanization, 2, 17, 28, 30, 67, 71, 122
    over-, 71
    without industrialization, 71

Velarde, Mike, 288
Villanueva, Eddie, 293
Villar, Manuel, 207–10, 212–26, 305–6
voluntary association, 8, 10, 17, 20, 22, 30, 31

voter education, vi, vii, 18, 121, 138–9, 143, 149–55, 246–8, 295–6

We Forum, 62
welfare state, 68, 244, 250–1, 253
World Bank, 28, 68, 70, 73, 75, 231, 282, 307
Wowowee, 65, 214, 224, 281

KYOTO-CSEAS SERIES ON ASIAN STUDIES
Center for Southeast Asian Studies, Kyoto University

List of Published Titles

The Economic Transition in Myanmar after 1988: Market Economy versus State Control, edited by Koichi Fujita, Fumiharu Mieno and Ikuko Okamoto, 2009

Populism in Asia, edited by Kosuke Mizuno and Pasuk Phongpaichit, 2009

Traveling Nation-Makers: Transnational Flows and Movements in the Making of Modern Southeast Asia, edited by Caroline S. Hau and Kasian Tejapira, 2011

China and the Shaping of Indonesia, 1949–1965, by Hong Liu, 2011

Questioning Modernity in Indonesia and Malaysia, edited by Wendy Mee and Joel S. Kahn, 2012

Industrialization with a Weak State: Thailand's Development in Historical Perspective, by Somboon Siriprachai, edited by Kaoru Sugihara, Pasuk Phongpaichit, and Chris Baker, 2012

Popular Culture Co-productions and Collaborations in East and Southeast Asia, edited by Nissim Otmazgin and Eyal Ben-Ari, 2012

Strong Soldiers, Failed Revolution: The State and Military in Burma, 1962–88, by Yoshihiro Nakanishi, 2013

Organising under the Revolution: Unions and the State in Java, 1945–48, by Jafar Suryomenggolo, 2013

Living with Risk: Precarity & Bangkok's Urban Poor, by Tamaki Endo, 2014

Migration Revolution: Philippine Nationhood and Class Relations in a Globalized Age, by Filomeno V. Aguilar Jr., 2014

The Chinese Question: Ethnicity, Nation, and Region in and Beyond the Philippines, by Caroline S. Hau, 2014

Identity and Pleasure: The Politics of Indonesian Screen Culture, by Ariel Heryanto, 2014

Indonesian Women and Local Politics: Islam, Gender and Networks in Post-Suharto Indonesia, by Kurniawati Hastuti Dewi, 2015

Catastrophe and Regeneration in Indonesia's Peatlands: Ecology, Economy and Society, edited by Kosuke Mizuno, Motoko S. Fujita & Shuichi Kawai, 2016

Marriage Migration in Asia: Emerging Minorities at the Frontiers of Nation-States, edited by Sari K. Ishii, 2016

Central Banking as State Building: Policymakers and Their Nationalism in the Philippines, 1933–1964, by Yusuke Takagi, 2016